This volume examines the impact of public policy on the long-term socioeconomic development of the Kingdom of Quito (now modern Ecuador) from 1690 to 1830. During the seventeenth century this Andean province gained greater regional autonomy as the institutional framework of the Spanish colonial state began its decline. The kingdom then began to establish links to an integrated network of secondary regional markets whose prosperity began to evolve more independently of the colonial export sector, which revolved around silver mining and the transatlantic trade. By the eighteenth century, however, global economic patterns, imperial reform policies, and a series of complex regional and local socioeconomic changes converged to reverse this trend towards greater autonomy and transformed development patterns in Quito.

This study focuses on how state policy contributed to these profound socioeconomic changes in the kingdom from the onset of the demographic and economic crises of the 1690s to the culmination of the independence movements in 1830. This examination of the Kingdom of Quito explores a fundamental but often ignored historical question: how did the colonial and early republican states contribute to shaping the political economy of Spanish America?

THE KINGDOM OF QUITO, 1690–1830

CAMBRIDGE LATIN AMERICAN SERIES

GENERAL EDITOR
SIMON COLLIER

ADVISORY COMMITTEE
MALCOLM DEAS, STUART SCHWARTZ, ARTURO VALENZUELA

80

THE KINGDOM OF QUITO, 1690–1830: THE STATE AND
REGIONAL DEVELOPMENT

THE KINGDOM OF QUITO, 1690–1830

THE STATE AND REGIONAL DEVELOPMENT

KENNETH J. ANDRIEN
The Ohio State University

CAMBRIDGE
UNIVERSITY PRESS

Published by the Press Syndicate of the University of Cambridge
The Pitt Building, Trumpington Street, Cambridge CB2 1RP
40 West 20th Street, New York, NY 10011–4211, USA
10 Stamford Road, Oakleigh, Melbourne 3166, Australia

First published 1995

Printed in the United States of America

Library of Congress Cataloging-in-Publication Data
Andrien, Kenneth J., 1951–
The Kingdom of Quito, 1690–1830 : the state and regional
development / Kenneth J. Andrien.
p. cm.
Includes bibliographical references and index.
ISBN 0–521–48125–2
1. Quito (Kingdom) – Economic conditions.   2. Quito (Kingdom) –
Politics and government.   I. Title.
HC202.A65   1995
338.9866'00903 – dc20   94–44080
                                                                  CIP

A catalog record for this book is available from the British Library

ISBN 0–521–48125–2 Hardback

*For Anne,
Jonathan,
and Elizabeth*

Contents

Acknowledgments

I began my work in Ecuadorian history nearly twelve years ago, and since then I have received generous support from a number of sources. A grant from The Ohio State University allowed me to begin archival work in 1983 at the Archivo General de Indias in Seville. Another grant, from the Fulbright-Hays program of the U.S. Department of Education in 1985, paid for my return to Spain and also for an extended visit to the Ecuadorian archives. A fellowship from the National Endowment for the Humanities provided an additional year of released time in 1991 to write the bulk of the study. Finally, the College of Humanities and the Center for Medieval and Renaissance Studies at The Ohio State University contributed funds for photocopying, research assistants, released time, and computer support at important stages of the project. Without such help and encouragement, this project would have taken much longer to complete.

My friends and colleagues in Spain and Ecuador also made the many months of archival research productive and enjoyable. As always, José Hernández Palomo offered hospitality, intellectual guidance, and counsel about caring for a family in Seville. Javier Ortiz de la Tabla and María Luisa Laviana Cuetos also spent many hours generously sharing their knowledge of Ecuadorian history. My old friends among the staff at the Archivo General de Indias gave much guidance. Manuel Romero Tallafigo, now on the faculty at the Universidad de Sevilla, was particularly helpful in locating some very important materials in the papers of the *Audiencia de Santa Fe*. In Ecuador, the staff of the various archives and libraries were always kind and helpful. Juan Freile Granizo, then director of the Archivo Nacional de Historia in Quito, proved a gracious and knowledgeable host. He freely shared information about archival holdings and provided material from his own genealogical studies. Gonzalo Cartagenova and the staff at the Fulbright commission in Quito also showed us every courtesy. My trip to Ecuador, however, would never have been as successful and enjoyable without the support and friendship of Christiana Borchart de Moreno and her husband, Segundo Moreno Yánez. They freely gave scholarly guidance, hospitality, and advice about living and working in Quito.

A number of my colleagues, students, and former teachers have given generously of their time and knowledge. In addition to the published works of colleagues in the field, I have also learned a great deal from my association with Rolena Adorno, Jacques A. Barbier, Maurice Brungardt, John H. Elliott, John R. Fisher, Brian R. Hamnett, Allan J. Kuethe, Anthony McFarlane, Robert Patch, Karen Powers, Luis Ramos Gómez, and Ann Twinam. My colleagues at various meetings of the Virginia-Carolinas-Georgia Colonial Latin American History Seminar (particularly Suzanne A. Alchon, Linda Arnold, Peter J. Bakewell, Rosemary Brana-Shute, Kendall W. Brown, Lyman L. Johnson, Susan M. Socolow, William B. Taylor, and John J. TePaske) also helped shape and refine my ideas. Two dedicated research assistants, Ana María Presta and Jeanne L. Friedman, also worked with me on coding, entering, and checking my computer data. Suzanne A. Alchon and Karen Powers shared their time, ideas, and data to help me complete this project. I also want to give special thanks to Christiana Borchart de Moreno, Simon Collier, Lyman L. Johnson, Randolph Roth, John J. TePaske, and two anonymous readers for Cambridge University Press, who generously took time away from their own work to read the entire manuscript and to make thoughtful, constructive criticisms. I only hope the final product justifies their generous efforts. Any errors of fact or interpretation which remain, however, are my own responsibility.

In the process of writing this book I decided to publish portions of the study as articles, and I would like to thank the editors for permission to reprint this material. Parts of Chapter 7 originally appeared in the following articles: "Economic Crisis, Taxes and the Quito Insurrection of 1765," *Past and Present*, 129 (November 1990): 104–31; and "Corruption, Self-Interest, and the Political Culture of Eighteenth-Century Quito," in Richard K. Matthews, ed., *Virtue, Corruption, and Self-Interest: Political Values in the Eighteenth Century* (Bethlehem, PA: Lehigh University Press, 1994), 270–96. Sections of Chapter 8 also appeared as "The State and Dependency in Late Colonial and Early Republican Ecuador," in Kenneth J. Andrien and Lyman L. Johnson, eds., *The Political Economy of Spanish America in the Age of Revolution, 1750–1850* (Albuquerque: University of New Mexico Press), 169–95.

Finally, I dedicate this book to my wife, Anne, and our children, Jonathan and Elizabeth. During our travels and the many solitary hours that I spent writing this book, their forbearance, confidence, and love sustained my efforts. I owe a very special debt to Anne B. Andrien, who has provided needed companionship and support throughout the years of travel, research, and writing. Jonathan and Elizabeth have also demonstrated their patience and love in innumerable ways over the years. While the time spent with my family often drew me away from this book, those happy moments made all the work seem worthwhile. Although hardly adequate recompense, I offer them this book as a token of my love and gratitude.

Introduction

This book examines the impact of public policy on long-term socioeconomic development in the Kingdom, or *Audiencia*, of Quito from 1690 to 1830.[1] It is an extension of the inquiry that resulted in my *Crisis and Decline: The Viceroyalty of Peru in the Seventeenth Century*. In that work I traced the political and economic causes for the fiscal decline of the Spanish colonial state in South America, which allowed provinces like Quito to gain greater regional autonomy. During this period the Kingdom of Quito became linked to an integrated network of secondary regional markets whose prosperity began to evolve independently of the more visible colonial export sector. By the eighteenth century global economic patterns, imperial reform policies, and a series of complex regional and local socioeconomic changes converged to reverse this trend towards greater autonomy and transformed development patterns in Quito. This study focuses primarily on how state policy contributed to these profound socioeconomic changes in the kingdom, from the onset of the demographic and economic crises of the 1690s to the culmination of the independence movements by 1830. Such a longitudinal examination of Quito can help to answer a fundamental but often ignored historical question: how did the colonial and early republican states contribute to shaping the political economy of Spanish America?

The major study of political economy in the Kingdom of Quito remains *La economía política del Ecuador durante la colonia* by José María Var-

---

1. The kingdom was also called the *Audiencia* or Presidency of Quito after the crown founded a high court in 1563 to head the imperial bureaucracy. The *audiencia* exercised jurisdiction over the provinces from Popayán in the north to Loja in the south, including the frontier regions of Atacames (in the northwest) and Quijos, Macas, Mainas, and Yaguarsongo or Jaén de Bracamoros (east of the Andes). After independence, the national government of Ecuador eventually lost control over Popayán and Pasto in the north and broad stretches of the Amazon frontier, so the core region of the *audiencia*, from Ibarra to Loja, formed the nucleus of the new nation. For a map picturing the provinces under the control of the modern nation of Ecuador and the colonial *audiencia*, see Suzanne Austin Alchon, *Native Society and Disease in Colonial Ecuador* (Cambridge, 1991), 1.

gas.[2] In recent years, however, a number of detailed regional studies have examined the variegated process of socioeconomic change throughout the Andean region, including the Kingdom of Quito.[3] Utilizing methods pioneered in social history, anthropology, demography, and economic history, this work has prompted a thoroughgoing reexamination of regional patterns of demographic change, land tenure, labor practices, market exchanges, manufacturing, social class formation, clerical activities, and resistance to the colonial order. Although a few of these studies are works of synthesis, many more are based on solid empirical evidence, drawn from extensive archival research.[4] My own book builds on these recent

2. José María Vargas, *La economía política del Ecuador durante la colonia* (Quito, 1957). Other classic works are: Federico González Suárez, *Historia general de la República del Ecuador* (Quito, 1970 edn.); and Juan de Velásco, *Historia del reino de Quito*, 2 vols. (Quito, 1971 edn.). See also Alberto Landázuri Soto, *El régimen laboral indígena en la Real Audiencia de Quito* (Madrid, 1959); Alquiles Pérez, *Las mitas en la Real Audiencia de Quito* (Quito, 1948); Darío Guevara, *Las mingas en el Ecuador* (Quito, 1957); and P. Peñaherrera de Costales and Alfredo Costales, *Historia social del Ecuador*, 4 vols. (Quito, 1964–65).

3. Three important recent reviews of contributions to Andean historiography dealing specifically with Ecuador are: Christiana Borchart de Moreno and Segundo E. Moreno Yánez, "La historia socioeconomica ecuatoriana (siglo XVIII): análisis y tendencias," *Revista de Indias*, 186 (1989): 379–409; Carlos Contreras, "Balance de la historia económica del Ecuador," *HISLA*, 5 (1985): 127–34; and Manuel Miño Grijalva, comp. *La economía colonial: relaciones socio-económicas de la Real Audiencia de Quito* (Quito, 1984), 9–85.

4. The only full study of Amerindian rebellions remains that by Segundo E. Moreno Yánez, *Sublevaciones indígenas en la Audiencia de Quito, desde comienzos del siglo XVIII hasta finales de la colonia* (Quito, 1985 edn.); an important new study of disease and population patterns is Alchon, *Native Society and Disease*; and a significant unpublished study of Amerindian migration is Karen Powers, "Indian Migration and Socio-Political Change in the Audiencia of Quito" (Ph.D. diss., New York University, 1990). The best recent study of the formation of colonial elites is Javier Ortiz de la Tabla Ducasse, *Los encomenderos de Quito, 1534–1660: origen y evolución de una élite colonial* (Seville, 1993). A selected list of recent major articles on landholding patterns, the transfer of land from Andeans to Spaniards, and the early *obrajes* is: Christiana Borchart de Moreno, "La transferencia de la propiedad agraria indígena en el corregimiento de Quito, hasta finales del siglo XVII," *Caravelle*, 34 (1980): 1–19; idem, "Composiciones de tierras en la Audiencia de Quito: el valle de Tumbaco a finales del siglo XVII," *Jahrbuch für Geschichte von Staat, Wirtschaft und Gesellschaft Lateinamerikas*, 17 (1980): 121–55; idem, "Composiciones de tierras en el Valle de los Chillos a finales del siglo XVII: Una contribución a la historia agraria de la Audiencia de Quito," *Cultura*, 5 (1980): 139–78; idem, "La tenencia de la tierra en el Valle de Machachi a finales del siglo XVII," *Antropología Ecuatoriana*, 2–3 (1983–84): 143–68; idem, "Capital comercial y producción agrícola: Nueva España y Quito en el siglo XVIII," *Anuario de Estudios Americanos*, 46 (1989): 131–72; idem, "La crisis del obraje de San Ildefonso a finales del siglo XVIII," *Cultura*, 24 (1986): 655–71: idem, "Las tierras de comunidad de Licto, Punín, y Macaxí: factores para su diminución e intentos de restauración," *Revista Andina*, 6:2 (diciembre 1988): 503–24; Carlos Marchán Romero, "El sistema hacendario serrano, movilidad y cambio agrario," *Cultura*, 19 (1984): 63–106; Hernán Ibarra, "Haciendas y concertaje al fin de la época colonial en Ecuador (Un análisis introductorio)," *Revista Andina*, 4 (1988): 175–200; Javier Ortiz de la Tabla, "Panorama económico y social del corregimiento de Quito (1768–1775)," *Revista de Indias*, 145–47 (1976): 83–98; and idem, "El obraje colonial ecuatoriano: aproximación a su estudio," *Revista de*

contributions by analyzing the impact of state policies and market forces on regional socioeconomic changes in the Kingdom of Quito during the crucial transitional period between the advent of the Bourbon Reforms and the independence era.

Indias, 149–50 (1977): 469–541; idem, "Las ordenanzas de obrajes de Matías de Peralta para la Audiencia de Quito: régimen laboral de los centros textiles coloniales ecuatorianos," *Anuario de Estudios Americanos,* 33 (1976): 471–541; and idem, "Obrajes y obrajeros del Quito colonial," *Anuario de Estudios Americanos,* 39 (1982): 341–65. The best survey of the textile economy remains Robson Brines Tyrer's unrevised doctoral dissertation, "The Demographic and Economic History of the Audiencia de Quito: Indian Population and the Textile Industry, 1600–1800" (Ph.D. diss., University of California at Berkeley, 1976). Other significant and more recent contributions are: Jaime Costales, "Los ordenanzas de obrajes," *Boletín de Informaciones Científicas Nacionales,* 119 (1986): 17–62; Manuel Miño Grijalva, "Capital comercial y trabajo textil: tendencias generales de la protoindustria colonial latinoamericana," *HISLA,* 9 (1987): 59–79; Alexandra Kennedy Troya y Carme Fauria Roma, "Obrajes en la Audiencia de Quito. Un caso de estudio: Tilipulo," *Boletín Americanista,* 32 (1987): 143–202. Segundo E. Moreno Yánez, "Formulario de las Ordenanzas de Indios: una regulación de las relaciones laborales en las haciendas y obrajes del Quito colonial y republicano," *Ibero-Amerikanisches Archiv,* 5:3 (1979): 227–41; Ricardo Muratorio, "La transición del obraje a la industria textil y el papel de la producción textil en la economía de la Sierra en el siglo XIX," *Cultura,* 24 (1986): 531–43; Jorge Villalba, "Los obrajes de Quito en el siglo XVII y la legislación obrera," *Revista del Instituto de Historia Eclesiástica Ecuatoriana,* 8 (1986): 43–212. Other studies of key industries are: Lawrence A. Clayton, *Caulkers and Carpenters in a New World: The Shipyards of Colonial Guayaquil* (Athens, OH, 1980); Frédérique Langue, "Minas ecuatorianas de principios del siglo XIX," *Revista del Archivo Nacional de Historia: Sección de Azuay,* 6 (1986): 101–24; and María Luisa Laviana Cuetos, "La Maestranza del astillero de Guayaquil en el siglo XVIII," *Temas Americanistas,* 4 (1983): 26–32. The commerce in agropastoral and manufactured goods from the south highlands has received attention in: Silvia Palomeque, "Loja en el mercado interno colonial," *HISLA,* 2 (1983): 33–45; and Martine Petitjean y Ives Saint-Geours, "La economía de cascarilla en el corregimiento de Loja," *Cultura,* 15 (1983): 171–207. An important study of the economic enterprises of the clergy is: Nicholas Cushner, *Farm and Factory: The Jesuits and the Development of Agrarian Capitalism in Quito, 1600–1767* (Albany, NY, 1982), and more recently, Jorge Villalba, "Las haciendas de los Jesuitas en Pimampiro en el siglo XVIII," *Revista del Instituto de Historia Eclesiastica Ecuatoriana,* 7 (1983): 15–60. Several key books exist dealing with the export boom along the Ecuadorian coast. See Michael T. Hamerly, *Historia social y económica de la antigua provincia de Guayaquil, 1763–1842* (Guayaquil, 1973); idem, *El comercio de cacao de Guayaquil durante el período colonial: un estudio cuantitativo* (Guayaquil, 1976); María Luisa Laviana Cuetos, *Guayaquil en el siglo XVIII: recursos naturales y desarrollo económico* (Seville, 1987); Julio Estrada Ycaza, *El puerto de Guayaquil,* 2 vols. (Guayaquil, 1973); and Manuel Chiriboga, *Jornaleros y gran propietarios en 135 años de exportación cacaotera (1790–1925)* (Guayaquil, 1980). Two thorough analyses of the urban development of colonial Ecuador are: Martin Minchom, *The People of Quito, 1690–1810: Change and Unrest in the Underclass* (Boulder, CO, 1994); and Rosemary D. F. Bromley, "Urban Growth and Decline in the Central Sierra of Ecuador (Ph.D. diss., University of Wales, 1977). Important demographic studies are: Martin Minchom, "Historia demográfica de Loja y su provincia desde 1700 hasta fines de la colonia," *Cultura,* 15 (1983): 149–69; idem, "The Making of a White Province: Demographic Movement and Ethnic Transformation in the South of the Audiencia of Quito (1670–1830)," *Bulletin de l'Institut Français d'Études Andines,* 12 (1983): 23–39; idem, "La evolución demográfica del Ecuador en el siglo XVIII," *Cultura,* 24 (1986): 459–80; Javier Ortiz de la Tabla, "La población ecuatoriana en la época colonial: cuestiones y cálculos," *Anuario de Estudios Americanos,* 37 (1980): 235–77; idem,

Political economy and dependency perspectives

Over the last thirty years much of the scholarly output dealing with the political economy of Spanish America has been influenced to some degree by the dependency paradigm.[5] Dependency perspectives provide a compelling theoretical approach linking the local, regional, and international dimensions of socioeconomic change.[6] Although no coherent "theory" of dependency exists, its advocates postulate that the expansion of international capitalism led to the economic subordination of Spanish America, resulting in widespread domestic inequalities and a legacy of structural

"La población tributaria del Ecuador colonial," *Cultura*, 24 (1986): 447–58. The best studies of politics and political economy are: Linda Alexander Rodríguez, *The Search for Public Policy: Regional Politics and Government Finances in Ecuador, 1830–1940* (Berkeley, CA, 1985); and Douglas Alan Washburn, "The Bourbon Reforms: A Social and Economic History of the Audiencia of Quito, 1760–1810" (Ph.D. diss., University of Texas at Austin, 1984); Rosmarie Terán Najas, *Los proyectos del Imperio Borbónico en la Real Audiencia de Quito* (Quito, 1988); María Luisa Laviana Cuetos, "Organización y funcionamiento de las Cajas Reales de Guayaquil en la segunda mitad del siglo XVIII," *Anuario de Estudios Americanos*, 37 (1980): 313–46, Leonardo Espinosa, "Política fiscal de la provincia de Cuenca: reseña histórico – presupuestaria – 1779–1861," in *Segundo encuentro de historia y realidad económica y social del Ecuador*, 3 vols. (Cuenca, 1978), 1:77–128; David J. Cubitt, "Economic Nationalism in Post-Independence Ecuador: The Guayaquil Commercial Code of 1821–1825," *Ibero-Amerikanisches Archiv*, 11:1 (1985): 65–82; idem, "La composición social de una élite hispanoamericana a la Independencia: Guayaquil en 1820," *Revista de Historia de América*, 94 (1982): 7–31; idem, "The Government, the Criollo Elite, and the Revolution of 1820 in Guayaquil," *Ibero-Amerikanisches Archiv*, 8:2 (1982): 257–81; and Kenneth J. Andrien, "The State and Dependency in Late Colonial and Early Republican Ecuador," in Kenneth J. Andrien and Lyman L. Johnson, eds., *The Political Economy of Spanish America in the Age of Revolution, 1750–1850* (Albuquerque, NM, 1994), 169–95. Two studies of the Quito Insurrection of 1765 are: Anthony MacFarlane, "The Rebellion of the Barrios: Urban Insurrection in Bourbon Quito," *Hispanic American Historical Review* 49 (May 1989): 283–330; and Kenneth J. Andrien, "Economic Crisis, Taxes and the Quito Insurrection of 1765," *Past and Present*, 129 (November 1990): 104–31. The treasury accounts for colonial Ecuador have been published; see Alvaro Jara and John J. TePaske, *The Royal Treasuries of the Spanish Empire in America:* Vol. 4, *Eighteenth-Century Ecuador* (Durham, NC, 1990). Several excellent master's theses completed at the Facultad Latinoamericana de Ciencias Sociales (FLACSO) in Quito are: Silvia Palomeque, *Cuenca en el siglo XIX: La articulación de una región* (Quito, 1990); Carlos C. Contreras, *El sector exportador de una economía colonial: la costa del Ecuador entre 1760 y 1830* (Quito, 1990); Galo Ramón Velarezo, *La resistencia andina: Cayambe, 1500–1800* (Quito, 1987); Rosario Coronel Feijóo, *El valle Sangriento: de los indígenas de la coca y el algodón a la hacienda cañera Jesuita: 1580–1700* (Quito, 1991); and Loreto Rebolledo, *Tierras y indios en la sierra ecuatoriana: el caso de Lumbisí colonial* (Quito, 1991).

5. For a discussion of the influence of the dependency literature on historians of colonial Latin America, see Lyle N. McAlister, *Spain and Portugal in the New World, 1492–1700* (Minneapolis, MN, 1984), 387–90.

6. Two path-breaking contributions to the dependency literature are: Andre Gunder Frank, *Capitalism and Underdevelopment in Latin America* (New York, 1970), and Fernando Henrique Cardoso and Enzo Faletto, *Dependency and Development in Latin America* (Berkeley, CA, 1971 edn.). For a discussion of the different variants of the dependency paradigm, see Ian Roxborough, *Theories of Underdevelopment* (New York, 1979), 44–53.

underdevelopment. Although most of the early dependency literature focuses on the nineteenth or the twentieth century, in their influential study Stanley and Barbara Stein trace the roots of dependency in Spanish America to the late fifteenth century.[7] In recent years Immanuel Wallerstein and Fernand Braudel have extended the dependency paradigm by taking as their unit of analysis a single world system, which links the expansion of European capitalism in the fifteenth century with the exploitation of Spanish America and other peripheral zones across the globe.[8] Regardless of their approach, however, most *dependentistas* tie the expansion of capitalism from the metropolitan or core nations in Europe (and later North America) to the historical underdevelopment of Spanish America.[9]

7. The Steins also argued that the renewal of royal authority during the Bourbon Reform period in the eighteenth century reinforced this dependency by "shoring up the gothic edifice" of Spanish colonialism. See Stanley J. Stein and Barbara H. Stein, *The Colonial Heritage of Latin America: Essays on Economic Dependence in Perspective* (New York, 1970), 104.

8. Immanuel Wallerstein has published voluminously, but his major works outlining the historical formation and evolution of the world system to date are the following: Immanuel Wallerstein, *The Modern World-System:* Vol. 1, *Capitalist Agriculture and the Origins of the World-Economy in the Sixteenth Century* (New York, 1974); Vol. 2, *Mercantilism and the Consolidation of the European World-Economy, 1600–1750* (New York, 1980); Vol. 3, *The Second Era of Great Expansion of the Capitalist World-Economy, 1730–1840s* (New York, 1989). More specific elaborations of Wallerstein's principal arguments may also be found in Terence K. Hopkins and Immanuel Wallerstein, eds., *World-Systems Analysis: Theory and Methodology* (New York, 1982), 41–82. In addition, two critical but concise descriptions of the main points covered in world-system theory are: Daniel Chirot and Thomas D. Hall, "World-System Theory," *Annual Review of Sociology*, 8 (1982): 81–106; and Charles Ragin and Daniel Chirot, "The World System of Immanuel Wallerstein: Sociology and Politics as History," in Theda Skocpol, ed., *Vision and Method in Historical Sociology* (Cambridge, 1979), 276–312.

9. Fernand Braudel is one of the few historians to integrate many basic principles of the dependency paradigm with empirical research, in his magisterial three-volume history of the world: *Civilization and Capitalism, 15th–18th Century*, Vol. 1, *The Structures of Everyday Life: The Limits of the Possible*, trans. Sian Reynolds (New York, 1981 edn.); Vol. 2, *The Wheels of Commerce*, trans. Sian Reynolds (New York, 1982 edn.); Vol. 3, *The Perspective of the World*, trans. Sian Reynolds (New York, 1984 edn.). Braudel also summarizes his arguments in the following study: Fernand Braudel, *Afterthoughts on Material Civilization and Capitalism*, trans. Patricia Ranum (Baltimore, MD, 1977). An excellent discussion of how economic theory can be utilized in the sort of historical studies covering long- or medium-range time periods advocated by Braudel is Luca Meldolesi, "Critical Economics and Long-Term History: An Introduction," *Review*, 9 (Summer 1985): 3–55. Another historian, Carlos Sempat Assadourian, has contributed substantially to integrating central portions of the dependency argument into his studies on the evolution of Andean regional markets during the colonial period. His most important works on this topic are: Carlos Sempat Assadourian, *El sistema de la economía colonial: mercado interno, regiones y espacio económico* (Lima, 1982); idem, "Modos de producción, capitalismo, y subdesarrollo en América Latina," in Carlos Sempat Assadourian et al., eds., *Modos de producción en América Latina* (Mexico City, 1973), 47–81; and idem, "La producción de mercancía dinero en la formación del mercado interno colonial: el caso del espacio peruano, siglo XVI," in Enrique Florescano, ed., *Ensayos sobre el desarrollo económico de México y América Latina (1500–1975)* (Mexico City, 1979), 223–92.

Despite its seductive heuristic power, most historians of colonial Spanish America now ignore the dependency paradigm or dismiss it as an ineffective tool for analyzing the past. Some critics fault *dependencia* for overemphasizing the importance of the international market or for failing to provide an adequate statistical substructure.[10] Other scholars, however, focus on a central paradox of *dependencia*: it is not a theory to be proven, but a paradigm, which cannot be verified through empirical research, and thus the various dependency perspectives require complete substantive and epistemological acceptance from adherents. Some of the most rigid *dependentistas* even question the legitimacy of criticism from those who do not accept the validity of the paradigm – a solipsism that the majority of empiricists find antithetical to the basic tenets of modern historical research.[11] In many cases dependency advocates view the work of social, economic, and ethnohistorians of colonial Spanish America as little more than raw data, used to illustrate and validate their ideological vision.[12] Research in primary sources and attempts to assess their meaning are, at best, secondary to explaining this dependency process.[13] As a result, historians unwilling to embrace the basic methodological and theoretical

10. Marxist scholars have been particularly critical of the paradigm's alleged overemphasis on the market instead of class structures or modes of production. David Brenner, for example, has argued that while bourgeois economists display a blind faith in the market to promote development, *dependentistas* display equal myopia in blaming underdevelopment solely on the evolution of the capitalist market economy. The net result is to promote a vision of "semiautarkic socialist development" instead of international solidarity in fighting for a world socialist revolution. See David Brenner, "The Origins of Capitalist Development: A Critique of Neo-Smithian Marxism," *New Left Review*, 104 (1977): 27, 92. Other critics, such as Steve J. Stern, have argued that dependency provides no convincing explanation for the socioeconomic development of Spanish America. Using the examples (critical tests) of silver mining and sugar production, Stern concludes that Wallerstein's approach fails to fit the empirical data. See Steve J. Stern, "Feudalism, Capitalism, and the World-System in the Perspective of Latin America and the Caribbean," *American Historical Review*, 93 (October 1988): 829–72; Wallerstein's reply may be found in: "Comments on Stern's Critical Tests," ibid., 873–85; and Stern's rejoinder in: "Reply: Ever More Solitary," ibid., 886–97. Two scholars criticizing the various dependency perspectives for lacking an adequate empirical or statistical substructure are: D. C. M. Platt, "Dependency in Nineteenth-Century Latin America: A Historian Objects," *Latin American Research Review*, 16 (1981): 113–29; 147–49; and Patrick O'Brien, "European Economic Development: The Contribution of the Periphery," *Economic History Review*, 2nd ser., 35 (February 1982): 1–18. Other criticisms vary, but a common theme is the rigidity, determinism, and lack of emphasis on culture or ethnicity. See, for example, Chirot and Hall, "World-System Theory," 97–103; and Ragin and Chirot, "The World System of Immanuel Wallerstein," 301–06.

11. Three excellent reviews and commentaries on this literature are: Robert Packenham, "Holistic Dependency," *New World: A Journal of Latin American Studies*, 2 (1987): 12–48; and Tulio Halperín Donghi, "Dependency Theory and Latin American Historiography," *Latin American Research Review*, 17 (1982): 115–30; and Roxborough, *Theories of Underdevelopment*, 44–53.

12. Ragin and Chirot, "The World System of Immanuel Wallerstein," 299–301; and Chirot and Hall, "World-System Theory," 99–101.

13. Ragin and Chirot, "The World System of Immanuel Wallerstein," 284–90.

parameters of the paradigm have downplayed or ignored its importance as an organizing framework in their scholarly work.[14]

Political economy in the post-dependency era

As the intellectual influence of the dependency paradigm has waned, many scholars have turned from studying political economy to examining an array of other important topics, particularly in ethnohistory and social history. Despite this trend, the need to understand regional socioeconomic patterns in Spanish America remains important, particularly for the period of political and economic transition (or even turmoil) between the onset of the Bourbon Reforms and the independence era. This necessitates the development of fresh approaches to studying the political economy of Spanish America that transcend the inherent limitations of the various dependency perspectives. In my opinion, the inspiration for such research can come from studies utilizing the broad socioeconomic perspectives employed by the *dependentistas* and also from the theoretical and empirical work dealing with the role of the state as an economic actor.[15]

Although too often plagued by a rigid ideological determinism, dependency perspectives have focused attention on the development of colonial market economies in Spanish America within a global framework. This is particularly true of the work of Fernand Braudel, who argues that much of economic history can be "boiled down to the market econ-

14. A number of authors have clearly been influenced by the *dependencia*, but they do not even list references to this literature in their notes. The following works appear to manifest this influence: John Lynch, *Spain under the Habsburgs, 1589–1700*, vol. 2 (Oxford, 1969 edn.), 160–228; idem, *The Spanish American Revolutions, 1808–1826* (London, 1973 edn.), 1–36; P. J. Bakewell, *Silver Mining and Society in Colonial Mexico: Zacatecas, 1546–1700* (Cambridge, 1971), 221–36; and John Coatsworth, "The Limits of Colonial Absolutism: The State in Eighteenth-Century Mexico," in Karen Spalding, ed., *Essays in the Political, Economic, and Social History of Colonial Latin America* (Newark, DE, 1982), 25–51; and idem, "Obstacles to Growth in Nineteenth-Century Mexico," *American Historical Review*, 83 (February 1978): 80–100.

15. Douglass C. North has made the most original theoretical contributions on the role of state institutions in shaping economic performance. In particular, see Douglass C. North, *Institutions, Institutional Change and Economic Performance* (Cambridge, 1990). The pioneering empirical work on the role of state institutions and economic development in colonial Spanish America has been done by John J. TePaske and Herbert S. Klein. For a review of their contributions and the empirical work of other scholars dealing with this topic, see: Herbert S. Klein and Jacques A. Barbier, "Recent Trends in the Study of Spanish American Colonial Public Finance," *Latin American Research Review*, 23 (1988): 35–62; and William B. Taylor, "Between Global Process and Local Knowledge: An Inquiry into Early Latin American Social History," in Olivier Zunz, ed., *Reliving the Past* (Chapel Hill, NC), 115–90. An interesting recent study is Peter Guardino and Charles Walker, "The State, Society, and Politics in Peru and Mexico in the Late Colonial and Early Republican Periods," *Latin American Perspectives*, 73 (Spring 1992): 10–43.

omy."[16] Although preindustrial markets remained small and "an imperfect link between production and consumption," they still served as the principal "motor" driving economic development in the Spanish Indies by the late colonial period.[17] Moreover, examining regional socioeconomic structures within the context of imperial and international market forces can provide the essential context for understanding historical processes of "subordination, production, and distribution" in peripheral societies such as Spanish America.[18]

To move beyond the sweeping generalizations of the *dependentistas*, however, historians must collect and analyze empirical data on socioeconomic patterns in Spanish America. According to economic historian Donald McCloskey: "mute facts unarranged by human theories tell nothing; human theories unenlivened by facts tell less than nothing."[19] Empirical data, gleaned from painstaking archival research, can provide vital information on the evolution of the diverse patchwork of regional markets in colonial and early republican Spanish America. This approach is particularly promising for studying an outlying province such as Quito, with its diverse economy based on agriculture, textile production, and extensive overland and sea commerce. Some of these economic activities, such as the production of foodstuffs or textiles, met local or regional needs, while the export of cacao satisfied imperial and international markets. In short, the regional socioeconomic evolution of Quito was intimately connected to colonial and international market forces and cannot be understood adequately in isolation.

Networks of production and exchange throughout Spanish America were also influenced by the institutions and policies of the colonial state.[20] Most dependency approaches, however, underestimate the historical role of the state in Spanish America's economic development. Immanuel Wallerstein, for example, argues that strong states evolved solely in the more developed European core regions, while peripheral zones (such as Spanish America) developed only small-scale, weak state structures.[21] Such an assertion cannot be sustained, however, once the theoretical assumptions of *dependencia* come into dialogue with the evidence.[22]

16. Braudel, *Afterthoughts on Material Civilization*, 17.

17. *Ibid.*, 44.

18. For a theoretical discussion of the need to study macrohistorical topics within a particular world system, see Charles Tilly, *Big Structures, Large Processes, and Huge Comparisons* (New York, 1984), 62–65.

19. Donald N. McCloskey, *Econometric History* (London, 1987), 21.

20. For a theoretical discussion of this concept, see Tilly, *Big Structures, Large Processes*, 63.

21. Hopkins and Wallerstein, *World-Systems Analysis*, 23–29.

22. Two recent anthologies that present a comparative array of essays on these themes are: Karen Spalding, ed., *Essays in the Political, Social, and Economic History*, and Andrien and Johnson, eds., *The Political Economy of Spanish America*.

Although small in scale, the institutions of the colonial state and its agents played a major role in determining the context for economic growth by allocating labor, providing access to essential raw materials, forcing consumption, and subsidizing many productive enterprises. By the late eighteenth century, the rejuvenated colonial state also expanded its interventions in the market economy, seeking to encourage some favored sectors, particularly export agriculture and mining, while discouraging others, such as most types of manufacturing. A principal goal of the Bourbon monarchs in this period was to use the public sector to control colonial market economies. This symbiosis between the state and the market economy would continue into the early republican era.

The role of the public sector in organizing and sustaining the connections among local, regional, and international markets is central to understanding socioeconomic development in the Kingdom of Quito. As the economic historian and Nobel Laureate Douglass C. North has argued, state institutions can define the range of economic choices and opportunities available to individuals and groups in any polity.[23] To understand the influence of the state on economic performance in Quito, I examine more than specific tax, monetary, or commercial policies in this study; I also analyze the cumulative impact of all pertinent government interventions in the market economy. Such an investigation of the kingdom's political economy can help to isolate the "internal" and the "external" dynamics of socioeconomic change during the period from the 1690s to 1830. This study also evaluates colonial political conflicts, examining how powerful individuals and partisan groups attempted to grapple with the broad socioeconomic changes that helped to shape their lives. This approach to political economy, dealing primarily with long-term structures and medium-range socioeconomic cycles, is not the only viable way to examine the transition from colonialism to independence. It will undoubtedly leave numerous important issues untouched, particularly in intellectual and cultural history. But in a field such as colonial Spanish American history, where much basic research remains to be done, I hope it will serve as a useful historiographical point of departure.

Sources and organizational framework

Given the paucity of empirical studies on colonial and early republican Quito, the foundations of this book rest primarily on materials found in extensive research conducted at the Ecuadorian and Spanish archives. The most important sources on the link between state power and socioeconomic development in the Kingdom of Quito are the various fiscal re-

23. North, *Institutions and Economic Performance*, 4.

cords dealing with the three major economic regions of the realm — Quito, Guayaquil, and Cuenca. Precisely because these data were generated by the colonial administration, they reveal the fiscal parameters of the state and provide a wealth of information on the outcome of government policies. Along with other more qualitative materials (such as government reports, notary records, diaries, business papers, legislation, official and private correspondence, and judicial records), this fiscal data can supply a wealth of information on the political economy of the Kingdom of Quito from 1690 to 1830. I will also evaluate these findings in conjunction with recently published secondary works on Ecuador, to place my study in the broadest possible historical context.

I use these rich sources to trace the impact of public policy on economic development in the key regional markets of Quito, Guayaquil, and Cuenca. The work itself is divided into two interrelated parts that survey both the evolution of socioeconomic changes in the kingdom and the link between state policies and economic development. The first chapter begins a section of the study that places state policies and regional socioeconomic developments (between 1690 and 1830) within the context of imperial and international market forces. Chapter 1 explains that natural disasters, epidemics, and Spanish trade policy prompted a long decline in traditional textile manufacturing sectors from the 1690s. Chapter 2 examines how the eclipse of the urban market of Quito and the overall economic stagnation of the entire north-central highlands prompted large-scale out-migrations from that region, contributing to the rise of formerly peripheral regions around Cuenca, and later Guayaquil. The third chapter provides more detail on this process by discussing how an archaic organizational structure, unfavorable crown policies, and international competition led to the decline of highland manufactures, while cottage textile production in the south highlands prospered and coastal shipbuilding followed the rhythms of the local export economy. Chapter 4 discusses the role of imperial trade policies and international market forces in the gradual decline of highland textile- and food-producing regions and in the corresponding prosperity of the coastal cacao export economy from the 1790s. Chapter 5 traces how ties to the decaying highland market economy forced many marginal Amerindian groups to migrate, first to the south sierra and later to the coast. High taxes and diminished economic opportunities also incited some of those who remained to rebel against Spanish authority by the late colonial period. The sixth chapter examines the influence of both crown policies and the vicissitudes of the internal economy in altering commercial patterns in the Kingdom of Quito between 1690 and 1830.

The seventh chapter begins the final section of the study, dealing with the link between structural socioeconomic changes and the bitter political struggles over the formation of public policy. Chapter 7 examines the failure of *Quiteño* elites to control the weakened judicial state during the first half of the century, culminating in the unsuccessful Quito Insurrection of 1765. The eighth chapter demonstrates how the legacy of social divisions after the insurrection of 1765 allowed the crown to impose a centralized bureaucracy, capable of intervening in the economy and enhancing the economic subordination of the kingdom. Even after the collapse of Spanish authority, the new republican governments failed to enact more enlightened policies that would have promoted investment, rewarded enterprise, and sustained autonomous development. Finally, Chapter 9, the conclusion, surveys the role of state policies and changing market forces in obstructing economic development in the Kingdom of Quito throughout the long period from the 1690s to 1830.

PART I

The state and socioeconomic development

1

The late seventeenth-century crises

By the seventeenth century the Kingdom or *Audiencia* of Quito had emerged from over a century of turmoil. It took the Inca state (Tawantinsuyu) until 1495 to conquer the region's six independent indigenous chiefdoms. Only forty years later the conquering forces of Sebastián de Belalcázar, Diego de Almagro, Juan de Salinas, and Gonzalo Pizarro established Spanish rule in the region. After founding a town council (*cabildo*) in their provincial capital of Quito in 1534, the new invaders started distributing the Amerindian settlements into grants of *encomienda*. This system allowed the Europeans to collect taxes and labor from the Andeans, in return for military protection and religious instruction. A generation of civil war among the conquistadors and periodic indigenous rebellions, however, impeded the consolidation of Spanish rule. It was not until 1563 that the crown established a high court (*audiencia*) in the city of Quito to head the newly implanted imperial bureaucracy. By then a stable Spanish society had formed in the region, laying the foundations for a vibrant regional economy based on the production of woolen textiles.

The Kingdom of Quito's textile sector was linked to a series of prosperous, integrated regional economies extending throughout the Viceroyalty of Peru during the seventeenth century. While silver mining connected the Spanish Andean colonies and the international economy, smaller regional markets supplied foodstuffs, wine and liquor, cloth, and labor for the burgeoning mining zones. Quito's textile economy played an important role among these evolving secondary regional markets for most of the seventeenth century. Local elites utilized the fertile lands in the narrow Andean valleys and wide stretches of *páramo* pasture lands to establish numerous textile mills (*obrajes*) in the north-central sierra from Otavalo to Riobamba. These mills supplied woolens to markets in Peru and New Granada in return for specie, which the small local elite used to maintain a comfortable European lifestyle. This pattern of socioeconomic development was typical of the complex internal markets that had evolved in the Spanish Andes.

By the late seventeenth century, crown policy and a number of catastrophic events combined to produce a prolonged economic decline in the textile sector. Along with diminished demand for cloth at the silver mines, a series of droughts, earthquakes, and epidemics disrupted regional markets throughout the Andes by the 1690s. These natural disasters proved particularly damaging to the textile economy of Quito, far removed from its sources of demand in Peru and New Granada. Epidemics and crop failures decimated the Amerindian population, which ended the period of cheap labor and made *Quiteño* producers susceptible to competition from colonial mills closer to the mines. Even more devastating, however, was the crown's decision to allow the introduction of cheap high-quality European cloth, first brought by French traders during the War of the Spanish Succession (1700–16). These European imports undercut *Quiteño* woolens, particularly in the lucrative Lima market, worsening the economic plight of the cloth industry. The crown exacerbated these problems after the war by easing trade restrictions, which allowed the continued influx of European textiles. In short, by the early eighteenth century Quito's place within the integrated colonial socioeconomic order had eroded.

The viceregal economy in the age of transition

Despite the contraction of the international economy during the seventeenth century, a number of factors combined to stimulate economic diversification in the Viceroyalty of Peru and to promote prosperity in regions like Quito.[1] A small home market, an overreliance on mining, and a dependence on European manufactured goods and luxuries had retarded any substantial growth in viceregal markets early in the colonial period. By the seventeenth century, however, the gradual decline of the

---

1. The long-standing debate over the nature of socioeconomic change in Spanish America (the so-called "crisis" of the seventeenth century) has also provoked sharp divisions among the dependency and world system advocates. Some of the early dependency advocates like Andre Gunder Frank have contended that decline in Europe promoted economic self-sufficiency and diversification in the peripheries. See Andre Gunder Frank, *Latin America: Underdevelopment or Revolution* (London: 1969), 3–30. More recent studies, however, have strongly disagreed. Immanuel Wallerstein and Carlos Sempat Assadourian, for example, argue that the world economic downturn of the seventeenth century led to economic autarky and decadence in the peripheral zones like Spanish America. See Immanuel Wallerstein, *The Modern World-System: Vol. 2, Mercantilism and the Consolidation of the European World Economy, 1600–1750* (New York, 1980), 144–55; and Carlos Sempat Assadourian, *El sistema de la economía colonial: mercado interno, regiones, y espacio económico* (Lima, 1982), 121–27, and passim. This theoretical perspective, however, fails to explain how regional centers like Quito could enjoy extended cycles of prosperity during the century, while the mining industry and the transatlantic trade declined. For a discussion of this phenomenon, see Kenneth J. Andrien, *Crisis and Decline: The Viceroyalty of Peru in the Seventeenth Century* (Albuquerque, NM, 1985), 1–41.

mining sector and of transatlantic trade prompted slow evolutionary changes, leading to a restructuring of the viceregal economy. Mining remained an important link to the international arena, but regional agricultural systems, manufacturing, and intercolonial trade networks became important elements in the increasingly diversified colonial economy. As mining and the transatlantic trade began their decline, these vibrant regional markets evolved more independently, promoting variegated patterns of economic growth. Andean markets became more tightly welded together than in the past, which provided the opportunity for some groups, such as the textile producers of Quito, to experience prosperity.[2]

Several factors combined to stimulate this shift from primitive export-oriented production to a more diversified economic base in the Andes. The growth of the Spanish population over the century, particularly in urban centers throughout the Andes, undoubtedly led to a rise in consumer demand for locally produced commodities, after the onset of a recession in the Atlantic trade by the 1620s. The Amerindian population also began to participate more actively as consumers and producers in regional economies by paying taxes, working in the mines and on Spanish estates, and buying local commodities. Sizable investments by clerical organizations and merchant bankers in regional enterprises promoted further economic development. Another important stimulus came from increased government spending, as the viceregal state retained an increasing share of public revenues to maintain fortifications, the Pacific fleet, local armories, and to pay bureaucratic salaries and subsidies for frontier provinces and the Huancavelica mercury mines. At the same time, shortages and high prices caused by the declining transatlantic trade encouraged merchants to extend trade links in legal and contraband goods throughout the Pacific basin and even to the Far East. In short, the rising consumer demand, public and private investment, and expanded trade links undoubtedly led to a rise in aggregate demand and a more efficient utilization of colonial resources.[3]

2. Studies that examine important elements of the regional prosperity of seventeenth-century Quito are: Robson Brines Tyrer, "The Demographic and Economic History of the Audiencia of Quito: Indian Population and the Textile Industry, 1600–1800" (Ph.D. diss., University of California at Berkeley, 1976); Karen M. Powers, "Indian Migration and Socio-Political Change in the Audiencia of Quito" (Ph.D. diss., New York University, 1990); Manuel Miño Grijalva, ed., *La economía colonial: relaciones socio-económicas de la Real Audiencia de Quito* (Quito, 1984), 15–70; Lawrence A. Clayton, *Caulkers and Carpenters in a New World: The Shipyards of Colonial Guayaquil* (Athens, OH, 1980); and John Leddy Phelan, *The Kingdom of Quito in the Seventeenth Century: Bureaucratic Politics in the Spanish Empire* (Madison, WI, 1967).

3. These internal stimuli to economic diversification and development were unforeseen by Wallerstein and Assadourian, who focus primarily the role of the international market in the evolution of peripheral zones. A major factor inhibiting economic growth in preindustrial societies, in both the core and the peripheral zones, was the underutilization of resources and a sluggish aggregate

The textile economy in the seventeenth century

Developments in the Kingdom of Quito, with its vigorous textile sector and regional trade links, typified the evolution of this new colonial economic order in the seventeenth century. Deposits of precious metals in Quito were small and had been exhausted by the sixteenth century, and rugged geographical barriers isolated the region from the principal silver-mining and commercial centers of the viceroyalty. Cut off from direct participation in the international economy, Quito could have become a decadent provincial backwater. Instead, the demand for cloth in the mining and urban centers of South America led to the foundation of numerous *obrajes* in the district by the late sixteenth century. During the textile economy's heyday, approximately 10,000 workers produced an average of over 200,000 *varas* of the region's famous blue cloth (*paño azul*), which garnered between 1 and 2 million pesos in the markets of Peru and New Granada.[4] According to one prominent member of the manufacturing elite, the Marqués de Maenza:

from the time of the pacification or conquest of these kingdoms it was assigned to this province [Quito] as its endowment the production of high-quality woolens (*paños*), that of lesser quality woolens (*bayetas*) to those regions of Upper Peru [Bolivia] that had no minerals; leaving to that of Lima the cultivation of vines and olive groves, so that in this manner the fruits and riches of each province were exchanged by means of a reciprocal trade and a fixed negotiation in which each looked after its own well being.[5]

In short, the Marqués saw the *Quiteño* textile economy as forming part of a regional market complex, extending throughout Spanish South America.[6]

The Kingdom of Quito possessed numerous advantages favorable to the development of the textile industry. The Andean valleys had an abun-

---

demand. Wallerstein, Assadourian, and other dependency or world-system advocates seldom analyze the ways in which capitalist development can stimulate aggregate demand over time, beyond the limits imposed by external stimuli from the international economy alone. Since "capitalist development creates its own demand," the character of economic growth can change over time, promoting regional diversification and prosperity, even in periods when international trade is contracting. This is precisely the process that I am attempting to describe here. For a more detailed discussion of this process for the Andean region, see Andrien, *Crisis and Decline*, 29–39. A discussion of these trends in Europe may be found in Jan DeVries, *The Economy of Europe in an Age of Crisis, 1600–1750* (Cambridge, 1976), 176–209.

4. Tyrer, "Demographic and Economic History," 313. The exact length of the *vara* is in dispute, but the most accurate estimate is 83.5 centimeters, or 33 inches. See Martin Minchom, *The People of Quito, 1690–1810: Change and Unrest in the Underclass* (Westport, CT, 1994), 268.
5. Quoted in Tyrer, "Demographic and Economic History," 280.
6. *Ibid.*, 232.

dance of fertile land and at higher elevations spacious expanses of *páramo* served as excellent pasture lands. After the large-scale introduction of merino sheep in the sixteenth century, local Spanish landowners established large- and medium-sized textile mills that produced many different types of cloth, particularly *paño azul*. Local merchants and clerical organizations provided most of the credit to finance these textile enterprises.[7]

The crown quickly began to regulate and control the evolution of this *obraje* economy in the kingdom. At first, the Madrid government opposed the establishment of colonial cloth manufactories, fearing that such competition with metropolitan producers might impede the transatlantic trade. King Philip II even gave Viceroy Francisco de Toledo (1569–81) secret instructions to close down any colonial mills operating in the Andes. As late as 1601 the crown also prohibited the use of forced Amerindian labor in the mills.[8] But the impracticality of discouraging colonial textile production became apparent by the late sixteenth century. European textile manufacturers could not meet the demand for cheap cloth in the Indies, and the crown had to adopt a more pragmatic policy towards the emerging Andean cloth industry. As a result, Spanish authorities opted to regulate local textile mills and to profit from their operation. Crown authorities in the kingdom sold licenses to selected creoles and peninsulars and provided the legal mechanisms to draft the forced and wage laborers needed to help establish textile enterprises.[9] These policies allowed the crown to restrict the participation of entrepreneurs in the marketplace and to subsidize labor costs at the mills. Whether by design or accident, crown policy makers effectively turned the textile business in the north Andes into an oligopoly, which nurtured selected colonial cloth producers.[10]

---

7. *Ibid.*, 213–15; 300–03; Archivo Nacional de Historia de Quito (hereafter cited as ANH-Q), Ropas, Caja 5, Testimonio de Nicolás Antonio de Carrión y Vaca, Quito, 30 julio 1766; ANH-Q, Obrajes, Caja 14, Autos de esperas pedidas por dn. Thomás de Arostegui a sus acreditiedores, Quito, 9 septiembre 1767. Additional information on the extent of clerical investment in land and *obrajes* may be found in the Archivo General de Indias (hereafter cited as AGI), Quito, 181. The entire bundle of documents deals with efforts by landowners to have their interest payments on church loans and liens lowered from 5 percent to 3 percent and provides much detail on the extent of the problem of encumbered properties and textile mills in the first half of the eighteenth century. Additional information may be found in the ANH-Q, in the section "Censos y Capellanías" and scattered information in the sections "Obrajes," "Haciendas," and "Temporalidades."

8. Tyrer, "Demographic and Economic History," 148–50.

9. The crown began selling licenses from the 1590s to the 1620s and renewed the policy in the 1680s; see *ibid.*, 150.

10. According to Tyrer, the "crown played no positive role in facilitating the growth of the textile industry." *Ibid.*, 150. I strongly disagree. Early crown ambivalence about colonial manufacturing

The large Amerindian population in the kingdom also proved a vital asset in the success of the *obrajes*. Unlike most Andean provinces, where the available labor force declined from epidemic diseases, in Quito the Amerindian population living in the north-central sierra (from Ibarra to Riobamba) grew from nearly 145,000 in 1591 to over 270,000 one hundred years later.[11] Apparently, migrations from adjacent lowland and marginal economic zones in the north and south accounted for this large increase in the Amerindian population.[12] Highland communities had long sent colonists to gain access to resources in these frontier areas, which quickly became a haven for refugees from the Inca and Spanish invasions of the late fifteenth and sixteenth centuries. These colonists and fugitives apparently returned to the north-central sierra afterwards to repopulate Andean communities hard hit in the sixteenth century by epidemic diseases, producing a seeming upsurge in the population.[13]

Spanish authorities took advantage of this situation by promoting fiscal policies encouraging Andeans to seek work in the textile mills. From the 1570s Spanish authorities began to assess extremely high tax rates on the traditional Andean communities, payable principally in specie. Tribute rates ranged from 4 to 9 pesos annually, an exorbitant amount for the modest indigenous agrarian economies of the highlands. Many Andeans had to seek work in the growing Spanish economy in urban centers, on rural estates, and in the textile mills to gain the money needed for their tax obligations.[14] As the century progressed, increasing numbers of workers left their communities permanently to seek the lower tax obligations afforded displaced migrants (*forasteros*).[15] In this way, Spanish fiscal policies ensured a large labor force for the *obrajes*, at least until the disastrous epidemics of the 1690s decimated the Amerindian population.

As mill owners used this Andean labor force to develop a prosperous textile economy, elites throughout the district began to participate in regional commerce. The mill owners themselves sent their higher-quality *paños* to Lima, where they exchanged them for European wares and Pe-

aside, the system of licensing and providing access to Andean laborers played the crucial role in establishing the *obrajes*.

11. Tyrer, "Demographic and Economic History," 35–38.
12. Powers, "Indian Migration and Socio-Political Change," 16–191. This important study by Karen Powers explains a great deal. The epidemics of the sixteenth century in Quito led to rapid population declines throughout the provinces of the Viceroyalty of Peru, including the Kingdom of Quito. The upsurge in the taxpaying Amerindian population during the seventeenth century cannot likely be explained by natural increase – given the relatively high death rate associated with preindustrial societies – so migration is the most satisfactory explanation.
13. *Ibid.*
14. *Ibid.*, 165–191; Tyrer, "Demographic and Economic History," 129–30.
15. Powers, "Indian Migration and Socio-Political Change," 187–91.

ruvian products.[16] The Lima merchant community then sent the textiles to the various mining centers in Peru and Upper Peru, particularly Potosí. The cheaper, low-quality textiles (*bayetas* and *jergas*) generally went north, transported by New Granada merchants from Popayán and Nieva to more distant markets such as Barbacoas, the Chocó, and even Antioquia. These northern merchants also took charge of introducing European goods from Cartagena into the Quito region.[17] The sale of *Quiteño* woolens in both of these markets financed the importation of European wares and provided the specie for domestic enterprise, regional trade, and the fiscal needs of the colonial state.[18]

The *Quiteño obraje* complex

The first Spaniards to open cloth manufactories in the Kingdom of Quito were the region's *encomenderos*, who sought viable sources of income after local placer gold deposits became exhausted by the 1560s. As epidemics decimated the Amerindian population in the years following the Spanish invasion – before migrations from the frontier began – tribute arrears mounted. In response, many *encomenderos* founded textile mills, called *obrajes de comunidad*, as money-making enterprises to supplement falling tribute returns. Typically, an *encomendero* established a mill in a prominent settlement under his jurisdiction, usually with the support of local ethnic leaders (*kurakas*) anxious to use cloth production to pay communal tax debts. Although these *obrajes de comunidad* were legally owned by the Andean communities, in reality the local Spanish *encomendero* treated them as his personal property.[19] By the early seventeenth century, this combination of circumstances had led to the foundation of fourteen community *obrajes* on *encomienda* grants and two additional mills in Otavalo, owned directly by the crown.[20]

The *encomenderos* in the kingdom had access to the capital and labor resources needed to construct, staff, and maintain a large *obraje de comu-*

16. Tyrer, "Demographic and Economic History," 283–94.

17. *Ibid.*, 260, 296–98.

18. *Ibid.*, 232, 241.

19. *Ibid.*, 111, 112–17.

20. The Otavalo mills were founded by the wealthy *encomendero* Rodrigo de Salazar in Andean villages as the communal mills. After Salazar died, however, the crown took direct control over the *encomienda* and its *obrajes*. The authorities allowed no competition in the province from privately owned enterprises, except the mill of San Joseph de Peguchi, founded by Pedro Ponce Castillejo in 1622. The crown mills in Otavalo remained extremely profitable for the crown. Javier Ortiz de la Tabla Ducasse, *Los encomenderos de Quito, 1534–1660: origen y evolución de una élite colonial* (Seville, 1993), 96–98; 214. The history of the San Joseph de Peguchi mill may be found in Rocío Rueda Novoa, *El obraje de San Joseph de Peguchi* (Quito, 1988).

nidad. Most mills usually consisted of one large stone or adobe structure and several small outbuildings. The main building could be as large as 250–300 meters in circumference, although some early mills were much smaller, even converted homes.[21] The outbuildings were often little more than small cottages or huts. The initial costs of construction varied considerably, depending on the size of the operation. In 1622, for example, Ponce de Castillejo employed twenty Andean laborers in Otavalo to convert his four-room house into a mill and to construct two smaller buildings, all for only 2,800 pesos.[22] Building costs for the larger *obrajes de comunidad*, however, could easily exceed 10,000 pesos.[23] After construction, the largest expense in outfitting the *obraje* was for the copper or bronze cauldrons used for dying the wool. After that the principal problem was attracting a large, resident labor force. With their political clout and access to Amerindian labor, however, the early *encomenderos* easily surmounted this last problem, which explains the proliferation of the *obrajes de comunidad* in the late sixteenth century.[24]

As the crown began to regulate the power of the *encomendero* elite throughout the Andean region during the sixteenth century, royal officials issued a wide range of laws controlling the operation of community mills in the Kingdom of Quito.[25] From the late sixteenth century, the viceroy in Lima began appointing special administrators to run the *obrajes* for the *encomenderos*; these officials received only a small annual pension from the profits of the mill. Although the Lima government designed these measures to ameliorate abuses and extend the viceroy's power, the administrators most often proved corrupt or inept. To rectify this problem, in 1621 a justice (*oidor*) of the *Audiencia* of Quito, Matías de Peralta, framed a series of laws (*ordenanzas*) governing the operation of the mills and the responsibilities of the administrators. Despite these regulations, the honesty and efficiency of the administrators failed to improve. In 1634 crown authorities despaired of reforming the system and began leasing the right to operate the mills for six-year terms to local elites, who replaced the viceregal appointees.[26]

21. Nicholas P. Cushner, *Farm and Factory: The Jesuits and the Development of Agrarian Capitalism in Colonial Quito, 1600–1767* (Albany, NY, 1982), 107–14.

22. Javier Ortiz de la Tabla y Ducasse, "El obraje colonial Ecuatoriano: aproximación a su estudio," *Revista de Indias*, 149–50 (1977): 501–04.

23. Cushner, *Farm and Factory*, 106–07.

24. Ortiz de la Tabla, *Los encomenderos de Quito*, 209–15.

25. The first laws regulating the mills were issued by Viceroy Francisco de Toledo. Phelan, *The Kingdom of Quito*, 71–72; Tyrer, "Demographic and Economic History," 114–15.

26. The Matías de Peralta *ordenanzas* are published and analyzed in: Javier Ortiz de la Tabla y Ducasse, "Las ordenanzas de obrajes de Matías de Peralta para la Audiencia de Quito, 1621: régimen laboral de los centros textiles coloniales ecuatorianos," *Anuario de Estudios Americanos*, 33 (1976): 875–931. They are also discussed, along with the introduction of the system of

Table 1.1. *Labor force of the communal obrajes, 1680*

Obraje	Province	Tributaries
Licto	Riobamba	250
Chambo	Riobamba	171
Quimiac	Riobamba	78
San Andrés	Riobamba	173
Cubijies	Riobamba	73
Yaruquies	Riobamba	67
Guasi	Riobamba	98
Puni-Macaxi	Riobamba	133
Penipe	Riobamba	61
Latacunga	Latacunga	384
Sigchos	Latacunga	300
Mulahalo	Latacunga	150
Alausí	Alausí	250
Otavalo	Otavalo	498
Peguche	Otavalo	300
Chimbo	Chimbo (closed 1666)	250
Total		3,236

Source: Robson Brines Tyrer, "Demographic and Economic History of the Audiencia of Quito: Indian Population and the Textile Industry, 1600-1800" (Ph.D. diss., University of California at Berkeley, 1976), 119.

Crown interest in the *obrajes de comunidad* also stemmed from their size and considerable output. Most community mills were located in the geographical heartland of the *obraje* economy, the provinces (*corregimientos*) of Riobamba and Latacunga, which had abundant fertile land and a dense Amerindian population (see Table 1.1). The crown provided annual allotments of Andean village laborers, often exceeding 200 men (see Table 1.1). These large enterprises often specialized in the production of higher-quality cloth, particularly *paño azul*. At their peak of productivity, over 3,200 laborers in the community mills produced approximately 100,000 *varas* of cloth, worth between 250,000 pesos and 400,000 pesos in the Lima market.[27]

Despite their early importance, the community mills became increasingly unprofitable during the seventeenth century. The cost of the crown-mandated administrative structure cut into earnings, as corruption and

leasing community mills to elite administrators, in: Tyrer, "Demographic and Economic History," 120–27. Abundant documentation on the leasing of the *obrajes de comunidad* may be found ANH-Q, Obrajes, Caja 9–10, 1689–1739.

27. Tyrer, "Demographic and Economic History," 120.

inefficiency among the elite administrators leasing the mills continued unabated. In addition, the salaries of local priests, magistrates (*corregidores de indios*), and the workers came from the mills' yearly income, which also added to the costs of operation. The abnormally high tribute rates established for communities with *obrajes de comunidad* also had to be deducted from yearly income.[28] Over time, these tax rates proved a heavy burden. A government investigation into the communal mills in the province of Riobamba (at Yaruquies, San Andrés, Puni-Macaxi, Cubijies, Chambo, Lito, Quimiac, and Penipe) found that none consistently produced profits capable of paying local tribute obligations.[29] In fact, few mills in the kingdom met more than half the communal tax assessment. By the late seventeenth century, these problems contributed to a 60-percent drop in the production of *paño* at the community mills.[30]

The decline of the *obrajes de comunidad* was probably inevitable. The crown sanctioned them primarily to extract high taxes from the Amerindians and to pay local crown officials, parish priests, and the pensions of *encomenderos*. Operating the mills to maximize both cloth output and profits was a secondary consideration. When the *audiencia* conducted a study of the communal mills in 1694, the investigators uncovered a stunning array of abuses and inefficiencies. The court attorney (*fiscal protector de indios*) decried the "tyranny" of the administrators, the excessive administrative costs, and the suffering of the indigenous people working in the mills. In the end, the court recognized the failure of the *obrajes de comunidad* and recommended the sale of these enterprises at public auction.[31] By the early eighteenth century, the crown began implementing this policy; in 1728 crown officials sold the last communal mills (Chambo and Puni-Macaxi) in Riobamba to the Leon y Mendoza family.[32]

By the seventeenth century, the most profitable and productive *obrajes* in the Kingdom of Quito were privately owned mills. Early in the century the crown had licensed only 41 of these private *obrajes*, but by 1690 the number had grown to over 100 – an indication of the profitability of the cloth industry.[33] Most of these mills were in the districts of Quito, Latacunga, and Riobamba (see Table 1.2). Although large *obrajes* existed elsewhere (particularly in Otavalo and Ambato), these three districts had

28. *Ibid.*, 122–28; Peruvian tribute rates were set at considerably higher levels than in New Spain; for a discussion of these differences, see Ronald Escobedo Mansilla, *El tributo indígena en el Perú* (siglos XVI–XVII) (Pamplona, Spain, 1979), 104.

29. ANH-Q, Obrajes Caja 9, Obrajes de comunidad venta a censo, 15 octubre 1694.

30. Tyrer, "Demographic and Economic History," 168.

31. ANH-Q, Obrajes Caja 9, El sr. Fiscal sobre los obrajes de comunidad se vendan a censo, 15 octubre 1694.

32. Tyrer, "Demographic and Economic History," 140, 145.

33. *Ibid.*, 152, 159.

Table 1.2. *Regional distribution of textile factories, 1600-1700*

Province	Private	Unlicensed	Communal	Total
Circa 1600				
Ibarra	0	unknown	0	0
Otavalo	0	unknown	2	2
Quito	20	unknown	0	20
Latacunga	7	1	3	11
Ambato	2	unknown	0	2
Riobamba	9	2	9	20
Chimbo	2	unknown	1	3
Alausí	0	unknown	0	0
Totals	40	3	15	58
Circa 1700				
Ibarra	1	6	0	7
Otavalo	2	5	1	8
Quito	37	37	0	74
Latacunga	20	8	3	31
Ambato	8	unknown	0	8
Riobamba	32	1	8	41
Chimbo	0	unknown	0	0
Alausí	0	0	1	1
Unknown location	4			4
Totals	104	57	13	174

Source: Robson Brines Tyrer, "Demographic and Economic History of the Audiencia of Quito: Indian Population and the Textile Industry, 1600-1700" (Ph.D. diss., University of California at Berkeley, 1976), 162.

abundant supplies of fertile land and the large Amerindian labor force needed for the growth of the industry. Such natural advantages explain why nearly 85 percent of the licensed *obrajes* (146 of the 174) were concentrated in these three provinces by 1700 (see Table 1.2).[34]

The crown made large sums by selling licenses for operating private *obrajes* to well-connected members of the regional elite, while prohibiting other entrepreneurs from participating in the industry. Between 1601 and 1628, the crown issued thirty-eight permits, which gave the mill operators (*obrajeros*) the right to conscript a servile labor force.[35] As with the *obrajes de comunidad*, heavy tax burdens forced many local Andean villagers to work as wage laborers in the mills to meet their tax obligations. For an additional fee, some licenses included the right to receive grants of forced laborers (*mitayos*). One *obrajero*, Juan de Santisteban, paid

34. *Ibid.*, 163.
35. *Ibid.*

4,000 pesos in 1644 for his grant of 112 forced laborers. In the case of the large complex at San Ildefonso in Ambato, the crown license also authorized the use of African slave laborers.[36]

Most of the wealthiest *obrajeros* established mills – employing upwards of 50 to 100 laborers – on rural properties, linked to food-producing estates and sheep ranches. The Jesuit estate complex in the Chillos Valley, for example, consisted of a sheep ranch at Tigua to furnish wool, a mill to make cloth, a *hacienda* at Pintag that supplied foodstuffs for the labor force, and another ranch at Ichubamba that raised mules to distribute the finished product.[37] Such integrated family-owned or clerical enterprises allowed *obrajeros* the flexibility of moving laborers from one estate to another, depending on the seasonal needs of the mill, agriculture, and grazing. Furthermore, they linked the key factors of production in one enterprise, which reduced the problems of recruiting laborers, minimized outlays of scarce specie for raw materials, and cut transaction costs.[38] As a result, these large integrated estates allowed mill owners to produce high-quality *paños* or coarser *bayetas* and *jergas*, which they could sell at competitive prices, despite their distance from the sources of demand in Peru, Upper Peru, and New Granada.

Apart from these large rural *obrajes*, a number of smaller enterprises developed during the seventeenth century. Most of these mills were un-licensed, employed under twenty workers, and developed on small rural holdings (*galpones*) or on the outskirts of urban areas. These more modest businesses, called *obrajuelos* or *chorillos*, were often marginal enterprises specializing in *bayetas* and *jergas*, most commonly sold in the New Gra-nada market.[39] Although seldom a threat to the profits of larger produc-ers, the small-scale operators had gained a secure market niche by the middle seventeenth century. The number of these unlicensed mills grew to at least fifty by the end of the seventeenth century, and they manu-factured a good deal of the coarse, cheap cloth in the *audiencia* district.[40]

The growth of these *obrajuelos* and *chorillos* eventually prompted bitter complaints from the larger mill owners. The wealthy *obrajeros* resented these small, illegal operations, particularly as the price of *paño* began to fall later in the seventeenth century. Many of the most vehement protests came from owners of large *obrajes* in the northern provinces, who re-

36. *Ibid.*, 153.
37. Cushner, *Farm and Factory*, 89.
38. Tyrer, "Demographic and Economic History," 141–42; 293–95, 320. Apparently not all *obrajes* were integrated complexes, with their own supplies of raw materials (particularly wool). This made them more vulnerable, since key inputs, such as wool, then had to be purchased with cash.
39. *Ibid.*, 160–61; 175.
40. *Ibid.*, 175; Powers, "Indian Migration and Socio-Political Change," 170–86.

sponded to falling *paño* prices by moving into the production of cheaper *bayetas* and *jergas* for the New Granada market. This put them in direct competition with the smaller enterprises, which naturally heightened tensions. In fact, the complaints of these *obrajeros* (and the lure of new licensing revenues) prompted the crown in the 1680s to begin selling permits for all mills operating in the kingdom and stamping out any illegal businesses.[41] Between 1690 and 1712, crown officials issued at least ninety-two licenses for *obrajes*, *obrajuelos*, and *chorillos* scattered throughout the north-central sierra, which produced over 70,000 pesos for the royal treasury.[42]

Regardless of this infighting, crown policy and the steady colonial demand for cloth allowed the woolen textile industry to thrive in the north-central sierra by the seventeenth century. The Spanish mercantile legislation tightly regulated the flow of European imports into South American markets. Spanish manufactories proved utterly incapable of meeting the colonial demand for cheap textiles, and the relatively high prices and irregular supplies of contraband imports often made them an impractical alternative for colonial consumers. As a result, cloth producers in Quito could use their political clout, abundant labor supplies, and raw materials to market their woolens throughout the Pacific trading system. By the 1690s, the *obrajes* in the Kingdom of Quito produced a combined total of 210,000 *varas* of *paño* and 425,000 *varas* of coarser cloth annually, worth approximately 3 million pesos in the markets of Peru and New Granada. In addition, the mills employed roughly one in every six tax-paying male Andeans during the period.[43] These large and small enterprises also made a wide range of cloth products like hats (*sombreros*), blankets (*fresadas*), and ponchos. This dynamic local textile industry served as the economic foundation of the Kingdom of Quito.

The onset of crisis

By the late seventeenth century, the conditions that had given rise to the economic prosperity of the textile manufactories in the Kingdom of Quito began to deteriorate. The gradual decline of the mining economy in Peru and Bolivia curtailed the demand for cloth in southern markets over time. The growth of textile mills closer to the mines, in provinces like Conchucos, Huaylas, Cajamarca, Cusco, and Cochabamba, also provided competition for Quito's *paños*, *bayetas*, and *jergas* at a time when the decline

---

41. Tyrer, "Demographic and Economic History," 175.
42. ANH-Q, Obrajes Caja 9, Autos de Indultos de Obrajes de la Ciudad de Quito y todo su provincia, 10 junio 1690.
43. Tyrer, "Demographic and Economic History," 166–68; 173–75.

of silver mining had already lessened the overall demand for American cloth. The earthquakes beginning in 1687 contributed further to the falling demand for *Quiteño* woolens by devastating the city of Lima and undermining its strength as a marketing center for over a decade.[44]

During this period a number of natural disasters also struck the Kingdom of Quito, causing thousands of deaths throughout the region. In 1691, a serious spring drought led to widespread hunger in the district, followed in September by an epidemic of measles (*sarampión*). The population, already weakened by famine and disease, had to endure further outbreaks of measles and smallpox (*viruelas*) in 1692, and fevers (*tabardillo*) the next year. These epidemics attacked both the urban and rural areas but struck with particular virulence among the Amerindian population. Efforts at public health measures and treatment were crude and unavailing; the pestilence continued unabated until 1695. Relief for the beleaguered population of the kingdom still proved illusive, however, as a devastating earthquake struck in June of 1698, causing additional deaths and great physical destruction in the provinces of Quito, Latacunga, Ambato, and Riobamba. Droughts also continued to plague the district until 1704.[45] Together, these natural disasters probably accounted for the death of almost one-third of the Amerindian labor force.[46] Such terrible losses effectively ended the period of cheap, available labor that had been so influential in the rise of the highland textile industry.

Colonial competitors, epidemic disease, drought, and earthquakes were followed by another serious threat to the *Quiteño* cloth industry – the importation of cheap, high-quality European cloth. As the legal fleet system serving Portobelo and Cartagena faltered during the War of the Spanish Succession (1700–16), French traders took the lead in introducing European textiles.[47] According to some estimates, the French had already supplied as much as two-thirds of the cloth sent by the Seville and Cádiz merchant monopolies through the legal fleet system. During the succession struggle, however, the French cleverly used their alliance with Philip V to wrest concessions. On 11 January 1701, for example,

---

44. For a more detailed discussion of this process, see Andrien, *Crisis and Decline*, 23–28.
45. Suzanne Austin Alchon, *Native Society and Disease in Colonial Ecuador* (Cambridge, 1992), 89–99.
46. Tyrer, "Demographic and Economic History," 39.
47. The classic study of the French Pacific trade in the early eighteenth century is Erik W. Dahlgren, *Les relations commerciales et maritimes entre la France et les cotes de l'Ocean Pacifique*: Vol. 1, *Le commerce de la Mar du Sud jusqu'a la Paix d'Utrech* (Paris, 1909). Two fine studies of the entry of European goods and the collapse of the Portobelo Fairs are: George Robertson Dilg, "The Collapse of the Portobelo Fairs: A Study in Spanish Commercial Reform, 1720–1740" (Ph.D. diss., Indiana University, 1975); and Geoffrey J. Walker, *Spanish Politics and Imperial Trade, 1700–1789* (Bloomington, IN, 1979). The most important recent work on the French trade, which has superseded all past studies, is Carlos Daniel Malamud Rikles, *Cádiz y Saint Malo en el comercio colonial Peruano (1698–1725)*.

the king decreed that French ships could enter colonial ports for provisioning, but this opening merely became a pretext for merchants to bypass Spanish intermediaries and to trade directly with the colonies.[48] The crown issued edits (*cédulas*) in 1706, 1708, 1712, 1713, and 1715 prohibiting any illicit trade with the empire, but to no avail.[49] By securing some legal licenses in Madrid, but mostly through direct contraband commerce, French traders began flooding the Pacific markets with European cloth.[50] In effect, this inundation of European imports ended the period of Spanish mercantile protection most responsible for the growth of the *Quiteño* cloth manufactories.

The French had many incentives to penetrate Spanish South American markets. The war debts accumulated by King Louis XIV had produced a serious shortage of specie, which trade with Spanish colonial markets in Peru could ease. Meanwhile, French cloth manufacturers and merchants sought outlets for their textiles, particularly from ports like Bayonne, Marsailles, and especially Saint-Malo.[51] These French interests had been involved with the Cádiz monopolists in supplying American markets, and the prospect of gaining direct access to Peruvian silver proved a powerful lure. The trade in legal and contraband goods in Peru provided the French over 3.5 million pesos annually in the peak years between 1703 and 1718. During the entire period from 1700 to 1725, the volume of France's trade in the Pacific probably totaled nearly 100 million pesos, approximately 68 percent of the viceroyalty's foreign trade.[52]

French merchants exploited their considerable economic advantages to undercut American textiles in Spanish South American markets. These traders could import a wide variety of different-priced European textiles to meet the specialized needs of colonial consumers. Upscale cottons, linens, and damasks from Rouen, Cambray, and Brittany were suited for elite tastes, while common woolen, cotton, and flaxen textiles met the demands of those with more modest incomes. In addition, since most French traders were contrabandists, they did not have to pay the heavy commercial taxes levied by the Spanish crown. Contemporaries estimated that selling 1,256 *varas* of French Rouen cloth through legal channels would yield a profit of 752 pesos (or 25 percent). By avoiding taxes, however, an illicit trader could earn a profit of 2,926 pesos (or 116 percent) for the same merchandise.[53] As the flood of European wares increased, the price of imports also declined in the major South American

48. Dilg, "Collapse of the Portobelo Fairs," 32; Malamud Rikles, *Cádiz y Saint Melo*, 120.
49. Malamud Rikles, *Cádiz y Saint Malo*, 121.
50. Ibid., 97–98; Dilg, "Collapse of the Portobelo Fairs," 39–40.
51. Malamud Rikles, *Cádiz y Saint Malo*, 55–67.
52. *Ibid.*, 81.
53. Dilg, "Collapse of the Portobelo Fairs," 49–50.

markets. In Upper Peru, for example, the selling price of Rouen linen fell dramatically between 1691 and 1716.[54] It is no small wonder that increasing numbers of colonial consumers began to substitute these relatively cheap, high-quality imported textiles for *Quiteño* woolens.

Despite this competitive edge, French contrabandists still needed the cooperation of colonial officials to gain steady access to American markets. The interim viceroy of Peru, Diego Ladrón de Guevara (1710–16), and most of the Lima *audiencia* were implicated to some degree in the contraband trade.[55] When an intrepid, newly appointed *oidor* in Lima, Bernardo Gómez Frigoso, naively tried to expose such widespread complicity in the contraband trade, he found himself a local pariah. On 27 January 1716, Gómez discovered a cache of illegal goods in Lima, ostensibly owned by several leading merchants. The *oidor* immediately had the goods seized and placed under guard, pending legal action. When Gómez returned the next morning, however, he found the guards dutifully in place before the locked door, but the walls of the building had been removed and the merchandise stolen. An exasperated Gómez tried to interrogate the guards, but they refused even to give their names and fled. Instead of sharing the justice's outrage, his colleagues on the *audiencia* berated Gómez for pressing charges in the case. Later, a mob of angry citizens attacked him in the street, forcing the frightened judge to take refuge in a local church. Fearing for his life, Gómez feigned illness and refused to leave the sanctuary. By the time local authorities began making inquiries, all the incriminating evidence had been sold, moved, or destroyed. In the end, only the unfortunate Bernardo Gómez Frigoso suffered; he was convicted, after having admitted that he had distorted evidence in the case.[56]

The new Bourbon dynasty eventually regained enough control over the bureaucracy and the Pacific shipping lanes to stem these French imports by 1725, but the cloth manufacturers of Quito continued to suffer losses, particularly in the important Lima market. As the crown eased trade restrictions, particularly after the end of the Portobelo Fairs in 1740, Spanish merchants began to export increasingly large quantities of European wares. Legal imports of European goods into the Spanish Indies rose from just over 175,000 tons between 1681 and 1709 to nearly

---

54. According to Enrique Tandeter and Nathan Wachtel, the price trends of Rouen linen were undoubtedly representative of those for all textile imports. The price index for Rouen linens fell from 406 in 1691 to only 60 in 1716. Enrique Tandeter and Nathan Wachtel, "Prices and Agricultural Production in Potosí and Charcas," in Lyman L. Johnson and Enrique Tandeter, eds., *Essays on the Price History of Eighteenth-Century Latin America* (Albuquerque, 1990), 202–10.

55. Walker, *Spanish Politics*, 61–62.

56. Dilg, "Collapse of the Portbelo Fairs," 36–38.

740,000 tons from 1748 to 1778.[57] Over one-third of this volume was clothing. In fact, between 1720 and 1751, Cádiz merchants exported 40,000 tons of textiles to the Indies.[58] With this steadily rising supply of imports, the price of European textiles continued to fall, which only encouraged more consumption.[59] In the end, this continued inflow of European cloth through the legal trade system dramatically undercut the market share of American textiles.

For regions like the Kingdom of Quito, developments in the colonial economy of the seventeenth century produced an era of sustained prosperity. As the productivity of the dominant silver-mining economy and commercial linkages to Europe slowly weakened, a more stable and self-sufficient network of regional economies evolved. Mining still dominated, but the development of wine, agricultural, grazing, and textile sectors gave the vast Peruvian viceroyalty a more diversified economic base. At the same time, trade in legal and contraband goods supplied thriving regional markets in South America and beyond – in Central America, Mexico, and even the Far East. These regional economies, such as Quito, maintained indirect ties to international markets, but they also developed a buoyancy and strength no longer so dependent on the international trade in silver. In short, the pillaging conquest economy based on silver mining had given way to a more stable, self-sufficient, and mature economic order. Ironically, the decline of commercial ties with Spain promoted unprecedented levels of regional prosperity in some important regions of the Viceroyalty of Peru, particularly the Kingdom of Quito.

From the late sixteenth century, crown policies worked to nurture the development of the *obraje* sector in the north-central highlands. Although officially hostile to colonial manufacturing, the Madrid government recognized that Spanish merchants could never supply the cloth needed in viceregal markets. This led crown authorities to license the *obrajes* of Quito and to provide the legal means to conscript Amerindian laborers. Then, local elites in the district could effectively marshall the region's labor, food, and livestock resources to establish a prosperous textile economy, until the crises of the late seventeenth century.

Although the natural disasters of the 1690s curtailed profits, the crown delivered the decisive blow to the *Quiteño* manufactories. New methods of textile manufacturing in Europe led to greater productivity and re-

57. Antonio García Baquero González, *Cádiz y el Atlántico (1717–1778)*, 2 vols. (Seville, 1976), I, 541.
58. *Ibid.*, 1:312.
59. Tandeter and Wachtel, "Prices and Agricultural Production," 207.

duced prices, making it feasible to sell larger quantities of relatively cheap, high-quality textiles in distant American markets. First through weakness and later by design, the Spanish crown abetted this process. From the War of the Spanish Succession, the Madrid government effectively abandoned two hundred years of mercantile protectionism by allowing French traders to introduce large quantities of cloth throughout the Pacific trading zone. After the failure of efforts to reestablish the monopoly fleet system, the crown eased its trade controls further, which only increased the importation of European wares. Colonial manufacturing centers, such as Quito, could not compete; European imports captured many of the most lucrative colonial markets. In essence, Spanish commercial policies sacrificed colonial manufactories to promote the transatlantic trade. The result was a prolonged period of economic decline that afflicted the north-central highlands of the kingdom and produced profound socioeconomic changes throughout the remainder of the colonial period.

2

The people and markets of the kingdom

The decline of the *obraje* sector had a profound demographic and economic impact in the Kingdom of Quito between 1690 and 1830. Many Andeans had left their traditional ethnic communities by the seventeenth century to work in Spanish *obrajes*, on *haciendas*, and in the chief cities. As manufacturing in the north-central sierra declined, however, increasing numbers of indigenous people lost their jobs and migrated from the north-central highlands to regions promising greater economic opportunities in the south sierra and later the coast.[1] From the 1690s the province of Cuenca benefitted from this influx of Amerindians to develop an economy providing textiles and foodstuffs for regional markets. Entrepreneurs in the southern region also profited from exports to Europe of *cascarilla*, a tree bark rich in quinine for medicines. The province of Guayaquil began attracting emigrants later in the eighteenth century, when the export of cacao, tobacco, and coffee led to a coastal economic boom.

State policies often influenced the direction of these important structural changes in the kingdom's market economy. By ending nearly two centuries of commercial protectionism, the crown effectively undermined manufacturing in Quito and the entire north-central highlands, which lessened employment opportunities and prompted the out-migration of many Amerindians. Even Cuenca and Guayaquil, which presided over a vibrant network of regional commercial exchanges, still had their economic development influenced by outside political and economic forces. Crown subsidies for mining in Peru indirectly helped provide the market for Cuenca's textiles, and the advent of imperial free trade (between 1778 and 1789) promoted the coastal export economy. In addition, the prosperity of both regional economies depended on large merchant houses in centers favored by the state (particularly Lima and Mexico City) to market

---

1. According to Jacob Price, the economic roles of most pre-industrial towns may be divided into four categories: (1) civil and ecclesiastical administration, (2) maritime transport and external exchange, (3) manufacturing, and (4) internal service. See Jacob Price, "Economic Function and the Growth of American Port Towns in the Eighteenth Century," *Perspectives in American History*, 8 (1974): 130.

their goods and to finance their economic growth. In short, state policies had a profound cumulative impact on shaping the links between regional markets in the kingdom and the wider imperial and international economies.

The human base of the kingdom

Tracing demographic changes in the Kingdom of Quito poses daunting methodological challenges.[2] The most abundant data are colonial tribute rolls, which record only numbers of tax-paying Amerindian males between the ages of eighteen and fifty. These materials are fragmentary until the late eighteenth century, and unscrupulous local officials often manipulated the figures to control tax assessments and the flow of public revenues.[3] Amerindian communities, fearing higher taxes, also resisted many efforts to update tribute lists.[4] As a result, the first official census of the kingdom did not occur until 1778–81, when the crown ordered the *fiscal* of the *audiencia*, Juan Josef de Villalengua y Marfil, to count

2. Some important studies of historical demography in the *Audiencia* of Quito are the following: Robson Brines Tyrer, "The Demographic and Economic History of the Audiencia of Quito: Indian Population and the Textile Industry, 1600–1800" (Ph.D. diss., University of California at Berkeley, 1976); Martin Minchom, *The People of Quito, 1690–1810: Change and Unrest in the Underclass* (Westport, CT, 1994); idem, "Demographic Change in Eighteenth Century Ecuador," in D. Delaunay and M. Portais, eds., *Equateur 1986*, 2 vols. (Paris, 1989), 1:179–96; idem, "The Making of a White Province: Demographic Movement and Ethnic Transformation in the South of the Audiencia of Quito (1670–1830)," *Bulletin de l'Institut Français d'Études Andines*, 12 (1983): 23–39; idem, "Historia demográfica de Loja y su provincia desde 1700 hasta finales de la colonia," *Cultura*, 15 (enero–abril 1983): 149–70; Michael T. Hamerly, *Historia social y económica de la antigua provincia de Guayaquil, 1763–1842* (Guayaquil, 1973); idem, "La demografía histórica del distrito de Cuenca, 1778–1838," *Boletín de la Academia Nacional de Historia*, 53 (julio–diciembre 1970): 203–29; María Luisa Laviana Cuetos, *Guayaquil en el siglo XVIII: recursos naturales y desarrollo económico* (Seville, 1987); Rosemary D. F. Bromley, "Urban Growth and Decline in the Central Sierra of Ecuador, 1698–1940" (Ph.D. diss., University of Wales, 1977); idem, "Disasters and Population Change in Central Highland Ecuador, 1778–1825," in David J. Robinson, ed., *Social Fabric and Spatial Structure in Colonial Latin America* (Ann Arbor, MI, 1979), 85–115. An important new study of migration in the sixteenth and seventeenth centuries is: Karen M. Powers, "Indian Migration and Socio-Political Change in the Audiencia of Quito" (Ph.D. diss., New York University, 1984). All of these works discuss critically the validity and the weaknesses of the available demographic sources.

3. The notorious corruption of the local magistrates led crown authorities to reform the tribute system in 1718 and later to sell the right to collect Amerindian tribute to private citizens between 1734 and 1778. This process made tribute rolls the private property of the tax farmers rather than public records. As a result, tribute lists for this period are rarely found in the archives. Archivo General de Indias (hereafter cited as AGI), Quito, 241, Certificación Dada por los Oficiales Rls de estas Cajas, dcto. 5, 1780.

4. For a full account of how attempts to enumerate rural and urban Amerindian groups could lead to violent protest, see: Segundo Moreno Yánez, *Sublevaciones indígenas en la Audiencia de Quito, desde comienzos del siglo XVIII hasta finales de la colonia* (Quito, 1985 edn.), passim.

the population. Villalengua relied on parish records, tax rolls, and *hacienda* accounting books to determine his population figures. Since Villalengua was concerned primarily with the number of Andean tributaries, his numeration combines the European, black, and caste populations into a single census category. Moreover, Villalengua's superiors hoped to use this census to increase taxes, so his totals tend to be inflated for most regions.[5] The census takers also failed to distinguish between permanent residents and migrants for some Amerindian parishes, and they usually present unreliable figures for urban areas, where rooting out taxpayers and determining their ethnicity proved most difficult.[6]

The only official state population counts began in 1778, with the censuses (*padrones*) ordered by the Madrid government. Unfortunately, no scholar has uncovered the original house-by-house census materials (if they were ever compiled), making the figures difficult to verify and any detailed demographic analyses impossible. Later censuses appear to be mere reproductions of early counts, replete with copying errors.[7] The earliest *padrones*, however, present minimal figures for each parish, which can be compared to the tribute lists and the Villalengua census to examine very basic demographic trends.[8] Population estimates based on such figures must remain extremely tentative, but they do reflect the changing size of different demographic groups (by sex, ethnicity, and civil status) and do provide some important information on migration patterns.

All of these census materials indicate that the population of the *Audiencia* of Quito experienced only minimal growth during the eighteenth century. The Amerindian population recovered slowly from the epidemics of the 1690s.[9] Birth rates remained high, but periodic epidemics, natural disasters, and the sluggish highland economy apparently inhibited any sustained demographic expansion for the kingdom as a whole.[10]

The official *padrones* indicate that even by the late eighteenth century most of the population (65 percent) still lived in the north and central sierra districts (see Table 2.1). Over 70 percent of these residents in the north-central highlands were Amerindians, who primarily engaged in

5. According to Martin Minchom, Villalengua's figures are inflated for most regions in comparison to the official *padrones*, except for the central sierra. Minchom, "Demographic Change in Eighteenth Century Ecuador," 182.

6. For a detailed discussion of the problems in using the Villalengua enumeration, see *ibid.*, 181–85. The summary figures for the Villalengua census are preserved in AGI, Quito 381 or 412.

7. These problems are explained in Bromley, "Disasters and Population Change," 88–89. Like Bromley, I have used average figures, compiled from several censuses to minimize the significance of any single error in the *padrones*.

8. This point is made clearly in Laviana Cuetos, *Guayaquil en el siglo XVIII*, 98.

9. Tyrer, "Demographic and Economic History," 51–62.

10. Bromley, "Disasters and Population Change," 99–115.

Table 2.1. *Social character of the population, Audiencia of Quito, in the late colonial period*

Province	Clerics	Europeans	Andeans	Castes	Slaves	Totals
Quito	960	18,758	42,098	969	550	63,335
Ibarra	97	7,075	8,460	122	1,203	16,957
Otavalo	33	2,481	25,230	5,096	264	33,104
Latacunga	55	11,543	37,978	372	20	49,968
Ambato	41	14,793	28,417	63	27	43,341
Riobamba	127	14,038	48,735	384	96	63,380
Guaranda	20	6,726	8,155		142	15,043
Subtotal	1,333	75,414	199,073	7,006	2,302	285,128
Alausí [a]						11,960
Cuenca	199	26,264	55,939	1,022	254	83,678
Loja	81	6,772	13,221	4,565	312	24,951
Subtotal	280[a]	33,036[a]	69,160[a]	5,587[a]	566[a]	120,589
Guayaquil	75	4,962	10,011	15,961	2,068	33,007
Total						438,724

[a] Detailed figures for Alausí are not available and are not included in these subtotals. This table also excludes Oriente province, which was thinly populated and played little role in the socioeconomic evolution of the *audiencia*. The total population of this frontier zone reached only 13,177 in 1780.

Sources: AGI, Quito, 242, Padrón de la Audiencia de Quito de 1782; Quito, 378A, Padrón de la Audiencia de Quito de 1783; Quito, 243, Padrón de la Audiencia de Quito de 1785; ANH-Q, Empadronamientos, Caja 15, Padrones de Ibarra, 1779, 1780, 1784, 1786; Padrones de Otavalo, 1779, 1780, 1785; Caja 5, Padrones de Latacunga, 1779, 1780, 1782, 1784; Caja 27, Padrones de Ambato, 1779-82, 1784, 1787, 1789; Caja 32, Padrones de Chimbo-Guaranda, 1778, 1780, 1789, 1791; Caja 17, Padrones de Loja, 1778, 1780, 1784, 1786, 1789, 1814; Caja 1, Padrón de Cuenca, 1780; Martin Minchom, *The People of Quito, 1690-1810: Change and Unrest in the Underclass* (Westport, CT, 1994), 117-52; Michael T. Hamerly, *Historia social y económica de la antigua provincia de Guayaquil, 1763-1842* (Guayaquil, 1973), 65-97; and María Luisa Laviana Cuetos, *Guayaquil en el siglo XVIII: recursos naturales y desarrollo económico* (Seville, 1987), 77-159, 376-77.

subsistence agriculture. A majority of the indigenous population worked on Spanish estates only in the provinces of Quito, Latacunga, and Riobamba – the regions of the north-central sierra most deeply involved in textile manufacturing.[11] The relatively small European and caste populations resided primarily in the cities and towns, with smaller numbers scattered in the rural zones. Only Ibarra in the north had a significant

11. The figures for Latacunga indicate that a majority of the Andean population resided on Spanish estates until the 1750s. By 1812, however, the tribute records indicate that 57 percent then lived in traditional villages. The same source indicates that 49 percent of the Andean population of Riobamba lived in their villages as late as 1792; by 1812 that figure had risen to 54 percent. Tyrer, "Demographic and Economic History," 435.

slave population, working principally on lowland sugar estates in the Chota and Mira river valleys (see Table 2.1).

The ethnic composition of the south sierra was similar to that of the rest of the highlands. The Andean population was by far the largest sector, accounting for 64 percent of the population. Likewise, the small European population generally settled in the cities and towns, or owned scattered rural properties. The only significant regional anomaly was the large caste population of over 4,500 in the province of Loja, south of Cuenca (Table 2.1). Only Otavalo in the north and Guayaquil on the coast had such large numbers of racially mixed residents (see Map 1).

The coastal region had the most distinct ethnic configuration.[12] The small Amerindian population lived in the provinces of Machala, Porto-viejo, and Santa Elena. The large caste population, at 48 percent of the total, resided throughout the coastal zone, serving principally as laborers and artisans. The Guayaquil district was also home for nearly half of the slaves living in the *audiencia*, who usually worked as laborers on local plantations or as domestic servants (see Map 1). Finally, the European population of nearly 5,000 comprised the regional elite, living principally in the city of Guayaquil and the rural plantations located throughout the coastal zone (Table 2.1).

Migration and socioeconomic change

Given the minimal growth of the population and the stable birth rates, migration undoubtedly accounted for the significant regional demographic shifts taking place during the eighteenth century.[13] The Inca invaders in the late fifteenth century had removed many of the native Cañari people from the south highlands, leaving the region sparsely populated when the Spaniards arrived a generation later. By the late eighteenth century, however, emigrants from the north-central highlands gave the Cuenca province a population density ranging from 7 to 8 persons per square kilometer.[14] Only the Loja region remained underpopulated,

12. Historians have uncovered only two complete *padrones* for Guayaquil, from 1780 and 1790. On the other hand, the detailed estimates from former governor Juan Antonio de Zelaya (1765) and the account of Francisco de Requena (1774) provide relatively reliable figures, along with the late colonial tribute returns, to verify the counts taken in 1780 and 1790. See Laviana Cuetos, *Guayaquil en el siglo XVIII*, 87–104; Hamerly, *Historia económica y social*, 65–97.

13. Bromley, "Disasters and Population Change," 99; Minchom, "Demographic Change in Eighteenth Century Ecuador," 184.

14. Despite these migrations, the principal Amerindian centers of the central sierra still had dense populations: Latacunga had nearly 10 persons per square kilometer, while the numbers for Ambato and Riobamba ranged between 13.5 and 14.2. These figures are presented in Linda Alexander Rodríguez, *The Search for Public Policy: Regional Politics and Government Finances in Ecuador, 1830–1940* (Berkeley, CA, 1985), 208–09.

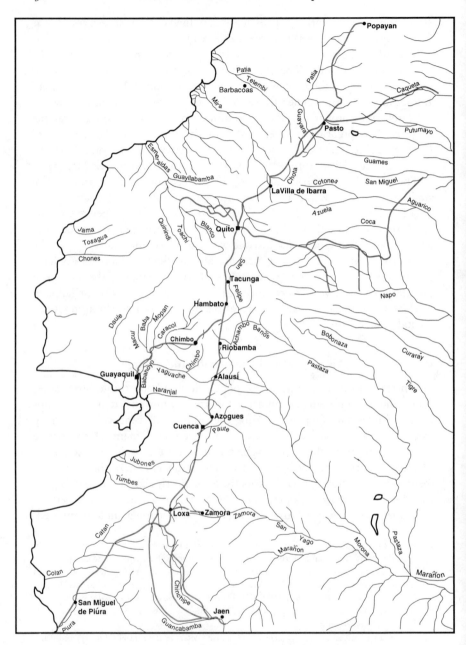

Map 1. Adapted from the map of the *Audiencia* of Quito by Pedro Vicente
Maldonado, 1750. *Source*: J. P. Deler and N. Gomez, *El manejo del
espacio en el Ecuador: etapas claves* (Quito, 1983).

Table 2.2. *Population changes, Audiencia of Quito, between 1779-80 and 1825*

Province	1779-81 Padrón	1825 Padrón	Percent Change
Quito	59,391	63,605	7%
Ibarra	16,585	25,492	54%
Otavalo	32,060	33,233	4%
Latacunga	49,919	55,814	12%
Ambato	42,372	37,495	-12%
Riobamba	66,766	51,137	-23%
Guaranda	14,368	15,006	4%
Alausí	11,960	10,338	-14%
Cuenca	83,678^a	75,785	-9%
Loja	23,810	34,305	44%
Guayaquil	30,343^a	55,048	83%
Total	431,252	457,258	6%

^{a} The figures for Cuenca and Guayaquil differ from those presented in Hamerly and are taken directly from the *padron* of 1780, found in ANH-Q, Empadronimientos, Caja 1, Azuay, 1776-1874, and Guayas, Caja 12, 1846-1871.
Source: Michael T. Hamerly, "La demografía histórica del distrito de Cuenca: 1778-1838," *Boletín de la Academia Nacional de Historia*, 53 (Julio–Diciembre 1970), 222.

with a density of just under 2 persons per square kilometer. The population of the coast never attained such density, but it did more than double between 1779–80 and 1825.[15] In short, population movements during the period from 1690 to 1830 reflected the significant socioeconomic changes taking place in the Kingdom of Quito.

The epidemics of the 1690s began this movement of Andean peoples from their homes in the north-central sierra. In Riobamba, for example, absenteeism reached 50–60 percent in most communities by the early eighteenth century.[16] This migration from the north-central highlands only escalated over the next century. Some regions of the central highlands, such as Riobamba and Ambato, lost between 12 percent and 23 percent of their population between 1779 and 1825 (see Table 2.2). In other regions such as Alausí, however, the out-migration of the Andean population began much later. According to the state tax rolls, the number of registered tributaries in Alausí rose from 1,506 in the late 1780s to over 1,900 by 1800.[17] Within 25 years, however, over 1,500 people had left the region (Table 2.2). Regardless of these regional variations, the

15. The population density of the coast jumped from .5 persons per square kilometer in 1779–80 to 1.2 in 1825. *Ibid.*
16. Powers, "Indian Migration and Socio-Political Change," 151–56; 161.
17. AGI, Quito, Cuentas de Tributos de Alausí, 1782–1800.

general movement of Andeans from the north-central highlands continued throughout the period 1690–1830 (see Map 1).

Leaving their home communities allowed tributaries (called *llactayos*)
to seek the legal status of emigrants, or *forasteros*, which gave them lower
tax assessments and exemptions from forced-labor drafts.[18] In many cases,
crown authorities never could locate these displaced Andeans and register
them on the tax rolls. This often proved a powerful economic incentive
for *llactayos* to migrate, particularly from those highland provinces most
hard hit by the worsening depression in the textile industry. In fact, by
the 1770s this process of migration was so advanced that enumerators
working on the Villalengua census classified numerous Andeans as crown
emigrants (*forasteros coronas*) or simply (*coronas*), indicating that their original home community could not be determined.[19] Many of these migrants
had abandoned their ethnic communities long before the 1780s. Those
who could not settle in a prosperous region of the south highlands or
the coast undoubtedly formed an impoverished lumpen proletariat moving throughout the kingdom in search of work.

The only regions in the north-central sierra to register any significant
gains in population were Latacunga (12 percent) and Ibarra (54 percent).
Latacunga benefitted from rich farmland and numerous Spanish estates,
which undoubtedly attracted new settlers. The region's *obrajes*, which
specialized in lower-quality cloth for the northern trade to New Granada,
were also less affected by the downturn in the textile industry.[20] Ibarra
had always been an underpopulated province of large Spanish estates involved in producing foodstuffs and sugar cane, not cloth (see Map 1). As
a result, the province remained largely untouched by the decline in the
obraje sector (see Table 2.2).[21]

18. The term *llactayo* was commonly used in the fiscal documentation to denote a tributary. The
    root word, *llacta*, however, usually referred to an Andean territorial entity (town, village, or
    province), its local deities (*huacas*), and the group of original inhabitants favored by the *huaca*.
    As a result, the word *llactayo* or *llactayuc* (in Quichua) originally meant much more than "original
    resident" or "taxpayer." See Frank Salomon and George Urioste, eds. and trans., *The Huarochirí
    Manuscript: A Testament of Ancient and Colonial Andean Religion* (Austin, TX, 1991), 23–24.
19. Villalengua's census tends to overcount the numbers of *llactayos*, apparently to maximize tribute
    receipts. Villalengua also began the process of having Amerindians pay tribute in their com-
    munities of residence, not their original village, to simplify collection procedures. Villalengua
    found the highest numbers of *coronas* in the Cuenca and Loja provinces; he did not count the
    Amerindian population of the coast, where he would undoubtedly have found some additional
    concentrations of migrants. The tribute rates for these *coronas* was usually around one-half the
    amounts collected from *llactayos*. For a comparison of the Villalengua figures and the lower
    figures taken from the *padrones*, see Minchom, "Demographic Change in Eighteenth Century
    Ecuador," 182–83. For the procedures used by Villalengua in assessing tribute rates and the
    numbers of *coronas* found in the enumeration, see AGI, Quito, 381, 412.
20. Bromley, "Disasters and Population Change," 102–03; Tyrer, "Demographic and Economic
    History," 319–20.
21. For a detailed regional study of Ibarra's economic evolution, see Rosario Coronel Feijóo, *El Valle*

Andean migrants began moving in large numbers to the south sierra by the late seventeenth century, lured by abundant supplies of vacant land. The Andean tributary population in Cuenca at first rose slowly from under 3,000 in the 1660s to nearly 4,500 by 1683.[22] By the 1690s, however, growth accelerated. A census in 1727 counted almost 9,000 tributaries, while the Villalengua enumeration registered over 11,000 taxpayers and a total Andean population of nearly 60,000.[23] In Loja the growth was less spectacular; the number of tributaries rose from just under 2,600 in 1764 to 3,200 by the 1780s.[24] In both provinces, however, this growth undoubtedly resulted from migration. By the late eighteenth century, over 75 percent of the Andean population in both Cuenca and Loja consisted of emigrants (classified either as *forasteros* or *coronas*).[25] Loja even continued as a favored location for migrants until the 1820s, a time when Cuenca's population already had begun its decline (see Table 2.2).

The tribute records of 1792 demonstrate that over 77 percent of the emigrants to the province of Cuenca had settled in the northern and eastern parishes.[26] In all likelihood, these *forasteros* came from the central sierra after the epidemics of the 1690s, particularly neighboring Riobamba.[27] The northern and eastern zones also contained 56 percent of the province's *llactayo* population, which resided primarily in relatively prosperous, traditional settlements. These same zones also accommodated over 68 percent of the Spanish estates in the province of Cuenca, which offered potential jobs for displaced migrants from the central sierra (see

Sangriento: de los indígenas de la coca y el algodón a la hacienda cañera Jesuita, 1580–1700 (Quito, 1991).

22. Tyrer, "Demographic and Economic History," 64.

23. AGI, Quito, 131, Padrón General de Indios que se hallen en la jurisdicción de la Ciudad de Cuenca, 1727; AGI, Quito, 412, Plan de la Numeración de Indios, Españoles, Mestizos, Negros, y Mulatos residente en el Govierno de Cuenca, 1782.

24. Minchom, "The Making of a White Province," 31; idem, "Historia demográfica de Loja," 164; and AGI, Quito, 412, Plan de la Numeración de Indios, Españoles, Mestizos, Negros, y Mulatos residente en el corregimiento de Loxa, 1783.

25. Archivo Nacional de Historia, Quito (hereafter cited as ANH-Q), Presidencia de Quito, 1785–1786, tomo 360, Expediente tramitido por Manuel Vallano y Cuesta . . . de pago y abonos a los indios del corregimiento de Loxa, 1786, 1792 (hereafter cited as Libros de tributos de Loxa); ANH-Q, Presidencia de Quito, 1792–1793, tomo 361, Expediente tramitido por el Admin. Principal de Cuenca dn Jose de Rengifo con . . . sobre el pago y abonos a los indios del corregimiento de Cuenca, 1792 (hereafter cited as Libros de tributos de Cuenca). These figures also appear in summary form in Tyrer, "Demographic and Economic History," 434.

26. ANH-Q, Presidencia de Quito, 1785–1786, tomo 360, Libros de tributos de Loxa; ANH-Q, Presidencia de Quito, 1792–1793, tomo 361, Libros de tributos de Cuenca. Tyrer, "Demographic and Economic History," 434.

27. In 1695, for example, *forasteros* from the *encomienda* of the prince of Esquilache in Riobamba settled predominantly in Quito and Cuenca provinces. Tyrer, "Demographic and Economic History," 87, note 59.

Map 1). By the late eighteenth century, the lure of good land, jobs in the local villages producing textiles, or even settling on Spanish estates all attracted emigrants from the troubled central sierra.[28]

The more sparsely populated province of Loja also drew a sizable number of emigrants. According to the tribute records of 1792, *forasteros* tended to disperse throughout the Loja region, particularly in zones where few traditional Andean villages had existed previously. Most either moved to regions with numerous Spanish estates or to zones with abundant supplies of vacant land.[29]

Emigrants apparently accounted for the considerable number of castes in Loja. The large number of *coronas,* who maintained no ties to their former communities, must have used their ambiguous social position to declare themselves *mestizos,* which freed them from the labor and tax obligations demanded of Amerindians. This phenomenon of "passing" was easier in an underpopulated and underpoliced province such as Loja, with its large and culturally less rooted *corona* population.[30]

The prosperous plantation economy of the coast began to supplant the south highlands as the principal magnet for *forasteros* by the 1790s. The provincial population of Guayaquil grew over 83 percent between 1780 and 1825 – a period when the population of Cuenca fell 9 percent (see Table 2.2). Emigrants to the coast seldom relocated near the traditional coastal Amerindian settlements. They moved instead to emerging centers of economic prosperity throughout the coastal plain, particularly the parishes of Babahoyo, Daule, La Canoa, Palenque, Portoviejo, and Pueblo-viejo.[31]

Despite the large-scale migration from the highlands to the province of Guayaquil, the numbers of coastal Amerindians registered on the tax rolls grew relatively slowly, from under 8,000 in the 1760s to nearly 12,000 by 1790.[32] The largest concentrations of Amerindians remained in the parishes of Portoviejo and Santa Elena, where the inhabitants con-

28. ANH-Q, Presidencia de Quito, 1792–1793, tomo 361, Libros de tributos de Cuenca, 1792.
29. Of the *forasteros,* 20 percent lived in the east around the city of Loja, 20 percent in the west, 34 percent in the north, and just under 20 percent in the south, where mining and the collection of *cascarilla* were centered. The *llactayo* population, by contrast, tended to be in the south (46 percent) and the west (26 percent). ANH-Q, Presidencia de Quito, 1786, tomo 360, Libros de tributos de Loxa, 1793.
30. For a detailed discussion of this phenomenon, see Minchom, "The Making of a White Province," 23–39.
31. Portoviejo was a region with a considerable Amerindian population, but generally the migrants tended not to move to these indigenous settlements. See Laviana Cuetos, *Guayaquil en el siglo XVIII,* 149; Hamerly, *Historia económica y social,* 66–67, 103, 105.
32. Laviana Cuetos, *Guayaquil en el siglo XVIII,* 126. This last figure for 1790 was drawn from the official *padrón* for that year. Records of the tribute administration listed a decline in the number of taxpayers between 1785 and 1800. The Amerindian population of the coast obviously experienced no upsurge. AGI, Quito, 483, Cuentas de tributos de Guayaquil, 1785–1801.

tinued in traditional occupations – fishing, crafts, wood and salt gathering, and farming.[33] Although some found work as urban domestics or plantation laborers, most remained involved in the subsistence economy and played little role in the export sector.

By contrast, the number of castes increased rapidly, from 11,120 in the 1760s to just over 19,200 by 1790, forming nearly 50 percent of the total population along the coast.[34] Most of this caste community settled in the city of Guayaquil and the prosperous centers of plantation agriculture (the parishes of Baba, Yaguache, Daule, and Portoviejo), contributing to the export economy as domestics, plantation workers, and artisans.[35] Although some of these castes were freed slaves and mulatos, most others were probably Andean emigrants from the highlands. The province of Guayaquil remained loosely supervised by crown officials until the 1780s and had a reputation for greater social mobility than the more hierarchical societies of the north-central sierra. As in Loja, many Andean emigrants probably succeeded in "passing" as *mestizos*, to avoid tribute and labor obligations.[36] In this way, they could find work and a refuge from high taxes in their highland communities.

The coastal European population also increased rapidly during the eighteenth century. Internal migration and newcomers from Spain pushed the number of Europeans from 2,300 in 1765 to just under 5,500 in 1790.[37] This relatively small number of creoles and peninsulars, however, never accounted for over 15 percent of the total population. Most of them settled in the city of Guayaquil (where they formed over 25 percent of the residents) or in parishes involved in the export economy.[38]

Although Guayaquil had the largest concentration of slaves in the kingdom, their numbers increased from 1,500 in 1765 to under 2,200 by 1825.[39] Over half these bondsmen resided in the city of Guayaquil by the 1790s, and a mere one-third worked on plantations or became involved in cutting and gathering wood.[40] Slaves in the port city probably worked as domestics, artisans, or manual laborers, while Andean emi-

33. Laviana Cuetos, *Guayaquil en el siglo XVIII*, 134, 149–51.
34. *Ibid.*, 136, cuadro XII.
35. *Ibid.*, 135.
36. Before proving this hypothesis, much additional demographic research must be undertaken. On the other hand, the relatively small caste population of the highlands (Tables 2.1, 2.2) makes it unlikely that any migration of castes to the coast accounted for an upsurge in the numbers of mixed bloods in the province of Guayaquil. In addition, the Andean population was more mobile, and its heavy tax burden made migration to prosperous, underpopulated, and under-policed regions such as the coast an attractive alternative.
37. Laviana Cuetos, *Guayaquil en el siglo XVIII*, 126, cuadro X.
38. *Ibid.*, 128–29.
39. The percentage of slaves in the total population actually fell from approximately 7 percent to 3 percent during this same period. *Ibid.*, 126; 140, cuadro XIV.
40. *Ibid.*, 138–39.

grants and castes performed much of the labor on the coastal cacao, tobacco, sugar, and coffee plantations. The cost of imported slaves made them an increasingly expensive alternative to meeting the coastal labor shortage, given the large numbers of displaced highlanders by the late eighteenth century.

Economic decline, natural disasters, and epidemic diseases served to impel this movement of Andeans and castes from many regions of the north-central sierra in the eighteenth century. The prolonged economic decline of the *obrajes* left many tributaries without the jobs needed to meet their heavy tax obligations, particularly in Riobamba and Quito. A series of earthquakes and volcanic disturbances only accentuated these dismal economic circumstances. The eruptions of Mount Tungurahua (near Ambato) in 1773 and 1777 and the massive earthquake of 1797 disrupted farmlands, destroyed fragile irrigation systems, promoted flooding, and killed thousands of people and their livestock. Equally devastating were major epidemics in 1785 and 1814, which had a particularly high mortality rate among Amerindian children. These economic and natural disasters forced many poor people living on the edge of subsistence to leave their homes in search of work in the south highlands and later the coastal parishes.

The urban markets of the Kingdom of Quito

Long-term demographic and economic trends also altered the structure and functioning of the urban economies in Quito, Cuenca, and Guayaquil between 1690 and 1830. In the seventeenth century, Quito served as the manufacturing, commercial, and administrative hub of the kingdom, and its economic orbit extended throughout the north-central sierra. After the slow deterioration of the textile trade, the capital's urban economy increasingly came to depend on the administrative and service sectors. These trends in the north-central sierra also encouraged Andean migrations, which helped transform Cuenca from a provincial backwater to a prosperous regional trading center. By the late eighteenth century, as the pattern of migration shifted from the highlands to the coast, the city of Guayaquil evolved from a small port and shipbuilding center into the nucleus of a burgeoning export economy.

The slow decline of Quito

Despite the falling output of the *obrajes*, the city of Quito and its hinterland (the Five Leagues) experienced a period of demographic recovery and stability between 1730 and 1780.[41] Fragmentary data on births and

41. The Five Leagues of Quito consisted of the following towns and villages: San Juan Evangelista

mortality from the city's parish records, for example, indicate slow but steady demographic growth during these fifty years, broken only by epidemics in the mid-1740s and 1760s.[42] By the 1780s, however, the capital's population began to decline from approximately 25,000 inhabitants to under 13,400 by 1825. During this period of urban flight, the population of Quito's hinterland stagnated, falling from 39,641 in 1781 to 37,216 in 1814 and then recovering to 39,719 by 1825.[43]

Population trends for the city of Quito mirrored the slow demise of textile manufacturing during the eighteenth century. A partial census of the Amerindian population in the 1730s demonstrates that over half the registered indigenous population still found employment in the textile mills.[44] This pattern had changed considerably, however, by the time the census of sales tax administrator Antonio Romero Tejada was made between 1768 and 1775. Only 2 of the city's 11 registered *obrajes* still functioned, and only 4–6 hat manufacturing plants (*sombrerías*) remained in business. In addition, the city listed just 1 major pottery shop and 3–5 tile factories. The census takers also found only 48 *pulperías* and 124 shops of varying sorts. Although many additional retailers and small manufacturing outlets escaped registration, these figures still indicate a relatively low level of traditional manufacturing and commercial activity for a city of over 20,000.[45]

The occupational data for the parish of Santa Bárbara in 1768 indicates that a variety of service-sector activities may have accounted for Quito's apparent demographic and economic stability between the 1730s and the 1780s. Traditional service occupations like artisan activities (29 percent), domestic services (29 percent), and food and marketing (14 percent) were the most common jobs for the middle- and lower-class citizens of the parish (see Table 2.3). These artisans (mostly carpenters, embroiderers, and cigar rollers) were involved generally in meeting local orders rather than manufacturing for sale outside of the province. Although Santa Bárbara never had many *obrajes*, only eleven people listed occupations related to textile manufacturing in 1768. Among the elite occupations in Santa Bárbara listed in Table 2.3 (the church, government, the professions, and commerce), all provided services rather than producing commodities.[46]

de Chimbacalle, María Magdalena, Chillogallo, Aloac, Aloasí, Machachi, Perucho, San Antonio de Lulubamba, Pomasque, Calacalí, Cotocollao, Guayllabamba, Zambiza, el Quinche, Yaruquí, Puembo y Pifo, Tumbaco, Cumbayá, Guápulo, Alangasí, Conocoto, Pintag, Sangolquí, Amaguaña, and Uyumbicho. Minchom, *The People of Quito*, 27; 125–44.

42. Minchom, "Demographic Change in Eighteenth Century Ecuador," 188–95.
43. Minchom, *The People of Quito*, 140, Table 6.4.
44. Tyrer, "Demographic and Economic History," 59–60; 414–15.
45. This census, found in AGI, Quito, 430, is analyzed in detail in: Javier Ortiz de la Tabla Ducasse, "Panorama económico y social del corregimiento de Quito (1768–1775)," *Revista de Indias*, 145–46 (1976): 83–98.
46. The only productive group were the small number of landowners (4 percent). This *padrón* has

Table 2.3. *Padrón of the Parish of Santa Bárbara, Quito, 1768*

Occupational sector	Amerindians	Europeans	Total
Services	58	5	63 (29%)
Artisans/Crafts	19	44	63 (29%)
Food and Market	14	17	31 (14%)
Industry (Textiles)	11		11 (5%)
Commerce	2	18	20 (9%)
Church		8	8 (4%)
Professions/Government		15	15 (7%)
Landowners		8	8 (4%)
Total[a]	104	115	219[a]

[a]The percentages total over 100% because of rounding off figures.
Source: "Censo de la Ciudad de Quito en 1768," *Museo Histórico (Quito),* 56 (1978): 93-122.

While the small elite of Quito could make a comfortable income from their estates, commerce, a profession, or the bureaucracy, the urban populace faced more restricted economic options as the textile mills closed down. Many of the city's racially mixed and Amerindian plebeian sector coped with these difficult economic times by participating in an evolving underground service economy. Plebeians operated small butcher and leather shops, opened stills and bars to manufacture and sell cane liquor (*aguardiente*) or corn wine (*chicha*), or ran family groceries (*chagras*). The number of peddlers (*gateras*) and hucksters (*regatonas*) – mostly women – selling produce from the surrounding small farms and large estates also proliferated.[47] Most of the goods and services went untaxed and unregulated by city authorities, which allowed the underground economy to provide work for many urban plebeians as manufacturing concerns began to shut down.[48] The presence of this subterranean economy also explains the small number of licensed *pulperías* and shops listed in the Romero Tejada census.[49]

been published in "Censo de la Ciudad de Quito en 1768," *Museo Histórico* (Quito), 56 (1978): 93–122; it has also been summarized in Minchom, *The People of Quito,* 184–86, Table 7.1.

47. The city's sex ratios indicate that there were only 53 men per 100 women in 1797. The predominance of women in the city suggests the diminished importance of traditionally male manufacturing jobs and the importance of service-sector jobs taken by women: domestic servants, *gateras, regatonas,* and grocery store clerks. Minchom, *The People of Quito,* 145–50.

48. The emergence of this underground economy is explained in Minchom, *The People of Quito,* 101–15.

49. According to these tax assessments of 1768–75, Quito had only 70 *pulperías,* while Caracas, a city of similar size, registered over 134. See Martin Minchom, "La economía subterranea y el mercado urbano: pulperos, 'indias gateras,' y 'regatonas' del Quito colonial (siglos XVI–XVII),

Apart from this subterranean service economy, a modest manufacturing and artisan sector emerged, exporting goods principally to New Granada. By the 1780s, merchants based in Quito had organized a cotton textile business employing the cottage or putting-out system of production. Merchants supplied cotton, which the Amerindian and *mestizo* weavers (working in small urban sweatshops or their homes) used to produce cloth, called *tocuyos* or *lienzos*. Sometimes these merchant-entrepreneurs even supplied fine European yarns to manufacture into higher-quality textiles for elite consumption in the north-central sierra, New Granada, and to a lesser degree Lima.[50] In addition, artisans in Quito and its hinterland produced paintings, decorated hides, and made large numbers of rosaries for export.[51] Although these humble enterprises failed to garner large profits, they did provide employment and export earnings for the urban economy during the late colonial period.

A network of socioeconomic ties between Quito and its hinterland gave some modest buoyancy to this urban economy. Peddlers, hucksters, and local store owners often maintained ties in both the city and the countryside. By selling foodstuffs from nearby villages, they linked small-scale Andean and caste farmers to the urban market and provided them with cash to meet their tax obligations. In addition, supplying urban artisans and elites with cheap food helped to ease the personal burdens of families in a declining economy. Members of the elite also benefitted from this emerging service sector. Some castes and Andeans worked as servants in wealthy households, while the network of illegal shops and bars provided an outlet for produce from neighboring elite estates or just cheap food for wealthier urban citizens.[52] In short, the operation of the urban marketplace helped to provide a network of reciprocal, interlocking ties emanating from the city throughout the Five Leagues.[53]

in Segundo Moreno Yánez, ed., *Memorias del primer simposio Europeo sobre antropología del Ecuador* (Quito, 1985), 176–78; and Minchom, *The People of Quito*, 112–14.

50. The head of the *Dirección general de alcabalas*, Carlos Presenti, wrote about such enterprises in his report on trade and manufacturing in the kingdom in 1780. AGI, Quito, Copia del Informe, 31 agosto 1780. The most detailed and sophisticated treatment of the subject is: Christiana Borchart de Moreno, "Más alla del obraje: la producción artesanal en Quito, 1780–1830," *The Americas* (forthcoming), and idem, "La economía quiteña en un periodo de transición: circulación y producción manufacturera y artesanal entre colonia y república" (paper delivered at the Latin American Studies Association meetings, 1992), both cited with the permission of the author.

51. *Ibid.*

52. For an interesting discussion of the development of such urban–rural ties, see Frank Salomon, "Indian Women of Early Colonial Quito as Seen through Their Testaments," *The Americas*, 44 (January 1988): 331–33; 337–40.

53. The evolution of such a subterranean economy tying the city to its hinterland was not unique to Quito. See Fernando Iwasaki Cauti, "Ambulantes y comercio colonial: iniciativas mercantiles en el virreinato del Perú," *Jahrbuch für Geschichte von Staat, Wirtschaft, und Gesselschaft Lateinamerikas*, 24 (1987): 179–211.

Despite these links between the capital and the internal economy, the slow transformation of Quito into more of an administrative and service center ultimately failed to promote any lasting growth and prosperity. Apart from producing moderate amounts of cloth and artisan goods, such an economy failed to generate much specie, and it required lax enforcement of market regulations and tax laws. From 1765, however, the crown began imposing higher taxes and administrative controls in the city, and the urban underground economy apparently experienced difficulties. *Gateras* and *regatonas* found it harder to sell their merchandise without paying taxes, while small- and medium-sized holdings in the hinterland had their taxes increased. Government controls over the sale of *aguardiente* and the licensing of all bars and groceries cut into the small profits of many family-run concerns and also disrupted the ties between the city and its hinterland.[54] The disorder caused by epidemics, natural disasters, and the wars of independence only contributed further to this decline. As a result, Quito's population began declining by the early nineteenth century, as the worsening condition of the urban economy led many people to abandon the city.

Cuenca and the internal economy

While Quito's economy slowly languished, Cuenca benefitted from demographic growth and economic prosperity in the south sierra. Government controls and taxes were minimal in the south highlands, which attracted emigrants and stimulated economic activity. During an inspection (*visita*) of Cuenca in 1735, for example, an *audiencia* justice, Pedro Martínez Arizala, found rich farming and pasturelands that supplied wheat, corn, barley, sugar cane, and various types of meat to local and regional markets. Despite this wealth, the local treasury office barely managed to collect 25,000 pesos annually in the 1730s. Most of these funds came from Amerindian taxes, but local tribute assessments were still much lower than in the north-central sierra. The regional elites paid very little to the crown.[55] It is hardly surprising that the region served as a magnet for the poor and dispossessed from the northern provinces.

As the large numbers of Andean settlers from the central sierra pushed the provincial population to over 80,000 by the 1780s, the city of Cuenca developed into an important regional manufacturing and service center

54. For a discussion of the role of government taxes and regulations in promoting the Quito Insurrection of 1765, see Kenneth J. Andrien, "Economic Crisis, Taxes and the Quito Insurrection of 1765," *Past and Present*, 129 (November 1990): 117–20.
55. For a description of the weak government presence in Cuenca in the mid-eighteenth century, see: AGI, Quito, 176, Visita de Cuenca de dn. Pedro Martínez de Arizola, Madrid, 5 septiembre 1737, and Pedro Martínez de Arizala to crown, Cuenca, 28 febrero 1736.

(see Table 2.1). During this period, the population of the city and its hinterland grew rapidly. In the 1740s Cuenca and its semi-rural parishes, San Sebastián and San Blas, had only 12,000–15,000 residents, but by the 1780s they had grown to over 31,000 people, according to the Villalengua census. The city was dominated by a small elite, drawn from a total European population that numbered nearly 12,000 in 1780. There were only 82 slaves and 430 castes. The bulk of the population (60 percent) was Andean and lived in the two parishes of San Sebastián and San Blas.[56]

Although no occupational data have been uncovered for the urban population, nearly 16,000 Amerindians undoubtedly formed the bulk of the city's weavers, domestics, manual laborers, petty traders, and low-level artisans. These relatively poor residents of San Sebastián and San Blas probably entered the urban labor market or retreated to its hinterland, depending on the job opportunities in the city. The less affluent Europeans and the castes dominated the artisan crafts, small-scale trading, and the more lucrative service-sector occupations.

Abundant natural resources in the south sierra allowed the city of Cuenca to attain prominence as a regional trading center during the eighteenth century. Farmers in Cuenca and Loja cultivated some cotton, a wide variety of fruits, grains, potatoes, and even sugar cane in the lowlands. In Loja a number of ranchers also raised mules for the overland trade route to Peru. Medium-sized Spanish estates (along with small Amerindian and *mestizo* holdings) near the city of Cuenca supplied the urban market with meat and foodstuffs, while larger *haciendas* in the less populated zones of the south and east specialized in grains, fruits, and sugar cane for export and local consumption.[57] Over 75 percent of the Andeans lived in their own villages, not on Spanish holdings. The largest of these settlements were located in the northern and eastern parishes of Cuenca and scattered throughout the province of Loja, where the inhabitants raised a variety of foodstuffs and animals. At the same time, the Andean villagers supplemented this subsistence economy by participating in a local cottage textile industry. The villagers sold their rough cottons and woolens to Spanish and creole merchants from Lima, northern Peru, and

---

56. The *padrón* of 1780 listed the official population as 28,346. ANH-Q, Empadronamientos, Caja 1, Azuay, 1776–1871. Some authorities do not count the large Andean population in the semirural parishes of San Sebastián and San Blas as part of the city's population, which would lower the 1780 count to 11,876 – indicating that little growth had occurred in the city since the 1740s. This viewpoint assumes, however, that the early census figures also excluded these Andean *barrios*. See Martin Minchom, "Demographic Change in Eighteenth Century Ecuador," 187, Table 2.

57. ANH-Q, Presidencia de Quito, 1793, tomo, 361, Libros de tributos de Cuenca, 1792; tomo 360, Libros de tributos de Loja, 1792.

the coast, who marketed them in mining centers such as Hualgayoc, near Trujillo.[58] The rich agricultural wealth and the cottage textile industry allowed the south sierra to support its growing population and to develop commercial ties with a number of thriving, nearby regional markets.

More tenuous links between the south sierra and the international market rested on the export of small amounts of precious metals and *cascarilla*. Minor deposits of gold in Sigsig (south of Cuenca) and silver in Cañar (to the north) continued to produce modest profits during the eighteenth century. The largest export product, however, was the bark of the *cascarilla* tree, rich in quinine. The region from the city of Cuenca southwards through the Cusibamba River basin (near Loja) to Jaén de Bracamoros yielded rich forests of *cascarilla*, which elite entrepreneurs gathered for export to Europe.[59] The practice became profitable enough for the crown to have royal officials supervise the supply of the bark and tax the industry's profits, from the 1780s.[60]

Although the demand for quinine in Europe remained steady, the forests of *cascarilla* quickly became depleted. Local elites usually hired gangs of 20–50 workers to live in the highland regions and gather the tree bark between April and August. The workers hacked off the bark with machetes and in the process usually managed to kill or severely damage the trees. Since *cascarilla* grew only in regions with a moderate climate (most often at medium altitudes, between 1,500 meters and 3,000 meters), the supplies rapidly declined.[61] By the 1790s, merchants operating in the region complained about the dwindling stock of *cascarilla*, which inhibited the international trade and promoted a shortage of specie.[62]

Within two decades, the disruption of trade patterns during the independence era also contributed to an overall decline in the manufacturing and agrarian sectors. As the economy of Cuenca fell into the doldrums, people left the region for the coast. By 1825, the provincial population had dropped to under 76,000. Although Loja continued to grow, from just under 24,000 people in 1780 to over 34,000 inhabitants

58. Silvia Palomeque, "Historia económica de Cuenca y sus relaciones regionales (desde fines del siglo XVIII a principios del XIX)," *Segundo encuentro de historia y realidad económica y social del Ecuador*, 3 vols. (Cuenca, 1978), 1, and passim; and Scarlett O'Phelan Godoy, "Vivir y morir en el mineral de Hualgayoc a fines de la colonia," *Jahrbuch für Geschichte von Staat, Wirtschaft, und Gesselschaft Lateinamerikas*, 30 (1993): 75–127.

59. Antonio de Alcedo, *Diccionario geográfico histórico de las Indias Occidentales o America*, 4 vols. (Madrid, 1967 edn.), 1:405–06; 2: 329–31.

60. For a discussion of royal projects to control the sale of *cascarilla*, see Martine Petitjean and Yves Saint-Geours, "La economía de la cascarilla en el Corregimiento de Loja," *Cultura*, 15 (enero–abril 1983): 172–75; 194–96.

61. *Ibid.*, 175–77.

62. AGI, Quito, 276, Matías López Escudero to crown, Cuenca, 15 octubre 1790.

by 1825 (a 44-percent increase), it remained too underpopulated to revive the troubled regional economy of the south sierra (see Table 2.2).[63]

Guayaquil and the export economy

Guayaquil and the coastal region experienced unprecedented economic and demographic growth from the late eighteenth century until the 1840s. Before that time the port of Guayaquil had supported a regional shipbuilding industry and served as the major trading outlet for the highlands. After the advent of imperial free trade between 1778 and 1789, however, coastal plantation owners could send their cacao (which accounted for 75 percent of all exports until the 1840s) directly to colonial and international markets.[64] The resulting export growth encouraged large-scale migration from the highlands, causing the coastal population to climb from 20,000 people in 1736 to almost 72,500 by 1825 – a growth rate of nearly 3 percent annually.[65] The population increase really accelerated, however, during the period from 1793 to 1805, when the annual growth rate nearly reached 5 percent.[66] Most of this demographic upsurge took place in the city of Guayaquil and the plantation zones of the interior, surrounding Baba-Samborondón, Babahoyo, Palenque, Balzar, Naranjal, Portoviejo, and Daule.[67]

The principal coastal marketing center was Guayaquil, situated at the base of the fertile Guayas River basin. The port city grew rapidly, from a mere 6,000 inhabitants in 1738 to nearly 14,000 by 1804 – still a modest urban center trailing both Quito and Cuenca in population. According to some preliminary analyses of records from the city's central parish (Sagrario) for 1832, birth rates remained high, but so did mortality. Fewer than 9 percent of the citizens in Sagrario lived beyond the age of fifty, and nearly 58 percent of the inhabitants were under the age of twenty-five. This youthful population, high death rates, and disproportionate numbers of women all point to migration (from the city's hinterland and especially the highlands) as the principal reason for urban growth during the period.[68]

---

63. Loja continued to trade modest amounts of cloth to Piura, even during the independence era, which probably explains why it also served as a haven for some migrants from Cuenca. See Silvia Palomeque, "Loja en el mercado interno colonial," *HISLA*, 2 (1983): 43.

64. Hamerly, *Historia social y económica*, 112.

65. Some population estimates for 1825 indicate that the coastal population may have exceeded 90,000 inhabitants. See Laviana Cuetos, *Guayaquil en el siglo XVIII*, 106.

66. *Ibid.*, 108, cuadro VI.

67. *Ibid.*, 118–20.

68. Hamerly, *Historia social y económica*, 76–78; 93.

Table 2.4. *Occupational breakdown: city and province of Guayaquil, 1832*

Occupational sector	City	Province	Total
Artisan/crafts	1,028 (56%)	330 (8%)	1,358
Commerce	440 (24%)	165 (4%)	605
Professions/service	177 (10%)	50 (.7%)	227
Agriculture	141 (8%)	3,588 (87%)	3,729
Industry[a]	34 (2%)	13 (.3%)	47
Total	1,820	4,146	5,966

[a] Industry/shipbuilding   359 (20%)   99 (2%)   458
This new category includes those craftsmen who worked in the city's shipyard, who are
listed under the "Artisan/crafts" category above.
Source: Michael T. Hamerly, *Historia social y económica de la antigua provincia de Guayaquil,
1763-1842* (Guayaquil, 1973), 113-19.

A partial occupational breakdown for Guayaquil and the interior provinces in 1832 indicates that the port was a prosperous shipping and
communications center serving its growing agrarian hinterland.[69] Artisan
and craft occupations accounted for 56 percent of the city's labor force.
Large and small commercial jobs employed 24 percent of the urban populace, with the professional and service sectors providing jobs for 10
percent. By far the smallest sector was industry, representing a mere 2
percent of the registered urban occupations (see Table 2.4). This figure
jumps to 20 percent, however, when the carpenters, metalworkers, and
charcoal makers – listed among the artisans in Table 2.4 – are added to
the industry category. Most of these craftsmen worked in the city's shipyard, the largest industrial employer during the period. Although shipbuilding declined in relative importance during the export era, it still
benefitted by providing small ships for coastal traders.[70] In short, the city
of Guayaquil furnished most of the commercial, artisan, and industrial
services needed by the largely rural export-oriented regions surrounding it.

The port city's rich tropical hinterland, spreading across the littoral,
was a cornucopia of tropical produce. Agriculture employed 87 percent
of the population in the interior, followed by artisans at 8 percent, commerce at 4 percent, professional services at 1 percent, and industry (see
Table 2.4). Virtually every parish produced at least some rice, fruits, corn,
and woods – not just exportable commodities such as cacao. The coastal

69. Export growth continued to 1842, so this material reflects the occupational structure of the city
    in the midst of its prosperity. See Hamerly, *Historia social y económica*, 99–121.
70. Laviana Cuetos, *Guayaquil en el siglo XVIII*, 260–301.

parishes, particularly those with a considerable Amerindian population, also supplied meat, grains, and large quantities of seafood. These goods from the outlying parishes flowed into Guayaquil daily, often carried by mule trains or floated downriver on crude balsa rafts. Roads passing through Naranjal, Yaguachi, and Babahoyo connected the coast with the highlands, which also supplied manufactured goods and additional food-stuffs. These goods were exchanged in the central market – created during the presidency of José García de Leon y Pizarro (1778–83) – or in a number of informal marketplaces, commonly located in the shanty towns ringing the more established central zones. In short, Guayaquil's rich and varied hinterland kept the port supplied with a wide range of foodstuffs, minimizing the need to import basic commodities.

Despite its prosperity, crown fiscal policies and the structure of the export trade restricted the growth of the coastal plantation economy. The crown closely regulated all exports and imposed heavy taxes, which cut into profits. Quite apart from these levies, however, a number of coastal citizens complained that a few local cacao planters and merchants used their political clout, particularly in the 1780s, to dominate the export business.[71] Despite the volume of regional exports, high labor costs and unpredictable fluctuations in the international price of cacao also limited profits.[72] Moreover, Guayaquil's planters and merchants faced considerable disadvantages in controlling the sale and marketing of regional exports. Coastal elites lacked the large capital resources and access to credit abroad needed to sell their exports in the most lucrative retail markets in Spain and the Indies. As a result, they could never hope to compete with the larger metropolitan and colonial merchant houses. The largest profits from the export trade also came from the sale of European imports, not the trade in cacao. Again, large merchant houses had the advantage of scale, making it impossible for most coastal planters or merchants to compete. Consequently, the coastal export economy prospered, but it lacked the potential to generate large profits capable of transforming the coast into a dynamic, diversified, and more independent economic center in the Pacific basin.

The demographic history of the Kingdom of Quito between 1690 and 1830 demonstrates the problems of attaining sustained, autonomous economic growth within the Spanish colonial system. In the north-central

71. Michael T. Hamerly, *El comercio del cacao de Guayaquil durante el periodo colonial: un estudio cuantitativo* (Guayaquil, 1976), 31.
72. According to several accounts, most affluent Guayaquil merchants and planters had assets of between 40,000 pesos and 50,000 pesos, while only the few wealthiest could boast of a total wealth of perhaps 200,000 pesos. See Michael Conniff, "Guayaquil through Independence: Urban Development in a Colonial System," *The Americas*, 33 (1977): 396–97.

sierra, metropolitan authorities undermined textile producers by allowing the importation of European cloth. The resulting slow decline of *obrajes* diminished economic opportunities in the urban and rural zones of much of the region. As a result, poverty, along with natural disasters and epidemic diseases, impelled the Andean peoples to leave their traditional homes in the highlands in search of jobs and a better life.

The influx of emigrants to the south highlands, the growth of the internal economy, and the export of *cascarilla* contributed to the prosperity of Cuenca. The region's favorable geographical location astride the overland trade routes to Peru and the coast allowed local producers to supply those regions with foodstuffs and textiles. In addition, abundant supplies of *cascarilla* tied the south highlands to the international economy. The dependency of local producers on large outside merchant houses (centered in Lima) to manage regional and international trading networks, however, proved a long-term weakness as the internal economy began to collapse during the independence era. As supplies of *cascarilla* dwindled and the demand for cloth in the mining towns of Peru declined, these outside merchant houses slowly abandoned their commercial enterprises in the south sierra. By the 1820s, the shrinking regional economy of Cuenca began losing population, as increasing numbers of Andeans left to seek jobs along the coast.

Guayaquil benefitted most directly from royal efforts to stimulate colonial export economies; the lifting of restrictions on colonial trade, beginning in 1778, led to the rapid growth of plantation agriculture, particularly cacao production. This development of the coastal region created acute labor shortages, however, met at first by importing African slaves and later by migrations from the highlands. Despite this prosperity, the high taxes, the fluctuating export prices, and the dependency on outside merchant houses limited profits for coastal elites. Foreign imports also discouraged long-term investments in broadening the regional economic base. Over time, the economy failed to diversify, for industry, commerce, and agriculture all depended on an export trade, which coastal merchants and planters could not control.

3

The state and manufacturing

European manufacturing and commercial expansion during the eighteenth century had a profound impact on economic development in the Kingdom of Quito. As new methods of cloth production lowered costs and expanded output, it became possible for European manufacturers to supply textiles in distant American markets. At the same time, the Spanish crown aided this process by liberalizing colonial trade policies, which allowed peninsular merchants to ship increasing amounts of these products to the Indies. The resulting importation of European wares captured regional markets in Pacific trading zones and undermined the competitive position of colonial manufacturing centers such as Quito. The local woolen textile economy suffered from a rigid, archaic organizational structure, primitive technology, and a scarcity of capital, making it impossible for it to compete with these European products. The only *Quiteño* mills capable of surviving over time were those manufacturing cheap, low-quality woolens for the northern markets in New Granada. As a result, the *obraje* economy entered a prolonged decline during the eighteenth century.

As the *obraje* sector decayed, a prosperous cotton and woolen textile industry emerged in the south sierra, principally in the *corregimiento* (and later *gobernación*) of Cuenca.[1] This industry was concentrated in the Amerindian villages of the southern highlands, where merchants (mostly from Lima) organized a cottage or putting-out system of manufacturing. The merchants usually supplied the raw cotton and wool, while the villagers – usually women – used traditional Andean methods of spinning and weaving to produce coarse cotton and woolen cloth. The merchant-entrepreneurs then used their commercial connections to market these cheap, low-quality textiles in the cities and mining centers of northern Peru. The industry won an increasing share of the regional market in

---

1. Cuenca remained a *corregimiento* until 23 May 1771, when the crown elevated it to the status of a *gobernación*. Federico González Suárez, *Historia general de la República del Ecuador* (Quito, 1970 edn.), 1120.

Peru for low-cost cottons and woolens until the early nineteenth century, when declining productivity at the Peruvian mines and the disruptions of the independence era led to a falloff in demand. By 1830 the once-thriving cottage textile industry had shrunk to virtual insignificance.[2]

The shipyard of Guayaquil was the only remaining manufacturing sector in the kingdom for most of the eighteenth century. The relative isolation of regional economies on the Pacific coast and numerous government contracts had stimulated the development of a small but thriving shipbuilding industry in the city of Guayaquil by the seventeenth century. Viceregal patronage, rich supplies of wood and naval stores, and the growth of intercolonial trade in the Pacific had combined to promote the modest prosperity of the yards. By the early eighteenth century, however, diminished viceregal financial support for the Pacific armada (*Armada del mar del sur*) and commercial decline in Lima led to an era of stagnation, until an upsurge in the coastal export economy revitalized the shipyard later in the eighteenth century. Thereafter, the prosperity of the industry became linked with the fortunes of the cacao economy.

The decline of the highland *obrajes*

Over the course of the eighteenth century, the *obrajes* of the north-central sierra underwent a prolonged decline, leading to a drop in output ranging between 50 percent and 75 percent.[3] This downturn resulted primarily from the falling price of *paño* in the formerly lucrative Lima market.[4] At the outset of the century, 1 meter of *paño azul* fetched 24–28 silver reales in Lima; by the period from 1750 to 1800 that price bottomed out at 16–18 reales.[5] Falling prices cut into profits, leading to numerous mill closures. The number of mills operating in the *audiencia* fell from 169 in 1700 to 125 in 1780, and the number of workers employed in the *obrajes* dropped from over 10,000 to 6,000 (see Table 3.1).[6] The decline was most severe in Quito and Riobamba, regions that specialized in *paño* production for the Lima market. In provinces such as Otavalo and La-

---

2. For an excellent discussion of this textile industry in the nineteenth century see Silvia Palomeque, *Cuenca en el siglo XIX: La articulación de una región* (Quito, 1980), 19–25.

3. Robson Brines Tyrer, "The Demographic and Economic History of the *Audiencia* of Quito: Indian Population and the Textile Industry" (Ph.D. diss., University of California at Berkeley, 1976), 323.

4. *Ibid.*, 223–24.

5. *Ibid.*, 187–90.

6. According to *audiencia* president Lope Antonio de Munive, the number of workers in the *obrajes* may have reached 30,000. AGI, Quito, 69, Informe del presidente Lope Antonio de Munive, 1681; also cited in Javier Ortiz de la Tabla y Ducasse, "El obraje colonial ecuatoriano: aproximación a su estudio," *Revista de Indias*, 37 (1977): 481.

Table 3.1. *The obrajes of the Audiencia of Quito, 1700 and 1780*

Province	Obrajes in 1700	Obrajes in 1780	% change
Ibarra	7	1	-86
Otavalo	8	11	38
Quito	74	36	-51
Latacunga	31	50	61
Riobamba	41	24	-41
Ambato	8	3	-63
Total	169	125	-26

Source: Robson Brines Tyrer, "The Demographic and Economic History of the Audiencia of Quito: Indian Population and the Textile Industry, 1600-1800" (Ph.D. diss., University of California at Berkeley, 1976), 315.

tacunga, *obrajeros* converted their mills to manufacture cheaper *jergas* and *bayetas* – initially less affected by European competition – for the New Granada market. The number of mills in both provinces actually increased slightly during the century. Still, the overall pattern was one of unmistakable decadence.[7]

The drop in woolen textile production in the north-central sierra took place incrementally over the course of the eighteenth century. Between the epidemics of the 1690s and approximately 1750, the *obrajes de comunidad* and the smaller mills, particularly those in urban areas, began to close down. The larger, private, rural *obraje*-estate complexes still managed to produce substantial amounts of textiles. By mid-century, however, the slow erosion of demand in southern markets led to a more serious drop in *paño* prices, which cut into the profits of even these *obrajeros*.[8] Then, only the largest and most well-funded enterprises survived, such as those run by the wealthy Jesuit order. After the expulsion of the Society of Jesus in 1767, however, crown officials found it difficult to run even these enterprises at a profit. By the 1780s, increased taxes and the dramatic influx of European wares following the advent of imperial free trade prompted additional mill closings. According to government officials, most of these imported goods were cheap English textiles (called *paños de segundo* or *paños de tercero*), which came via the Cape Horn route and dramatically undercut *Quiteño* woolens in American markets.[9] Finally, the disruptions of the wars of independence in the early nineteenth cen-

7. Tyrer, "Demographic and Economic History," 314–15.
8. *Ibid.*, 187.
9. AGI, Quito, 240, José García de Leon y Pizarro to Josef de Gálvez, Quito, 18 septiembre 1780.

tury signaled the near total collapse of woolen production in the *audiencia* district.[10]

Foreign cloth imports effectively increased the competition in American markets for textile products, particularly upscale American woolens like *paños*. The demand for lower-quality, less expensive American products, like *bayetas* and *jergas*, was less affected by the imports, at least until the influx of English *paños de segundo* in the 1780s.[11] Overall, escalating quantities of relatively low-priced European textiles increased the number of suppliers in American marketplaces, prompting a gradual shift in consumer preferences: buyers substituted European cloth for American *paños*.[12] The resultant drop in the price of *paños* slowly eroded the profits of *obrajeros* in the kingdom, producing an economic decline in those regions of the north-central sierra most dependent on the production and sale of higher-quality *Quiteño* textiles.

Despite the scale, complexity, and productivity of their enterprises, most of the *obrajeros* in the Kingdom of Quito failed to meet the challenge of European competition. Nevertheless, their mills did employ a sophisticated division of labor, and some, such as the *obraje* at San Ildefonso, provided work for over 400 people (making them larger than most contemporary European mills).[13] The principal mystery of the *obrajes* remains why competition from abroad failed to provide the incentive for technological and organizational changes, capable of lowering production costs and increasing product quality. In short, why did these large factory-like enterprises fail to serve as the foundation for a *Quiteño* industrial revolution?

10. Despite this general trend, a few *obrajes* continued making cloth well into the nineteenth century, particularly for local or regional consumption. See Alexandra Kennedy Troya and Carme Fauria Roma, "Obrajes en la Audiencia de Quito. Un caso estudio: Tilipulu," *Boletín Americanista*, 32 (1987): 181–92

11. The production of various sorts of cloth varied according to consumer demand. At the large *obraje* of San Ildefonso, for example, managers changed the amounts of different types of cloth produced throughout the late colonial period. See Christiana Borchart de Moreno, "La crisis del obraje de San Ildefonso a finales del siglo XVIII," *Cultura*, 24 (1986): 660.

12. In essence, this involved a change in the elasticity of demand for Quito's *paños*. Trying to calculate such changes in the elasticity of demand for textiles, however, using the available evidence, is fraught with difficulty. For an example of the ambivalent results obtained from such an effort, see Richard J. Salvucci, "Entrepreneurial Culture and the Textile Manufactories in Eighteenth-Century Mexico," *Anuario de Estudios Americanos*, 39 (1982): 412–17.

13. There was no consistent pattern of moving from cottage to mechanized factory production in Europe. In fact, some European textile production became concentrated at an early period, well in advance of mechanization, while other producers continued cottage production into the early nineteenth century. The literature on this subject is immense, but some effective treatments that summarize much of it are: Pat Hudson, *The Industrial Revolution* (London, 1992), 101–32; Myron P. Gutmann, *Toward the Modern Economy: Early Industry in Europe, 1500–1800* (New York, 1988).

The key to resolving this dilemma lies in the inflexible organizational structure of the *obrajes*, which evolved in the state-regulated business environment of the late sixteenth century. Given the inability of Spanish manufactories to supply American markets and the geographical constraints on the development of a viable market economy in the Andes, the crown promoted an oligopoly situation in the *audiencia*, which restricted competition and nurtured selected elite producers in the north-central sierra. The most successful *obrajeros* in Quito flourished in this environment by establishing family-owned rural enterprises, which linked the clothing mill with food-producing estates and sheep ranches. Such rural *obraje*-estate complexes displayed considerable flexibility, allowing owners to move laborers from one property to another depending on the seasonal needs of the mills and agriculture. Furthermore, land was cheap in Quito, which permitted many mill owners to integrate the key factors of production relatively inexpensively in one enterprise. This reduced most cash outlays needed for wages, raw materials, and transportation. In essence, colonial *obrajes* internalized many market functions, supplying labor, capital, and raw materials needed for production.[14] This rigid organizational structure served mill owners well in the protected colonial markets of the sixteenth and seventeenth centuries but made them unable to increase the quality of their cloth and lower prices to compete with European textiles. In short, by liberalizing trade restrictions and allowing the introduction of high-quality imports, the crown effectively ended the traditional oligopolistic arrangement responsible for the prosperity of Quito's mills.

The business of woolen cloth manufacturing

Elite families and the church played a major role in the development of the *obrajes* during their heyday. Few individual entrepreneurs could obtain the information needed to run a textile mill, and family connections often proved essential in transacting business. Accumulating large rural estate complexes required a knowledge of changing consumer tastes, local land values, transportation routes, and, most importantly, access to credit. In the absence of well-organized banking structures, a scarcity of capital also predominated. Under such conditions, entrepreneurs relied on family ties to secure from clerical organizations or merchants the loans needed to buy land and to operate an *obraje*. Given the lack of financial publications, company annual reports, and trade organizations, families also provided

---

14. This point has been demonstrated clearly by Richard J. Salvucci in his seminal work on the *obrajes* of Mexico. See Richard J. Salvucci, *Textiles and Capitalism in Mexico: An Economic History of the Obrajes, 1539–1840* (Princeton, NJ, 1987), especially chapter 2.

crucial business information.[15] Finally, gaining an *obraje* license itself and controlling access to Amerindian laborers required political clout, which could only come from well-developed elite family networks.[16] Although small, and usually illegal, sweatshops existed throughout the colonial period in Quito, they never dominated woolen textile manufacturing as did the large enterprises of local magnates.

By the late sixteenth century, a small, tightly knit nexus of elite families and wealthy clerical organizations (such as the Jesuits) controlled the *obraje* economy and made substantial fortunes. In the *corregimiento* of Quito, for example, seven or eight families controlled over 50 percent of the *obrajes* in operation between 1607 and 1776. In Riobamba, Ambato, and Latacunga four *obrajeros* dominated cloth manufacturing by 1680. Many of these families traced their lineage to the conquest, when they had received lucrative *encomiendas* and founded the first *obrajes de comunidad*.[17] Most consolidated their positions through intermarriage and alliances with newly arrived, peninsular-born bureaucrats and merchants. By the mid-eighteenth century, the principal families – the Villacis, Sánchez Orellanas, Guerreros, Pérez Ubillus, Larreas, Maldonados, Ramírez de Arrelanos, Galarzas, and Londoños – were related through a complex array of business and social connections.[18] Members of the regular clergy, particularly the Jesuits, also entered the textile business to support their varied pastoral, educational, and missionary activities.[19] Only these lay and clerical mill owners could muster the capital and the political power needed to dominate cloth manufacturing in the kingdom.

Obraje owners oversaw a complex production process, usually involving a large mill, several outbuildings, and upwards of 100 laborers. Turning wool into finished *paños*, *jergas*, and *bayetas* involved four basic steps: preparing the wool, spinning, weaving, and finishing. The process usually began outdoors, where laborers unloaded the raw merino wool and soaked it in a solution of water and urine (a natural source of ammonia) to remove the grease, yolk, and dirt. It was then rinsed, dried, and taken into the mill, usually a large building divided into several rooms arranged around a central patio. Once inside the principal building, the wool was

15. Salvucci makes these points cogently in his study on the Mexican mills. *Ibid.*, 93–95.

16. According to Salvucci, the oligopolistic system of licenses in Quito had no corollary in Mexico. Given that Mexican *obrajes* produced for markets in closer proximity than their counterparts in Quito, it is not surprising that the Andean producers needed this added political assistance to survive over time. *Ibid.*, passim.

17. See Ortiz de la Tabla, "El obraje colonial ecuatoriano," 521–22.

18. *Ibid.*, 521–30; 537–41; and Javier Ortiz de la Tabla Ducasse, "Panorama económico y social del corregimiento de Quito (1768–1775), *Revista de Indias*, 145 (1976): 91–93.

19. The most complete discussion of a clerical order's involvement in the textile business is Nicholas P. Cushner, *Farm and Factory: The Jesuits and the Development of Agrarian Capitalism in Colonial Quito, 1600–1767* (Albany, NY), 89–115.

ready for carding or combing – a process that involved aligning the wool fibers, for spinning, with a hand-held implement.[20] Workers then took the carded wool into one of several rooms set aside for spinning it into yarn, using either traditional Andean spindles or European-style spinning wheels.[21] After the yarn had been spun and treated, it was taken to the dying rooms. Indigo, the dye most commonly used in preparing *paño azul*, was ground and mixed in one room and placed in large, heated, copper cauldrons with the yarn. The dyed yarn then went to the largest department of the mill for weaving. The weavers used smaller looms for the cheaper *bayetas* and *jergas*, while larger looms produced the finer *paños*. Then the cloth was ready for fulling or milling (a process that involved cleaning, shrinking, and beating or felting the woolen cloth), which most often took place in a separate outbuilding. The entire process was time consuming, labor intensive, and involved no sophisticated machinery.[22] It did not change significantly throughout the colonial period.

Inventories of the *obrajes* taken by crown officials during the late seventeenth and eighteenth centuries manifest the low level of technology used in cloth production in the kingdom. The *visita* of the *obrajes* carried out by royal officials in the 1690s indicated that their total fixed capital (buildings and equipment) usually ranged between 2,500 pesos and 3,500 pesos.[23] Equipment usually accounted for only 20 percent of these amounts, demonstrating minimal use of machinery and other technology in production.[24] By the 1760s, inventories of confiscated Jesuit mills carried out by the new government agency empowered to administer or sell them, the *Administración de temporalidades*, show that the ratio of building to equipment costs had not changed significantly. The single largest expenditure for equipment involved the purchase of copper or

20. Shorter wools were carded, a process that involved a hand-held wire brush to align the fibers. Longer or worsted wools were combed – a heated metal comb was drawn by hand through the wool to separate the long fibers and align them. See Salvucci, *Textiles and Capitalism*, 50.
21. This task involved three or four times as many spinners as weavers to keep the production process efficient. At the Yaruquí mill, run by the Jesuits, of the 236 workers employed, 104 were spinners (44 percent), 32 were carders (13 percent), and 27 were weavers (11 percent). Cushner, *Farm and Factory*, 100. At the *obraje* of San Bartolomé from 1761 to 1765, there were 56 spinners (48 percent), 16 carders (14 percent), 9 dyers (8 percent), 3 wool felters (3 percent), 9 hat makers (8 percent), 23 weavers (20 percent), 2 pressers (2 percent), 2 finishers (2 percent), and 6 wood cutters (5 percent). See ANH-Q, Obrajes, Caja 12, Libro de socorros de los Indios del Obraxe de San Bartolomé de la Marquesa de Solanda que corre desde 15 junio 1761–65.
22. A general discussion of the production process is found in Kax Wilson, *A History of Textiles* (Boulder, CO, 1979), 7–107. Another useful summary of the process in Mexico may be found in Salvucci, *Textiles and Capitalism*, 45–55. The manufacture of cloth on the Jesuit estate of Chillo is discussed in Cushner, *Farm and Factory*, 94–99.
23. These costs did not include the buildings needed to house the *obraje*, which might increase the figures to as high as 10,000 pesos. Ortiz de la Tabla, "El obraje colonial ecuatoriano," 501–04.
24. *Ibid.*

bronze vats for dying, hardly a significant addition to the technology of cloth production.[25] The use of such primitive methods over the period 1690 to 1830 made it unlikely that *obrajeros* could increase output, enhance product quality, or lower production costs.

Despite their size, the *obrajes* also enjoyed few economies of scale in producing cloth. The persistence of small *obrajuelos* during the seventeenth century indicates that the large mills could never lower costs to drive out small competitors. In addition, extant inventories of the *obrajes* show that the ratio of working capital (inventories of raw materials, finished goods, and worker indebtedness) to fixed capital could be 2:1 or higher.[26] This relatively high level of working capital demonstrates that the principal advantage of the larger *obrajes* was apparently controlling the supply of raw materials and finished cloth in the face of an uneven supply-and-demand structure in the "thin" (meaning few buyers and sellers), imperfect colonial markets of the Andes.[27]

Another major advantage of the *obraje* was its ability to control the supply and cost of labor. The annual wages paid by mill owners in the seventeenth and eighteenth centuries remained virtually unchanged.[28] In

25. According to Cushner, the Yaruquí mill (not including salaries paid to labor) was valued at 14,228 pesos; only 2,478 pesos (17 percent) were invested in equipment, with the rest going for the buildings. The Chillo mill (also excluding labor costs) was valued at 9,802 pesos, with 4,370 pesos (45 percent) invested in equipment. This included 1,957 pesos for new copper cauldrons. Once that extraordinary amount was subtracted, the funds invested in equipment fell to 2,413 pesos (25 percent). Cushner, *Farm and Factory*, 106.

26. This evidence is drawn from the records of the *Administración de temporalidades*, and it is difficult to interpret. The inventories in the late eighteenth century tend to vary from year to year, reaching highs of 50 percent of production. In most years, the practice of paying workers in cloth apparently led to a shrinking in inventories for many years. Likewise indebtedness rose and fell, depending on the year. Nevertheless, the level of working capital to fixed capital probably remained relatively high in Quito. The sources used to estimate these figures for Quito were taken from the following: Cushner, *Farm and Factory*, 105–07; ANH-Q, Haciendas, Caja 15, Cuentas de Yaruquí, Julio 1777–Octubre 1779; ANH-Q, Haciendas, Caja 16, Cuentas de San Ildefonso, Agosto 1777–Marzo 1780; ANH-Q, Haciendas, Caja 18, Cuentas de Tacunga, Marzo 1778–Abril 1780; ANH-Q, Haciendas, Caja 20, Cuentas de San Ildefonso, Marzo 1780–Enero 1787; ANH-Q, Haciendas, Caja 21, Estado de Yaruquí, Enero 1782–Junio 1783; ANH-Q, Haciendas, Caja 22, Estado de Chillo, Junio 1783–Octubre 1785.

27. This ratio of working capital to fixed capital was considerably higher in the Mexican mills, however, reaching levels of 10:1 in some cases. Apparently the Mexican producers could more easily use their large reserves of cloth to control the supply of produce in regional markets, a more difficult proposition for the *Quiteños*, who sold the bulk of their woolens in distant Peru or New Granada. It is not surprising that the *obrajeros* in the kingdom needed crown support to continue the oligopoly arrangement in cloth production in order to remain profitable. Only by limiting competition could the *Quiteños* hope to duplicate the control over cloth supplies needed to repeat the success of the Mexican mills. See Salvucci, *Textiles and Capitalism*, 42–43.

28. The wages paid to dyers (*tintoreros*), carders and combers (*cardadores*), pressers (*prensadores*), spinners (*hiladores*), finishers (*dispinseros*), and *tejedores* all remained virtually identical. The amount

addition, workers even in skilled occupations such as dying, weaving, and finishing received low wages – barely distinguishable from more low-skill manual labor jobs such as pressing or carding. Moreover, owners made few concessions to improving working conditions in the mills, which most contemporary observers found abysmal. Beatings, jailings, child labor, dangerous working conditions, and long hours characterized textile work. In short, the *obrajes* were little more than large sweatshops, where men, women, and children worked for minimal wages in physically demanding jobs.

As the textile industry experienced hard times in the late eighteenth century, mill owners attempted to cut labor costs even further. In his *visita* of the mills between 1775 and 1777, *fiscal* Juan Josef de Villalengua uncovered a shocking array of abuses designed to lower costs. At the *obraje* of Calera in Latacunga, for example, the workers voiced a common complaint: they were never paid in specie but cloth, which the foreman valued above the market price. Paying workers in cloth minimized cash outlays and allowed mill owners to dispose of their inventory at relatively high prices. Likewise, allocations of foodstuffs (*socorros*) were often inedible, overpriced, and distributed at *haciendas* 5 leagues away. Workers at Calera also complained that shop foremen forced spinners to work seven days each week, with no time off for holidays.[29] At the mill of Tigua in Riobamba, foremen allegedly coerced the wives and children of workers to labor four days each week for a small portion of barley. Mill workers at Ysinchi in Riobamba claimed that the owner, the Marqués de Villa Orellana, even cut their wages to half the legal level, set 150 years earlier.[30]

In response to this widespread chorus of complaints, Villalengua tried, with little success, to ameliorate the most exploitative labor practices. He first demanded an end to all abuses and then raised wages above the seventeenth-century levels. Despite these reforms, the problems apparently continued, as *obrajeros* dealt with the shrinking market for cloth by squeezing more work for less pay from their laborers. Government officials routinely ignored the problem and failed to enforce Villalengua's edicts. In fact, when the city council of Riobamba registered a complaint

earned by warpers (*urdidores*) and spoolers (*canileros*) actually declined a few pesos. Only wages of wool beaters (*bergueadores*) and wood cutters (*leñateros*) increased slightly. Data on wages has been taken from: ANH-Q, Obrajes, Caja 12, 1742–56, Libro de socorros de los indios del obraje de San Bartolomé de la Marquesa de Solanda que corre desde 15 Junio 1761–65; Tyrer, "Demographic and Economic History," 200; and Cushner, *Farm and Factory*, 100.

29. Shortages of laborers to spin the yarn itself could bring production to a halt. See Salvucci, *Textiles and Capitalism*, 51.

30. For the results of this *audiencia*-wide *visita*, see ANH-Q, Obrajes, Caja 15, Autos de la Visita de los Obrajes de Latacunga, Hambato, y Riobamba, 1775–1779.

in 1793, the *audiencia* even ordered the minimal wage increases imposed by Villalengua returned to the original levels set in 1621.[31] Local authorities clearly had no commitment to protect the rights of beleaguered *obraje* workers.

Mill owners throughout the *audiencia* district also used debt peonage to maintain control over their work force. Given the high tribute rates in the kingdom, *obrajeros* could often lure laborers by offering advances of cash (usually 10 pesos), food, and clothing.[32] These workers began their jobs in debt, a condition which usually increased over time. Low wages and the tendency to pay workers in kind only forced laborers deeper into debt, making it virtually impossible for them to leave the mills. The Jesuits were particularly skillful in using debt peonage to keep their laborers at work. According to the accounts for 1753 at Yaruquí, the 142 workers at the mill owed 5,572 pesos, an average debt of nearly 40 pesos for each employee.[33] Given the deplorable working conditions in the *obrajes*, mill owners found debt peonage a viable way to recruit and maintain their labor force in the *obrajes*.

Despite the lack of serial data on indebtedness, numerous account books from the mills indicate that debt peonage was not used universally in the eighteenth century. At the *obraje* of Macaji, account books listed only 22 of 177 workers in debt by 1753; at the mill of San Bartolomé between 1761 and 1765 only 47 of 116 workers had debts. Moreover, most debts were small, ranging from 10 pesos to 20 pesos.[34] These mills may have been operated more humanely or, more likely, declining profits kept them in operation only part of the year. Under these circumstances it made little sense to keep a large, indebted, and underemployed resident labor force on the premises. Debt peonage after all, had its costs. It was a useful way to keep laborers working at low-paying undesirable jobs, but only if the mills operated at full capacity.[35] As the profits from manufacturing woolens declined, some mill owners undoubtedly found it cheaper to abandon debt peonage, but probably not for any humanitarian reasons.

31. ANH-Q, Obrajes, Caja 20, Protector de naturales al corregidor de Riobamba, Quito, 24 octubre 1793.

32. For the example of the Jesuits, see Cushner, *Farm and Factory*, 103–05.

33. *Ibid.*, 103.

34. ANH-Q, Obrajes, Caja 12, Libro de Rayas y Socorros de los Indios Labrantes del Obraje de Macaji, 1753; Libro de socorros de los Indios del Obraje de San Bartolomé de la Marquesa de Solanda que corre desde 15 junio 1761–65.

35. The relatively high productivity of the Jesuit mills during this period probably explains why debts remained commonplace in Yaruquí and San Ildefonso during this same time period. Cushner, *Farm and Factory*, 103.

Table 3.2. *Costs and profits in Manufacturing 56* varas *of* Paño Azul, *1650-1800*
(in pesos de ocho)

Expenses	Obraje de comunidad	Private Obrajes		
	1630-1710	1650-1700	1700-1750	1750-1800
Materials	49.0	48.5	47.0	47.0
Labor	45.0	26.0	26.5	26.5
Administration	2.5	3.0	3.0	3.0
Transport and Taxation	17.5	18.0	19.0	22.0
Sales commission	8.0	8.0	6.5	5.5
Interest	20.0	16.0	16.0	16.0
Total costs	142.0	119.5	118.0	120.0
Gross sales	182.0	182.0	147.0	119.0
Net profit	40.0	62.5	29.0	- 1.0

Source: Robson Brines Tyrer, "The Demographic and Economic History of the Audiencia of Quito: Indian Population and the Textile Industry, 1600-1800" (Ph.D. diss., University of California at Berkeley, 1976), 218-20.

The economics of decline

Saddled with an outdated and inflexible organizational structure, *obrajeros* could do little to lower production costs. As the figures provided by Robson Tyrer (presented in Table 3.2) indicate, the total cost of making a bolt (56 *varas*) of *paño azul* changed little from 1650 to 1800. The most expensive materials used in cloth manufacturing – wool and dye – could vary in price, but only dye had to be imported. Larger mill owners often raised their own merino sheep, which helped in controlling the cost of wool.[36] As a result, despite periodic increases in the price of indigo, the cost of raw materials actually declined slightly from 1650 to 1800.[37] Wages too continued virtually unchanged. Given the lack of any technological innovations, labor and administrative expenses also remained stable during the period.[38] Although *obrajeros* could save small amounts of money by delaying salaries or paying workers in cloth, the number of man-hours needed to produce a bolt of *paño azul* stayed at approximately

36. Given the variable prices of wool, those *obrajeros* who did not own sheep ranches operated at a considerable disadvantage.
37. According to Robson Tyrer, the average price of indigo rose from 12 reales to 20 reales from the seventeenth to the eighteenth century. The average price of wool during this same period declined, however, from 21 reales to 16 reales. The drop in wool prices nearly compensated for the rising indigo prices. See Tyrer, "Demographic and Economic History," 195.
38. "Administrative" costs refer to management and supervisory costs. *Ibid*, 199.

281–301 workdays (*rayas*).[39] Without significant labor-saving devices, mill managers could only squeeze so much in cost savings from their poorly paid and overworked employees.

Transport and marketing costs also remained stable during the period. Mill owners and merchants had to send their cloth overland to Guayaquil and then ship it by sea either directly to Lima or to Tumbes. From Tumbes it would be forwarded overland to Lima, the viceregal capital. The Tumbes route was slightly more expensive, but regardless of the route chosen, the costs of transport, insurance, warehousing, credit, and sales commissions changed little between 1650 and 1700. Taxes rose after 1750 (from 7.5 pesos to 11 pesos), but the declining price of credit and sales commissions apparently compensated.[40]

The principal problem in maintaining the profitability of cloth manufacturing involved falling prices in the Lima market, not rising costs. The declining cost of imports during this period prompted a corresponding downward trend in the price of American textiles. The selling price of *paño azul* in Lima, for example, declined from 28 reales in 1650 to 16–18 reales by 1750, which proved a crippling blow to the industry (see Table 3.2).[41] The income from selling of 56 meters of *paño* was 182 pesos from 1650 to 1700 but only 119 pesos between 1750 and 1800. By the last fifty years of the eighteenth century, foreign competition had undercut the price of *paño azul*, trimming the profits from over 62 pesos (between 1650 and 1700) to a net loss by 1800 (see Table 3.2). In short, European textile imports and changing consumer tastes simply made the demand for Quito's *paños* more elastic, prompting a decline in prices and profits.

The difficulty in turning a profit from operating an *obraje de comunidad* is also manifest from the statistics presented in Table 3.2. The average profit for communal mills was only two-thirds that garnered in privately owned operations. The high price of labor was the principal reason for increased production costs and smaller profits (see Table 3.2). According to the system of leasing an *obraje de comunidad*, the person with the highest bid for an "official" work year of 312 days received the contract.[42] In effect, this bidding determined labor costs at the mills, which tended to

---

39. *Ibid.*, 197.

40. *Ibid.*, 202, 204–12.

41. Individual enterprises could prove exceptions to these general trends. The *obraje* of Macaxi, in Riobamba, produced a net profit of over 5,000 pesos for the Leon family according to a series of judicial proceedings in 1782. See ANH-Q, Obrajes, Caja 16, Autos de Liquidación de Cuenta hecha por los contadores nombrados en la causa seguida pr Dr Dn Gregorio de Leon con Da Antonia Carselen, 23 October 1782.

42. Given the number of festival days and holidays, it is extremely unlikely that any laborer worked 312 days annually.

push prices upwards.[43] By the early eighteenth century, rising bids for labor cut further into profits, since administrative costs and salaries for all local officials and clergy were figured into yearly labor costs. Indeed, an inspection of community mills in 1694 found these amounts so high that the *obrajes* were incapable of meeting the Amerindians' tribute obligations or paying the pensions of local *encomenderos*.[44] In fact, most ran at a deficit.[45] As mill output declined nearly 50 percent by 1700, the crown eventually sold or leased these unprofitable operations to private citizens.

The most prosperous *obrajes* during the eighteenth century were the larger, privately owned mills, situated on rural estates complexes. Material, labor, and administrative expenses accounted for approximately 67–75 percent of the cost of producing *paño azul* (see Table 3.2). A large, rural *obraje* complex could meet most of these costs without having to expend any specie, a considerable advantage in the perennially cash-starved *Quiteño* economy. Wool came from the owner's nearby sheep ranches, while supervisors and laborers often collected their pay in cloth, not cash. Owners only paid out cash to meet the costs of marketing, transportation, credit, and taxes.[46] Since the larger *obrajeros* usually traded their own cloth for specie and European wares, even these costs could be minimized.[47] In short, although the larger cloth manufacturers could not produce *paño* much more cheaply than smaller urban shops, their ability to minimize cash payments proved a powerful long-term advantage.

Although the crown refused to stem rising European cloth imports, the decision to impose the *repartimiento de mercancías* (forced distribution of goods to Amerindian communities) in Peru also effectively subsidized those larger *obrajes* in Quito favored with crown contracts. These *repartimientos*, officially sanctioned between 1753 and 1781, always included significant amounts of *paño* produced in the *audiencia* district. The contract (*arancel*) of 1753 (shown in Table 3.3) provided for distributions of 73,700 meters of *paño* from Quito. Most of the cloth went to the provinces of Canas y Canches, Conchucos, Lambayeque, Lampa, Quispicanchi, Sicasica, Tarija, and Tarma. The official price of 3–8 pesos, established in the *arancel*, exceeded the amounts *obrajeros* had ever received in the Lima market.[48] The total value of this crown subsidy to the *obrajeros* of

43. Tyrer, "Demographic and Economic History," 124.
44. ANH-Q, Obrajes, Caja 9, Obrajes de comunidad venta a censo, 15 Octubre 1694.
45. The mills either turned a minuscule profit or ran at a deficit; in either case, by the time expenses were deducted they paid little of the tribute quotas for the local communities providing the labor force. *Ibid.*
46. Tyrer, "Economic and Demographic History," 212–16.
47. *Ibid.*, 295–96.
48. During this period the market price for *paño azul* was 2 or 2.5 pesos. See Alfredo Moreno

Table 3.3. *Minimal figures for Quiteño cloth in the Arancel of
the Repartimiento de Comercio del Perú, 1753*

Province	Paño de Quito (varas)	Paño de Quito (peso value)
Aimaraes	1,000	(7,800)
Andahuailas	1,500	(11,500)
Angaraes	500	(2,700)
Arequipa	2,500	(9,500)
Arica	1,500	(5,500)
Atacama	200	(1,600-1,400)
Azángaro	1,500	(11,500)
Berenguela	600	(4,200-3,600)
Cailloma	1,000	(5,600)
Cajamarca	0	0
Cajamarquilla	Not specified	
Cajatambo	800	(4,300)
Calca y Lares	800	(6,200)
Camana	1,000	(5,600)
Canas y Canches	1,500	(11,500)
Canta	Not specified	
Cañete	200	(1,000)
Carabaya	1,000	(7,800)
Carangas	300	(2,100-1,600)
Castrovirreyna	1,000	(5,600)
Cercado	0	0
Cochabamba	4,000	
Conchucos	2,000	(10,000)
Condesuyos	1,200	(6,800)
Cotabamba	1,000	(7,800)
Cuzco	1,000	(5,800)
Chachapoyas	Not specified	
Chancay	0	0
Chayanta	800	(6,400-5,600)
Chilques y Masques	1,200	(9,400)
Chucuito	1,000	(7,000-6,000)
Chumbibilcas	1,000	(7,800)
Huamalies	4,000	(20,000)
Huamanga	1,200	(5,800)
Huanta	1,200	(6,800)
Huánuco	Not specified	
Huarochirí	0	0
Huailas	600	(3,000)
Lambayeque	6,000	(30,000)
Lampa	3,000	(23,000)
Larecaja	1,000	(7,000-6,000)
Lipes	200	(1,600-1,400)
Lucanas	1,200	(6,800)
Luya y Chillaos	Not specified	
Misque	300	(2,400-2,100)

Table 3.3. *(cont.)*

Province	Paño de Quito (varas)	Paño de Quito (peso value)
Moquegua	1,500	(4,500)
Omasuyo	600	(4,200-3,600)
Oruro	500	(3,500-3,000)
Paria	500	(3,500-3,000)
Parinacochas	1,000	(5,600)
Paucarcolla	800	(5,600-4,800)
Paucartambo	800	(6,200)
La Paz	500	(3,500-3,000)
Pilaya y Paspaya	300	(2,400-2,100)
Piura	500	(2,000)
Porco	400	(2,800)
Quispicanchi	2,800	(21,600)
Santa	500	(2,500)
Sicasica	2,700	(18,900-16,200)
Tarija	1,500	(12,000-10,500)
Tarma	8,000	(41,500)
Urubamba	500	(3,900)
Vilcashuaman	1,000	(5,600)
Yamparaes	200	(1,600-1,400)
Yauyos	300	(1,500)
Yca y Pisco	Not specified	
Total	73,700	424,300-412,300

Source: Alfredo Moreno Cebrián, *El corregidor de indios y la economía peruana en el siglo XVIII (Los repartos forzosos de mercancías* (Madrid, 1977), 317-58.

Quito probably ranged from 410,000 pesos to 425,000 pesos each year. Such contracts for *paño* undoubtedly went to the larger, more politically well-connected cloth producers in Quito, which helped them continue producing in the diminished economic circumstances of the eighteenth century. This important crown subsidy to the *Quiteños* effectively ended, however, with the Tupac Amaru Rebellion in 1780, worsening the plight of the manufactories.

The decline of the textile business accelerated with the increasing volume of foreign imports (particularly cheap English *paños de segundo*) following the proclamation of imperial free trade between 1778 and 1789. Some producers in regional centers such as Otavalo could use their favorable geographical location to keep the expense of transportation down, while the relatively low cost of labor in Latacunga aided cloth producers. Both areas had abundant raw materials and specialized in making cheaper, low-quality *bayetas* and *jergas* that proved competitive in the New Granada market.[49] Mills producing *paño*, however, suffered. Many formerly wealthy *obrajeros* began to lease their mills, and when renters became scarce, eventually closed them down for at least part of the year. The failure of the *Administración de temporalidades* to run the former Jesuit mills profitably only hastened this process, since most of the Society's mills had specialized in *paño* production. The majority of the smaller workshops, particularly in urban areas, had gone bankrupt years before. The city of Quito, for example, boasted over fifty clothing mills in the seventeenth century, but by 1768 census takers found only two small *chorillos* and nine hat plants (*sombrerías*) still in operation.[50]

The decline of the *obraje* sector greatly exacerbated the dearth of specie. This problem became so acute that members of the merchant community often entered the textile business to produce cloth needed to finance imports. *Obrajeros* always had problems with liquidity and finding adequate credit; without selling their cloth, they could not hope to buy European imports. After mid-century, mercantile houses had the best access to capital for operating the mills, and many merchants realized the link between textile production and selling imports.[51] As a result, a number of wealthy traders, such as Tomás de Arostegui, began buying rural *obraje* complexes to support their mercantile enterprises. By 1767 Arostegui owned the *obraje* of Colimbuela, which he rented to the Conde de Lagunas, and operated his own integrated *obraje*-estate complex in Chillogallo, as well as his merchant stores in Quito.[52] In the end, this movement of mercantile capital into the textile business proved inadequate; without some sustained recovery of the industry, the merchants could not support both textile production and their import-export businesses.[53]

By the 1780s, declining productivity from the *obrajes* encouraged New Granada merchants (many based in Quito) to organize a cottage industry producing cotton textiles. The merchants supplied the raw cotton, grown

49. Tyrer, "Demographic and Economic History," 299–300; 321–22.

50. *Ibid.*, 317.

51. *Ibid.*, 301–04; Richard Salvucci comments on a similar pattern in Mexico; see Salvucci, *Textiles and Capitalism*, 91–92.

52. ANH-Q, Obrajes, Caja 14, Autos de esperas pedidas por dn. Tomás de Arostegui a sus acretiedores, Quito, 9 septiembre 1767.

53. As Robson Tyrer observed, "without other sectors of society being involved as well, the merchants would have ended up as the only significant consumers of imported goods." Tyrer, "Demographic and Economic History," 303.

along the Mira River basin, to Amerindian and *mestizo* weavers, who used it to make cheap *tocuyos* or *lienzos*.[54] Sometimes merchants even supplied fine European yarns to produce higher-quality textiles for elite consumption. Most of this cloth production centered in small sweatshops or individual homes in the city of Quito and its surrounding villages. There is also evidence that merchants organized a similar, but smaller-scale, putting-out system farther south in Latacunga and Ambato. The merchant-entrepreneurs then used their trade connections to sell the textiles principally in northern markets such as Pasco, Popayán, Barbacoas, the Chocó, or Antioquia in New Granada. Although modest in scale, such cottage production did provide jobs and some export earnings for the depressed north-central sierra.[55]

Despite the gains in this cottage industry, *Quiteño* textiles never regained their former share in the important Lima market, which proved disastrous for the long-term commercial life of the north-central sierra. During the seventeenth century, most wealthy *obrajeros* from the kingdom had transported their own *paños* to Lima and exchanged them for European goods and Peruvian products. Earnings from such transactions could be substantial, since the *Quiteños* controlled the sale of their textiles and the importation of many European goods into the district.[56] Although the northern cloth trade to New Granada maintained much of its vigor even after the 1780s, it offered more modest profits than the Lima market. New Granada merchants purchased mostly cheaper cloth and also took charge of introducing European goods from Cartagena into the Quito region.[57] As a result, the falling demand for *paños* in Lima cut into profits, restricted imports of European goods, and damaged commercial life in the north-central highlands.[58]

---

54. Merchant entrepreneurs also provided raw wool, which local weavers used to produce woolen *bayetas* and *jergas*. The bulk of this production, however, seems to have been in cotton, not woolen cloth.

55. Little has been uncovered about this cottage industry in the Quito region until recently. See Christiana Borchart de Moreno and Segundo Moreno Yánez, *Los circuitos del textil: producción y circulación en la Audiencia de Quito (1780–1830)* (forthcoming); Christiana Borchart de Moreno, "Más alla del obraje: la producción artesanal en Quito, 1780–1830," *The Americas* (forthcoming); and idem, "La economía quiteña en un periodo de transición: circulación y producción artesanal entre colonia y república" (paper delivered at the Latin American Studies Association meetings, 1992), cited with permission of the author. There are some allusions to the topic in the report of the director of the *Dirección general de alcabalas*, Carlos Presenti, in 1780. See AGI, Quito, Copia del Informe, 31 agosto 1780.

56. *Ibid.*, 283–95. ANH-Q, Ropas, Caja 5, Testimonio de Nicolás Antonio de Carrión y Vaca, Quito, 30 julio 1766.

57. Tyrer, "Demographic and Economic History," 296–98.

58. *Ibid.*, 232, 243.

The cottage textile industry of the south sierra

A prosperous cottage textile industry emerged in the south sierra, centered in the *gobernación* of Cuenca to meet the demand for cheaper cloth in Peruvian markets. The development of this industry required a dense population of Andean peasants to spin and weave the cloth. It also needed a well-organized merchant community to arrange the putting-out system of production, to facilitate the supply of raw materials, and to market the finished goods. This pattern of industrial organization, modeled on European cottage textile manufacturing, mirrored developments throughout the Spanish Indies, where an available labor force and proximity to regional markets encouraged production.[59]

The cottage textile industries in the south sierra and elsewhere in the kingdom emerged after the onset of decline in the *obraje* sector. The oligopoly enjoyed by *obrajeros* in the north-central sierra had driven most indigenous cotton producers from the market by the seventeenth century. Amerindian producers did not have the political influence of the *obrajeros*, and they lacked the advantages enjoyed by the large, concentrated woolen textile mills. The *obraje* was a successful solution to the problem of producing cloth in the thin, poorly integrated markets of the Andes in the seventeenth century. Once these mills began to close down, however, colonial merchants could use the more advanced network of regional markets that had evolved by the eighteenth century to develop a putting-out system, producing cotton and woolen cloth in the urban areas and indigenous settlements of the kingdom. Efforts by the crown to stimulate mining production in New Granada and Peru created a steady demand for cheap textiles, which the European *paños de segundo* had not completely filled.[60]

The cottage textile industry in the south highlands benefitted from numerous economic advantages. Good land and freedom from excessive tribute and *mita* obligations attracted numerous emigrants to the south sierra throughout the eighteenth century. The city of Cuenca also served as the principal marketing and service center for the region. Those emigrants who did not move to the city, however, located on Spanish *ha-*

---

59. For an overview of this process, see Manuel Miño Grijalva, "Capital comercial y trabajo textil: tendencias generales de la protoindustria colonial latinoamericana," *HISLA*, 9 (1989): 59–79. For a description of an analogous cotton-based textile industry, which developed in Cochabamba, see Brooke Larson, "The Cotton Textile Industry of Cochabamba, 1770–1810: The Opportunities and Limits of Growth," in Nils Jacobsen and Hans Jürgen Puhl, eds., *The Economies of Mexico and Peru during the Late Colonial Period, 1760–1810* (Berlin, 1986), 150–68.

60. Miño Grijalva, "Capital comercial y trabajo textil," 59–73. For a discussion of how the crown tried to stimulate mining production in the Viceroyalty of Peru, see J. R. Fisher, *Silver Mines and Silver Miners in Colonial Peru, 1776–1824* (Liverpool, 1977).

ciendas or on vacant lands. As the supplies of available land diminished, however, newcomers often had to settle in relatively less productive agricultural zones.[61] This provided an added incentive for rural villagers to supplement meager agricultural incomes by accepting commissions to spin or weave cloth for merchant suppliers. Much of this work could be done in the home by women and children.[62] This employment, often part-time, provided additional income and greater freedom than working in the loathsome *obrajes*.

This economic potential of the south sierra gradually attracted merchants eager to organize a putting-out system. These entrepreneurs apparently introduced cotton and raw wool from northern Peru or Jaén de Bracamoros or simply purchased them locally to supply the Andean villagers. The traders then used their commercial connections to sell local cotton *tocuyos* or woolen *jergas* throughout the mining and urban centers of South America.[63] In 1802, the Cuenca region exported 598,000 *varas* of cottons and 125,700 *varas* of baize. Merchants sent these goods to Lima (35 percent), Guayaquil (34 percent), Chile (19 percent), northern Peru (9 percent), and Panama (1 percent).[64] On the return trip, the entrepreneurs also introduced European products and imported colonial goods and raw cotton into the kingdom.[65]

Although modest in scale, profits from this import–export trade could be considerable. According to figures compiled by Silvia Palomeque, a merchant selling 20,044 *varas* of Cuenca's white cottons (*tocuyo blanco*) in Piura or Lima could net a profit of nearly 1,000 pesos.[66] Merchants often preferred to travel along the slower overland route through Piura, because it required a smaller initial outlay of cash than hiring space on a ship from Guayaquil. Regardless of the route taken, however, traders usually returned with European luxury items and raw cotton to sell in Cuenca. The cost of buying and transporting 180 mule loads (*cargas*) of cotton and European wares could reach 6,200 pesos; these same goods then sold in Cuenca for over 7,800 pesos, producing a net gain of 1,600 pesos. In short, over the course of the two-year round trip, entrepreneurs could

61. Silvia Palomeque, "Historia económica de Cuenca y sus relaciones regionales (desde fines del siglo XVIII a principios del XIX), *Segundo encuentro de historia y realidad económica y social del Ecuador*, 3 vols. (Cuenca, 1978), 1:106.

62. Miño Grijalva, "Capital comercial y trabajo textil," 66; Palomeque, "Historia económica de Cuenca," 88.

63. Silvia Palomeque, "Loja en el mercado interno colonial," *HISLA*, 2 (1983): 35–36.

64. Palomeque, "Historia económica de Cuenca," 87, 113, 128.

65. *Ibid.*, 96–100, 112–15.

66. The initial investment in cloth was 4,760 pesos 4 reales; transport, commissions, and taxes brought the total expense to 5,827 pesos 4.5 reales. The cloth could be sold for nearly 7,000 pesos. Palomeque, "Loja y el mercado interno," 38.

earn 25–30 percent annually on their original investment.[67] This compared very favorably to the rates of return made by *obrajeros* in the seventeenth century but with less risk. The original outlays needed to purchase over 20,000 *varas* of *tocuyo* seldom exceeded 5,000 pesos, while investing in an *obraje* required much more capital simply to purchase the mill and hire the necessary laborers.

Despite its prosperity, the cottage textile industry of the south highlands remained dependent on outside merchant houses, principally based in Lima. These merchants had the capital to organize the putting-out system, to advance needed supplies of cotton or wool, and most importantly, to market local *tocuyos* and *bayetas*, particularly in the mining centers of Peru.[68] Commercial houses from Lima also introduced nearly 69 percent of all European imports in 1802, while merchants from northern Peru and Guayaquil specialized in importing colonial merchandise to the south sierra.[69] Local elites in the south highlands simply lacked the mercantile connections and capital needed to control the textile business. As a result, they continued investing in land, leaving cloth production to outsiders.

This reliance on distant merchant houses eventually contributed to the decline of textile production in the south highlands by the nineteenth century. The end of the Peruvian mining boom, disruptions to colonial trading routes during the independence wars (1809–25), and the introduction of cheaper English cloth in the nineteenth century all encouraged merchants gradually to abandon the industry. This loss of mercantile organization promoted a decline in textile exports in the Cuenca region from 705,700 *varas* in 1802 to 284,765 *varas* in 1828; by 1849 local producers exported only 89,240 *varas* of cloth.[70] The cottage textile industry in Cuenca was too limited in scale and lacked the resources to survive without its outside merchant backers. It simply had no real potential to promote long-term regional economic growth in the diminished economic order following the independence era.

Shipbuilding in the coastal export era

The only other significant industrial enterprise in the Kingdom of Quito was the shipyard (*astillero*) of Guayaquil. From the late sixteenth century, abundant natural resources along the coast and the distance from Europe produced the Pacific's most extensive shipbuilding industry. The ship-

---

67. *Ibid.*, 38–39.
68. Palomeque, "Historia económica de Cuenca," 99–100, 114.
69. *Ibid.*, 97, 114–15.
70. Palomeque, *Cuenca en el siglo XIX*, 21–22.

yard's skilled workers organized into a guild structure (*gremio*), whose numbers had reached 335 men by 1777.[71] Most of the employment for these guild members came initially from the viceregal government, seeking ships for the southern armada (*Armada del mar del sur*). Contracts for smaller ships came from coastal merchants, usually based in Lima. By the eighteenth century, however, declines in viceregal orders left the shipyard in the doldrums, until an upsurge in the coastal export economy by the 1780s. Orders for new constructions from Lima merchants and repairs on the existing coastal merchant marine revitalized the industry, whose prosperity became inextricably linked thereafter to the prosperity of Guayaquil's export economy.

Apart from iron for nails, the coastal zone surrounding Guayaquil possessed important raw materials for shipbuilding, all within easy reach through an extensive coastal riverine system. Hardwood trees such as *guachapelí* (like oak) and *palos maría* (a wood similar to pine, used for masts) proved suitable for sailing vessels and grew in abundance throughout the coastal plain, especially in the forests of Bulabulu.[72] Highland textile manufacturers in Cuenca or the north coast of Peru produced the cotton cloth for sails, while the fibrous *cabuya* plant (comparable to sisal or hemp) provided cordage. A local tar-like substance (*copey*) served as pitch, and the principal caulking material (*estopa*) came from the skin of a locally grown coconut.[73] Members of the shipbuilder's guild fashioned these materials into sailing vessels renowned for their longevity in the Pacific commerce.[74]

The guild list (*matrícula*) of 1777 indicates that the majority of the carpenters and caulkers in the shipyard were castes, whose already low salaries declined throughout the eighteenth century.[75] In 1723, for example, a master carpenter earned between 20 reales and 24 reales daily, while in 1819 that wage had fallen to 12 reales. Most of the shipyard's employees, however, earned much less. In addition, steady work depended on new ship construction and repair orders, which seldom kept guild members busy all year long. The head of the guild – always a peninsular or creole – and Spanish authorities justified these declining wages because of the low cost of living in Guayaquil. Food was abundant and cheap

---

71. María Luisa Laviana Cuetos, *Guayaquil en el siglo XVIII: recursos naturales y desarrollo económico* (Seville, 1987), 266–67.

72. For a summary of the natural resources found in the Guayaquil region used in shipbuilding, see: *ibid.*, 227–60; Lawrence A. Clayton, *Caulkers and Carpenters in a New World: The Shipyards of Colonial Guayaquil*, (Athens, OH, 1980), 82–86.

73. This product was replaced for larger vessels by Chilean hemp (*cáñamo*). See Clayton, *Caulkers and Carpenters in a New World*, 85.

74. *Ibid.*, 69–72.

75. Laviana Cuetos, *Guayaquil en el siglo XVIII*, 266–67.

along the coast.[76] Nevertheless, the pay of most master carpenters by the nineteenth century was approximately equivalent to that of day laborers on local cacao plantations.[77] The castes who worked in the yards clearly had low-status and poorly paid jobs, despite the considerable skills involved in this important local industry.

Low labor costs and the unpredictable cycle of ship orders discouraged any long-term investments in organizational or technological innovations, which might have lowered costs and increased the quality of the ships produced. The *matrícula* of 1777 listed 254 carpenters (*carpinteros*) and only 81 caulkers (*califates*) laboring in the yards, indicating that many carpenters worked building wooden houses in Guayaquil during the long weeks or months between ship orders.[78] Whether working on home construction or in the shipyard, the workmen seldom employed any sophisticated planning or equipment. Indeed, the shipbuilders of Guayaquil were notorious for ignoring the techniques and regulations established in Europe, improvising with each new construction.[79] Shipbuilders remained tied to their traditional, labor-intensive procedures. Although the shipyard provided employment and benefits for over 300 men, the industry failed to produce sufficient profits to fund its own modernization.

The declining financial base of the viceregal government in Lima and the resulting decay of the *Armada del mar del sur* hindered the development of the Guayaquil shipyard throughout the early eighteenth century. The Lima government placed only four major ship orders during the entire century – for the frigate *El Fermín* (1730), the ship-of-the-line *La Limeña* (1740), the frigate *La Liebre* (1750), and the ship-of-the-line *San José el Peruano* (1756). Periodic scandals about cost overruns on these larger contracts only discouraged additional orders and blackened the reputation of the Guayaquil shipyard.[80] Most ship purchases during this period came from private merchants, who tended to order small, cheaper vessels and to be intolerant of cost overruns. In 1772, even before the export boom, local authorities estimated that agricultural exports produced 300,000–400,000 pesos annually for the province, while shipbuilding yielded only 100,000 pesos.[81]

The upsurge of cacao exports in the 1780s ended the relative stagna-

76. *Ibid.*, 270–73.

77. *Ibid.*, 270.

78. Most of the private dwellings in the city were constructed of wood, and periodic fires in the city and the port's growth during the cacao boom provided alternate employment for good carpenters. In 1802 the Callao shipyards listed 96 carpenters and 82 caulkers. *Ibid.*, 266–69.

79. Some observers even complained that the shipyards produced ungainly vessels, which met no standards for design or construction. Clayton, *Carpenters and Caulkers in a New World*, 65–67.

80. Laviana Cuetos, *Guayaquil en el siglo XVIII*, 281–84.

81. *Ibid.*, 285, note 116.

tion in ship construction. Between 1779 and 1788, the shipyard completed 75 jobs, worth a combined total of 1,528,024 pesos. This produced an annual intake of approximately 190,000 pesos, nearly twice the amount of income estimated by viceregal authorities for 1772. Only 12 of these orders involved new construction; 70 percent of the contracts concerned repairs for existing naval and merchant vessels.[82] Despite this renewed construction boom, most large orders came from Lima merchants, not local traders. In short, the shipyard became a service industry, meeting mostly the repair needs of merchants from Lima and elsewhere, who controlled the export of cacao during the boom years.[83] Technological innovation never characterized the industry, and by the mid-nineteenth century the yards could not adjust to manufacturing competitive steam-powered vessels.

Throughout the period 1690 to 1830, manufacturing in the Kingdom of Quito remained dependent, labor-intensive, and, in the long run, uncompetitive. Nevertheless, *Quiteño* entrepreneurs had few viable alternatives; innumerable obstacles blocked any potential efforts to adopt manufacturing techniques that had begun to revolutionize production in Europe. The most productive European manufactures benefitted from advances in market integration, an improving transportation system, a skilled labor force, available credit facilities, and innovations in technology and work organization. Moreover, entrepreneurs employed these advantages in very different ways; there was no single model for manufacturing anywhere in Europe.[84] Even if the *Quiteños* had tried to revamp their manufacturing system, merely gathering and analyzing information about the latest European innovations was a daunting task. Secrecy, government patents, legal barriers, and communication problems all impeded the flow of reliable information. There was also the problem of how to adapt European methods to the very different business environment of eighteenth-century Quito.[85] In fact, virtually none of the conditions prompting Europe's industrial upsurge existed anywhere in

82. *Ibid.*, 289–94.
83. By the early nineteenth century, the revived income of the yards still produced only one-fifth the wealth generated by the export sector. *Ibid.*, 300.
84. Much of the work on the European Industrial Revolution emphasizes the interaction of several causal factors. See, for example, Maxine Berg, *The Age of Manufactures, 1700–1820* (New York: 1986), passim, and Hudson, *The Industrial Revolution*, passim.
85. For a discussion of the technological and organizational innovations transferred between Europe and North America during this period, see Thomas C. Cochran, *Frontiers of Change: Early Industrialism in America*, 50–77. An important revisionist treatment of the historical role of technology and mass production in industrialization is Charles Sabel and Jonathan Zeitlin, "Historical Alternatives to Mass Production: Politics, Markets and Technology in Nineteenth-Century Industrialization," *Past and Present*, 108 (August 1985): 133–75.

Spanish South America. Finally, any attempt to imitate European advances faced the hostility of the Spanish crown, whose policies encouraged imports, not colonial manufacturing enterprises. In short, *Quiteños* had no realistic chance to restructure their manufactories to compete successfully with European imports.

The *obraje* sector faced the greatest challenges in overcoming the competitive edge of European textile producers. These oligopolistic enterprises emerged to produce cheap cloth in the thin, imperfect Andean markets of the sixteenth century. Although the *obrajes* superficially resembled later European textile enterprises, their archaic organizational structure made it impossible for mill owners to lower production costs or increase product quality – the principal purpose of modern factory organization. Instead, the *obrajes* used their size to fulfill many functions of the market, controlling the supply of labor, capital, and raw materials needed to produce cloth. Any attempt to implement the few available technological innovations in woolen manufacturing from Europe would have involved a radical restructuring of the work place, a reeducation of the labor force, and large influxes of capital.[86] The incentives and facilities for utilizing such production methods in the Kingdom of Quito simply did not exist. As a result, the *obrajeros* tried to take the only realistic, available option; they repeatedly and unsuccessfully petitioned the crown to stop the importation of European textiles.

The prospects for transferring European advances to the kingdom's labor-intensive cottage textile industry, centered in the south highlands, were equally dismal. Although the putting-out system superficially resembled many European textile manufactories, any attempt to utilize advanced techniques such as water-powered jennys for weaving, mules or frames for spinning, and carding machinery faced daunting obstacles. The English, who pioneered these technologies, were loathe to share any information about them with potential competitors. In addition, implementing such innovations required technological sophistication, a reasonably skilled labor force, access to capital, and a reliable market demand; none existed in the Kingdom of Quito. As a result, the cottage industry remained wedded to traditional production methods. When the independence wars disrupted regional markets, the demand for these crude cotton and woolen textiles eroded. By 1830, merchant-capitalists had completely abandoned the decaying industry.

The shipyard of Guayaquil proved equally labor-intensive, and dependent. The yard developed in the late sixteenth century to supply ships for the viceregal fleet and the Pacific trade. When the patronage of the

---

86. An important summary of the woolen textile industry in England is D. T. Jenkins and K. G. Ponting, *The British Wool Textile Industry, 1770–1914* (London, 1987), 1–76.

viceregal government and colonial merchants declined by the early eighteenth century, so too did the prosperity of the shipyard. The industry did not revive until the coastal export boom in the Guayaquil province after 1778, and thereafter its prosperity remained tied to the cacao economy. The boom-or-bust nature of the business, low profits, inadequate capitalization, and cheap labor costs all discouraged technological innovations that might have renovated this sector. By the advent of steam power in the mid-nineteenth century, the shipyard could no longer compete and fell into complete decadence.

Despite their relative size, complexity, and longevity, the textile and shipbuilding industries always operated in a business environment circumscribed by the dictates of the colonial state. Government controls limited the evolution of business enterprise, capital accumulation, and market integration, ensuring that manufacturing sectors could never promote any prolonged economic growth. After Spanish commercial policies led to the decadence of the *obrajes*, the cottage textile industry of the south sierra and later the shipyard of Guayaquil flourished. Nevertheless, these manufacturing enterprises had little potential for long-term expansion in this state-regulated economic system. When the colonial order slowly collapsed between 1809 and 1825, cottage textile production and shipbuilding rapidly declined. They simply lacked the scale, profit potential, and sophistication to promote any self-sustaining economic growth in the diminished markets of the early independence era.

4

Spanish agriculture and the rural economy

From the late sixteenth century, Spanish estates formed an essential link between colonial market centers and the rural zones of the north-central highlands. These agrarian enterprises had organized abundant land and labor resources in the interior to produce woolen textiles for export to Peru and New Granada. As a result, the diminishing demand for locally produced *paños* in the eighteenth century led to declining profits for rural estates in much of the region. The internal markets of the Andes also offered few alternatives to the traditional commerce in woolen cloth. High transport costs limited the ability of most *hacendados* to move from exporting textiles to selling their bulk crops in more distant regional markets. Over time, most successful rural estates were large enterprises, such as the holdings of the religious orders or the wealthiest members of the elite. Damaging Spanish commercial policies and rugged geographical barriers combined to force much of the rural economy in the north-central zone into greater isolation and stagnation.

In contrast, the agricultural economy of the south sierra experienced steady growth from the 1690s, as Andean migrants from depressed northern provinces provided a cheap labor force. The prosperity of most Spanish estates was linked to the demand for agricultural products and textiles in the local highland markets, Guayaquil, and northern Peru. Although the landholding elite played little role in cottage textile manufacturing, the cloth trade did stimulate the local agrarian economy, which helped pay for European imports. Some Spanish landowners also prospered by exploiting regional supplies of *cascarilla*. When the trade in textiles and *cascarilla* collapsed during the independence era, however, many Spanish estates continued to flourish, especially those holdings lying along the major overland trade routes.

The coastal export economy began to prosper when the crown allowed free trade within the empire between 1778 and 1789. The loosening of trade regulations was part of an ongoing effort by King Charles III and his advisors to stimulate imperial commerce, particularly in precious metals and tropical produce. Peninsular and creole elites established increasing numbers of *cacao* plantations along the extensive river system of the littoral, exporting their produce to South America, Mexico, and Europe. These rural plantations linked the coastal economy to international trade cycles. Even the disruptions of the independence era did not curtail the demand for chocolate in Mexico and Europe permanently, and cacao exports continued their uneven growth until the 1840s.

Spanish estates in the north-central sierra

Although the mountain valleys from Ibarra to Riobamba possessed some of the richest farming and pasture land in the Andes, Spanish landowners faced daunting challenges. The narrow mountain valleys of the kingdom were traversed by an extensive system of rivers, producing a varied, disorderly pattern of climatic and soil conditions.[1] Most larger estates occupied lands at markedly different altitudes and climates, which made specializing in a single, lucrative cash crop unfeasible. The high cost of transporting basic foodstuffs across this rugged terrain also impeded exports. To profit in these conditions, Spanish landowners often consolidated their holdings into large estate complexes, supplying food for local markets and textiles for export throughout South America. When the demand for locally produced woolens began declining, most landowners either attempted unsuccessfully to revive the textile trade or to find an export crop capable of earning specie.

These long-term economic problems proved particularly damaging in the Quito basin, which had a diverse rural economy revolving around the production of food and textiles. The province registered 346 *haciendas* in 1784, the largest number in the kingdom (see Table 4.1). Estates in warmer regions along the lower Guayabamba River valley raised sugar cane, fruits, grains, potatoes, vegetables, and livestock. In slightly more elevated lands in the northern part of the valley, Spanish landowners grew wheat, corn, and barley and bred livestock. In the remainder of the Quito basin, farmers raised a similar array of crops and livestock, depending on the climate and altitude of their holdings. Since high transport costs prohibited most farmers from exporting such bulk commodities to distant markets, larger landholders continued organizing their estates around textile manufacturing, even after the industry began to experience hard times in the eighteenth century.

1. The Ecuadorian sierra is among the narrowest portions of the Andean mountain range, at some points compressed to a width of no more than 81 miles. At their widest point, the Andes extend to only 137 miles in Ecuador – compared to 469 miles across Bolivia and northern Chile. David Basile has described the changing altitudes in the sierra as "producing a 'crazy quilt' pattern of microclimates that prevail over short distances." David Giovanni Basile, *Tillers of the Andes: Farmers and Farming in the Quito Basin* (Chapel Hill, NC, 1974), 5, 6, 19.

Table 4.1. *Number of Andean laborers on Spanish estates in the highlands during the late colonial period*

| Province | Year | Number of estates/Percentage of conciertos | | | Total |
		1-10 conciertos	11-50 conciertos	51+ conciertos	
Ibarra	1784	54 (50%)	52 (48%)	2 (2%)	108
Otavalo	1784	36 (49%)	32 (44%)	5 (7%)	73
Quito	1785	198 (57%)	140 (40%)	8 (2%)	346
Latacunga	1756	149 (50%)	114 (39%)	33 (11%)	296
Ambato	1823	96 (70%)	39 (28%)	3 (2%)	138
Riobamba	1812	78 (35%)	130 (60%)	10 (5%)	218
Cuenca[a]	1792	2 (2%)	99 (94%)	4 (4%)	105
Loja	1784	92 (84%)	17 (16%)	0	109

[a] Represents figures from only a partial list of parishes for the Province.
Source: Robson Brines Tyrer, "The Demographic and Economic History of the Audiencia of Quito: Indian Population and the Textile Industry, 1600-1800" (Ph.D. diss., University of California at Berkeley, 1976), 432-34.

Over 60 percent of the Andean population in the province worked as resident laborers (*conciertos*) on these Spanish holdings.[2] Nearly 200 estates had 1–10 *conciertos*, while the remainder employed a larger rural labor force (see Table 4.1). Estates in the warmer zones around the Guayabamba River basin tended to be smaller but quite profitable.[3] Great estates, specializing in textiles and mixed farming, clustered in the Tumbaco and Chillos Valleys, while both medium and larger holdings predominated in the Machachi Valley (see Map 2).[4] By the late seventeenth century, for example, only 12 estates in the Tumbaco Valley dominated 65 percent of the arable land; in the Chillos Valley large holdings of the religious

2. Robson Brines Tyrer, "The Demographic and Economic History of the Audiencia of Quito: Indian Population and the Textile Industry, 1600–1800" (Ph.D. diss., University of California at Berkeley, 1976), 435.

3. One outstanding exception to this generalization was the large *hacienda* of Cusubamba, owned by Pablo Unda in Guayabamba, which employed 59 *conciertos*. See ANH-Q, Presidencia de Quito, Tomo 360, 1785, Expediente tramitado por dn José de Rengifo . . . sobre el paso y abono a los indios que existen sueltos en los pueblos y en las haciendas del corregimiento de Quito, 1784 (hereafter cited as Libros de tributos de Quito).

4. ANH-Q, Presidencia de Quito, Tomo 360, 1785, Libros de tributos de Quito. Christiana Borchart de Moreno, "La tenencia de la tierra en el Valle de Machachi a finales del siglo XVII, "*Antropología Ecuatoriana*, 2–3 (1983–84): 148–49; idem, "Composiciones de tierras en el Valle de los Chillos a finales del siglo XVII: una contribución a la historia agraria de la Audiencia de Quito," *Cultura*, 5 (1980): 147; idem, "Composiciones de tierras en la Audiencia de Quito: el valle de Tumbaco a finales del siglo XVII," *Jahrbuch für Geschichte von Staat, Wirtschaft und Gesellschaft Lateinamerikas*, 17 (1980): 134.

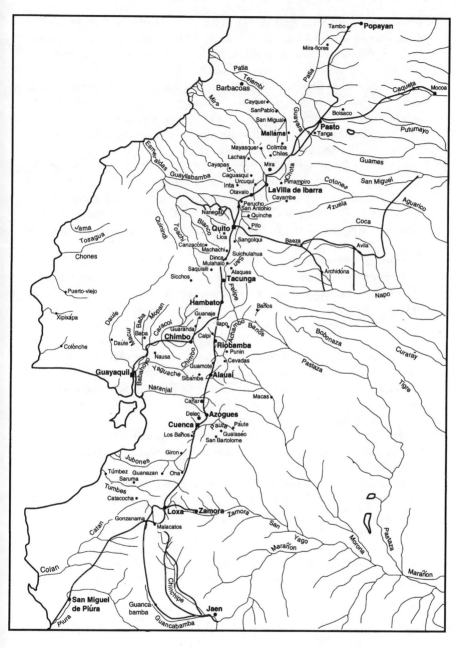

Map 2. Adapted from the map of the *Audiencia* of Quito by Pedro Vicente
Maldonado, 1750. *Source*: J. P. Deler and N. Gomez, *El manejo del
espacio en el Ecuador: etapas claves* (Quito, 1983).

orders held more than half the farmland.[5] As late as 1784, the former Jesuit properties of Chillo and Pedregal in Sangolquí still employed nearly 230 *conciertos*, despite the decline of these properties since the order's expulsion seventeen years earlier.[6]

The more diversified rural economies in Otavalo and Ibarra, to the north of Quito, generally fared well during the eighteenth century. In the northern and western zones, the warm, wet lowlands along the Mira and Chota Rivers proved excellent for growing sugar cane. Large estates, often owned by *Quiteños* and the religious orders, dominated the countryside by the late seventeenth century. From the town of Otavalo southward mixed farming prevailed, as Spaniards grew foodstuffs, bred extensive herds of livestock, and maintained a moderately prosperous textile industry. The *obrajeros* of Otavalo produced cheaper *bayetas* and *jergas*, utilizing their favorable geographical location to cut shipping costs to markets in New Granada.

Large holdings dominated the landscape in the north sierra. The two northern provinces had 181 registered estates in 1784, and over 50 percent of these *haciendas* listed 11 or more permanent laborers (see Table 4.1). In Ibarra only 44 percent of the sparse Andean population resided on Spanish estates, forcing the landowners to use African slave labor on their large sugar plantations.[7] Although some extensive sugar estates existed in the parishes of Cotacache, Urcuquí, and Tumbaviro in Otavalo, large holdings organized around textile production prevailed elsewhere. One such complex of rural estates, owned by Joaquín Sánchez, employed over 350 Andean laborers in the 1780s, producing a wide variety of food products and woolen textiles.[8] Nevertheless, over 50 percent of Otavalo's Amerindian population still lived in their traditional settlements, where they produced foodstuffs and worked in the large state-run *obrajes* founded in the sixteenth century.[9]

The textile industry also prospered in the province of Latacunga during the eighteenth century. Apart from some sugar production in the lowlands around Angamarca, most rural properties grew foodstuffs and raised livestock (mostly sheep). Larger estates often manufactured cheaper textiles for the New Granada market, which helped local landowners avoid the worst of the economic downturn that afflicted Quito to the north. The province maintained 296 Spanish estates in 1756, while the number

5. Borchart de Moreno, "La tenencia de la tierra en el Valle de Machachi," 148–49; idem, "Composiciones de tierras en el Valle de los Chillos," 147.

6. ANH-Q, Presidencia de Quito, Tomo 360, 1785, Libros de tributos de Quito, 1784.

7. Tyrer, "Demographic and Economic History," 436.

8. ANH-Q, Presidencia de Quito, Tomo 360, 1785, Libros de tributos de Quito, 1784.

9. Tyrer, "Demographic and Economic History," 436.

of *obrajes* increased 61 percent during the century (see Table 4.1).[10] Many of these rural enterprises hired small numbers of *conciertos*, but 50 percent listed 11 or more resident laborers (see Table 4.1). As the prosperity of Latacunga's rural estates and textile mills continued, more Andean laborers migrated there to find jobs in the rural economy. In fact, the number of *conciertos* increased from 30 percent of the Amerindian population in 1745 to over 57 percent in 1828.[11]

To the south, fertile lands in the province of Ambato supported a modest rural economy. By 1823 authorities identified only 138 Spanish estates – less than half the number in Latacunga. The bulk of these rural enterprises (70 percent) tended to be small- or medium-sized, employing 10 Andean laborers or fewer (see Table 4.1). Nevertheless, a few massive estate complexes like the former Jesuit estate complex of San Ildefonso continued to operate at reduced levels during the early nineteenth century. Apart from a wide variety of food products and producing some textiles, Ambato's Spanish landowners also grew sugar cane in the lowlands around Patate and Pilileo; a small cochineal business also flourished. The bulk of the indigenous population (56 percent) remained in their traditional settlements, involved in subsistence agriculture and artisan activities.[12]

The province of Riobamba was affected most severely by the declining textile business. Although the rural economy still supported over 218 Spanish estates in 1812, the number of textile mills in the province had declined markedly since the late seventeenth century (see Table 4.1).[13] The large *obrajes de comunidad* in Riobamba either closed down or passed to private entrepreneurs, such as Nicolás Carrion, whose mills employed nearly 240 Andeans in the parish of Licto in 1782.[14] Most *obrajeros* tried to shift away from the traditional production of *paños* to cheaper cloths, but according to contemporaries, high transportation costs and competition from Cuenca's cottage industries limited profits. Landowners still raised livestock and foodstuffs; they even grew some sugar cane in the southern lowlands. Over 65 percent of these estates employed 11 or more Andean laborers by 1812, with the largest holdings in Licto and Guamote (see Table 4.1).[15] The declining economy and high provincial trib-

10. *Ibid.*, 315.

11. *Ibid.*, 435.

12. *Ibid.*

13. The number of mills in Riobamba declined from 41 in 1700 to only 24 in 1780. See *ibid.*, 315.

14. ANH-Q, Presidencia de Quito, Tomo 359, 1783, Libro real para el cobro de tributos de los indios de la encomienda de Licto, Chambo, y Quimiag . . . por el año de 1782 (hereafter cited as Libros de tributos de Riobamba).

15. *Ibid.*

ute rates forced many Andeans to migrate south to Cuenca. Others undoubtedly settled on Spanish estates, which registered nearly 4,000 *conciertos*.[16] This movement to local *haciendas* reflected the overall weakness of the textile business, however, rather than any real dynamism in the rural sector.

The remaining provinces of Chimbo and Guaranda had few large estates, less fertile soil, and a sparse Andean population; they remained only marginal contributors to the rural economy of the north-central sierra. The few Spanish estates in these regions usually raised livestock and some food products for traders traveling the major thoroughfares to the coast. Large-scale textile production on rural estates had never taken root there.

The rural elite of the north-central highlands

A relatively small but closely knit group of elite families controlled rural society in the north-central sierra. The traditional success of large estate complexes organized around an *obraje* concentrated great economic power and social status in these provincial magnates. According to the tax records of 1768–75, less than 1 percent of the population of the city of Quito owned 34 percent of the land in the province.[17] Many of the largest holdings fell under the control of the hereditary aristocracy.[18] In 1692, for example, the Conde de Selva Florida (Manuel Ponce de Leon Castillejo) had accumulated extensive properties in Tumbaco and Cotocollao, which remained in the family throughout the eighteenth century.[19] Most of these aristocratic families maintained lands in several provinces, but they usually concentrated their holdings in a single region. The Marqués de Miraflores, for example, owned substantial properties in the Machachi Valley near Quito, but the largest family estates remained in Latacunga.[20] These aristocratic families frequently intermarried, which expanded their access to land, wealth, and political power in the kingdom.

Not all the powerful and wealthy *hacendados* were titled nobility. Old, prominent families such as the Merisaldes, Monteseríns, Peñaherreras, and de la Peñas also held important social positions. One descendant of the conquistadors, José Antonio Sancho de la Carrera, for example, owned

16. Tyrer, "Demographic and Economic History," 433.
17. See Javier Ortiz de la Tabla, "Panorama económico y social del corregimiento de Quito (1765–1775)," *Revista de Indias*, 145–46 (1976): 91.
18. For a listing of the titled nobility in the Kingdom of Quito, see J. A. Guzmán, *Títulos nobiliarios en el Ecuador* (Madrid, 1957).
19. Borchart de Moreno, "Composiciones de tierras en la Audiencia de Quito," 131.
20. ANH-Q, Presidencia de Quito, Tomo 360, 1785, Libros de tributos de Quito, 1784.

extensive properties in Machachi and Cayambe, where he even founded an entail (*mayorazgo*) in 1700.[21] Although entry into this elite was limited, some parvenu families did gain access to the upper reaches of power and status. By the mid-eighteenth century, merchants such as Tomás de Aróstegui began buying lands and *obrajes* to diversify their investment portfolios. Later in the century a peninsular emigrant, Joaquín Sánchez, also found it possible to accumulate large landholdings and *obrajes*.[22] Although these men seldom penetrated the highest echelons of the establishment during their own lifetimes, their children often attained social acceptance among the elite.

Important landowners also played a major role in the commercial life of the north-central sierra. Fifty-six of Quito's leading families (less than 1 percent of the capital city's population) accounted for nearly 32 percent of all purchases and sales registered in the region from 1779 to 1803.[23] The most important transactions (64 percent) involved rural properties, while 32 percent entailed the sale of houses, usually in urban areas.[24] Transactions by elites also accounted for nearly 44 percent (by value) of all the *hacienda* purchases and 80 percent of the purchases of *obrajes*.[25] The only large mill, which sold for 10,166 pesos, went to the Montúfar family (the Condes de Selva Alegre).[26] In short, members of established elite families arranged the most important business deals in the north-central sierra.

Credit, debt, and the declining rural economy

Despite the aggregation of wealth and power by highland elites, the rural economy's gradual decline led to bitter squabbles over interest rates charged on rural credit transactions. Landowners had frequently borrowed from clerical organizations to finance their estates or imposed liens against rural properties to support church activities, such as chantries (*capellanías*), religious brotherhoods (*cofradías*), or pious works (*obras pías*). Most

21. Borchart de Moreno, "La tenencia de la tierra en el Valle de Machachi," 147.

22. ANH–Q, Presidencia de Quito, Tomo 360, 1785, Libros de tributos de Quito. Jorge Moreno Egas, "Resumen alfabético del segundo libro de matrimonios de españoles de la Parroquia de El Sagrario de Quito 1764–1805," *Revista del Centro Nacional de Investigaciones Genealógicas y Antropologías*, 3 (Noviembre 1981): 267.

23. The data from this section are taken from the meticulous research of Montserrat Fernández Martínez in *La alcabala en la Audiencia de Quito, 1765–1810* (Cuenca, 1984), 143.

24. The transactions involving rural properties included the sale and purchase of *haciendas, obrajes, chacras, estancias,* land (*tierras*), and credit (*imposiciones de censos*). *Ibid.*, 127–42.

25. Many of these *haciendas* undoubtedly had textile mills on their grounds, so the distinction between the sale of *obrajes* and *haciendas* is, to some degree, meaningless. *Ibid.*

26. *Ibid.*

of these encumbrances, known as *censos*, required the landowners to pay yearly interest payments (*réditos*) of 5 percent on the principal.[27] By the early eighteenth century, however, such encumbrances exceeded 3 million pesos in principal and 150,000 million pesos annually in interest – a heavy burden during an era of economic decline.[28] In response, members of the landholding elite, particularly in the hard-hit provinces of Quito and Riobamba, agitated to lower the interest rate on *censos* from 5 percent to 3 percent.[29]

Complaints about the interest burden from liens and loans became even more intense after bad harvests. In the 1720s, landowners complained that an attack of a wheat fungus (*polvillo*) cut crop yields dramatically in Urcuquí and Tumbaviro in Ibarra; Cotacache, Cayambe, and Tontaqui in Otavalo; the Chillos, Machachi, and Guayabamba Valleys in Quito; and parts of Riobamba and Latacunga.[30] According to many farmers in those regions, farming costs had doubled as crop yields fell 50–75 percent.[31] One *hacendado*, Joseph de Aguirre, claimed that escalating debts and interest payments forced him to sell his estate in the Quito region at a loss of 8,000 pesos.[32] Even after the immediate crisis had subsided, farmers raised dire warnings about the collapse of regional agriculture if the crown did not ease the credit burden on rural properties.[33]

27. An important article on credit in the early colonial period for the Loja region is Chantal Caillavet, "Les rouages économiques d'une sociètè minière: échanges et crédit. Loja: 1550–1630," *Bulletin l'Institut Français d'Études Andines*, 13:3–4 (1984): 31–63. Two interesting articles on whether or not the church was a net consumer or lender of rural capital are: Arnold J. Bauer, "The Church in the Economy of Spanish America: *Censos* and *Depósitos* in the Eighteenth and Nineteenth Centuries," *Hispanic American Historical Review*, 63 (November 1983): 707–33; and Agueda Jiménez Pelayo, "El impacto del crédito en la economía rural del norte de la Nueva Galicia," *Hispanic American Historical Review*, 71 (August 1991): 501–29. The most recent contributions to this debate for the Andean region are: Alfonso W. Quiroz, "Reassessing the Role of Credit in Late Colonial Peru: *Censos, Escrituras*, and *Imposiciones*," *Hispanic American Historical Review*, 74 (May 1994): 193–230; and idem, *Deudas olvidadas: instrumentos de crédito en la economía colonial peruana, 1750–1820* (Lima, 1993).
28. AGI, Quito, 181, Autos seguidos para el prior gral de la ciudad de Quito sobre minoración de censos, 1755, f. 1r–v.
29. *Ibid.*, ff. 14–150v.
30. *Ibid.*, ff. 250–53v.
31. *Ibid.*, ff. 230v., 240v., 250v.
32. According to Aguirre, he paid 14,000 pesos for the property and sold it for only 6,000 pesos. *Ibid.*, f. 2r.
33. Resentment over the church's role as a consumer rather than a net provider of rural funds may have added to the bitterness among lay landowners in Quito. No systematic study of rural credit markets in Quito has been undertaken, but the problem is complex. Data in the ANH-Q, Censos y Capellanías, is not a complete listing of such credit transactions and may not even be a representative sampling. The best data would be found dispersed in the notary records. It seems probable, however, that the overall economic downturn and specie shortages in the kingdom made it unlikely that a significant amount of credit in cash was available from the church

Landowners used their political power to good effect in 1726, when they convinced the *audiencia* to lower all interest payments on *censos*. The judges declared that encumbrances on all wheat estates and sheep ranches would be lowered to 3 percent, while the rate on cattle ranches and sugar plantations was adjusted to 4 percent. The beleaguered *obraje* owners would pay only 2 percent.[34]

The response from church organizations was swift and negative. Clerical creditors claimed that interest rates on all *censos* had been negotiated in perpetuity and that the *audiencia* had no authority to lower them without their approval. Indeed, some clergymen warned that lowering interest rates on *censos* might impoverish nuns and chaplains, who depended on these payments for their subsistence.[35] The resulting imbroglio was not resolved until 1755, when the crown heeded the advice of the kingdom's landowners and cut the interest rate on all *censos* to 3 percent.[36]

Although lowering the interest rate on *censos* did provide some relief to rural landowners, the problem of heavy encumbrances continued. The declining textile business continued curtailing rural exports, profits, and access to specie. As a result, landowners still borrowed against their estates. Between 1769 and 1779, for example, the administrator of the *obraje* and estates of the Conde de Real Agrado in Riobamba spent over 5,100 pesos for interest on *censos* and direct loans (*préstamos*) and to pay debts for estate improvements and back salaries for servants, supervisors, and laborers.[37] In short, easing the credit burden on rural estates hardly altered the long-term economic plight of farmers, ranchers, and textile producers in the north-central sierra.

Taxation and the rural economy

Although the declining textile trade undoubtedly had an impact on rural production, no reliable documentation on agricultural output exists for

for the rural economy. Most chantries, pius works, and even some dowries for nuns entering convents probably would have been established with liens on rural properties, rather than cash outlays. After all, most landowners in the north-central sierra had little specie or the economic means to secure it. As a result, the clerical organizations probably had little cash to lend during the period 1690–1830. The subject, however, awaits further investigation.

34. AGI, Quito, 181, Autos seguidos para el prior gral de la ciudad de Quito sobre minoración de censos, 1755, f. 313. The *audiencia* first called for similar reductions in 1705.

35. *Ibid.*, ff. 157r–168v. ANH-Q, Censos y Capellanías, Caja 31, 1760–64, Autos seguidos por el sr. Fiscal con el cavildo de esta ciudad sobre la rebaja de censos del 5% a 3%, 22 julio 1760.

36. AGI, Quito, 105, Consulta, Madrid, 21 junio 1755; 8 agosto 1755.

37. ANH-Q, Haciendas, Caja 11, Quenta General de cargos y descargos que . . . presenta dn Vicente de Villavicencio como arrendador que fue de los fundos y fincas de sus padres los senores Condes de el Real-Agrado . . . por el tiempo de dies años, cinco meses, y quince dias que tubo dichas fincas en arrendamto desde 8 marzo de 1769 años en que resivio asta 23 de agosto de 1779 en que las entrego.

any region of the Kingdom of Quito. The only serial data, auction values for the tithe or *diezmo* (a 10-percent duty on most rural produce paid to the church), too often reflect changes in basic commodity prices, bureaucratic corruption or zeal, and shifts in the annual mix of the crops produced in each region.[38] The bids these prospective tithe collectors (*diezmeros*) offered every two years for the tax farming contract depended on their expectations for the coming harvests. As a result, the auction values from the tax farmers represent a crude estimation by contemporaries of *expected* rural production. More importantly, however, these tithe figures measure the biannual *tax revenues* paid by each rural parish in the region over time.

The tithe remittances from the north-central sierra demonstrate the overall importance of the rural sector in generating tax revenue during the eighteenth century. From 1721 to 1806, remittances for the Bishopric of Quito (which encompassed the entire north-central sierra) fluctuated between 45,000 pesos and 140,000 pesos (see Graph 1).[39] These tithe figures show an upward trend until the mid-1750s, followed by an overall decline, broken only by a short recovery from 1769 to 1772. These amounts far exceeded the relatively stable tithe revenues collected in the south highlands and the coast during this period.

By the 1790s, remittances from the north-central sierra, the south highlands, and the coast show dramatic increases, continuing into the early nineteenth century (see Graph 1).[40] The average growth rate for tithe remittances during this period was 4.7 percent annually for the Bishopric of Cuenca (including both the south sierra and the coast) and just over 4 percent for Quito. At the same time, the remittances also indicate the overall decline of the north-central sierra relative to the coast and the south highlands. Despite its larger population and geographical

---

38. For a recent article assessing the controversy over tithe remittances as an index of rural production, see: Arij Ouweneel and Catrien C. J. H. Bijleveld, "The Economic Cycle in Bourbon Central Mexico: A Critique of the *Recaudación del diezmo líquido en pesos,*" *Hispanic American Historical Review*, 69 (August 1989): 479–530, and "Comments on 'The Economic Cycle in Bourbon Central Mexico': A Critique of the *Recaudación del diezmo líquido en pesos* by Ouweneel and Bijleveld," by David Brading, John H. Coatsworth, Héctor Lindo-Fuentes, and the response by Arij Ouweneel and Catrien C. J. H. Bijleveld, *Hispanic American Historical Review*, 69 (August 1989), 531–57.

39. The tithes for the Bishopric of Quito included remittances from Pasto and Barbacoas, which are not included in these figures. These provinces were not really part of the mainstream political and economic life of the *Audiencia* of Quito.

40. The tithe auction values may be found in ANH-Q, Diezmos, Caja 1, Remates de diezmos, 1725–1780; AGI, Santa Fe 971, Remates de Diezmos de Quito, 1791–1806; Remates de Diezmos de Cuenca, 1789–1812; and ANH-Q, Diezmos, Caja 7, Remates de Diezmos, 1799–1810. The Bishopric of Cuenca was established in 1779. See Federico González Suárez, *Historia general de la República del Ecuador* (Quito, 1970 edn.), 1244.

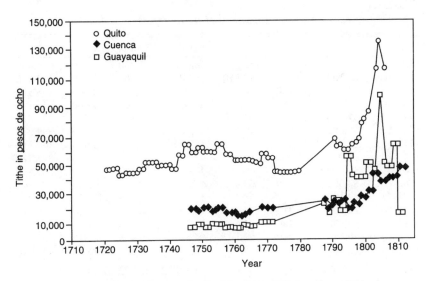

Graph 1. Tithe remittances for the Kingdom of Quito, 1721–1810.
Source: ANH-Q, Diezmos, Cajas 1–3, Remates de Diezmos, 1725–1780; Caja 7, Remates de Diezmos, 1799–1810; AGI, Santa Fe, Remates de Diezmos de Quito y Cuenca, 1789–1806; and Remates de Diezmos de Cuenca, 1789–1812.

area, by the 1790s tithe revenues from the north-central sierra failed to keep pace with the combined total for the coast and the south highlands.[41]

Fluctuations in tithe remittances for the north-central sierra depended largely on the contributions of two key provinces, Quito and Ibarra.[42] Between 1721 and 1806, these two provinces sent over 2,300,000 pesos, accounting for 51 percent of the total auction value for the Bishopric of Quito (see Table 4.2). Despite its much larger population and land area, Quito's rural economy sent less in tithe revenues than its northern neighbor by the 1790s, an indication of its relative economic decline. Latacunga and Riobamba yielded less than half the amounts of the two leading provinces. Ambato and Chimbo lagged even farther behind, producing only 16 percent of the total tithe (see Table 4.2).

For the Quito region, tithe remittances reflect the economic difficulties faced by Spanish estate owners. The richness of the land, the overall demographic stability of the province, and the chronic specie shortage kept food prices low until the mid-1760s, when they began a very slow

41. The north-central sierra had a population of 285,127 by the late eighteenth century, compared to 141,565 for the coast and south sierra. See Table 3.1.
42. For the purposes of tithe collection, Ibarra and Otavalo were counted as a single province.

Table 4.2. *Tithe remittances, Archbishopric of Quito, 1721-1810*

Year	Ambato	Chimbo	Ibarra-Otav.	Latac.	Quito	Riob.	All
1721-25	27,000	12,100	52,250	38,000	65,830	38,850	234,030
1726-30	27,500	10,550	50,750	38,000	63,305	35,550	225,655
1731-35	33,250	11,130	56,500	45,000	72,742	34,700	253,322
1736-40	30,350	10,980	60,000	46,800	71,766	34,300	254,196
1741-45	31,500	15,250	63,540	43,650	83,125	38,750	275,815
1746-50	38,600	17,000	72,250	44,200	90,475	45,750	308,275
1751-55	38,200	14,400	77,581	46,800	89,755	39,575	306,311
1756-60	33,925	12,000	73,400	47,500	83,920	46,475	297,220
1761-65	31,700	10,300	60,800	47,000	75,082	44,650	269,532
1766-70	33,300	12,900	67,460	46,200	69,231	44,850	273,941
1771-75	29,100	12,412	57,300	43,135	62,608	42,250	246,806
1776-80[a]	25,700	10,312	47,000	42,585	66,064	37,250	228,912
1791-95	36,980	18,786	85,631	52,477	80,343	46,284	320,501
1796-1800	40,699	21,749	92,197	67,570	89,478	48,815	360,508
1801-05	52,737	24,469	116,147	76,364	116,575	71,624	457,916
Total	510,541	214,339	1,032,806	725,281	1,180,299	649,673	4,312,939

[a]The years 1781 to 1790 are not available in the AGI, Seville, or the ANH, Quito.
Source: ANH-Q, Diezmos, Caja 1, Remates de Diezmos de Quito, 1721-1780; AGI,
Santa Fe 971, Remates de Diezmos de Quito, 1791-1805.

decline. Wheat fetched high prices, but periodic blights could reduce harvests (as in the 1720s) by 50 percent. The only crop capable of bringing consistently high prices was sugar cane, which landowners manufactured into a popular cane liquor, *aguardiente*.[43] When the crown established direct state control over the manufacture and sale of *aguar-*

43. Between 1750 and 1780, for example, corn averaged only 15 reales/*fanega* (1.5 bushels), beans only 17 reales/*fanega*, and potatoes 7 reales/*costal* (bag). Wheat averaged 30 reales/*fanega*, while *aguardiente* sold for an average of 85 reales/bottle before 1765; after 1765 the price of cane liquor fell dramatically to between 56 reales and 40 reales/bottle. Price data are scattered throughout the ANH-Q and a few secondary works. The price data used in this chapter come from the following sources: ANH-Q, Haciendas, Caja 3, Estado de las haciendas de Chaquibamba y Lloa; Caja 5, Libro de Recivos de la hacienda de San Antonio de Quaxara desde 1 agosto hasta fin de septiembre 1767; Caja 8, Libro de recivo de estas haciendas de San Yldefonso del Colegio Mayor de Sn. Luis, que empieza a correr desde 1 dic. 1759, siendo hacendero Joseph Sánchez; Caja 14, Cuentas de las haciendas de San Xavier, El Palmar y San Pedro, 1774–1780; Cuentas adjustadas a dn Francisco Auzeco Echea de las haciendas de Santiago, Carpuela, Chaluayaco, Caldera, Concepción, Chamanal, y Tumbaviro, desde 12 junio 1776 hasta 28 marzo 1778: Cuentas Ajustadas a dn Simon Fuentes y Vivero, Comisionado de las Temporalidades de Tacunga desde 31 diciembre 1776 hasta 5 mayo 1778; Caja 20, Cuentas ajustadas del Obraje y Haciendas de Sn Ildefonso al Admr. Ramon Puente desde 30 marzo 1780 hasta 31 enero 1787; ANH-Q, Temporalidades, Caja 8, Cuentas dadas por dn Joaquin de Merizalde y comisionado de la Temporalidades de Cuenca, año 1772; and Tyrer, "Demographic and Economic History," 188.

diente in 1765, however, even the price of cane liquor dropped over 50 percent.[44] In short, no single agricultural crop could substitute for profits previously earned from textiles in the province of Quito.

By the 1790s, the parishes most responsible for rising tithe remittances in the province of Quito were located in the Machachi Valley (in the south) and the central region encompassing the parishes of Cotocollao, Chillogallo, Zambiza, Pomasque, and San Antonio.[45] Tithe collections in the Machachi region had risen steadily since the 1770s, while funds from the central region apparently did not begin to increase until the 1790s.[46] Estates in the Machachi Valley tended to be large, specializing in mixed farming, livestock raising, and some textile manufacturing. Large or medium holdings dominated the central parishes and produced a similar variety of foods, livestock, and textiles. A few estates also grew sugar cane in low-lying regions near San Antonio and Pomasque.

In Otavalo and Ibarra, sugar cane and textile manufacturing zones contributed to increased tithe revenues. Large sugar-producing estates surrounding the city of Ibarra, and the parishes of Pimampiro, San Antonio, Tumbaviro, and Urcuquí sent the largest tithe remittances throughout the period from 1790 to 1806. Farther south, the region surrounding the town of Otavalo and the parish of Tabacundo paid sub-

---

44. The crown ordered the establishment of the monopoly in 1739 to provide funds for the maintenance of the palace of the local *audiencia*. It was not established until 1746 and remained a permanent impost, despite the renovation of the building. It was always tax farmed, however, until 1765. See ANH-Q, Presidencia de Quito, tomo 58, Melchor de Rivadeneyra to oficiales reales, Quito, no date, f. 30. While the monopoly remained under the control of local tax farmers, the high profits from *aguardiente* production in Quito and Ibarra continued, attracting numerous *Quiteño* elites and members of the clerical corporations. By the 1750s numerous land disputes developed over the scramble to acquire the best cane fields. See Juan Romualdo Navarro, "Idea del reino de Quito," in Manuel Miño Grijalva, ed., *La economía colonial: relaciones socioeconómicas de la Real Audiencia de Quito* (Quito, 1984), 127. The most interesting land disputes involved Joseph de Grijalva y Recalde. See AHN–Q, Tierras, Caja 67, Autos de Joseph de Grijalva con Joseph de Osejo, Quito, 27 octubre 1752; Caja 72, Autos de Francisco Mariano de Arboleda con Joseph de Grijalva, Quito, 1755–1760. For an analysis of the role of sugar in the rural economy of mid-eighteenth-century Quito, see Kenneth J. Andrien, "Economic Crisis, Taxes, and the Quito Insurrection of 1765," *Past and Present*, 129 (November 1990): 115–20. After the fall in prices, sugar and *aguardiente* production continued to thrive in Ibarra, but many lowland estates in Quito became less profitable. See Jorge Juan and Antonio de Ulloa, *Relación histórica del viaje a la América meridional*, 2 vols., ed. Miguel M. Rodríguez Navarro and Miguel Rodríguez San Vicente (Madrid, 1978), Libro I, Título VI, Capítulo I, ff. 417–19. Among the principal sugar-producing parishes of Quito during the eighteenth century, only Chillogallo showed any marked increase in its tithe remittances after 1790 – an indication that many sugar zones of the Quito province proved less profitable after the fall in *aguardiente* prices after 1765. See AGI, Santa Fe 971, Remates de Diezmos de Quito, 1791–1806.
45. AGI, Santa Fe 971, Remates de Diezmos de Quito, 1791–1806.
46. AGI, Santa Fe 971, Remates de Diezmos de Quito, 1791–1806; AHN–Q, Diezmos, Caja 1, Remates de Diezmos, 1721–1780.

stantial tithes.[47] Both zones had large estates involved in mixed farming, livestock raising, and textile production.

The tithe figures for Quito, Ibarra, and Otavalo provide some tantalizing clues about the agricultural cycles of the north-central sierra.[48] These provinces had a climate, topography, and economic structure representative of the entire north-central highlands, and their rural economies contributed a majority of the tithe revenues. In all three provinces, tithe contributions rose from the 1790s in parishes where large- and medium-sized holdings predominated. Some of these estates produced primarily sugar cane, but most specialized in foodstuffs, livestock, and textiles for sale in local or regional markets. Spanish farmers in the region apparently found no new export crop or method of estate management to reverse their economic fortunes; instead the most successful landowners had larger estates, using cheap labor to supply the kingdom's internal markets.

Spanish estates in the south sierra

Spanish estates in the south sierra benefitted from the region's demographic and economic growth during the eighteenth century. In the provinces of Cuenca and Loja, the cottage textile industry was seldom an important activity on Spanish estates; urban artisans and Andean villagers spun and wove the cotton and woolen cloth exported from the region. Instead, Spanish estates – occupying the high- and medium-altitude lands – furnished food, livestock, and *cascarilla*. Estates in the lowlands grew sugar cane, cotton, fruits, and tropical produce. These Spanish landholdings generally supplied markets within the region, along the coast, and in the mining zones of northern Peru.

In the province of Cuenca, larger estates prevailed; all but 2 of the 105 Spanish estates employed 11 or more *conciertos* (see Table 4.1). Many of the biggest estates were located in the north, particularly the parish of Cañar. The *hacienda* of Francisco de Rada outside of Yzabieja, for example, provided work for 94 resident workers in 1792. Estates to the south and east in Cañaribamba, San Bartolomé, Nabón, Pagcha, Guachapala, Paute, Jaday, Cumbe, and Oña tended to be somewhat smaller, employing 20–30 *conciertos*.[49] Most of these holdings grew a variety of

---

47. AGI, Santa Fe 971, Remates de Diezmos de Quito, 1791–1806; AHN–Q, Diezmos, Caja 1, Remates de Diezmos, 1721–1780.

48. Tithe data from the remaining provinces were often recorded in annual summaries rather than by parish. This makes parish-by-parish comparisons over time impossible, except for the two largest tax contributors, Quito and Ibarra. AGI, Santa Fe 971, Remates de Diezmos de Quito, 1791–1806; AHN–Q, Diezmos, Caja 1, Remates de Diezmos, 1721–1780.

49. ANH-Q, Presidencia de Quito, Tomo 361, 1792–93, Expediente tramitido pro el Admin Prin-

grains, fruits, and, in the warmer lowlands, sugar cane. Spanish estates in the higher-altitude zones of Oña and San Bartolomé raised livestock, while *haciendas* in the southeast specialized in harvesting *cascarilla*.[50]

Despite the dominance of large Spanish estates, smaller holdings thrived in the central parishes. Spaniards, castes, and Andeans owned these farms, supplying food to the urban markets of Cuenca and Azogues. In the fertile lands surrounding Gualaseo and Sigsig, very small farms (*minifundia*) also predominated, despite the presence of a few large estates.[51]

In the southernmost province of Loja, the sparse population inhibited the development of estates with large numbers of *conciertos*. Over 85 percent of the Spanish estates employed 1–10 *conciertos*; over 75 percent of the Andean population remained living in their villages (see Table 4.1).[52] The majority of these *haciendas* clustered around Loja and San Juan del Valle in the east, Malacatos in the southeast, and Cotacache in the west.[53] In the lowlands landowners grew sugar cane, *yerba maté, añil*, and *maní*; estates at higher altitudes specialized in grains, beans, *ají*, vegetables, and fruits. In the more barren regions, Spaniards raised mules for the overland traffic in cloth and food products to Peru; many landowners in the eastern highlands also organized the gathering of *cascarilla*.

The rural elite in the south highlands

A network of peninsular and creole families dominated the rural society of the south sierra. Powerful clans such as the Valdiviesos, Veintemillas, Otandos, Bermeos, Crespos, Astudillos, and Ochoas owned the largest landed estates, and they maintained their wealth and power through skillful business and marriage connections.[54] The largest landowner of the late colonial period, Francisco de Rada, for example, married his daughter to Fernando Valdivieso y Carrera, scion of an old and distinguished provincial family.[55] The established families also made alliances with wealthy merchants, miners from northern Peru, and members of the political

---

cipal de Cuenca dn José de Rengifo con . . . sobre el pago y abonos a los indios del corregimiento de Cuenca . . . 1792 (hereafter cited as Libros de tributos de Cuenca).

50. Silvia Palomeque, *Cuenca en el siglo XIX: la articulación de una región* (Quito, 1990), 124–26.

51. *Ibid.*

52. Tyrer, "Demographic and Economic History," 436.

53. ANH-Q, Presidencia de Quito, 1785–86, Tomo 360, Expediente tramitido por Manl. Vallano y Cuesta . . . de pago y abonos a los indios del corregimiento de Loxa, 1786, 1792 (hereafter cited as Libros de tributos de Loxa).

54. For a genealogy of the elite in the south sierra, see Maximiliano Borrero Crespo, *Orígenes Cuencanos*, 2 vols. (Cuenca, 1962).

55. Palomeque, *Cuenca del siglo XIX*, 155–56.

establishment.[56] After all, the south sierra formed part of an emerging complex of regional markets, which made such ties very useful in conducting business.[57]

The rural elite in the province of Cuenca seldom gained noble titles or founded entails, but they remained a potent regional economic force, supplying food and livestock to overland traders and the towns. The leading rural landowners were also active in provincial business, buying and selling luxury imports, land, and even urban houses throughout the period.[58] Others took part in the harvest and export of *cascarilla*.[59]

Loja had few large landholders and supported a very small provincial elite. After a short mining boom in the sixteenth century, the regional economy revolved around *cascarilla* and supplying internal trade routes – to Cuenca in the north and Peru to the south. *Haciendas* and ranches in the north, near Saraguro and Yúruc, provided food and mules for the northern route. Estates around Catacocha and Malacatos also served the southern roads to Peru. The five largest *haciendas*, which employed over ten *conciertos* in 1792, were clustered near these two routes.[60]

While the decline of the cloth and *cascarilla* trades hurt some rural landowners, most simply shifted to supplying regional markets or the coast. The most hard-hit members of rural economy were the small-scale *mestizo* and Andean farmers, who lost the ability to supplement their meager agrarian incomes by producing cloth. Many sold their holdings over the nineteenth century and migrated to areas promising more economic opportunity, such as the coast.[61] Their relative isolation from the export trade, however, left most Spanish landowners insulated from the slow regional decline in the early nineteenth century. By that time, 10 percent of Cuenca's *hacendados* had accumulated 85 percent of the arable land; these estates proved a powerful asset following the decline of regional commerce and manufacturing.[62]

Taxation and the rural economy

Tithe remittances from the south sierra produced approximately half the revenue generated in the north-central highlands. Despite the economic

56. *Ibid.*
57. Scarlett O'Phelan Godoy, "Vivir y morir en el mineral de Hualgayoc a fines de la colonia," *Jahrbuch für Geschichte von Staat, Wirtschaft, und Gesellschaft Lateinamerikas*, 30 (1993): 75–127.
58. In 1788, for example, landowners Francisco de Rada, Francisco Veintemilla, Francisco Andrade, and Mariano Alvarez all took part in substantial land transactions. Sometimes these transactions involved selling land, but often they simply represented families transferring properties to consolidate estates. AGI, Quito, Alcabalas de Cuenca, Escrituras y Contratos Públicos, 1788.
59. Palomeque, *Cuenca en el siglo XIX*, 150.
60. ANH-Q, Presidencia de Quito, 1785–86, Tomo 360, Libros de tributos de Loxa, 1792.
61. Palomeque, *Cuenca en el siglo XIX*, 128–38.
62. *Ibid.*, 128–29; 155–68.

growth of the southern provinces during the eighteenth century, the region still had only 40 percent of the population living in the northern provinces, and its rural economy remained moderate in scale. Cuenca and Loja also had fewer Spanish estates (214) than the single province of Riobamba (218) (see Table 4.1). Moreover, indigenous communities paid the tithe only on certain commodities (crops of indigenous origin were normally exempt). As a result, by the 1790s the amounts collected in these southern parishes approximately equaled the combined tax revenues collected in Quito and Ibarra.[63]

Auction values for the tithe income remained stable from 1745 until 1795, when they began an uneven rise until 1812 (see Graph 1). This upswing occurred despite a decline in the textile and *cascarilla* trades in the early nineteenth century. Very few estate owners participated in selling *cascarilla*, and fewer still took an active role in the cottage textile business. As a result, rising tax remittances from the rural economy remained unaffected by the general decline in these sectors.

The parishes most responsible for the increasing tithe remittances were located on the major southern trade routes. The parishes of Cañar, Azogues, Biblián, Deleg, Paute, Paccha, San Juan del Valle, Exido, and Nabón in Cuenca; Saraguro in Loja; and Sibambe and Tigsan in Alausí together accounted for nearly 75 percent of the increased remittances from 1795 to 1812.[64] All clustered around major trade routes to the north and the coast, except Nabón in the south, which lay on the road to Loja (see Map 2). The parishes that had produced *cascarilla* sent lesser tithes each year.[65]

Cacao and the coastal export boom

The reform of Spanish commercial policy from the 1770s began an unprecedented escalation in coastal agricultural production. In 1774, the crown allowed free trade among the Pacific colonies, and it expanded the provision to include most of the empire in 1778. Fearful of competition from Guayaquil's growers, cacao interests in Venezuela lobbied successfully to have the crown impose a limit of 8,000–10,000 *fanegas* annually on the amount of the coastal crop exported to Mexico, the principal Indies market for chocolate.[66] This quota was not abolished until 1789.[67]

63. According to colonial law, local custom governed whether the Amerindians paid the tithe. In most locales, the Amerindians paid the tithe only on crops of European origin. See *Recopilación de leyes de los reynos de las Indias* (Madrid, 1973, 1681), libro I, título 16, leyes 2–8, 13; and Clarence Haring, *The Spanish Empire in America* (New York, 1947, 1963), 263–64. AGI, Santa Fe, 971, Remates de Diezmos de Cuenca, 1789–1812; Remates de Diezmos de Quito, 1791–1806.

64. AGI, Santa Fe, 971, Remates de Diezmos de Cuenca, 1789–1812.

65. *Ibid.*

66. One *fanega* equaled approximately 1.5 bushels. See Cushner, *Farm and Factory*, 193.

67. For a summary of the advent of free trade along the kingdom's coast, see: Michael T. Hamerly,

Without these trade restrictions, cacao production expanded rapidly along the coast, from 56,000 *quintales* (hundredweight) annually in the 1780s to 150,000 *quintales* by 1810.[68] Although estates on the fertile coastal plain produced copious amounts of tobacco, hardwoods, and sugar, the cultivation and export of cacao became the most lucrative regional economic activity. The crown further encouraged this export boom in 1779 by halving the port taxes (*almojarifazgos*) on all goods leaving Guayaquil and on all shipments of cacao entering other American ports.[69] As a result, from the 1790s the province and port of Guayaquil could participate directly in both colonial and global markets for cacao, which ensured regional prosperity until the rapid decline in world prices for the crop by the 1840s.

The expansion of export agriculture along the coastal river valleys and littoral encouraged the development of large- and medium-sized plantations, particularly in the parishes of Baba, Babahoyo, Palenque, and Machala. In the northern parishes (Baba, Babahoyo, and Palenque) abundant rainfall, a hot climate, and an extensive river system all encouraged production.[70] The southern parish of Machala benefitted both from an inland river system and its proximity to the Pacific; its cacao crop was the cheapest in the entire *gobernación*. By 1774, these four parishes alone accounted for 94 percent of the regional cacao production; this domination continued into the next century.[71] In fact, the coastal census in 1832 listed over 280 plantation owners in these four wealthy parishes alone.[72]

A few Spanish estates in the parishes of Daule, Balzar, and Yaguache also grew cacao, but most specialized in tobacco, sugar cane, and cotton. The census of 1832 registered 237 plantation owners in these parishes, but most of these estates were smaller and less profitable than the cacao plantations in Machala and the northern zones.[73] Nevertheless, these regions produced 230,568 *mazos* (bundles; one *mazo* equals approximately ten tobacco leaves) of tobacco in 1784, before a series of blights cut the

Historia social y económica de la antigua provincia de Guayaquil, 1763–1842 (Guayaquil, 1973), 124–25; idem, *El comercio del cacao de Guayaquil durante el período colonial: un estudio cuantitativo* (Guayaquil, 1976), 26–28; María Luisa Laviana Cuetos, *Guayaquil en el siglo XVIII: recursos naturales y desarrollo económico* (Seville, 1987), 167–69.

68. Hamerly, *Historia social y económica*, 122; Laviana Cuetos, *Guayaquil en el siglo XVIII*, 182.

69. The crown lowered the port tax on all cacao leaving Guayaquil to 1.25 percent and cut the levy on all shipments entering other Indies ports to 2.5 percent. Hamerly, *El comercio del cacao*, 27; idem, *Historia social y económica*, 124; Laviana Cuetos, *Guayaquil en el siglo XVIII*, 168.

70. Hamerly, *Historia social y económica*, 109–10; Laviana Cuetos, *Guayaquil en el siglo XVIII*, 175–77.

71. Hamerly, *Historia social y económica*, 109–10; Laviana Cuetos, *Guayaquil en el siglo XVIII*, 175–77.

72. Hamerly, *Historia social y económica*, 113, Table 21.

73. *Ibid.*

crop to only 62,438 *mazos* by 1790. Although tobacco production did recover to 132,400 *mazos* in 1805, growers complained that selling their crop at fixed prices to the government monopoly (*estanco*) hurt profits and forced production cutbacks.[74] The cultivation of sugar cane was never so extensive. The sugar crop probably never exceeded 14,000 *arrobas*, which growers sold each year to the government *estanco*.[75] The agency then manufactured it into *aguardiente* for local consumption.[76]

Coastal farms of all sizes owned by Spaniards, Amerindians, and castes raised large quantities of fruits, vegetables, and livestock for local consumption. Near Puná and Punta de Santa Elena, Amerindian villagers also caught fish, cut hardwoods, produced artisan goods, grew foodstuffs, and raised livestock. All of these producers generally sold their goods in the port city and the regional towns.[77]

The coastal elite

The rapidly expanding coastal export economy allowed greater social mobility than the more established highland societies. Opportunities for profit in the deregulated cacao economy prompted the rapid alienation and exploitation of arable lands during the 1780s. During this decade landowners planted 250,300 new cacao trees in Babahoyo, 210,200 in Baba, 102,550 in Palenque, and 98,310 in Machala. A small number of wealthy *costeños* planted the bulk of these new trees; only 15 percent of the landowners accounted for 63 percent of the total. Five men alone, José del Campo, Francisco Garaicoa, José Ortega, Juan de Aguirre, and Silvestre Gorostiza Villamar planted 277,310 new trees – 40 percent of the total. Gorostiza, the lieutenant governor of Machala, planted over 90,000 trees on his plantations in Balao and Tenguel, which had formerly belonged to the Jesuits.[78] Francisco Garaicoa, another powerful politician, used his political and social connections to gain control over a large cacao plantation with over 50,000 trees in Babahoyo.[79] In short, the export sector's growth led to an unprecedented expansion of the rural economy, enriching a landholding elite who became the region's "barons" of cacao.

Early in the cacao boom, political and commercial connections pro-

74. Laviana Cuetos, *Guayaquil en el siglo XVIII*, 192–95.
75. One *arroba* equaled approximately 11.3 kilograms. See Cushner, *Farm and Factory*, 193.
76. Laviana Cuetos, *Guayaquil en el siglo XVIII*, 206–09.
77. *Ibid.*, 209–26.
78. *Ibid.*, 178–79.
79. *Ibid.*; AGI, 232, Hoja de Servicio de Francisco Ventura Garaicoa, 1797. Garaicoa was appointed administrator general of the tobacco monopoly in Guayaquil by the powerful *audiencia* president-regent José García de Leon y Pizarro in 1778, and by 1787 he had already consolidated his landed holdings in Babahoyo. He came to Guayaquil from La Coruña and married into a wealthy local family.

vided the most secure avenue to wealth and social status. The amazing success of the mulatto merchant-politician Bernardo Roca provides an apt illustration. Roca came to the port from Panama in the 1760s, probably as part of the militia sent to put down the Quito Insurrection of 1765.[80] When the crown ordered the creation of a disciplined militia in Guayaquil in 1774, Roca linked his fortunes to Captain Víctor Salcedo y Somodevilla, the man entrusted with implementing the military reforms. Roca quickly rose to become commander of the caste (*pardo*) battalion.[81] After Salcedo left Guayaquil, the ever opportunistic Roca turned to a new patron, Governor Ramón García Pizarro.[82] According to several disgruntled cacao planters, Roca, García Pizarro, and their cronies (Manuel Barragan, Jacinto Bejarano, Martín Icaza, Miguel García, Francisco Garaicoa, Nicolás Cornejo, Joseph Mejía) used their powers ruthlessly to establish a virtual monopoly over the export trade in cacao.[83] Even after the crown transferred García Pizarro to Salta in 1789, Bernardo Roca continued as a prosperous and well-connected merchant; by 1809 he was also a respected citizen (*vecino*) of Guayaquil, who styled himself "don" Bernardo, despite his lowly social origins.

After the downfall of the export monopoly run by García Pizarro and his allies, most of the coastal plantation owners relied on established commercial houses (usually based in Lima and Mexico City) to market their produce. Occasionally, however, a wealthy merchant became involved in agriculture. Martín de Icaza, for example, originally made his fortune as the local representative in Guayaquil of his family's powerful Mexico City merchant house, which served as a major importer of coastal cacao.[84] Later, Icaza diversified his interests by purchasing the large food-producing *hacienda* of Cacharí in Babahoyo and additional estates in Palenque, which produced 325,000 *matas* of cacao annually.[85] This union of commercial and landed wealth was unusual, however, since most planters lacked the connections and resources needed to market cacao abroad.[86]

---

80. Bernardo Roca was born in Panama in 1740. Laviana Cuetos, *Guayaquil en el siglo XVIII*, 132–33.

81. Roca quickly gained a reputation as a "man who could be trusted to handle the *pardos*." In fact, Salcedo did not even bother to follow the royal instructions calling for a separate "white" command structure for all *pardo* units – an indication of his confidence in Bernardo Roca. Allan J. Kuethe, *Military Reform and Society in New Granada, 1773–1808* (Gainesville, FL, 1978), 62.

82. Bernardo Roca even served as one of the bondsmen for Ramón García Pizarro, the governor of Guayaquil. Laviana Cuetos, *Guayaquil en el siglo XVIII*, 132.

83. AGI, Quito, 271, Anonymous author to crown, Guayaquil, 4 diciembre 1787.

84. John E. Kicza, "Mexican Merchants and Their Links to Spain, 1750–1850," in Kenneth J. Andrien and Lyman L. Johnson, eds., *The Political Economy of Spanish America in the Age of Revolution, 1750–1850* (Albuquerque, NM, 1994), 115–36.

85. Hamerly, *Historia social y económica*, 109–10.

86. Unlike highland farmers, who usually relied on the church for credit, most coastal planters used

By 1830, a well-established coastal elite of politicians, large plantation owners, and merchant families controlled much of the regional economy. Although some social mobility still existed, a few landowners – Martín de Icaza, Domingo Santisteban, Josefa Pareja, Francisco Vitores, and General Juan José de Flores – now controlled the production of over 1 million *matas* of cacao, representing 25 percent of the total crop.[87] Some of these landowners, such as Icaza, were also prominent merchants, while General Flores used his extensive political powers to consolidate his landholdings in the region. This elite dominated the major economic transactions involving land, urban property, and slaves, and they also served as major consumers of luxury goods.[88] After independence, these wealthy families continued to exert great influence in coastal political, social, and economic affairs.[89]

Taxes and the coastal export economy

Auction values for the tithe reveal the magnitude of the export boom and provide an indication of the relative magnitude and tax burden of the coastal economy. Tithe remittances increased rapidly after 1795, reflecting both the extension of cacao cultivation along the coast and the resulting rise in rural production (see Graph 1). On the other hand, the tax revenues generated by the coastal export economy were only slightly larger than the tithes collected annually in the south sierra. This is hardly surprising. The low population density of the coast and the restriction of cacao cultivation to zones near the rivers curtailed any greater economic expansion. Although the tithe collections reveal the dynamism of the export economy, they also indicate the relatively modest scale of coastal agriculture. The principal value of the cacao economy was its ability to generate hard cash. In the Kingdom of Quito, cacao was the only commodity capable of easing the specie shortage accompanying the decline of the textile trade.

Coastal tithe remittances remained sluggish from the 1740s, until the dramatic upsurge in the cacao economy in the mid-1790s (see Graph 1).

merchant capital, leading to frequent conflicts over interest rates. For a revealing case about merchant–planter conflicts over credit, see AGI, Santa Fe 971, Silvestre Gorostiza to crown, copy of original made in Madrid, 20 junio 1796. According to Gorostiza, a politician and leading planter, merchants tried to charge 6-percent interest on loans, when 5 percent was normal on the coast (3 percent was the legal interest rate on all clerical *censos* after 1755).

87. Manuel Chiriboga, *Jornaleros y gran propietarios en 135 años de exportación cacaotera (1790–1925)* (Guayaquil, 1980), 15, 16, 20.

88. For an indication of just how active the elite was in the commercial life of the coast, see AGI, Quito 478, Alcabalas de Guayaquil, Escrituras y contratos públicos, 1769–1808.

89. David J. Cubitt, "La composición social de una élite hispanoamericana a la independencia: Guayaquil en 1820," *Revista de Historia de América*, 94 (1982): 14–16.

After 1795, the tithes tended to fluctuate unevenly, in all likelihood reflecting periodic changes in the price of cacao.[90] After 1810, however, tithe income began to drop significantly, as a series of droughts, floods, and a falling demand for cacao during the Napoleonic Wars curtailed production and profits.[91] This situation lasted until 1819, when tithe remittances rose again, reflecting the return of prosperity to the regional export economy.

The parishes most responsible for the rising tithe revenues were Baba, Babahoyo, Palenque, and Machala – all centers of cacao production. These four parishes alone generated 55–67 percent of the tithe revenues collected in the province. Only the rural economies of Balzar and Daule generated significant amounts of revenue, producing 9–11 percent of the annual totals. These two parishes grew some cacao, but their rural economies depended more heavily on tobacco, sugar, fruits, and some foodstuffs. Although important, these crops figured less prominently in the overall economic upsurge in the Guayaquil region.

Clerical landholding: the Jesuits

While most elite landowners concentrated their holdings in one province, clerical corporations often held large estates scattered throughout the realm. This was especially true of the Jesuits, the largest and most successful clerical landowners in the kingdom. By 1767, the order had acquired extensive properties, through direct purchase, grants (*mercedes*) from local *cabildos*, gifts, and occasional mortgage foreclosures or litigation.[92] The Colegio Máximo held the largest number of estates, stretching from Ibarra to Latacunga, while the smaller colleges tended to concentrate their holdings in one or two regions (see Appendix 1).[93] Their large

---

90. Although no complete price series exists for the coast, the price of cacao, the major coastal crop, probably exercised much influence on the tithe receipts in cash. The cacao crop in the mid–1780s fetched only 1.5 pesos/*carga* but increased slowly to 7–10 pesos/*carga* in the next decade. By the late 1790s, the price of cacao then stabilized at 4 pesos/*carga* – despite some seasonal fluctuations, leading to temporary prices hikes to 7 pesos/*carga* – until the 1840s. See Laviana Cuetos, *Guayaquil en el siglo XVIII*, 180–83.

91. David J. Cubitt, "The Government, the Criollo Elite and the Revolution of 1820 in Guayaquil," *Ibero-Amerikanisches Archiv*, 3 (1982): 271–72.

92. In the province of Ibarra, where the Jesuits had extensive landholdings, the order secured over 56 percent of its land by direct purchase from Spanish and Amerindian owners. Most of these transfers came between 1680 and 1740. See Rosario Coronel Feijóo, *El valle sangriento: de los indígenas de la coca y el algodón a la hacienda Cañera Jesuita: 1580–1700* (Quito, 1991), 59.

93. The Jesuits constantly bought and sold property to consolidate their holdings and to dispose of unprofitable lands. As a result, the exact configuration of *obrajes, haciendas*, and plantations under their control constantly shifted. The list in Appendix 1 is only a partial list of the major holdings in 1767, not a complete accounting of all the properties owned by the Jesuits during their tenure in the kingdom. A further complication involves the names assigned to the estates – the

estates allowed the Jesuits to control land and water resources across different ecological zones, recruit needed laborers, and dominate many local markets for rural produce. These networks of estates supported the thirteen Jesuit colleges operating in the kingdom and the frontier missions along the Mainas and Marañon Rivers. After the Society's expulsion in 1767, however, the state agency (*Administración de temporalidades*) that administered the properties and a series of private owners failed to duplicate the Jesuit's long-term successes. As a result, examining the structure and functioning of these Jesuit estates – before and after 1767 – provides important information about the factors promoting success or failure for rural enterprises in the Kingdom of Quito.[94]

The Jesuits organized their rural holdings throughout the *audiencia* district into integrated estate complexes producing a wide array of products. The Colegio Máximo's huge textile and food-producing holdings in the Chillos Valley, for example, were linked to its large estates in Ibarra – Santiago, Carpuela, Chaluayaca, and Caldera. These northern plantations, ranches, and farms were organized around the production of sugar cane and *aguardiente*.[95] An inventory of the estates in 1776 listed over 500 *cuadras* of sugar cane, tended by 398 slaves and numerous part-time Andean laborers.[96] Only the Jesuits had the capital to purchase the large numbers of expensive slave laborers needed to solve the perennial labor shortage in the north sierra.[97] Some northern properties also raised foodstuffs, while over 9,500 head of livestock grazed on their nearby ranches (*hatos*) of Chunchi, la Comunidad, and Alor. Whatever the northern estates could not grow came at low prices from the Colegio's properties in the Chillos Valley.[98]

Smaller landholdings producing crops and livestock also formed an

order maintained a series of integrated estate complexes, with each having its own name. Usually the largest estate gave its name to the entire complex, but not always. As a result, the estates listed in Appendix 1 may vary from other lists of Jesuit assets, depending on what estate names are used in the documentation.

94. The largest number of estates listed in Appendix 1 were located in the north-central sierra, the traditional agrarian heartland of the kingdom. After all, the Jesuits were expelled in 1767, before the economy of Cuenca reached its peak and nearly twenty years before the cacao boom along the coast. Nevertheless, the Jesuits did have colleges and estates in the south sierra and the coast, maintaining a viable presence throughout the realm.

95. Cushner, *Farm and Factory*, passim; Coronel, *El valle sangriento*, 96.

96. Each *quadra* was equal to the size of an urban plaza one block around. Cushner, *Farm and Factory*, 193.

97. Coronel, *El valle sangriento*, 83–88.

98. Likewise, the more modest estates of the Jesuit College of Guayaquil – San Xavier, El Palmar, and San Pedro – put 95 slaves to work tending nearly 52,000 cacao trees. These estates also grew food, raised livestock, and met the remainder of their basic needs by trading or purchasing goods from other Jesuit estate complexes. ANH-Q, Haciendas, Caja 12, Inventario de las haciendas de San Xavier, El Palmar, y San Pedro, 1774–1777.

integral part of a more extensive estate network owned by the various Jesuit colleges. The Colegio Máximo's estates of Tanalagua, Guatos, and Niebli in the province of Quito were typical of these labor-intensive agrarian enterprises (see Appendix 1).[99] The Jesuits began acquiring these lands in 1648, adding plots of varying sizes until the entire estate consisted of 440 *caballerías* by 1767.[100] The properties were bounded on the north and east by the Perucho River and stretched from the villages of Perucho and Conrogal southward to the small towns of Puellaro and Alchipichi (see Map 3). The estates of Ignacio Barreto, Juan de Hacha, and the Dominicans formed the southern border. Over 94 *caballerías* of land on the east of Tanalagua were devoted to growing grains. Between 1778 and 1779 these lands alone produced 4,100 bags (*costales*) of corn, 27 *fanegas* of barley, 8 of wheat, 76 of beans, and 272 *costales* of potatoes. Scattered along the outer fringes of the complex were 325 *caballerías* of grazing lands that supported 2,347 head of livestock. The Jesuits devoted 21 *caballerías* of land on the northern portion of the estate, stretching between the villages of Guatos and Niebli, to sugar cane, fruits, and livestock raising.[101] All of this varied produce supplied local markets and the needs of the Colegio Máximo's more specialized properties, especially the sugar plantations in Ibarra.

According to data generated by the *Administración de temporalidades*, their vast rural holdings allowed the Jesuits to finance a wide range of pastoral obligations in the five years before their expulsion.[102] Total income from all the Jesuit properties ranged between 168,075 pesos in 1766 and 222,896 pesos in 1765. In some years (such as 1764) the Jesuits made a handsome profit of 60,000 pesos, while in others years (such as 1762 and 1766) their expenses exceeded income. The extensive holdings of the Colegio Máximo generated the largest income from 1762 to 1766, while the college in Ibarra and the provincial college registered the high-

---

99. See also Coronel, *El valle sangriento*, 154.

100. ANH-Q, Temporalidades, Caja 19, Expediente sobre la venta de las haciendas conocidas con los nombres Tanlagua, Guatos, y Niebli, pertenes. a el Colegio Máximo, 1783. One *caballería* equaled approximately 16 *cuadras*. Cushner, *Farm and Factory*, 193.

101. *Ibid.*

102. The agency had a vested interest in making low estimates of the order's profits. This would allow state administrators to minimize their own failures or magnify their successes. As a result, the agency probably made low or extremely conservative estimates of the Society's income and profits. The agency's estimate of profits under the Jesuits for the Chillos estate complex certainly seems low in comparison to the figures cited by Nicholas Cushner, which he took directly from accounts in the Jesuit archives in Quito and Rome. See Cushner, *Farm and Factory*, 145–70. At the same time, Cushner's high profit figures have been criticized for failing to take note of investments in land, inputs, and improvements undertaken by the order. See Coronel, *El valle sangriento*, 117.

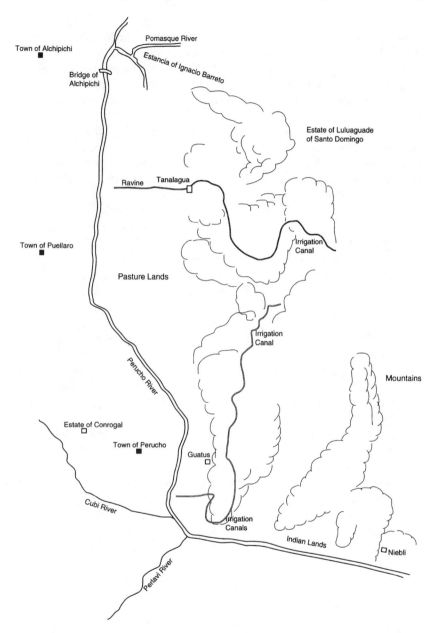

Map 3. Hacienda complex of Tanalagua, Guatus, and Niebli. *Source*: ANH-Q, Temporalidades, Caja 19, 1783–1784, Expediente sobre la venta de las haciendas conocidas con los nombres de Tanalagua, Guatus, y Niebli, pertentes. a el Colegio Maximo.

est profits, mainly from their sugar-producing estates in Ibarra.[103] Apparently sugar and *aguardiente* production were particularly lucrative before the crown established the cane liquor monopoly in 1765. Apart from these estates, the richest individual properties were the large holdings in the Chillos Valley and the complex of San Ildefonso in Ambato, which generated annual profits during the period of 6,095 pesos and 5,246 pesos respectively.[104]

Patient investment and management strategies often allowed the Jesuits to sustain temporary losses resulting from unwise purchases or rundown properties. When the Casa de Exercicios purchased the *hacienda* of San Ignacio de Chaquibamba in 1744, for example, the property took years to turn a profit. The Jesuits paid 5,616 pesos in cash and assumed encumbrances on the estate worth 8,300 pesos. The *hacienda* operated at a deficit in the first four years totaling 20,249 pesos; it was not until 1755 that the administrator (*mayordomo*) managed to complete needed repairs, to retire most of the encumbrances, and to make a small profit. By the 1760s, however, the estate generated annual profits ranging from 400 pesos to 1,100 pesos.[105] The persistence of the order in committing resources during the decade-long process of renovation and debt repayment ultimately led to a successful investment.

After the Jesuit's expulsion in 1767, the *Administración de temporalidades* failed to duplicate the careful and patient management that had led to the success of San Ignacio de Chaquibamba. The state agency too often employed corrupt or inefficient administrators to run the former Jesuit properties. A *visita* of the large estate complex in the Chillos Valley, for example, uncovered operating deficits of over 8,000 pesos during the stewardship of Manuel Araujo in 1779. Araujo blamed bad weather, his predecessors, the dishonesty of underlings, missing livestock, and poor harvests; none of his explanations proved adequate. As the investigation demonstrated, his utter mismanagement had turned this showpiece of the Jesuits into a rundown, unprofitable enterprise.[106] Even when state administrators did equal the profits of the Society, they often did so by selling off livestock, deferring needed improvements, or firing laborers, rather than through skillful management. In fact, between 1779 and

103. AGI, Quito 242, Estado que manifiesta los productos de las Haciendas, Fincas, y Rentas que gozaron los Regulares expatriados de la Provincia de Quito . . . y los gastos ordinarios y extraordinarios de cada Colegio, Quito, 15 noviembre 1784.

104. *Ibid.*

105. ANH-Q, Haciendas, Caja 3, 1714–1722, Visita de la hacienda de San Ignacio de Chaquibamba, 1744–1767, Quito.

106. ANH-Q, Temporalidades, Cajas 12, 13, Informe de la Contaduría de Temporalidades, Quito, 20 abril 1779, 20 agosto 1779.

1796 – despite selling the most unprofitable Jesuit estates – the *Administracíon de temporalidades* registered scarcely one-half to one-third the annual income garnered by the order from 1762 to 1766.[107]

The state also lacked the warehouses, mercantile connections, and capital reserves used by the Jesuits to operate their estates. The order frequently stored woolens and other produce from its large estate complex at San Ildefonso in its Lima warehouses until prices reached an acceptable level. Without these advantages, the *Administración de temporalidades* earned annual profits from San Ildefonso that were over 1,000 pesos less than the Jesuits'. As an inspection of the estate uncovered in 1798, however, even these reduced profits came only by deferring repairs and renovations. The entire complex was organized around textile and sugar production, but with the falling price of *paño*, successive administrators had allowed the *obraje* to fall into a deplorable state. The investigators found that a fire in 1797 had left the mill with broken equipment and badly damaged buildings, and that the herds of sheep on the ranches of Llangagua, Cunucyacu, and Pacobamba had thinned considerably. The sugar mills and the *haciendas* of Tontapi, Patalo, and Quinchibana were in better shape, but their produce was unable to compensate for the loss of income by the *obraje*. In fact, the crown inspectors declared that San Ildefonso's properties were "unsalable as separate parts, because they are mutually dependent auxiliaries of the *obraje*."[108] In the end, the government sold the estate for 128,000 pesos to Agustín Valdivieso in 1800, despite valuing the properties at over 192,000 pesos (see Appendix 2).

By the 1780s, exasperated crown officials decided to cut their losses by selling the Jesuit properties at public auction. These transactions ostensibly brought nearly 1,800,000 pesos to the treasury (see Appendix 2). The estates fetching the most substantial sums were usually very large enterprises, particularly the profitable sugar plantations in Ibarra. Most of the sale price, however, was not collected in cash. Given the shortage of specie in the kingdom, buyers usually relied on modest cash outlays and financed the remainder of the purchase price with *censos*. Although Pedro Calixto offered 140,000 pesos for the estates of Chalguayaco, Cotacache, Laguna, and Agualongo in Ibarra, he agreed to pay only 30,000 pesos in cash – the first 20,000 pesos over six months, and the remaining

107. ANH-Q, Temporalidades, Caja 25, Copia del Inventario que en testimonio se presenta con estas cuentas y comprehende todo el Dinero, efectos, y mas especies sobre que se funda el cargo del Director Antonio Azpiazu . . . desde 11 abril 1779 hasta 21 diciembre 1794, Quito.

108. AHN–Q, Obrajes, Caja 21, Visita de San Ildefonso, Quito, 21 Julio 1798. For a concise narrative of the problems at San Ildefonso and the destructive earthquake of 1797, see Christiana Borchart de Moreno, "La crisis del obraje de San Ildefonso a finales del siglo XVIII," *Cultura*, 24 (1986): 655–71.

10,000 pesos within two years. He financed the rest, 110,000 pesos, with long-term encumbrances.[109] In cases where the purchasers failed to meet their interest payments, government officials had to confiscate the property and resell it, usually at a lower price.[110] In short, government efforts to administer and later to sell the Jesuit properties proved a difficult and complicated undertaking.

Private purchasers usually fared no better than the state in making money from the former Jesuit holdings. Some purchasers profited by acquiring *haciendas* near their own properties. The Marqués de Miraflores, for example, bought four smaller Jesuit estates near his traditional family estates in Latacunga – Saquisilí, San Blas Pamba, Ylito, and Tacaló. Such successes, however, were uncommon.[111] Efforts by more ambitious purchasers to duplicate the large, integrated rural enterprises run by the Society invariably failed.

The merchant Carlos Araujo was typical of these unsuccessful entrepreneurs. Araujo began his career as an itinerant, small-scale merchant, traveling from Lima to Quito and Popayán. After making a fortune in commerce, this *nouveau riche* merchant began acquiring rural properties in Quito and Ibarra in 1772. His accumulation of property culminated ten years later when he purchased the large sugar-producing estates of Quajara and Chamanal from the *Administración de temporalidades* for 80,000 pesos. The 266 slaves on these estates posed a serious problem for Araujo; they had to be fed and clothed. The Jesuits had resolved the problem by shipping supplies from their estates in the Chillos Valley, an option not open to Araujo. Undaunted, the enterprising merchant purchased the estate of Cochicaranqui in 1785 to provide the needed supplies, but the transaction badly overextended his finances. Araujo first tried to pool resources with another merchant, Antonio Freyre de Andrade, but even this measure proved inadequate. Now desperate, Araujo began selling his slaves, provoking a near riot among the bondsmen, who opposed having their families separated. In the end, Carlos Araujo defaulted on his mortgages and lost everything, typical of many private entrepreneurs who

109. ANH-Q, Temporalidades, Caja 22, Creditos activos por venta de haciendas de Cotacachi, Agualongo, Caldera, Chaguayaco, Calera, y obraje de La Laguna, Quito, 16 septiembre 1784.
110. After Mariano Donoso defaulted on his mortgages for the *hacienda* of Santiago, for example, the state sold the property to Juan Saldumbide. For the case of Donoso and others who defaulted or fell behind in their interest payments, see ANH-Q, Temporalidades, Caja 22, Cuentas de la Caja de Temporalidades, Quito, 15 noviembre 1797.
111. ANH-Q, Temporalidades, Caja 13, Expediente sobre la venta de las haciendas de trapiche nombrado Tacaló pertenecente al Colegio de Latacunga, 23 Agosto 1782; Caja 14, Expediente sobre la venta de al hacienda de Ylito pertenecente a el Colegio de Latacunga, no date; Expediente de la venta de la hacienda de Saquisilí, no date.

tried to duplicate the techniques of the Society of Jesus in the *Audiencia* of Quito.[112]

Although their expulsion in 1767 spared the Jesuits from dealing with the worst years of the economic recession (from the 1780s), the order's economic achievements indicate the sort of strategies needed to prosper in eighteenth-century Quito. Given the scale of its operations, the order could absorb temporary losses, invest in repairs and other capital improvements, and integrate its estate complexes. By transferring food, livestock, supplies, and even laborers, Jesuit administrators had each estate contribute to the success of the other. In addition, the Jesuits could use their warehouses in Lima and Cartagena to store goods until prices rose. In short, the Society's extensive resources allowed it to overcome the many problems imposed by geographical barriers, state regulations, and the thin, poorly integrated Andean regional markets. The state and most private landowners simply lacked the capital, experience, or expertise to duplicate this system.

State policy and the rugged Andean geography limited growth in the rural economy of the north-central sierra. The textiles produced on Spanish estates formed a key link between these rural zones and colonial markets in Peru and New Granada. As Spanish commercial policies led to a declining demand for Quito's *paños*, a downward economic spiral began for the local agrarian economy. Geographical barriers produced small, fragmented colonial markets, which inhibited any efforts at shipping food products outside the region. Moreover, attempts to find another viable export, such as *aguardiente*, proved impractical for most provinces. Only wealthy elites and the religious orders could muster the political clout and economic resources needed to profit over time.

Spanish estate owners in the south sierra circumvented such problems by serving growing regional markets. The *hacendados* seldom took part in the cottage textile industry and concentrated instead on developing estates along the major trade routes, meeting the local and regional demand for food, livestock, and *aguardiente*. Only those few Spanish landowners engaged in harvesting *cascarilla* became involved in selling to international markets. This strategy allowed landed elites in the south highlands to prosper and dominate local society, even after the collapse of the cottage textile industry by 1830.

112. This section on Carlos Araujo has been drawn from the extensive research and publications of Christiana Borchart de Moreno on the administration of the former Jesuit properties. For a more detailed version of the Araujo case, see Christiana Borchart de Moreno, "Capital comercial y producción agrícola: Nueva España y Quito en el siglo XVIII," *Anuario de Estudios Americanos*, 46 (1989): 131–72.

When the crown eased its trade restrictions from 1778, the coastal export economy began its sixty-year era of prosperity. The extensive river system permitted plantation owners to ship cacao, tobacco, and sugar cane cheaply to the port of Guayaquil. In addition, migrations of Andeans from depressed regions in the highlands eased local labor shortages, allowing landowners to curtail their dependence on more expensive slave workers. The emerging plantation system organized productive forces in the coastal hinterland and linked them to colonial and international markets. Nevertheless, the coastal elite still depended on merchant houses in Mexico City and Lima to sell their crop and provide imported goods. In the end, the wealth generated by the export economy primarily benefitted just a few mercantile and landed families.

Throughout the late colonial period, Spanish rural estates organized the land and labor resources of rural zones to produce commodities for the small, state-regulated markets in the Andes. The strategies needed to prosper in this environment over time usually involved creating very large estates, organized around producing a single export commodity such as textiles, sugar cane, or later cacao. In the end, this led to a system of inefficient *latifundia*, dominated by a narrow elite. By 1830, such a system of rural estates was ill prepared to compete in the deregulated, volatile regional and global markets of the post-independence era.

5

Amerindians and the market economy

By the eighteenth century, the economic fortunes of most Amerindians in the Kingdom of Quito had become tied to fluctuations in the colonial market economy.[1] From the outset of Spanish colonial rule, the disruptions caused by disease and warfare, heavy state tax and labor obligations, and divestment of their traditional resources compelled large numbers of Amerindians to participate actively in market exchanges. By the eighteenth century, much of the Amerindian economy still revolved around subsistence agriculture, but increasingly villagers had to supplement farming incomes by selling commodities in regional markets. Many Andeans also left their traditional settlements to work for Spanish landowners, *obrajeros*, and in local urban centers. The degree of this integration into the evolving colonial markets differed in each region of the kingdom, but few communities could thrive over time by depending only on subsistence agriculture. As a result, the economic evolution of the three major colonial markets in the kingdom – Quito, Guayaquil, and Cuenca – had a profound long-term impact on the material welfare of most Amerindians.[2]

The overall decline of industrial and agrarian sectors in the north-central sierra led to particularly difficult times for Amerindians during the eighteenth century. The region from Otavalo to Riobamba remained the demographic center of the indigenous population, which had long provided most of the labor force for Spanish enterprises. The slow deterioration of the textile business had repercussions throughout these provinces, severely restricting economic choices for Andeans. Job oppor-

---

1. An intriguing recent study of Amerindian participation in the markets of the southern Andes is Olivia Harris, Brooke Larson, and Enrique Tandeter, eds., *La participación indígena en los mercados surandinos: estrategias y reproducción social. Siglos XVI a XX* (La Paz, 1987).

2. The material presented in this chapter deals with the Amerindians living within range of these three colonial markets. Some groups on the peripheries, in provinces like Esmeraldas or Jaén de Bracamoros, obviously were less affected by market forces. On the other hand, the bulk of the Amerindian population lived in the highlands and the coast, where their lives were influenced by the evolution of these three major market centers.

tunities lessened in the *obrajes* and on Spanish estates, while the low prices of agricultural produce limited profits from selling community surpluses in local markets. By the late eighteenth century, the reforms of the Bourbon dynasty heightened fiscal pressure on all the Andean peoples, amidst this overall economic decline. Amerindians found it harder to earn the specie needed to meet their escalating tax obligations, forcing many of the poorest villagers to migrate in search of a better life. The economic problems facing the indigenous people who remained behind often worsened, culminating in periodic violent rebellions against the fiscal demands of the colonial state in the north-central sierra.

In contrast, the relatively prosperous market economies of the south sierra and the coast provided more options for Amerindians. The emergence of a thriving cottage textile industry and regional Spanish estates furnished jobs, while the sparseness of the indigenous population (native to the region) left ample supplies of arable land. As a result, the southern highlands served as a magnet for migrants from the declining northern provinces until the disruption of regional trade routes in the independence era. Likewise, the cacao economy and the growing port city of Guayaquil provided a market and jobs for numerous highland emigrants and even some coastal Amerindians. The distance of the coastal indigenous towns from the cacao-producing zones, however, meant that many of these Amerindians faced little competition from Spaniards for their lands, which the indigenous peoples devoted to traditional agriculture and grazing. Most Amerindians native to the coast left work on the local plantations to slaves and Andean emigrants. Instead, they gained some modest profits from meeting the growing internal market's demand for foodstuffs, local hardwoods, salt, and artisan crafts.

Amerindian settlements and the market economy

Despite the virulent epidemics of the 1690s and the erosion of the *obraje* economy, most Amerindians still resided in the north-central highlands by the late colonial period. In addition, over half of these indigenous taxpayers were registered as *llactayos*, not migrants (see Table 5.1). Only the province of Quito had a *forastero* population nearing 50 percent. Nevertheless, the numbers of registered tributaries (living on Spanish estates and in traditional settlements) continued to decline in most of the north-central highlands, even into the late colonial period. In the period from 1785 to 1800, for example, only the relatively prosperous provinces of Otavalo and Latacunga registered gains in the numbers of tributaries.[3]

---

3. In the period from 1785 to 1789, the tax lists for Otavalo registered an average of 4,734 tributaries and Latacunga an average of 8,610 tributaries. By the period from 1795 to 1799, those

Table 5.1 *Amerindian population trends, Audiencia of Quito, late colonial period*

Province	Tributaries	Total Amerindians	Llactayos-Forasteros	
Quito	8,476	42,098	51%	49%
Ibarra	2,529	8,460	60%	40%
Otavalo	5,173	25,230	54%^{a}	44%^{a}
Latacunga	7,703	37,978	57%^{a}	43%^{a}
Ambato	5,539	28,417	55%	45%
Riobamba	8,076	48,735	56%^{a}	44%^{a}
Guaranda	1,936	8,155	59%	41%
Alausí	1,915	13,671^a	30%^{a}	70%^{a}
Cuenca	10,309	55,939	25%	75%
Loja	2,961	13,221	25%	75%
Guayaquil	2,577	10,011	no data	
Total	57,194	291,915		

^{a}These figures come from the Villalengua census. (See the source note to this table).
Note: Blank cells represent lack of data.
Sources: All of the figures for tributaries are averages derived from the available tributary lists in the records of the Dirección general de tributos. AGI, Quito, 435, Cuentas de tributos de Quito, 1779-1802; AGI, Quito, 494, Cuentas de tributos de Ibarra, 1780-1801; AGI, Quito, 506, Cuentas de tributos de Otavalo, 1781-1801; AGI, Quito, 504, Cuentas de tributos de Latacunga, 1780-1801; AGI, Quito, 447, Cuentas de tributos de Ambato, 1779-1801; AGI, Quito, 492, Cuentas de tributos de Guaranda, 1783-1799; AGI, Quito, 537, Cuentas de tributos de Riobamba, 1780-1792; AGI, Quito, 460, Cuentas de tributos de Cuenca, 1779-1801; AGI, Quito, 500, Cuentas de tributos de Loja, 1784-1799; AGI, Quito, 448, Cuentas de tributos de Alausí, 1782-1800; AGI, Quito, 483, Cuentas de tributos de Guayaquil, 1785-1801. The total figure for the Amerindian population is taken from Table 2.1. The figures for *llactayos* and *forasteros* are from Robson Brines Tyrer, "Demographic and Economic History of the Audiencia of Quito: Indian Population and the Textile Industry, 1600-1800" (Ph.D. diss., University of California at Berkeley, 1976), 434. The figures marked ^{a} in the table come from the Villalengua census, and vary from those presented by Tyrer. AGI, Quito, 381 or 412, Census of Juan Josef de Villalengua y Marfil, 1778- 1781. The figures from Alausí are not available from the *padrones* and were taken from the Villalengua census, which explains the low number of tributaries for the total population. That census listed only 2,621 tributaries, however, which is still low for the 13,671 total population.

The sizable *forastero* population in Cuenca, Loja, and Alausí also provides strong evidence that the south sierra served as the principal receptor

numbers had climbed to 5,772 and 8,920 respectively. These data come from the records of the *Dirección general de tributos*. AGI, Quito, 435, Cuentas de tributos de Quito, 1779–1802; AGI, Quito, 494, Cuentas de tributos de Ibarra, 1780–1801; AGI, Quito, 506, Cuentas de tributos de Otavalo, 1781–1802; AGI, Quito, 504, Cuentas de tributos de Latacunga, 1780–1801; AGI, Quito, 447, Cuentas de tributos de Ambato, 1779–1801; AGI, Quito, 492, Cuentas de tributos de Guaranda, 1783–1799; AGI, Quito 537, Cuentas de tributos de Riobamba, 1780–1792.

of these migrants from the north, leading to the repopulation of the Amerindian villages and the development of Spanish estates (see Table 5.1). No large-scale migrations from the highlands to the coast began until the onset of the cacao boom in the 1790s.

The distribution of the Amerindian tributary population in the north-central highlands reflected the overall evolution of the market economy. The Andean peoples concentrated around major cities and towns and the principal agricultural and textile-producing regions. The city of Quito and the provincial capitals, for example, accounted for nearly 18 percent of the tributaries registered in the north-central highlands.[4] Apparently the lure of jobs in the towns and the need to supply urban centers with food attracted many Andeans. While most Amerindians living around Ibarra labored on nearby Spanish estates, in other urban centers, such as Quito and Otavalo, the bulk of the indigenous population worked in the towns or cultivated communal lands and small freeholds, supplying produce for urban markets.[5]

Apart from the urban areas, the rural Amerindian population remained scattered throughout the fertile highland valleys of the north-central sierra. In Ibarra, the majority of the Andean population concentrated around the northern towns of Mira and Puntal, while in Otavalo the largest number lived around Cotacachi (west of Otavalo) and Cayambe (to the south).[6] The rural centers of Quito's Amerindian population were the Machachi, Chillos, and Tumbaco Valleys, along with the central towns of Cotocallao and Zambiza.[7] In Latacunga the largest numbers of Andeans lived on the west side of the San Felipe River, from Saquisilí to Ysinlivi.[8] Nearly 80 percent of Ambato's indigenous peoples lived around the provincial capital or the rural towns of Píllaro, Pelileo, Santa Rosa, and Quisapincha.[9] Most tributaries in the rural zones of Riobamba remained in Licto, Punín, Guamote, Calpi, and San Andrés (see Map 2).[10]

4. *Ibid.*

5. Approximately 309 Amerindians worked on Spanish estates in Ibarra, and 276 lived in traditional villages. ANH-Q, Presidencia de Quito, tomo 359, Libros de tributos de Ibarra, 1782. In the city of Quito and its suburban parishes, only 76 of 756 could be identified as serving on Spanish *haciendas*, in small *obrajes*, or in dye shops. ANH-Q, Presidencia de Quito, tomo 360, 1785, Libros de tributos de Quito. Around the *asiento* of Otavalo, 655 Amerindians worked on Spanish estates, and 806 lived in traditional settlements or the town. AHN-Q, Presidencia de Quito, tomo 359, Libros de tributos de Otavalo, 1784.

6. Another important concentration of Amerindians was in San Antonio, just south of Ibarra. AGI, Quito, 494, Cuentas de tributos de Ibarra, 1780–1801. AGI, Quito, 506, Cuentas de tributos de Otavalo, 1781–1802.

7. AGI, Quito, 435, Cuentas de tributos de Quito, 1779–1802.

8. AGI, Quito, 504, Cuentas de tributos de Latacunga, 1780–1801.

9. AGI, Quito, 447, Cuentas de tributos de Ambato, 1779–1801.

10. AGI, Quito, 537, Cuentas de tributos de Riobamba, 1780–1792.

A majority of the Andeans in the north-central sierra lived in traditional settlements, not as *conciertos* on Spanish estates. Only the provinces
of Quito and Riobamba registered a majority of *conciertos*. Both of these
provinces had been centers of the textile business in the seventeenth
century, and many Andeans left their own lands to seek work in local
obrajes.[11] Detailed data from the tribute lists, which exist just for the
corregimiento of Quito, indicate that only María Magdalena and Zambiza,
north of the city, and the towns of Conocoto and Alangasí to the southeast had a majority of the population living permanently in villages.[12]
In the remainder of the province, most Andean tributaries were registered
as *conciertos*, working on Spanish *haciendas* and in *obrajes*. Many Andeans
living around the capital city itself either worked as servants, artisans, or
cultivated small plots of land in the suburban parishes.[13] In short, the
data for the *corregimiento* of Quito indicate how the attraction of colonial
markets prompted the integration of the Spanish and Amerindian economies.

Patterns of Amerindian settlement differed markedly in the south sierra. The bulk of the *forastero* population moved southward from depressed regions such as Riobamba and settled in the northern and eastern
parishes. The city of Cuenca proved particularly attractive to migrants,
and many Andeans settled in towns or on small freeholds supplying the
city's markets with foodstuffs. These small- and medium-sized farms extended from Cuenca's suburban parishes through the eastern regions of
Gualaceo and San Bartolomé. A similar concentration of small Andean
holdings ringed the provincial town of Azogues.[14] The small provincial

---

11. Robson Brines Tyrer, "The Demographic and Economic History of the Audiencia of Quito:
    Indian Population and the Textile Industry, 1600–1800" (Ph.D. diss., University of California
    at Berkeley, 1976), 435–36.
12. The reasons for the persistence of densely populated Andean settlements surrounding these towns
    are unclear. In all likelihood, the villagers in María Magdalena and Zambiza were close enough
    to the urban markets of Quito to survive by supplying cheap food to the city. Few large Spanish
    estates developed in those regions. Likewise, in Conocoto, there were few large Spanish holdings
    in the region, and it too was close enough to Quito to benefit from supplying the urban market.
    The town of Alangasí, however, was located amidst the large holdings of the Jesuits and lay
    hacendados in the Chillos Valley. The villages surrounding the town had a reputation for weaving
    cotton cloth, on the putting-out system, similar to the Amerindian towns of the south sierra,
    rather than supplying foodstuffs to the Quito market. The Amerindians of Alangasí undoubtedly
    used these cloth sales to gain allies among the *Quiteño* merchant community. Along with their
    own profits from the cloth sales, these connections probably allowed the people of Alangasí to
    resist pressure from Spanish landowners in the region. In short, their successful participation in
    colonial markets probably preserved the corporate integrity of Andean villages in these four
    zones. The remaining records from the Libros de tributos do not provide this detailed data for
    an entire province of the north-central sierra. ANII-Q, Presidencia de Quito, tomo 360, Libros
    de tributos de Quito, 1785.
13. *Ibid.*
14. AGI, Quito, 460, Cuentas de tributos de Cuenca, 1779–1801; AGI, Quito, 448, Cuentas de

capital of Loja did not attract such large numbers of Andean settlers, and most of the indigenous population remained scattered throughout the *corregimiento* (see Map 2).[15]

In contrast to the northern provinces, in the south sierra the majority of Andeans lived in traditional settlements, not on Spanish estates.[16] Over 75 percent of the Andeans in Cuenca and 81 percent in Loja lived on their own lands. In fact, only the parishes of Cañar, Cañaribamba, and Cumbe (in Cuenca) and Catacocha and Chuquiribamba (in Loja) had a majority of the population living on Spanish holdings.[17] This does not, however, indicate the weakness of the Spanish *hacienda* system in the south. Instead, it reflects the importance of the cottage textile industry, centered in the Andean settlements. The manufacture of rough cottons and woolens in the south sierra provided economic opportunities for Amerindian villagers, which allowed indigenous communities to survive and even prosper during the eighteenth century.

The principal Amerindian villages along the coast remained concentrated in the region from Puná to Portoviejo, and extending as far west as Daule.[18] Apart from some villages near Portoviejo and Machala, these population centers were far from the cacao-producing zones, and apparently few coastal Amerindians worked on Spanish plantations. Slaves and migrants from the north-central sierra engaged in these laborious tasks. The coastal Amerindians continued working in subsistence agriculture, livestock raising, wood cutting, salt gathering, and artisan crafts. Much of their surplus production was sold to plantation owners, in provincial towns, and in the port city of Guayaquil.

The state and the Amerindian settlements

The state's escalating tax and labor demands, along with tighter commercial regulations, placed a heavy burden on the kingdom's Amerindian peoples by the late eighteenth century. The head tax, or tribute, proved a particularly onerous levy on indigenous agrarian communities, since the state seldom adjusted the rates during periods of dearth or following

   tributos de Alausí, 1782–1800. See also Silvia Palomeque, *Cuenca en el siglo XIX: la articulación de una región* (Quito, 1990), 124–28.
15. AGI, Quito, 500, Cuentas de tributos de Loja, 1784–1799.
16. ANH-Q, Presidencia de Quito, Tomo 361, Libros de tributos de Cuenca, 1792; Tomo 360, Libros de tributos de Loxa, 1786, 1792.
17. *Ibid.*
18. The principal towns with a large percentage of tributaries in the province were: Modno (9 percent), Chanduy (6 percent), Santa Elena (10.3 percent), Punta (10.2 percent), Coloche (5 percent), Daule (9.5 percent), Jipijapa (23.7 percent), and Montecristi (6.4 percent). AGI, Quito, 483, Cuentas de tributos de Guayaquil, 1785–1801.

natural disasters and population losses from migration or disease. The same problems obtained with state corveé labor obligations, which also weighed heavily on the indigenous population. When the colonial government did begin a thoroughgoing reevaluation of these obligations in the 1770s, the net result was to increase tax and labor burdens, not ease them. Likewise, royal efforts to regulate and tax overland trade disrupted internal markets and diminished the ability of Amerindians to earn the specie needed to pay their taxes. In short, the fiscal and commercial reforms of the Bourbons only increased economic burdens on the beleaguered Amerindian peoples, particularly in the depressed north-central sierra provinces.

By the late eighteenth century, colonial officials recognized the need for a complete reform of the tribute system. From the sixteenth century, crown authorities had established exorbitant annual tax rates of 6–9 pesos per capita for communities with *obrajes de comunidad* and 4–6 pesos elsewhere.[19] As the *obrajes* declined, Amerindians often found it impossible to secure the specie to pay these onerous taxes, forcing many to emigrate and claim the lower tax and labor obligations of *forasteros*.[20] The dramatic upsurge in the *forastero* population made tribute collection a nightmare for crown officials, who even leased the right to collect the levy to local tax farmers from 1734. Colonial officials ultimately found this system impossible to regulate, since only the tax farmers – not the crown – knew the actual size of the tributary population.[21] As a result, government policy makers decided to return tribute collection to state control. Before implementing this reform, however, the crown dispatched the *fiscal* of the *audiencia*, Juan Josef de Villalengua y Marfil, to conduct an accurate census in the highland provinces between 1778 and 1781.[22]

Villalengua clarified the tax status of Amerindians, adjusted tribute rates for each community, and enrolled thousands of Andeans on the tax rolls who had previously evaded paying taxes.[23] Following the Villalengua

---

19. Tyrer, "Demographic and Economic History," 130.
20. *Forasteros* in the Kingdom of Quito enjoyed lower tribute rates and an exemption from *mita* service, and they did not pay any clerical fees. See Loreto G. Rebolledo, *Comunidad y resistencia: el caso de Lumbisí en la Colonia* (Quito, 1992), 114.
21. Tyrer, "Demographic and Economic History," 47.
22. The figures from the Villalengua census may be found in AGI, Quito, 381 or 412.
23. Villalengua set the tribute rates for *llactayos* between 6 pesos 3 reales in Quito and 5 pesos 4 reales in Riobamba and Latacunga. The rates for *forasteros* ranged between 4 pesos 3 reales in Otavalo and 3 pesos in Riobamba and the south sierra. This actually lowered the rates in some communities, but his efforts to enroll all eligible Amerindians more than compensated for such adjustments. Villalengua was recalled to assume other duties and never extended his census to the coast. The relatively small size of the Amerindian population and its overall poverty, however, probably also led the crown to worry less about a census of the coastal population until the establishment of the *Dirección general de tributos*. By 1780 local authorities incorporated *for-*

census, the crown also established a special government agency, the *Dirección general de tributos*, to collect these levies and keep updated tax lists. In the north-central sierra, for example, the number of tributaries listed on the tax rolls soared from 11,451 in 1779 to a high of 40,143 in 1789.[24] These innovations produced a dramatic upsurge in the tax burden on Amerindians in the region, where tribute receipts increased from 51,050 pesos in 1778 to 195,596 pesos in 1801, despite the ongoing economic depression.[25] Given the overall stability of wages on Spanish estates and of prices for foodstuffs or artisan goods, Amerindians could not hope to compensate for any large tax increases by gaining more money from market exchanges. As a result, reform only meant heavier fiscal obligations.

The crown's efforts to maintain accurate census materials also increased the burden of state-sponsored corveé or *mita* labor. Although the kingdom had no significant mining operations, colonial officials assigned forced-labor drafts to public works, textile mills, even Spanish estates.[26] Generally one-fifth (*quinto*) of the tributaries from each Amerindian settlement would work as *mitayos* for periods ranging from a few weeks to a year.[27] Each tributary was also supposed to serve only once every five years, but as population losses from disease or migration occurred, the terms often came about more frequently. *Kurakas* and migrants were traditionally exempt from *mita* labor, which provided another powerful incentive for tributaries to flee and seek *forastero* status.[28]

The Villalengua census and subsequent tributary counts also permitted royal officials to regularize the *mita* obligations of Amerindian communities more effectively. In Ambato and Guaranda, for example, census enumerators used the new population counts to make accurate labor assignments of agricultural workers (*gañanes*) to local Spanish estates. Royal officials found 3,907 tributaries in Ambato and 1,380 in Guaranda. They

asteros on the tribute rolls in their place of residence and in 1790 abolished their exemption from paying clerical rents. See Rebolledo, *Comunidad y resistencia*, 134–35.

24. After 1789, the numbers began to decline as epidemics and migrations to areas of greater economic opportunity began to offset these initial gains from tighter registration efforts following the Villalengua census. See, AGI, Quito, 435, Cuentas de tributos de Quito, 1779–1802; AGI, Quito, 494, Cuentas de tributos de Ibarra, 1780–1801; AGI, Quito, 506, Cuentas de tributos de Otavalo, 1781–1802; AGI, Quito 504, Cuentas de tributos de Latacunga, 1780–1801; AGI, Quito, 447, Cuentas de tributos de Ambato, 1779–1801; AGI, Cuentas de tributos de Guaranda, 1783–1799; AGI, Quito 537, Cuentas de tributos de Riobamba, 1780–1792.

25. AGI, Quito, 419–428, Cuentas de la caja de Quito, 1778–1801. The summary figures for these accounts have been published in Alvaro Jara and John J. TePaske, *The Royal Treasuries of the Spanish Empire in America*: Vol. 4, *Eighteenth-Century Ecuador* (Durham, NC, 1990), 140–65.

26. Nicholas P. Cushner, *Farm and Factory: The Jesuits and the Development of Agrarian Capitalism in Colonial Quito, 1600–1767* (Albany, NY, 1982), 117–23.

27. *Ibid*; ANH-Q, Indígenas, Caja 95, Autos sobre el nuevo repartimiento de indios gañanes de este asiento de Ambato y pueblos de su jurisdicción, Hambato, 27 marzo 1778.

28. Cushner, *Farm and Factory*, 118–19.

apportioned one-fifth of the tributaries, 712 *gañanes* annually, in Ambato – ranging from small allocations of a single laborer to an assignment of 103 *mitayos* to the former Jesuit properties at San Ildefonso. The census also determined that Guaranda had only 276 tributaries eligible to serve every 5 years, despite having supplied 302 corveé laborers in most previous years. Census takers lowered the quota for the province, usually making allotments of *gañanes* involving under 10 laborers. The largest assignment of *mitayos* in Guaranda was 33 tributaries to the *haciendas* of the Monasterio de la Concepción in Riobamba. In essence, the Villalengua census ensured that at least 20 percent of the Amerindian male labor force between the ages of eighteen and fifty served for varying periods as *mitayos* – an additional heavy economic burden on their settlements in Ambato and Guaranda.[29]

By the eighteenth century the indigenous population was connected to the major colonial markets by a complex network of internal trade routes that remained virtually unregulated by the colonial state. Since the kingdom never imposed a forced distribution of European wares like the *repartimiento de mercancías* of Peru, itinerant traders and peddlers usually made the arduous trek overland carrying goods for Amerindians and local *hacendados*.[30] Most of these small-scale traders (*traficantes*) were Amerindians or *mestizos*, carrying one or two mule loads (*cargas*) of American or European merchandise (usually cloth, cacao, salt, or dried fish). They either conveyed these goods directly to villagers and *hacendados* or sold them in weekly open-air markets in nearby towns. The Amerindians and the traders often congregated at dawn and haggled over exchanges of merchandise for local foodstuffs, cloth, livestock, sugar, tallow, or salt until late afternoon. These small-time merchants then returned with Amerindian artisan goods, local woolen or cotton cloth, and food for sale in the larger regional markets of the highlands or the coast. In the south sierra these itinerant traders also participated in the textile trade. Such commercial ties extended throughout the kingdom, supplying a wide variety of merchandise and tying Amerindians, *mestizos*, and Spaniards in the interior to merchant houses in the major urban centers.[31]

The colonial government began to regulate this extensive internal

29. ANH-Q, Indígenas, Caja 95, Autos sobre el nuevo repartimiento de indios gañanes de Ambato y pueblos de su jurisdicción, Hambato, 27 marzo 1778; Repartimiento de indios de Guaranda, Guaranda, 6 agosto 1778.

30. There were three principal overland trade routes from the coast to the highlands. One followed the Babahoyo River north and then proceeded overland to Chimbo and Riobamba, where it connected with the major north–south routes. Another route went from Yaguache to Naranjito and Alausí, and then to the north–south roads. Finally, the road from Naranjal to Cuenca connected the coast directly to the south highlands. See Map 1.

31. ANH-Q, Ropas, Caja 5, Petición de Nicolás Carrión y Baca, Juez Diputado del Comercio de Quito, Quito, 9 noviembre 1764.

economy from the 1760s by expanding its network of customs offices (*aduanas*) to collect the sales tax (*alcabala*) on such market transactions. In addition, crown officials administered these customs houses directly, instead of leasing the right to local tax farmers. This process began in 1764, when the viceroy of New Granada dispatched a special commissioner, Juan Díaz de Herrera, to begin implementing these reforms in the *Audiencia* of Quito. Since it proved virtually impossible to assess the value of every mule load passing along the mountain roads of the kingdom, the commissioner imposed a flat rate of 35 pesos on each *carga* of merchandise. He also demanded that every trader pass through Quito, post a security bond (*fianza*), and secure a licence (*guía*) to sell his merchandise.

Merchants complained that all the new laws were outrageously impractical. Too often the value of a mule load did not warrant a tax of 35 pesos, which might account for 12 percent of the total sale price of the goods, not the mere 3 percent required by law. In addition, detouring to Quito could cost the *traficantes* 16 days on a trip from the coast to Riobamba, 8 days to Ambato, and 6 days to Latacunga. It also added an additional 6 days to the trip from the Naranjal road to Cuenca and 7 to Loja. Local merchants in Quito further complained that no sane citizen in the capital would post a security bond for the nomadic *mestizo* and Amerindian traders traveling the interior trade routes. Even the system of licenses drew criticism. Merchants argued that many peddlers operated alone or in small groups, making as many as fifty separate stops to sell their merchandise. Trying to keep track of such activities was impossible and would only disrupt trade links between large merchant houses and the internal market. Apart from easing the number of regulations about licenses and security bonds, however, government authorities chose to ignore such complaints.[32]

The crown also began to regulate another profitable sector of the internal economy in the 1760s, the provisioning of cities and towns in the kingdom. Amerindian villagers and small freeholders (both Andean and *mestizo*) often competed successfully with local Spanish *hacendados*, supplying foodstuffs to marketplaces in the larger cities and towns. Such small-scale farmers could produce commodities at low cost by devoting more communal or family labor to cultivation, and less capital, than the Spanish estates.[33] They also relied on local Andean peddlers (*gateras*) and

32. *Ibid.* The merchants of Quito also complained that a royal *cédula* of 19 February 1735 gave them privileges that were being contradicted in the *alcabala* reforms of Díaz de Herrera.
33. The theoretical explanation for how peasant communities can supply foodstuffs to markets at lower prices by maximizing their labor resources is a variant on the unequal exchange thesis called "permanent primitive accumulation." For a more detailed explanation of the theory, see Kostas Vergopoulis, "Capitalism and Peasant Productivity," *Journal of Peasant Studies*, 5 (1978): 446–65.

hucksters (*regatonas*) to sell their goods in the city. As Amerindians, both the producers and the sellers traditionally paid no sales tax, which also allowed them to sell goods at lower prices than most Spanish landowners. The large concentrations of Amerindians near Quito, for example, played a significant role in provisioning the capital city. In all likelihood, the considerable numbers of Andeans surrounding provincial capitals like Otavalo, Cuenca, and Guayaquil performed a similar function.

The reform of the sales tax, begun in 1764, undercut the economic advantages of the Amerindians and *mestizos* supplying the urban centers of the kingdom. The *alcabala* was actually several taxes, all related directly or indirectly to the sale of goods. Two assessments, the *alcabala del cabezón* and the *alcabala del viento* proved particularly disruptive to the functioning of the urban marketplace. The *alcabala del cabezón* was a tax on every rural and suburban landholding, based on the predicted value of its annual yield. The *alcabala del viento* was a levy collected on all local goods entering the city gates. Amerindians were traditionally exempt from both levies unless they grew or sold produce and livestock originally imported from Europe, like wheat, barley, or sheep.[34] Since these commodities sold well in city markets, however, most Amerindians did raise them for sale in the cities by local *gateras* and *regatonas*.

Higher sales tax assessments and more rigorous enforcement procedures led to widespread unrest. Local merchants complained bitterly about excessive regulation, bureaucratic red tape, and lower profits. Likewise, Amerindian and *mestizo* cultivators feared that higher tax rates on their lands and stricter enforcement of the taxes levied at the city's gates would raise the price of their goods and restrict the activities of peddlers and hucksters. Such policies would have undoubtedly curtailed the comparative advantage of many small-scale producers in the urban marketplace. In fact, the imposition of these reform measures in 1765 played a key role in the popular insurrection against the royal government in Quito. Although the crown did cease implementing many of the most objectionable tax policies in the rebellion's aftermath, by the 1780s royal officials renewed efforts to impose such reforms. In the end, these fiscal innovations disrupted the operation of the kingdom's internal economy, which had proven so important to the material welfare of Amerindians.

Amerindians and Spanish estates

By the late eighteenth century, the economic decline of traditional indigenous economies had prompted large numbers of Amerindians to seek work on Spanish estates. Although wages could be pitifully low and debt

34. For a discussion of the sales tax in the second half of the eighteenth century, see Montserrat Fernández Martínez, *La alcabala en la Audiencia de Quito, 1765–1810* (Cuenca, 1984).

peonage was commonplace, many Amerindians had little alternative. This was particularly true in the provinces of Quito and Riobamba, where a majority of the Andean population resided on Spanish rural holdings as *conciertos*. Working for Spanish *hacendados* or *obrajeros* was a hard life, but at least the Andeans could meet their basic material needs. For many of these poor *llactayos* and *forasteros* who chose not to migrate to the coast or the south highlands, it was the only alternative.

Spanish estate owners in the highlands used a variety of devices to lure Amerindians to work in their mills, farms, or ranches. Landowners usually offered *conciertos* a small plot of land to cultivate, an allotment (*socorro*) of cash, food, or tools, and they guaranteed the payment of each worker's tribute obligations. The cost of each "benefit" was deducted from the wages of the worker.[35] The customary wages for most rural laborers ranged between 18 pesos and 25 pesos (see Table 5.2).[36] Some jobs, like tending pigs, paid a mere 12 pesos annually, while a hard-working miller could gross 40 pesos in a year. The highest-skilled jobs, such as that of manager (*mayordomo*) of an estate, could pay 70–150 pesos, along with advances of food and clothing.[37] Salaries for workers on coastal plantations tended to reach higher levels; even laborers received 4–8 reales daily on the more productive cacao estates.[38] Most Spanish landowners, however, paid their workers the lowest possible salaries.[39]

These meager wages led numerous Andean laborers to fall deeply into debt. Tribute payments averaged 5–6 pesos, and most *socorros* – usually food or tools – cost an additional 5–10 pesos. This left little from an annual wage of 18 pesos to support the worker and his family on an estate.[40] Moreover, in times of economic distress *hacienda* laborers often

35. This point is made clearly in Cushner, *Farm and Factory*, 123–29, and in the numerous *hacienda* account books found in the Archivo Nacional de Historia de Quito, in the "Haciendas" and "Temporalidades" sections.

36. These wages were comparable to the amounts paid to *obraje* workers. This is hardly surprising, since many rural estates in the north-central sierra usually employed workers to do both agricultural and textile work. For data on wages for labor in the mills, see: ANH-Q, Obrajes, Caja 12, 1742–56, Libro de socorros de los indios del Obraje de San Bartolomé de la Marquesa de Solanda, que corre desde 15 Junio 1761–65; Tyrer, "Demographic and Economic History," 200; and Cushner, *Farm and Factory*, 100.

37. ANH-Q, Haciendas, Caja 28, Libro de socorros y salarios de los Indios y sirvientes de la Hacda de sn Izidro de Malchinqui, 24 marzo 1794; Caja 6, Libro de los Oficiales de la Caja, Texar y Molina, 1 junio 1749; Caja 11, Libro de la Hacienda de Llanagua, 1 mayo 1770; Caja 12, Cuentas de indios de Patalo, 1774.

38. María Luisa Laviana Cuetos, *Guayaquil en el siglo XVIII: recursos naturales y desarrollo económico* (Seville, 1987), 172.

39. Often the lowest-paid workers received 15 pesos, not the 18 pesos listed in the "Formulario de las Ordenanzas de Indios." See, for example, ANH-Q, Haciendas, Caja 2, Libro de Rayas de la Hacienda de Tanalagua, 1713–1728.

40. See Cushner, *Farm and Factory*, 123–27.

Table 5.2. *Wage rates for rural workers, according to the*
"Formulario de las ordenanzas de Indios", 1737

Job or position	Wage
Arriero (muleteer)	20 pesos/year, 5 *varas jerga blanca*
Albañil (mason)	2.5 reales/day
Boyero (livestock herder)	20 pesos/year, 5 *varas jerga*
Chagracama (farmer worker)	18 pesos/year
Carillero (carter)	24 pesos/year
Dispensero (dispenser)	24 pesos/year
Gañan (farm worker-shepherd)	18 pesos/year
Guasicama (cowboy)	18-20 pesos/year
Yeguarizo (mare herder)	20-25 pesos/year
Mayoral (foreman)	20-25 pesos/year
Molinero (miller)	20-40 pesos/year
Moledor de aceite (olive oil maker)	18 pesos/year
Moledor de caña (sugar cane grinder)	18 pesos/year
Obejero (shepherd)	20 pesos/year
Pastor de cabras (goatherd)	20 pesos/year
Pastor de cerdos (pig herder)	12 pesos/year
Quesero (cheese maker)	20 pesos/year
Trasquilador (shearer)	0.5 real/10 shearings

Source: Segundo E. Moreno Yánez, "El 'Formulario de las ordenanzas
de Indios': Una regulación de las relaciones laborales en las
haciendas y obrajes del Quito colonial y republicano," *Ibero-
Amerikanisches Archiv,* 5 (1979): 227-41.

worked less than a full year and received a smaller annual wage. Any
further loans or penalties, such as the loss of some livestock under a
worker's supervision, normally led to an additional surcharge, and indebtedness. The tendency of many *hacendados* or *obrajeros* to pay their
workers in kind rather than cash only exacerbated the problem.[41] An
inventory of the Jesuit *hacienda* of Tanalagua (near Perucho) from 1713
to 1728, for example, indicated that most of the estate's 311 workers
owed the order 40–60 pesos in debts.[42] Whenever there was a regional
labor shortage, Spanish landowners often found debt peonage a viable
way to keep a compliant labor force working their lands.

Despite the prevalence of peonage, some workers managed to escape

41. *Ibid*; ANH-Q, Haciendas, Caja 2, Libro de Rayas de Tanalagua, 1713–1728; Caja 4, Libro de
socorros de la Hacienda de Tanalagua, 1728–1734; Libro de Rayas de la Hacienda de San Pablo
Antiguo Laguna; Caja 6, Libro de los Oficiales de la Caja, Texar y Molina, 1749–1761; Caja
11, Libro de la Hacienda de Llanagua, 1770.
42. ANH-Q, Haciendas, Caja 2, Libro de Rayas de la Hacienda de Tanalagua, 1713–1728.

the burden of indebtedness, particularly later in the eighteenth century. At the Jesuit sheep ranch of Llanagua (in the province of Quito), for example, the 173 *conciertos* had accumulated debts ranging from 50 to 80 pesos by the 1770s. The amount each worker owed, however, often fluctuated from 50 pesos to only a few pesos, within a short time span.[43] Apparently the workers could sell food or animals raised on their small holdings, have family members work on neighboring estates, or sell artisan crafts in local markets to gain the funds needed to repay debts. It is also possible that Spanish landowners withheld salaries to force workers to pay any outstanding debts or encouraged them to work part-time on nearby enterprises in times of economic distress.[44]

A variety of business considerations governed the economic viability of debt peonage on Spanish estates. Many rural estate complexes in the seventeenth century linked food-producing properties with ranches and an *obraje*, which allowed landowners to keep a labor force of indebted workers busy all year. As profits from textile manufacturing declined, coerced labor would have become less profitable, except on estates producing labor-intensive crops such as sugar cane or corn.[45] On the Jesuit complex at Tanalagua, for example, debt peonage apparently endured because the estate grew large amounts of corn, which required extensive labor demands during the three- or four-month plowing and tillage period.[46] On the other hand, if an estate raised livestock or a crop that required relatively fewer days of attention – such as wheat or potatoes – the need for indebted peons would have diminished as cloth production declined.[47] This probably explains why estate managers at the Jesuit sheep ranch of Llanagua failed to impede workers from repaying their debts by the 1770s. After all, debt peonage was a costly way to keep large numbers of workers on the job, and landowners might well liqui-

---

43. ANH-Q, Haciendas, Caja 11, Libro de la Hacienda de Llanagua, 1770.

44. Cushner, *Farm and Factory*, 124–26.

45. The formula that expresses this theory is $W(r) \cdot D(l) < W(dp)$, where $W(r)$ is the wage rate of free labor, $D(l)$ represents the labor days required by the staple, and $W(dp)$ represents the cost of debt peonage. This argument is presented as an explanation of why slave labor endured in parts of the United States, but it may also be applied to the persistence or disappearance of debt peonage, another form of coerced labor. For a detailed discussion of this idea, see Carville Earle, "To Enslave or Not to Enslave: Crop Seasonality, Labor Choice, and the Urgency of the Civil War," in *Geographical Inquiry and American Historical Problems* (Stanford, CA, 1992), 226–57.

46. According to the Jesuit estate inventories, between 1778 and 1779 Tanalagua produced over 4,000 *costales* of corn and lesser amounts of barley, wheat, beans, and potatoes. AHN–Q, Temporalidades, Caja 19, Expediente sobre la venta de las Hacdas. conocidas con los nombres Tanlagua, Guatos, y Niebli, perttes. a el Colegio Máximo, 1783.

47. Earle, "Crop Seasonality," 234–35.

date debts, lay off unneeded laborers in bad times, and hire seasonal labor.[48] Too often, the quality of life for rural workers depended on just such impersonal economic considerations, which were well beyond their control.

Despite the burdens of low wages, poor working conditions, and debt peonage, at least some *conciertos* managed to reconstitute family and ethnic ties on the *haciendas*. In Cayambe, for example, Galo Ramón found that by 1720 nearly 94 percent of the region's *forasteros* worked on *haciendas*, apparently recruited by landowners from settlements stretching from Pasto to Riobamba.[49] Most of these workers came with their extended family or kin groups. Over time these workers forged important cultural and family ties through marriage, godparentage, and the acculturation that came from living and working together over generations. On the *hacienda* of Cangahua, the number of surnames for *conciertos* working on the estate fell from 105 in 1720 to only 89 by 1804.[50] Although hardly conclusive, these data suggest that some *conciertos* began to adapt, intermarry, and reconstitute their own cultural and social identity.

As Amerindians throughout the kingdom experienced hard times, many indigenous communal landholdings fell under Spanish control. Economic difficulties in meeting state tribute and labor demands forced many highlanders to sell their lands, particularly in economically depressed regions. *Kurakas* often sold community lands left vacant by migrants and used the proceeds to pay tax arrears or gain favor with local Spanish landowners eager to acquire choice acreage. In some cases, the clan leaders even pocketed the proceeds themselves. Regardless of the mechanism, however, migrations of Amerindians to Spanish estates or to distant villages in the south sierra often facilitated the gradual transfer of land from Andeans to Europeans.

Spaniards also used a number of their own strategies to buy, usurp, or gain access to the lands of Andean settlements throughout the north-central sierra. The law required the *audiencia* and local authorities to supervise any transaction involving the sale of Andean property to Europeans. Many clever Spaniards circumvented this judicial supervision by having Amerindians represent them in such sales. The Jesuits, for example, used Andean employees on their estate at Saquisilí to make initial purchases from indigenous landholders, which were later transferred le-

---

48. Galo Ramón has indicated that in Cayambe some *hacendados* owed considerable sums to their workers, which also served to keep them working on the estates; see Galo Ramón Valarezo, *La resistencia Andina: Cayambe, 1500–1800* (Quito, 1987), 249–52.

49. Ramón, *La resistencia Andina*, 181.

50. *Ibid.*, 224–29.

gally to the order.[51] In the parishes of Alóag, Aloasí, Pifo, and Sangolquí (in Quito), some European and *mestizo* men even married Andean women, which gave them access to their holdings and a potential business partner in any subsequent land transactions.[52] *Hacendados* also withheld access to water or pasturage to force villagers to sell their holdings. Finally, Spaniards acquired land directly from local *kurakas* in Licto, Punín, and Macaxí (in Riobamba) by the late eighteenth century. These *kurakas* treated the land as their own personal possession, an indication that traditional forms of communal landholding in Riobamba had passed to individual private ownership.[53] Where such communal landownership patterns had broken down, Spaniards could more easily purchase, expropriate, or even conspire to inherit Amerindian properties.

Some Andean communities used the colonial legal system successfully to resist any Spanish efforts at divesting them of communal lands or exploiting their labor. When Spanish landowners and *kurakas* in Chimbo conspired to force Andean men and women to perform illegal *mita* labor, for example, the local communities gained redress in the courts. On 3 August 1778, the *audiencia* ruled that all tributaries performing forced labor on Spanish estates had to receive the same wage as *conciertos*, payable only in cash. In addition, the court ended the forced, unpaid *mita* service demanded of many Andean women and *forasteros*. Finally, the judges prohibited estate owners from using debt peonage to entrap *mitayos* into permanent servitude on their lands.[54]

The Andean communities in Lumbisí, near the town of Cumbayá (within the Five Leagues surrounding Quito) used a variety of different stratagems for over one hundred years to protect their lands and legal rights. Spanish settlers began alienating land throughout the parish of Cumbayá from the sixteenth century, except in the remote section of Lumbisí.[55] Here the indigenous population actually increased over the eighteenth century; the region served as a refuge for a heterogeneous mixture of displaced Andeans. Some of the Amerindians worked on the

51. Segundo Moreno Yánez, "Traspaso de la propiedad agrícola indígena a la hacienda colonial: el caso de Saquisilí," *Jahrbuch für Geschichte von Staat, Wirtschaft und Gesellschaft Lateinamerikas*, 17 (1980): 97–119.

52. Christiana Borchart de Moreno, "La transferencia de la propiedad agraria indígena en el corregimiento de Quito hasta finales del siglo XVII," *Caravelle*, 34 (1980): 5–19.

53. Christiana Borchart de Moreno, "Las tierras de comunidad de Licto, Punín, y Macaxí: factores para su disminución e intentos de restauración," *Revista Andina*, 6:2 (diciembre 1988): 503–24.

54. ANH-Q, Indígenas, Caja 95, Autos sobre quitar los abusos introducidos en el modo de enterar gañanes en esta provincia de Chimbo, Guaranda, 3 agosto 1778.

55. The parish included the towns of Cumbayá, El Quinche, Yaruquí, Pifo, Puembo, Tumbaco, and Guápulo. The Lumbisí region itself was isolated by the ravines of Guangopolo in the southeast, the hills of Ilumbisí in the west, and the San Pedro River on the east. Only a relatively poor road connected the area to Quito via Cumbayá. See Rebolledo, *Comunidad y resistencia*, 28, 47.

only large Spanish estate of Lumbisí, owned by the nuns of La Concepción. Most, however, lived in traditional settlements, raising a variety of fruits and grains for the Quito market.[56] From the 1730s, this diverse Amerindian population united in a series of protracted disputes over land and labor obligations with the administrators of the Lumbisí estate. The indigenous peoples skillfully used their commercial connections in Quito and the colonial court system to protect their interests; when these efforts failed, they simply refused to abide by any unacceptable rulings. If that did not work, they even threatened rebellion.[57] Despite periodic reversals, the indigenous peoples of the Lumbisí region managed to survive, and by 1824 they still owned over 40 *caballerías* of land and over 4,150 livestock.[58]

Disputes over land and labor obligations usually proved less troublesome in the south sierra during most of the eighteenth century. The large numbers of emigrants to Cuenca and Loja found abundant supplies of land around the traditional Andean settlements or attached themselves to the growing Spanish estate complexes.[59] Moreover, the colonial state was comparatively weak in the south highlands for most of the century, and the new emigrants either paid the lower rates assigned to *forasteros* or even escaped paying taxes altogether. The cottage textile industry also offered employment for emigrants, and, in all likelihood, the protection of powerful merchants who organized the business. As a result, pressure from Spanish landowners was probably not as intense as in most regions of the north-central sierra.[60]

These more favorable economic circumstances for Andean villagers in the south sierra began to dissipate as the textile business declined in the early nineteenth century. Most Andean communities in the south farmed small communal holdings or private freeholds, and many supplemented their incomes by spinning and weaving cloth for merchant entrepreneurs. In Cuenca and Girón, for example, small Amerindian and *mestizo* proprietors accounted for 66 percent of the landowners, but they actually owned only 12 percent of the arable land.[61] Once the textile industry declined, these small Andean landholders had to subsist on their meager agricultural incomes alone. In many areas this proved impossible, partic-

---

56. From the sixteenth century, Lumbisí became a heterogeneous mix of original villagers, *yanaconas*, and *forasteros* from Riobamba and the surrounding region. *Ibid.*, 207–15; 228.

57. *Ibid.*, 220–24; 242–44.

58. *Ibid.*, 242. One *caballería* equaled approximately 16 *cuadras*, which the Quito *cabildo* measured as approximately the size of an urban plaza. The estate of the nuns of La Concepción measured just under 8.5 *caballerías*. See also Cusner, *Farm and Factory*, 193.

59. Palomeque, *Cuenca en el siglo XIX*, 124, 129, 169.

60. *Ibid.*, 169.

61. *Ibid.*, 130.

ularly given the more efficient tax system imposed by the Bourbons in the 1780s. By the early nineteenth century, numerous Amerindians from the south sierra left for the coast in search of greater economic opportunities.[62] The Amerindian settlements of the coast remained poor, and available evidence suggests that they generally suffered less pressure from Europeans wishing to acquire their lands. The export economy continued to prosper, but of the traditional indigenous population centers, only parts of Portoviejo became involved heavily in cacao production. The other indigenous regions – Punta de Santa Elena, Jipijapa, Modno, Chanduy, Coloche, Montecristi, and a portion of Daule – accounted for 80 percent of the coastal Amerindian population, but the land here was generally unsuitable for cacao cultivation.[63] In regions like Machala, the indigenous peoples even produced cacao themselves, supplementing their income by selling it to local Spanish merchants.[64] The principal effect of the cacao economy was to allow these village communities to supply the plantations and the port city of Guayaquil with food surpluses, hardwoods, salt, and artisan goods.

Resistance and rebellion

Escalating fiscal pressures on Amerindian settlements in the economically depressed regions of the kingdom prompted several violent uprisings during the eighteenth century. According to Segundo Moreno Yánez, a number of different causes sparked these Andean uprisings early in the century: the loss of lands, the objectionable behavior of ecclesiastical authorities, excessive *mita* and tribute obligations, and injustices in the *obrajes*.[65] Although such abuses continued, Moreno Yánez demonstrates that increased taxes and more rigorous collection procedures were the salient theme in all Andean upheavals in the north-central sierra from the late 1770s.[66] These efforts to siphon more resources from Amerindians came when economic decline had already eroded the productive capacity of indigenous communities, especially in the north-central highlands. Local *kurakas* usually proved powerless to mitigate these policies, and, in many cases, even collaborated with the increasingly exploitative colonial

---

62. *Ibid.*, 128–38, 168–84.
63. AGI, Quito, 483, Cuentas de tributos de Guayaquil, 1785–1801; for a discussion of the coastal Amerindian population centers, see Laviana Cuetos, *Guayaquil en el siglo XVIII*, 150.
64. Carlos C. Contreras, *El sector exportador de una economía colonial: la costa del Ecuador entre 1760 y 1820* (Quito, 1990), 67.
65. Segundo E. Moreno Yánez, *Sublevaciones indígenas en la Audiencia de Quito: desde comienzos del siglo XVIII hasta finales de la colonia* (Quito, 1985 edn.), 1–152.
66. *Ibid.*, 152–338.

state. For many desperate Andeans, violent protest seemed the only recourse.

One of the largest and bloodiest of these revolts occurred in Otavalo in 1777, when crown officials tried to conduct a census of the Amerindians.[67] Any attempt to count the Andean population always promised higher taxes, which indigenous people in Otavalo could ill afford. The provincial Amerindian population was evenly split between villagers and *conciertos*, who paid moderately high tribute rates – 5 or 6 pesos for *llactayos*, while *forasteros* paid 4 pesos.[68] In addition to their high tribute obligations, the relative prosperity of the province had attracted substantial numbers of emigrants. According to government census records, the province had 3,685 *llactayos* (54 percent of the tax-paying population) and 3,104 *forasteros* (46 percent of the taxpayers). Although census takers listed 1,060 of these migrants as *coronas*, who had lived in the province long enough to lose any effective ties with their home communities, 2,044 *forasteros* had arrived more recently in Otavalo, mostly from Pasto, Ibarra, and Quito.[69] As a result, the relatively well-established *llactayos* and *coronas* had to compete for jobs and land with a large, and probably very poor, group of more recent émigrés.[70]

The new census threatened every indigenous group in Otavalo. For *llactayos* and *coronas* it represented higher taxes at a time when competition with the new emigrants for resources was intense. The emigrants probably also feared having to pay heavy tribute levies to their home communities, rather than the lower rate of 4 pesos accorded to *forasteros*.[71] These very real threats were compounded by rumors that royal authorities intended to establish a new customs house (*aduana*) after the census was completed.[72] Rumor mongers speculated that customs

67. The royal *cédula* ordering the census throughout the *Audiencia* of Quito was issued on 10 November 1776. *Ibid.*, 152.

68. Tribute rates for *llactayos* ranged from over 6 pesos in Quito, Chimbo, and Ibarra to just over 4 pesos in those same provinces by the 1770s. *Llactayos* in the rest of the highlands generally paid approximately 4–5 pesos. Rates for *forasteros* were usually around 3 pesos. AGI, Quito, 381 or 412, Census of Juan Josef de Villalengua y Marfil, 1778–1781.

69. Thirty-six percent of the migrants came from Pasto and Tulcán, 28 percent originated from Quito, and 5 percent migrated from Ibarra. Together these provinces accounted for 70 percent of the *forastero* population; the remaining 22 percent came from Latacunga (21 percent), and Riobamba and Cuenca. Data for these calculations came from the Villalengua census: AGI, Quito, 381 or 412, Census of Juan Josef de Villalengua y Marfil, Otavalo, 1778–1781.

70. *Ibid.*

71. According to the Villalengua census, for example, the tribute rate for Quito's indigenous population ranged between 4 pesos and 6 pesos 3 reales. Attaining *forastero* status in Otavalo would have lowered these levies to 4 pesos 3 reales, apart from any work the migrants from Quito might have found in the more prosperous northern province. *Ibid.*

72. Moreno Yánez, *Sublevaciones indígenas*, 155–56.

officers would begin collecting the sales tax from Andeans, which would effectively raise taxes even higher and disrupt local commerce in the internal economy of the north sierra. In short, the census posed a potentially serious economic threat to the beleaguered Amerindians of Otavalo.

News of the census came to Otavalo with the arrival of the Conde de Cumbres Altas, Gregorio Hurtado de Mendoza y Zapata, who had returned from Spain to take up his post as an *oidor* in the *audiencia*.[73] The justice rested on his journey to Quito at the *hacienda* of Nicolás de Guerra in Cotacachi, where the *oidor* began making preliminary preparations for beginning a census. When Hurtado de Mendoza ordered the clergy to prepare census lists from their parish registers, discontent about rumored tax increases and the establishment of a customs house spread quickly among the villagers of Cotacachi. Such mistrust was only exacerbated because the *oidor* chose to stay with Guerra, an unpopular creole notorious for abusing the *conciertos* on his estates.[74]

The uprising began on 9 November 1777 in the parish church of Cotacachi, on the very morning the local priest had chosen to announce the impending census. A group of prominent Andean women, mostly relatives of ethnic leaders, began the uprising by declaring the parish priest an unfit representative of the church and badly beating him. The violence spread when protesters captured Pedro de Leon, the nephew of Nicolás de Guerra. The rioters suspected that Guerra would head any new provincial *aduana*, and they vented their rage on his nephew, beating him to death, disemboweling him, displaying his corpse publicly, and later feeding his remains to the dogs. Within a day the uprising had spread, as local villagers recruited *hacienda* and *obraje* workers and sacked Spanish properties. They also forced local *mestizos* to choose between joining their ranks or fleeing with the terrified peninsular and creole population. When the protesters drove back a small force from Otavalo under the command of the *corregidor* and tribute collector Joseph Posse Pardol, the violence spread rapidly to the provincial capital of Otavalo and southward to Cayambe.[75]

Throughout the month-long uprising, the rebels directed their violence in a systematic fashion against creoles, peninsulars, some *mestizos*,

---

73. The Conde de Cumbres Altas had purchased a post on the Quito tribunal in 1750 for 19,810 pesos. He served on an ad interim basis until the Quito Insurrection of 1765. Like many justices on the *audiencia*, he was implicated in the uprising and left the city for Lima and later Spain to clear his name. He had just returned to take a *número* position as *oidor* in 1777 when the Otavalo revolt occurred. AGI, Quito, 399, Consulta, Madrid, 29 abril 1772.

74. Moreno Yánez, *Sublevaciones indígenas*, 159.

75. *Ibid.*, 172.

and even a few Andean political leaders.[76] They singled out individuals suspected of complicity with the census and sacked Spanish estates and *obrajes*, particularly the extensive holdings of magnates like the Marqués de Villa Orellana, Miguel de Jijón, Ramón Maldonado, and Nicolás de Guerra. The rebels also killed or intimidated any local clan leaders suspected of collaborating with colonial authorities. The indigenous governor of Otavalo, Juan Manuel Balensuela, for example, was beaten to death in the town of Alsedos, apparently because of his long association with the government. Leaders like Balensuela often collected tribute and became wealthy in their own right serving the state.[77] These incidents apparently led most clan leaders, even those spared by the rebels, to play no active role in the uprising. In fact, many community leaders preferred to help the colonial authorities restore order in its aftermath.[78] In short, the rebels directed their ire against anyone they perceived as guilty of crimes against the indigenous communities, sparing neither Europeans nor Andeans.

The rebellion apparently had no commonly accepted central leadership, moving spontaneously in all directions from Cotacache. Although the rebels succeeded in gaining control of the southern and central portions of the province from Otavalo to Cayambe, they met stubborn resistance from the Spaniards in Ibarra. The *corregidor* of that province, Juan de Zarzana y Cuellar, rapidly organized a well-equipped force of 70 men to defend the provincial capital, when a ragged group of nearly 2,000 disorganized, poorly armed rebels moved northward. The two forces clashed on the fourteenth of November near the *hacienda* of Agualongo, where the Spaniards won a convincing victory. Zarzana and his troops killed nearly 40 Amerindians, executed 3 ringleaders, and imprisoned nearly 100 more rebels.[79]

After the defeat at Agualongo the rebellion quickly dissipated, which allowed the *audiencia* president, Joseph de Diguja, to restore order throughout the province by the end of November. After regaining control, Diguja executed only prominent leaders, preferring in most cases to mete out brutal lashings, exile, and imprisonment. He wisely left most participants in the rebellion unpunished. As he stated, "the matter of a counting or census, has been a very delicate one in these provinces, and each time that different agents have attempted it, one has experienced

---

76. Despite the important work of Moreno Yánez, no scholar has studied the ritual aspects of the revolt, particularly the uses of violence.
77. Moreno Yánez, *Sublevaciones indígenas*, 181–86.
78. *Ibid.*, 185.
79. *Ibid.*, 175–81.

very fateful consequences."[80] In addition, the president had only a small force under his command, and he recognized the danger of the uprising spreading throughout the highlands.

The problems giving rise to the Otavalo rebellion afflicted numerous Andean communities in the north-central sierra by the late eighteenth century. High taxes and the abusive treatment of Andean *conciertos* kept relations between the indigenous peoples and the Spanish-creole elites tense. In all likelihood, the influx of *forasteros* from Ibarra, Quito, and Pasto only exacerbated the problems of *Otavaleños*, by providing more competition for any jobs available in the Spanish sector. Fears about the census and new taxes, especially the establishment of a customs house, proved sufficient to provoke the villagers and *conciertos* alike into a desperate, spontaneous uprising. Higher tribute and more efficient collection procedures threatened to take money that Andeans could ill afford to pay. Moreover, any new customs duties would impede local trade networks supplying the province and also violated the long-standing crown policy of exempting Amerindians from the sales tax. This explains much about why the rebels directed their anger towards anyone connected to the fiscal system. In short, the census seemed an intolerable economic burden and a violation of the few traditional liberties left to *Otavaleños*. The result was a desperate revolt, directed against the oppressive colonial elite and the state.

By the eighteenth century, Amerindians in the Kingdom of Quito were connected to colonial urban markets through an integrated network of overland trade routes. Goods from large merchant houses passed on by itinerant merchants tied even remote estates and villages to the kingdom's three major marketing centers – Quito, Guayaquil, and Cuenca. Traditional Amerindian settlements survived and even prospered when they could participate effectively in these market exchanges to supplement their agricultural incomes. Concentrations of village lands and small freeholds surrounding the capital city of Quito also endured for much of the century by supplying foodstuffs and artisan goods to the nearby urban marketplace. Such communities and small farmers could utilize their labor resources, tax advantages, and local hucksters and peddlers to sell produce at costs competitive with local Spanish estates. In other communities near Cuenca, the Andeans used their connections with local merchants to make cotton and woolen cloth, which was sold in colonial markets along the coast and in northern Peru. Even the relatively poor, marginal Amerindian villages of the coast supplied goods to local plantations and urban centers. Where the indigenous peoples could not find

---

80. *Ibid.*, 154.

any marginal advantages in the colonial market economy, however, they often lost their lands to Spanish estate owners. This was particularly true in regions like Riobamba or Quito, where the pressure from the *obraje* economy had proven intense during the seventeenth century. In addition, when the market economy experienced hard times, many villagers and estate laborers found it impossible to make a living, prompting periodic waves of Amerindian migration during the eighteenth century, particularly from depressed regions in the north-central sierra.

The relationship between Amerindians and the market economy also depended on the policies of the colonial state. As crown commercial policy undermined the *obraje* economy of the north-central sierra, the economic prospects for Andeans in those provinces eroded. Such problems only intensified in the late eighteenth century when the crown increased the tribute and *mita* burdens on the Amerindian population and taxed trade goods passing through the internal economy. These policies prompted migrations and, later, violent upheavals directed against the state and local elites. In short, these government taxes and commercial regulations affected the material welfare of most Amerindians who took part in market exchanges.

By participating as producers and consumers in the state-regulated regional markets, the Amerindian peoples played an integral role in the economic evolution of the Kingdom of Quito. Where they survived, indigenous settlements often supplied labor for both the agricultural and manufacturing sectors and provided low-cost food to urban markets. Their migrations to more prosperous colonial regions, such as the south sierra, also allowed agriculture, business, and trade to develop and flourish in that region. This interweaving of subsistence sectors with the regional market system gave added dynamism, flexibility, and higher profits to the colonial economy. Whatever benefits the Amerindians derived from this participation in the market economy, however, hardly matched their contributions. The subordinate social and political position of Amerindians meant that their exchanges with the rest of the economy were always "unequal." The state also imposed heavy taxes, which drained additional resources from the Amerindians. Nevertheless, when the nexus of regional markets in Spanish South America began to unravel between 1809 and 1830, the Amerindian population undoubtedly faced even more difficult economic circumstances. Their dependency on these markets bound them increasingly to cyclical fluctuations in the colonial economy.

6

Commerce and economic patterns

Crown policies and structural economic changes had profound repercussions on commercial patterns in the Kingdom of Quito between 1690 and 1830. As falling prices for *paño* forced many *obrajes* in the north-central sierra to close down, the traditional textile trade gave way to a more diversified network of commercial transactions. European imports continued squeezing *Quiteño* woolens from the Lima market, but cloth producers in the kingdom still managed to supply ample amounts of cheaper textiles to New Granada. At the same time, the cottage cloth industry in the south sierra flourished until the early nineteenth century, providing low-cost cottons and woolens for markets in Peru. The most important commercial changes, however, occurred along the coast. At the end of the seventeenth century, the modest economy of Guayaquil revolved around shipbuilding and the trade in highland cloth. Nevertheless, within one hundred years the port had developed into a major Pacific trade center, exchanging cacao and a wide range of other coastal and highland exports for European and colonial imports.[1]

The crown attempted to regulate these changing trade patterns in the kingdom with a series of commercial reforms. As metropolitan authorities liberalized trade policies from 1778 to 1789, they also established an extensive network of customs houses (*aduanas*) to tax and monitor market exchanges throughout the kingdom. Moreover, the crown placed these new customs stations under direct state control, rather than farming out the duties to colonial elites and vested interest groups. As the custom's accounts demonstrate, these policies succeeded in dramatically extending the state's fiscal and regulatory power, and commercial tax receipts reached new heights, at least until the independence era. Then

---

1. The increase in port traffic to and from Guayaquil had begun even before the advent of *comercio libre*. From 1735 to 1774 the number of ships entering the port annually more than doubled, and the departures also rose significantly. See Archivo General de Indias (hereafter cited as AGI), Quito, 263, Josef Gazan y Miguel de Cueto, Ofic. Rls. de Guayaquil a Julián de Arriaga, Guayaquil, 18 febrero 1775.

tax revenues slowed to a trickle as the colonial state slowly collapsed, disrupting regional markets, intercolonial trade networks, and bureaucratic and service sectors in the kingdom. Only exports of cacao to Mexico and the international economy continued at high levels, which ensured the prosperity of the coast until the demand for chocolate declined in the 1840s.

Spanish commercial and fiscal reforms, 1700–1789

The pressing need for commercial and fiscal reforms became apparent after the final victory of Philip V in the succession wars by 1715. As the transatlantic trade in American silver reached its nadir, policy makers in Madrid searched for ways to reinvigorate the commercial ties with the colonies and increase revenues for the empty royal coffers. The growth of a more diversified network of regional economies in New Spain and South America supplying foodstuffs, export crops, and manufactured goods promised to bolster flagging mining and commercial receipts, but only if the crown could regulate and tax them. In short, the colonial state apparatus, fashioned in the sixteenth century to tax mining profits and the Atlantic trade, had to be overhauled in order to tap the resources of more diverse regional market economies. The task was difficult but necessary. Spain required colonial raw materials and tax revenues to revive the metropolitan economy and to repay the debts accumulated by generations of war and misrule.

The crown first attacked the problem of commercial reform by attempting to rejuvenate the traditional fleet system for South America. From the sixteenth century the crown had restricted trade with the Indies to Spanish vessels, which proceeded in periodic armed convoys from Seville to a few licensed trading sites, such as Portobelo, whose trade fair served most South American markets. The number of convoys and trade fairs had declined considerably during the seventeenth century, however, which allowed French contrabandists to ply Pacific trade routes with impunity during the succession wars. Moreover, the Treaty of Utrecht (1714) gave England the right to supply slaves and send a ship of 500 tons to each Portobelo trade fair, and British merchants used this privilege to furnish contraband for colonial markets. The first discussions on how to address these commercial problems took place in 1705 and 1706 between Spanish statesmen and merchants and two French envoys, seeking to lobby for trade concessions in the Indies. Whereas the Frenchmen urged abandoning the convoy system for individual licensed sailings, the Spanish representatives favored only minor changes: more frequent convoy departures, better defense measures, and a new system of taxing the trade.² Despite the disappointing commercial profits from the trade fair of 1707, entrenched mercantile and political interests in Spain persuaded the new monarch to move towards merely reforming the established fleet system.

Such conservative efforts to revive the old system of *flotas y galeones* culminated in the reform proposal (*proyecto*) of 1720. Although only three years earlier the Lima *consulado* had urged that all new fleets take the Cape Horn route, the new *proyecto* reaffirmed the traditional convoy system and the trade fairs at Portobelo. The reform simply called for more frequent sailings, with the proviso that all imports of merchandise should cater to consumer demand in the Americas, to avoid saturating colonial markets. The crown also expanded the system of licensed register ships to Buenos Aires and other regions not effectively serviced by the fleets. The proposal further adjusted rates for the convoy tax (*avería*) and instituted the *palmeo* system, which valued merchandise for taxation by cubic volume.³ A 1725 statute (*reglamento*) called for yearly fleet sailings, and a final proclamation in 1735 adjusted the mechanics of holding trade fairs, in order to meet the specific objections of colonial merchants.⁴

Despite these innovations, attempts to resuscitate the fleet system had failed miserably by the late 1730s. Contraband flowed freely into Caribbean ports and Buenos Aires. Under the pretext of their slave concession, the British placed commercial representatives and warehouses throughout the major Spanish American ports and introduced merchandise at the trade fairs far exceeding the legal limit of 500 tons. In 1722, for example, British merchants from Jamaica held their own exchange, and nine years later they dominated the fair, selling 1,000 tons of merchandise, worth over 9 million pesos. Distraught Spanish merchants had to force Peruvian traders to take cloth consignments from the royal factory at Guadalajara.⁵ The introduction of legal and contraband goods (through Buenos Aires and the Portuguese outpost of Colonia do Sacramento) also provided a steady stream of goods to colonial markets, further undercutting the fairs.⁶

2. George Robertson Dilg, "The Collapse of the Portobelo Fairs: A Study in Spanish Commercial Reform, 1720–1740" (Ph.D. diss., Indiana University, 1975), 66–69.

3. Antonio García-Baquero González, *Cádiz y el Atlántico (1717–1778)*, 2 vols. (Seville, 1976), 1:152–58; Dilg, "Collapse of the Portobelo Fairs," 70, 83–88. The *palmeo* system was designed to curb tax evasion and the time-consuming process of registering cargoes at the ports. See John Fisher, *Commercial Relations between Spain and Spanish America in the Era of Free Trade, 1778–1796* (Liverpool, 1985), 10, 12.

4. García-Baquero, *Cádiz y el Atlántico*, 1:158–61; Dilg, "Collapse of the Portobelo Fairs," 221–22, 230.

5. Dilg, "Collapse of the Portobelo Fairs," 74, 113–14; and Fisher, "Commercial Relations between Spain and Spanish America," 11.

6. Dilg, "Collapse of the Portobelo Fairs," 76, 90, 122.

Competition from this contraband trade forced colonial merchants to haggle endlessly with Spanish suppliers over the price of merchandise. Paying too much in Portobelo could ruin them. The resulting friction between Peruvians and Spaniards climaxed in 1731, when the peninsulars demanded and received crown permission to bypass the colonial merchants and sell their goods directly in viceregal ports.[7] As a consequence, when the outbreak of the War of Jenkins' Ear (1739–48) disrupted the projected trade fair of 1739, the old fleet system had few defenders in Spain or the Indies.[8] The crown wisely abandoned it in 1740 in favor of individual sailings by registered merchantmen from Cádiz.[9]

Ending the moribund system of *flotas y galeones* stimulated a tremendous increase in trade between Spain and the American colonies. Peninsular merchants shipped 738,758 tons of merchandise to the Indies in 2,365 ships between 1748 and 1778.[10] Colonial commerce received an added boost when King Charles III proclaimed the statute of free trade within the empire (*reglamento de comercio libre*) in 1778. The crown licensed thirteen Spanish ports to trade directly with the colonies, excluding only Venezuela and Mexico from the new trade system (until 1788 and 1789 respectively).[11] This trade liberalization led to a tremendous upsurge in Spanish exports to the Indies, from 9,314,495 pesos in 1778 to a high of 22,883,784 pesos in 1785.[12]

Such an escalation in European imports prompted a significant realignment of commercial patterns in the Kingdom of Quito. Manufactured goods, particularly cloth, probably formed over half of the European wares sent to the colonies, which further squeezed *Quiteño* woolens from the Lima market.[13] Cloth production continued its decline in the highlands, except in Otavalo, Latacunga, and Cuenca, which served stable regional markets. On the other hand, agricultural exports, such as coastal cacao, grew rapidly after the imposition of imperial free trade. Before *comercio libre*, uncertain departure dates and the limited carrying capacity of the galleons and register ships promoted high storage costs and led to periodic losses from spoilage, which discouraged exports of more perishable

---

7. *Ibid.*, 200–01, 213–22, 285.

8. *Ibid.*, 211–61.

9. The crown suspended sailings of register ships for New Spain in 1754; from 1757 to 1776 six fleets traveled to the colony, carrying over 7,000 tons of merchandise. Fisher, *Commercial Relations between Spain and Spanish America*, 13.

10. García-Baquero, *Cádiz y el Atlántico*, 1:541.

11. Fisher, *Commercial Relations between Spain and Spanish America*, 13–15. For a facsimile edition of the original *reglamento*, see Bibiano Torres Ramírez and Javier Ortiz de la Tabla, eds., *Reglamento y aranceles reales para el comercio libre de España a Indias de 12 de octubre de 1778* (Seville, 1979 edn.).

12. Fisher, *Commercial Relations between Spain and Spanish America*, 46.

13. *Ibid.*, 49–50.

cash crops.[14] By the late eighteenth century, however, trade reforms encouraged more frequent ship sailings from America to Spain, leading to the profitable export of bulk agricultural goods such as cacao, *cascarilla*, tobacco, and sugar.[15] Thus markets for agricultural exports expanded, while overall sales of colonial textiles diminished.

As the crown loosened commercial regulations, colonial authorities also began extending a network of customs houses throughout the kingdom, placing them under direct state control. This process began in 1765, when the viceroy ordered an end to tax farming for the sales tax (*alcabala*) in the *corregimiento* of Quito. The unpopularity of this policy, however, delayed any additional efforts to increase state control over commercial levies until 1778. Then the government allowed the tax farming contracts in Guayaquil to lapse and took over the administration of the customs office.[16] Colonial authorities later established a network of new *aduanas* throughout the highlands and the coast under the control of a newly created state agency, the *Dirección general de alcabalas* in 1787.[17]

By the late eighteenth century, the crown had created a centralized bureaucracy directly responsible for monitoring and taxing all land and sea commerce in the Kingdom of Quito. Each customs house in the provincial capitals supervised smaller suboffices located in every sizable town in the district. In Guayaquil, for example, the *aduana* in the port oversaw smaller customs stations in Babahoyo, Balzar, Daule, Palenque, Puná, Yaguache, Naranjal, and Punta de Santa Elena.[18] Each of these suboffices remitted annual tax receipts and fiscal accounts to the treasury in Guayaquil, which answered to the *Dirección general de alcabalas* in Quito. As a result, the main office in Quito supervised a network of thirteen provincial offices and over fifty subordinate offices.[19]

Although small by modern standards, this expansive network of cus-

14. Dilg, "Collapse of the Portobelo Fairs," 275–76.
15. For a discussion of the quantities of agricultural goods and their percentage of total American exports, see *Ibid.*, 66–71.
16. AGI, Quito, 409, Instrucción y Ordenanza para el Regimen y Govierno del la Dirección general de las Reales Rentas de Tabacos, Alcavalas, Aguardiente, Polvora, y Naipes de Quito, Quito, 3 junio 1783 (hereafter Instrucción y Ordenanza); Montserrat Fernández Martínez, *La alcabala en la Audiencia de Quito, 1765–1810* (Cuenca, 1984), 49.
17. The state took direct control over the customs houses in Otavalo and Ibarra in 1785 and in the south sierra by 1787. Fernández Martínez, *La alcabala en la Audiencia de Quito*, 49.
18. AGI, Quito, 478, Cuenta de la Aduana de Guayaquil, 1780.
19. AGI, Quito, 409, Instrucción y Ordenanza, Quito, 3 junio 1783; AGI, Quito 407, Razon de los empleos de Rl Hacda que hay establecidos en Quito y sus Provincias y los sujetos destinados en ellos, segun proviene la Real Orden de 12 Marzo de este año de 1783; AGI, Santa Fe, 803, Informe sobre la ordenanza que formó para el mejor arreglo y establecimiento que hizo del Ramo de Alcavala en aquella ciudad y corregimientos sujetos a sus Reales Caxas (hereafter cited as Razon de los empleos), Madrid, 13 abril 1799.

toms offices gave the colonial state unprecedented fiscal control over commercial life in the kingdom by 1787. Some fraud undoubtedly continued but at much reduced levels. These offices collected taxes and also forced merchants to carry trade permits (*guías*), listing the origin and destination of all trade goods moving through the *audiencia* district. After selling their goods, the merchants then obtained a receipt (*tornaguía*) stating that they had reached their appointed terminus, sold their merchandise, and paid the required *alcabala*. When the system functioned properly, it allowed the state to exercise considerable authority over the network of commercial routes extending from modest regional market towns to major trading cities such as Guayaquil. Moreover, the extant accounts of the main customs offices provide the best, most detailed record of changing trade patterns and the degree of government fiscal control over commerce in the kingdom during the late colonial period.[20]

The state and the coastal commercial boom

Tax receipts at the Guayaquil customs office clearly reflected the upsurge in the coastal export economy. Annual revenues at the city *aduana* rose from 53,288 pesos in 1780 to 149,283 pesos in 1786, the peak year for customs income during the colonial period. Taxes on the import–export trade constituted nearly 72 percent of these revenues.[21] The rest came from charges on rural properties, legal transactions, and local consumption. These amounts collected at the port dwarfed the sums registered at the *aduanas* of either Quito or Cuenca, indicating the growing importance of the coast in the kingdom's economy after the advent of *comercio libre*.

The coastal import trade

Although the customs accounts do not reveal the structure of the import trade, merchants in Guayaquil apparently exchanged the typical mixture of European goods for coastal cacao, agropastoral commodities, and artisan goods. Approximately half of these goods sent from Spain to the Indies between 1778 and 1796 originated from other European countries, not the metropolis. Most were manufactured goods, particularly cloth from Britain, France, and the Low Countries. Goods sent to America from Spain itself, however, were a mixture of manufactured products (55 percent) and agricultural commodities (45 percent), such as olive oil, nuts,

---

20. Accounts for the provincial treasuries of Quito, Cuenca, and Guayaquil are found in the Spanish and Ecuadorian archives. To date, the only records of the subordinate offices that I have uncovered are for Ambato for 1780 (in AGI, Quito, 445, Cuentas de Alcabalas de Ambato) and Latacunga for 1780 (in AGI, Quito, 507, Cuentas de Alcabalas de Latacunga).
21. AGI, Quito, 478–482B, Cuentas de la Aduana de Guayaquil, 1781–1808.

flour, wines, sherries, and brandies.[22] A study of commerce in the kingdom in 1780, prepared by Carlos Presenti – the head of the *Dirección
general de alcabalas* – confirmed that the European goods sold in Guayaquil
fit this overall pattern. Presenti reported that over half of the European
imports were textiles, usually from Britain and France, not Spain. Spanish
merchants also sent small amounts of textiles, along with iron products,
artisan goods, paper, flagstones, and wines.[23]

Merchants operating in Guayaquil also imported cloth, agricultural
produce, and raw materials from the highlands and the other Spanish
colonies. The bulk of all highland imports was rough cotton and woolen
textiles, predominantly from Cuenca.[24] Most other colonial imports came
from the Viceroyalty of Peru. Carlos Presenti reported that these Peruvian
goods included olives, olive oil, nuts and nut oils, lead, wax, cinnamon,
wine, and brandy. These colonial and highland commodities represented
over half the goods imported in 1780.[25]

After the beginning of imperial free trade in 1778, the state-controlled
aduana in Guayaquil registered a tremendous upsurge in tax income from
European imports. The only tax accurately representing levies on imports
from abroad was the *almojarifazgo*, and receipts from this duty rose rapidly after 1780.[26] The *almojarifazgo* on European imports ranged from 3
percent on Spanish goods to 7 percent on all commodities from elsewhere in Europe.[27] *Almojarifazgo* receipts on these European goods coming into Guayaquil increased from 5,520 pesos in 1780 to 63,063 pesos
by 1786 (see Table 6.1). Thereafter, the level of these import duties usually ranged between 20,000 pesos and 40,000 pesos (accounting for
50–80 percent of total import taxes), until they began an uneven decline

22. The breakdown of Spanish imports is as follows: cottons and linens, 27 percent; silks, 16 percent;
    other textiles and manufactures, 12 percent; and agricultural goods, 45 percent. Fisher, *Com-
    mercial Relations between Spain and Spanish America*, 49–50.
23. AGI, Quito, 240, Copia del Informe que hace el Admin Gen'l de Alcabalas de la Ciudad de
    Quito y sus Subalternas relativo a la Real Orden de 18 Octobre de 1779 que proviene se remitan
    a las Rs manos de S.M. las Listas de los frutos y Mercaderías más gastables en estas Provincias
    y de sus producciones que puedan entrar en el tráfico Marítimo, Quito, Carlos Presenti, 31
    agosto 1780 (hereafter cited as Copia del Informe).
24. AGI, Quito, 478–482B, Cuentas de la Aduana de Guayaquil, ramo de efectos de la sierra,
    1780–1808.
25. AGI, Quito, 240, Copia del Informe, 31 agosto 1780.
26. The other major tax on imports was the sales tax (*alcabala*). This tax was assessed at 3 percent
    of the market value of the goods. A number of goods entering the port, which were later
    reexported, however, did not pay the sales tax. As a result, the *almojarifazgo* probably represents
    a more accurate measure of the value and volume of imported merchandise.
27. The crown dropped the *palmeo* system of assessing tax value in favor of taxing a fixed percentage
    of the assessed value of the imports after 1778. Fisher, *Commercial Relations between Spain and
    Spanish America*, 15.

Table 6.1. *Almojarifazgo on goods imported into Guayaquil, 1780-1808 (in pesos de ocho reales)*

Year	Highland Goods Amount	%	Colonial Goods Amount	%	European Goods Amount	%
1780	1,398	10.5	6,397	48.0	5,520	41.5
1781	1,866	8.0	6,420	29.0	13,824	63.0
1782	2,061	7.5	7,041	25.5	18,436	67.0
1783	1,675	5.0	9,504	29.0	21,967	66.0
1784	1,144	2.0	10,408	22.0	35,979	76.0
1785	947	2.0	13,129	31.0	27,910	67.0
1786	1,524	2.0	15,937	20.0	63,063	78.0
1787	1,324	2.0	13,336	17.0	61,711	81.0
1788	1,621	3.0	10,825	19.0	43,964	78.0
1789	1,197	3.0	7,985	17.0	37,235	80.0
1790	1,198	2.8	8,096	18.6	34,256	78.6
1791	1,270	2.7	8,396	17.5	38,204	79.8
1792	1,374	3.0	8,521	16.0	42,926	81.0
1793	1,600	3.0	9,241	18.0	41,231	79.0
1794	1,764	5.0	8,832	23.0	27,437	72.0
1795	1,833	4.0	12,172	25.0	33,760	71.0
1796	12		14,048	27.0	37,881	73.0
1797	1,312	4.0	11,070	33.0	20,785	63.0
1798	2,591	11.0	13,777	57.0	7,628	32.0
1799	2,436	12.0	15,184	74.0	2,890	14.0
1800	2,991	9	14,748	44.0	15,947	47.0
1801	2,661	7.5	14,282	40.5	18,277	52.0
1805[a]	2,363	6.0	10,937	27.0	27,868	67.0
1806	2,345	5.0	20,372	46.0	21,433	49.0
1807	3,349	10.0	16,846	50.0	13,622	40.0
1808	3,271	8.5	13,379	35.0	21,564	56.5
Total	47,127	4.0	300,883	28.0	735,318	68.0

[a] The years 1802 to 1804 are not available in the AGI, Seville, or the ANH, Quito.
Note: The blank represents a value of under 1 percent in the percent column for "highland goods" for 1796.
Source: AGI, Quito, 478-482B, Cuentas de la Aduana de Guayaquil, 1780-1808.

after the onset of war with Britain in 1796 (see Table 6.1). Levies on European imports typically proved the most lucrative source of revenue for the Guayaquil customs office, but the quantities of goods entering the port varied dramatically depending on disruptions in international trade and fluctuations in local demand for luxury items.

Taxes on colonial and highland imports also increased significantly after 1780, but they demonstrated greater stability over time than levies collected on European goods. The *almojarifazgo* on colonial imports, assessed at 5 percent, rose gradually from 6,397 pesos in 1780 to 15,937 pesos in 1786. The trade in colonial goods suffered fewer sharp downturns

Table 6.2. *Origin of European goods imported into Guayaquil,*
1781-1808 (%)

Year	Viceroyalty of New Spain	Viceroyalty of Peru
1781	1.0	99.0
1782	55.0	45.0
1783	30.5	69.5
1784	1.5	98.5
1785	3.5	96.5
1786	1.0	99.0
1787	1.5	98.5
1788	1.0	99.0
1789	0.5	99.5
1790	12.5	87.0
1791	2.5	97.5
1792	3.5	96.5
1793	3.0	97.0
1794	1.0	99.0
1795	4.0	96.0
1796	2.5	97.5
1797	5.0	95.0
1798	6.5	93.5
1799	100	0.0
1800	16.0	84.0
1801	19.0	81.0
1807	8.0	92.0
1808	11.0	89.0
Total	7.0	83.0

[a] The years 1802 to 1806 are not available in the AGI,
Seville, or the ANH, Quito.
Source: AGI, Quito, 478-482B, Cuentas de la Aduana de
Guayaquil, 1781-1808.

even during wartime.[28] Highland goods, which paid only a 3-percent
sales tax, also produced consistent customs receipts. Trade goods from
the sierra arrived overland and normally provided from 1,000 pesos to
3,000 pesos in tax revenues annually (see Table 6.1).

The vast majority of the goods imported into Guayaquil came from
the Viceroyalty of Peru. From 1781 to 1808, Peru provided 83 percent
of the European imports, while only 7 percent came from New Spain.
Apart from 1782–83, the northern viceroyalty shipped only insignificant
amounts of European wares until the late 1790s (see Table 6.2). Despite
the importance of markets for cacao in New Spain, merchants from Mex-

---

28. Despite the stability of tax income from these American imports, they represented between 16
percent and 74 percent of all import duties, because of the wartime disruptions in the flow of
European goods (see Table 6.1).

ico City made few lasting inroads into the Guayaquil import market until very late in the century.

Even after *comercio libre*, the bulk of the kingdom's commerce with the other Spanish colonies still proceeded along traditional trade routes long dominated by Lima merchant houses. Peruvian wines, brandies, olive oil, and cinnamon flowed steadily into Guayaquil throughout the colonial period. Even the overland trade in textiles from the south sierra was controlled by Lima commercial houses. At least 75 percent of this cloth came from Cuenca, where Lima merchants financed the local cottage textile industry and also managed the marketing of southern cloth in both Guayaquil and Peru. Commercial reforms only increased the volume of this trade without lessening the dependency on Peruvian commercial houses.

Imports of European and colonial goods after 1778 also prompted a serious debt problem at the Guayaquil customs house. The rapid expansion of the import trade following the Anglo-Spanish War of 1783 encouraged merchants to introduce unprecedented quantities of European goods, particularly between 1786 and 1796 (see Table 6.1). In all likelihood, this led to a temporary saturation of the market, and custom's inspectors found it increasingly difficult to collect the full value on *almojarifazgo* assessments. Merchants importing European wares compiled yearly debts to the state, reaching 68,758 pesos in 1787. Even commercial houses attempting to sell colonial goods in the city amassed debts ranging from 7,000 pesos to nearly 15,000 pesos annually. Most of these amounts were repaid after a year or two, but the overall level of indebtedness recorded in the *aduana* accounts increased whenever imports reached very high levels. Apparently the kingdom's coastal and highland economies could not absorb these imports rapidly enough in the first twenty years of imperial free trade.[29]

The coastal export trade

Comercio libre also stimulated the export trade from Guayaquil. The *reglamento* of 1778 exempted cacao, the principal export crop, from paying the *almojarifazgo de salida* (a 2.5-percent tax on most colonial exports), and in 1789 the crown lifted the last restrictions on shipping coastal cacao to New Spain.[30] The result was an upsurge in cacao production as

---

29. Another possible explanation might involve the value assigned by customs inspectors to imports during this period. It is possible that these values were set artificially high from 1786 to 1796 and changed thereafter, which would also explain the rise in indebtedness. Any more definitive answer awaits further investigation of the import-export trade in Guayaquil and elsewhere in the Indies. AGI, Quito, 478B, Cuentas de la Aduana de Guayaquil, 1780–1808.

30. Torres and Ortiz de la Tabla, eds., *Reglamento para el comercio libre*, article 24, p. 12. This is cited

coastal planters now found markets for their produce in New Spain, Peru, and Europe. Merchants also shipped increasing quantities of *cascarilla*, indigo, cochineal, wood, hides, artisan goods, and highland woolens. In fact, the value of coastal exports between 1790 and 1800 had nearly doubled since the decade 1770–80.[31]

Export tax receipts from Guayaquil reflect the rapid growth of the coastal economy in the late colonial period. Returns from the 3-percent *alcabala* levied on cacao fluctuated from 1780 to 1792, when growth accelerated rapidly (see Table 6.3). This growth in tax receipts from the cacao trade slowed after the onset of war with Britain in 1796 but picked up again after 1800. According to additional *aduana* records preserved in Lima, the next drop in cacao production came between 1811 and 1816, followed by steady growth until the 1840s.[32] Cacao apparently accounted for at least 40–60 percent of the kingdom's total exports by the late colonial period.[33]

The merchants operating in Guayaquil also exported a wide range of other coastal products. Returns from the *almojarifazgo de salida*, levied against most coastal exports (other than cacao) grew slowly and evenly from 1780 to 1800, reaching a short-lived peak of 13,454 pesos in 1806 (see Table 6.3). Products like tobacco, coffee, rice, agave, wax, wood, hides, and artisan goods accounted for the bulk of these goods.[34] Although elite landowners grew most of these export commodities, crown monopolies regulated the sale of some products, such as tobacco, sugar, and coffee. The indigenous population also participated in the export growth. The Amerindians produced a number of commodities – hats, hides, agave, and wax – which merchants shipped in small amounts throughout the Pacific trading zone.[35]

Apart from selling agricultural and artisan goods, merchants operating in Guayaquil still reexported some highland commodities and European wares. Scattered data from the 1780s indicate that textiles and *cascarilla*, predominantly from the south sierra, accounted for nearly 30 percent of the port's total exports in some years.[36] In addition, merchants reexported small amounts of European goods, although by the early nineteenth cen-

---

in Carlos C. Contreras, *El sector exportador de una economía colonial: la costa del Ecuador entre 1760 y 1820* (Quito, 1990), 29.

31. A variety of coastal goods, such as flour and bread, and any goods produced by the indigenous population were also granted exemptions from the *almojarifazgo de salida*. Contreras, *El sector exportador*, 29.

32. *Ibid.*, 52–53, 143–44.

33. This estimate is taken from data compiled by Carlos Contreras for the years 1779–1801, 1803–06, 1808, 1810–11, 1813, 1817, 1820–25. *Ibid.*, 143–45.

34. *Ibid.*, 156–59.

35. *Ibid.*, 99–116.

36. *Ibid.*, 142.

Table 6.3. *Taxes on exports from Guayaquil, 1780-1808*

Year	Cacao 3% Alcabala		Other exports 2.5% Almojarifazgo	
	Amount	%	Amount	%
1780	4,635	37.5	7,720	62.5
1781	5,421	50.5	5,316	49.5
1782	6,863	53.0	6,131	47.0
1783	9,597	53.5	8,352	46.5
1784	10,956	55.0	8,958	45.0
1785	4,681	43.0	6,291	57.0
1786	10,422	57.0	7,943	43.0
1787	3,378	34.0	6,569	66.0
1788	2,295	29.0	5,721	71.0
1789	4,921	41.0	7,001	59.0
1790	6,816	49.0	7,205	51.0
1791	5,992	52.0	5,471	48.0
1792	8,255	57.0	6,317	43.0
1793	12,402	64.0	6,993	36.0
1794	17,342	72.0	6,780	28.0
1795	24,412	74.0	8,396	26.0
1796	13,810	69.0	6,197	31.0
1797	9,265	61.0	6,012	39.0
1798	7,771	71.0	3,172	29.0
1799	11,954	67.0	5,782	33.0
1800	9,826	64.0	5,544	36.0
1801	10,322	72.0	4,071	28.0
1805[a]	18,748	70.0	8,037	30.0
1806	12,130	47.0	13,454	53.0
1807	10,775	55.0	8,765	45.0
1808	12,939	64.0	7,357	36.0
Total	255,928	59.0	179,555	41.0

[a] The years 1802 to 1804 are not available in the AGI, Seville, or the ANH, Quito.
Source: AGI, Quito, 478-482B, Cuentas de la Aduana de Guayaquil, 1780-1808.

tury this modest reexport trade accounted for only 4 percent of the port city's total commerce.[37] After the advent of *comercio libre*, the city of Guayaquil did much more than exchange European imports for highland products; in most years over two-thirds of all its exports were coastal products.[38] By the late colonial period the port city had evolved into a major Pacific trading center in its own right, relying fundamentally on the export of coastal goods.

37. *Ibid.*, 141.
38. *Ibid.*, 44.

Table 6.4. *Destination of exports from Guayaquil, 1780-1808 (%)*

Year	New Spain	New Granada	Peru	Spain	Other
1780	33.0		67.0		
1781	59.5	0.5	40.0		
1782	56.0	0.3	40.7	3.0	
1783	13.5	0.5	77.0	9.0	
1784	26.0	0.4	73.6		
1785	24.0	1.0	75.0		
1786	16.0	1.0	83.0		
1787	12.0	1.0	87.0		
1788	18.0	3.0	79.0		
1789	20.0	0.5	79.5		
1790	13.0	0.5	86.5		
1791	50.0	3.0	47.0		
1792	40.0	2.0	54.0	4.0	
1793	32.0	2.0	66.0		
1794	40.0	1.0	51.0	8.0	
1795	36.8	0.2	27.0	36.0	
1796	31.0	0.4	38.0	30.6	
1797	54.0	1.0	34.0	11.0	
1798	71.0	18.0	11.0		
1799	27.0	39.0	34.0		
1800	17.0	39.0	35.0		9.0[a]
1801	64.0	1.0	35.0		
1805[a]	34.0	35.0			31.0[a]
1806	40.0	26.0	6.0		26.0[a]
1807	57.0	41.0	2.0		
1808	42.0	44.0	8.0		6.0[a]
Total	36.5	0.5	50.0	9.0	4.0

[a]The exports went to Montevideo in 1800, Boston in 1805-1806, and Manila and Hamburg in 1808. The years 1802 to 1804 are not available in the AGI, Seville, or the ANH, Quito.
Source: AGI, Quito, 478-482B, Cuentas de la Aduana de Guayaquil, 1780-1808.

After *comercio libre*, the Viceroyalty of Peru slowly lost its position as the principal market for goods from Guayaquil. Before 1778, crown legislation required all coastal exports to pass through Lima, allowing the viceregal capital to handle over 90 percent of Guayaquil's export trade.[39] According to the *aduana* records of the port (presented in Table 6.4), the percentage of goods shipped to Peru began declining in the 1790s, and by 1807 it had fallen to only 2 percent.

By the 1790s, merchants operating in Guayaquil began to ship their goods to a wide range of markets, particularly in New Spain (see Table

39. *Ibid.*, 80.

6.4). From 1795, coastal exporters also sent escalating amounts – upwards of 30 percent – of their produce directly to Europe. Most of these goods went to Spain until the early nineteenth century, when the beleaguered crown allowed neutral vessels to carry colonial merchandise directly to foreign ports, such as Boston and Hamburg.[40] On the other hand, until the late 1790s New Granada consumed an insignificant share of the port's exports, rarely exceeding 3 percent of the total (see Table 6.4).

The decline of Peru as a market for coastal goods is most apparent in the export of cacao. The largest demand for cacao had always been in New Spain, and even the small amounts sent to Lima before 1778 usually had been reexported there. After 1789, however, merchants could trade directly with colonial and European markets, which took an increasing share of the coastal crop. The customs records from Guayaquil indicate that nearly 40 percent of the cacao exports went to Acapulco or Realejo in New Spain.[41] The amounts sent directly to Spain also reached 50–60 percent in the peak years from 1795 to 1800. Meanwhile, the share of the cacao crop shipped to Peru slowly declined from a high of 82 percent in 1787 to a low of 6 percent in 1798.[42]

Although Peru no longer served as the primary destination for cacao exports, other coastal products continued going to the southern viceroyalty. The customs records indicate that nearly 65 percent of the remaining coastal exports went to markets in Peru, primarily Lima. New Spain consumed approximately 26 percent of the total. Spain and New Granada were unimportant markets for such coastal commodities, each importing less than 1 percent of the total. The remaining trade goods went to other European countries or the United States, but only during the periods when the crown allowed neutral trade (1797–99, 1801–02, 1804–08).[43]

40. For a discussion of neutral trade, see Jacques A. Barbier, "Comercio neutral in Bolivaran America: La Guaira, Cartagena, Callao, and Buenos Aires," in Reinhard Liehr, ed., *América Latina en la época de Simón Bolívar: la formación de las economías nacionales y los intereses económicos europeos, 1800–1850* (Berlin, 1989), 363–77.

41. Central American ports accounted for slightly over 8 percent of the cacao exports, while Acapulco took nearly 32 percent. AGI, Quito, 478–482B, Cuentas de la Aduana de Guayaquil, 1779–1808.

42. The percentages of cacao shipped to different markets are drawn from the customs records of Guayaquil in Spain. AGI, Quito, 478–482B, Cuentas de la Aduana de Guayaquil, 1780–1808. These figures differ slightly from those compiled from customs records in Peru and published data compiled by Carlos Contreras. The accounts are not always precise about the origin and destination of goods, as customs officers sometimes listed the next port of call and other times the final destination. The records are also occasionally internally inconsistent, having different totals in colonial workbooks from the final accounts sent to Spain. These problems explain the relatively minor differences in the figures; the overall trends explained here and in Contreras's work, however, are strikingly similar. See Contreras, *El sector exportador*, 79–82, 135–53.

43. The reasons for the differences from the figures presented in Contreras, *El sector exportador*, 116–19, 156–66, are similar to those given in note 42. The data were taken from AGI, Quito, 478–

Despite the diversification of markets for coastal exports during the late colonial period, trade from Guayaquil was controlled by a few large commercial houses, mostly based in Lima and to a lesser extent in New Spain. This was particularly true of cacao exports. In 1804, ten merchant houses shipped nearly 90 percent of the regional cacao harvest, and in 1811 the eleven largest exporters accounted for over 80 percent of the cacao sold abroad.[44] These large mercantile concerns had the business connections in the colonies and abroad to market the crops; smaller coastal merchants and planters could seldom compete. Given the dominance of Peruvian merchants in the import trade, it is only logical that they controlled much of the city's export commerce, except cacao, where Mexico City merchants made significant inroads.

While the bulk of the *aduana*'s revenues came from taxes on the import-export trade, the crown also levied charges on rural properties (*alcabala del cabezón*), legal transactions (*escrituras y contratos públicos*), commerce with the interior, and internal consumption. The trade in highland cloth and remittances from the suboffices (*recepturías*) in the interior provided stable but modest yearly sums, averaging under 1,000 pesos annually.[45] The only other significant source of revenue was the tax on *escrituras y contratos públicos*, which usually involved local elites buying and selling real estate, slaves, or making business partnerships. The remaining taxes on wood, meat, grocery stores (*pulperías*), tobacco, and *cascarilla* yielded very small sums.[46]

Despite its prosperity, the kingdom's coastal region apparently faced daunting trade deficits during the decade 1784–94.[47] Although the complex method of assessing taxes on imports and exports makes it impossible to calculate accurately their overall value or the port's balance of trade, the rising level of European imports outstripped export earnings by approximately 600,000 pesos during the decade.[48] This disparity was

482B, Cuentas de la Aduana de Guayaquil, 1780–1808. On the different phases of neutral trade, see Barbier, "Comercio Neutral," 366–77.

44. Contreras, *El sector exportador*, 68.

45. AGI, Quito, 478–482B, Cuentas de la Aduana de Guayaquil, 1780–1808.

46. *Ibid.*

47. Some commodities were exempted from taxes. In other cases, European goods imported into another colonial port, such as Lima, paid the *almojarifazgo* only at the first stop. When goods were reexported, they paid port duties only when they fetched a higher price in the second port. The *almojarifazgo* was only charged on the price difference, not the full value of the good. This surcharge was called the *mayor aumento*. For a discussion of this problem, see AGI, Santa Fe, 803, Informe del Consejo de Indias, Madrid, 20 abril 1773. Goods paying only this amount would appear to have an artificially low value. In practice, however, few imports paid only the *mayor aumento*. Nevertheless, reexports and exempted goods can make calculating total import or export values a hazardous proposition.

48. Projections of total imports and exports based on *aduana* records are extremely speculative. Nevertheless, a crude approximation of the value of Guayaquil's total exports between 1784 and 1794 runs at approximately 402,000 pesos annually. Similarly crude values for imports

moderated by over 50,000 pesos in profits from the sale of European goods in the highlands.[49] In addition, an influx of orders for the shipyard during this period provided approximately 100,000 pesos annually, while government spending for defense and bureaucratic salaries added an additional 100,000–115,000 pesos annually.[50] Together these highland trade links and invisibles (services) cut the apparent trade deficit substantially. After 1794 this problem rapidly diminished, as import and export earnings tended to coincide, evidently ending any trade deficits on the current account.[51]

Like many export economies in Spanish America, the coastal region benefitted from the Bourbon monarchy's emphasis on reviving colonial trade. Imperial free trade prompted a tremendous increase in the volume of commerce by the 1790s. The port city of Guayaquil extended its commercial links with Lima and New Spain, thereby becoming part of a larger network of colonial and international markets. At the same time, the port retained its traditional ties with the sierra, exchanging cloth, *cascarilla*, and other highland products for European and colonial imports. The state network of customs houses not only taxed this trade but also attempted to direct it through legally approved channels. As a result, the prosperity of the Guayaquil region rested on a lively import–export trade, nurtured, protected, and regulated by the colonial state. Despite this overall prosperity, outside merchant houses, centered in Lima and Mexico City, reaped much of the profit from the coastal trade.

Quito and the recession in the north-central highlands

The Quito customs accounts clearly demonstrate the relative decline of manufacturing and commerce in the north-central highlands. From 1780,

during this same period would be about 1,034,000 pesos. These figures are projections based on the *almojarifazgo* and *alcabala* statistics found in AGI, Quito, 478–482B, Cuentas de la Aduana de Guayaquil, 1780–1808.

49. Part of the apparent trade deficit may be explained by a tendency among custom's inspectors in Guayaquil and elsewhere to undervalue exports for taxation, particularly at the beginning of the cacao boom. In Spain, for example, John Fisher notes a similar disparity between 1778 and 1796: Spanish exports were valued much less than colonial imports, the reverse of the situation in Guayaquil. Fisher, *Commercial Relations between Spain and Spanish America*, 46–47, 60–64.

50. For the large number of ship orders placed at Guayaquil during those years, see María Luisa Laviana Cuetos, *Guayaquil en el siglo XVIII: recursos naturales y desarrollo económico* (Seville, 1987), 289–300. The figures on government spending can be estimated from documentation found in AGI, 478–482B, Cuentas de la Aduana de Guayaquil, 1779–1808; AGI, Quito, 470–73, Cuentas de la caja de Guayaquil, 1761–1803; AGI, Quito, 486, Cuentas de la dirección de tabacos, pólvora, y naipes, 1778–91; and AGI, Quito, 407, Razon de empleos, Quito, 12 marzo 1783.

51. For an interesting discussion of the problems in calculating the trade balance on the current account (imports minus exports plus invisibles) particularly the problem of estimating invisibles, see James F. Shepherd, *A Balance of Trade for the Thirteen Colonies, 1768–1772* (New York, 1985 edn.), passim.

the Quito office supervised a network of regional *aduanas* scattered throughout the sierra, from Ibarra to Riobamba, which collected the 3-percent sales tax on all European and colonial imports.[52] Customs officers also collected levies on rural properties, legal transactions, and internal consumption.[53] Nevertheless, the total customs receipts flowing into the capital ranged between 21,427 pesos in 1779 and 50,163 pesos in 1787 (see Table 6.5). This was approximately one-third of the annual intake of the Guayaquil *aduana*, which supervised a region with scarcely 12 percent of the population.[54] By the late colonial period, the coastal export economy had clearly eclipsed the formerly dominant textile sector.

Imports to the north-central highlands

The populace in the north-central sierra consumed only modest amounts of European and colonial trade goods. The customs records show that import taxes increased slowly to a high of only 17,682 pesos in 1786 and then averaged approximately 10,000 pesos for the remainder of the period (see Table 6.5). The relatively low value of these receipts also suggests the magnitude of the regional recession. Apparently local elites could not afford to buy large quantities of European luxury items or even colonial imports, despite their prestige value as consumer goods. In most years, taxes on local trade and production even exceeded the amounts collected on imports. As in Guayaquil, however, a substantial tax debt resulted when imports peaked during the period 1787–95 (see Table 6.5). Despite the moderate level of imports, apparently the market quickly became saturated, making it difficult for customs officers in Quito to collect the full sales tax.

Merchants introduced a wide variety of European, Peruvian, and local merchandise into Quito during the late colonial period. The most popular consumer goods were cloth from Britain, France, the Low Countries, and Spain, along with paper, iron goods, jewelry, guns, masonry, dyes, and art work.[55] In 1780, Carlos Presenti estimated that merchants sold 320,000 pesos worth of European wares annually in the north-central sierra, accounting for over 80 percent of total imports.[56] Peruvian olive

---

52. The single suboffice of Ambato maintained its own *recepturías* in Pillaro, Patate, Pelileo, Quero, Fisaleo, Mocha, Rosa, and Quisapincha. See AGI, Quito, 445, Alcabalas de Ambato, 1780.
53. These other *ramos* include: *escrituras y contratos públicos* on legal transactions, the *cabezón* on rural properties, the *viento* collected on foodstuffs and other commodities at the city gates, the *carnecería* on butchers, *tabaco y aguardiente* on local sales of tobacco and cane liquor, and remittances from the *recepturías* or provincial offices. See Fernándaz Martínez, *La alcabala en la Audiencia de Quito*, 71–117.
54. AGI, Quito, 478–482B, Cuentas de la Aduana de Guayaquil, 1778–1808.
55. AGI, Quito, 240, Copia del Informe, 31 agosto 1780.
56. *Ibid.*

Table 6.5. *Sales tax revenues in the North-central sierra, 1779-1803*

Year	Total Revenues	Imports	Local Trade[a]	Debts
1779	21,427	2,430	5,189	13,808
1780	36,838	9,458	10,754	16,626
1781	28,052	6,628	15,193	6,231
1782	30,470	6,100	18,632	5,738
1783	34,414	10,374	18,185	5,855
1784	37,781	9,490	22,214	6,077
1785	32,837	13,792	13,871	5,174
1786	43,490	17,682	21,673	4,135
1787	50,163	16,656	22,659	10,848
1788	44,390	13,344	18,493	12,553
1789	41,872	10,475	16,651	14,746
1790	28,545	3,155	10,384	15,006
1791	29,990	12,139	9,669	8,182
1792	29,571	9,762	8,635	11,174
1793	28,652	9,875	10,648	8,129
1794	30,829	12,084	10,805	7,940
1795	29,891	9,910	9,962	10,019
1796	28,071	8,958	11,197	7,916
1797	27,112	9,916	9,417	7,779
1798	26,202	6,301	11,748	8,153
1799	27,703	7,679	13,033	6,991
1800	29,355	11,430	11,964	5,961
1801	32,798	13,299	12,543	6,956
1802	30,747	10,827	12,367	7,553
1803	32,545	15,238	12,497	4,810
Total	813,745	257,002	338,383	218,060

[a]The figures for internal trade include remissions from the subtreasuries from 1781-1790, which explains the rising level of tax revenues on internal trade during those years. These subtreasuries at Latacunga, Ambato, Guaranda-Chimbo, and Alausí began remitting income in 1781; Ibarra and Otavalo did not do so until 1785. After 1790, however, these offices sent income directly to the *caja real* in Quito, instead of the *Dirección general de rentas*.
Source: Montserrat Fernández Martínez, *La alcabala en la Audiencia de Quito, 1765-1810* (Cuenca, 1984), 71-118; 157-67.

oil, nuts, lead, wax, and cinnamon also found buyers in the highlands. In addition, merchants sold highland cloth, foodstuffs, and coastal goods like cacao, dried fish, shellfish, salt, and artisan goods.[57]

For most years the customs accounts combined revenues from European, Peruvian, and local imports, making it impossible to determine

57. Archivo Nacional de Historia de Quito (hereafter cited as ANH–Q), Alcabalas, Caja 22, Libro manual de Quito, 1786.

with any precision the yearly fluctuations in each category. Nevertheless, for those years where the entries can be separated, tax revenues from European imports tended to rise over time.[58] In 1781, for example, taxes on the sale of European goods produced 3,103 pesos, or 60 percent of the total import revenues. The rest was split evenly between levies on Peruvian and local merchandise.[59] By the period from 1798 to 1808, however, customs revenues from the sale of European wares had risen to an average of 9,700 pesos, accounting for over 80 percent of import receipts. During these same years the sale of Peruvian merchandise dropped precipitously. In 1781 taxes on imports from the southern vice-royalty amounted to 1,031 pesos, but by 1798 they had dwindled to only 24 pesos. Tax revenues on sale of local merchandise, however, remained steady throughout the late colonial period, fluctuating between 1,300 pesos and 2,000 pesos annually.[60]

Imported merchandise came to Quito primarily from Guayaquil and New Granada. Merchants shipped European and Peruvian goods through Guayaquil and then overland to the highland capital.[61] The bulk of the imported merchandise from New Granada came by mule train from Car-

---

58. The customs accounts of the Quito office do not differentiate clearly among European, Peruvian, and local commodities. From 1768 to 1780, for example, the accounts list local and Peruvian goods in the same category (*ramo*), and between 1780 and 1798 the customs officers lump European and Peruvian imports together. Separating the entries is a painstaking process that can only be undertaken for selected years, even using the daily workbooks of the customs officers. See Fernández Martínez, *La alcabala en la Audiencia de Quito*, 83–95.

59. ANH–Q, Alcabalas, Caja 20, Libro principal de la contaduría de la administración general de alcabalas de Quito, en donde se lleba cuenta, y razón de todo cobrado en ella y que deude el Real Dro sobre los distintos ramos de que se compone esta Renta, que sirve desde 1 de enero de 1781 al cargo de contador dn Josef Guarderas.

60. *Ibid.*; ANH–Q, Alcabalas, Caja 21, Libro Matris Real Común, en donde por menor se lleva cuenta, y Razon del Valor del Real Dro que satisfacen a S.M. todos los Ramos de que se compone esta Renta, con un Resumen circunstanciado de las partidas de Cargo y Data del producto liquido, que por todos Ramos resulta en este Administración General, a beneficio de la Real Hacienda, en cumplimiento de las ordenanzas e instrucciones dicatadas por el Sor Don José García de Leon y Pizarro, Presidente, Regente, Visitador y Comandante General de estas provincias para su mas perfecto arreglo y establecimiento, 1782–84, 1786, and 1788; Alcabalas, Caja 24, Libro Común y Gral. de la Administración Principal de la Real Rta de Alcavalas de Quito del Cargo de Dn Bernardo Darquea Adminr Gral, Dn Domingo de Echeverria, Contador Principal (hereafter cited as Libro Común), 1791, 1793, and 1796; Alcabalas, Caja 25, Libro Real Común 1798–99; Alcabalas, Caja 26, Libro Rl. Comun y Gral . . . , 1801, and 1803; Alcabalas, Caja 27, Libro Comun y Gral, 1804–06; Alcabalas, Caja 28, Libro Manual de Alcavalas, 1807–1808; and Fernández Martínez, *La alcabala en la Audiencia de Quito*, 89.

61. Goods sent to interior cities like Quito were liable to pay only the *mayor aumento* if they had paid the full *alcabala* earlier. There is even some evidence that merchants lobbied successfully to pay only this lesser tax in Quito. See, for example, ANH–Q, Alcabalas, Caja 12, Quaderno de Abaluos de Mayor Aumento, 1796 y 1797. Such entries are exceedingly rare in the customs house records, however, leading me to believe that goods were most often charged the full 3-percent tax.

tagena through Popayán and Pasto. The customs accounts do not always specify clearly the port of entry for European imports, but in the 1780s most entered through Guayaquil. In the decade from 1786 to 1796, the influx of European wares at the coastal port reached new heights, and merchants apparently sent considerable quantities of the merchandise to the highlands. During this decade, 70–80 percent of the European products sold legally in Quito came from the coast. By the late 1790s, however, customs inspectors reported that only 50–60 percent of the European imports entered through Guayaquil; the remainder entered through New Granada. By the early nineteenth century, about half the European goods sold in the city came from the coast and half from Popayán.[62] In short, when Guayaquil was glutted with European wares, coastal merchants could dominate the highland markets, but as the war in Europe disrupted the Pacific trade, an increasing share of these goods came via New Granada.

Tax receipts on rural estates, local trade, internal consumption, and legal transactions also confirm the prolonged economic malaise in the region. The amounts raised from these levies account for just 12–25 percent of the funds raised by such taxes in Guayaquil (see Table 6.5).[63] Despite the much larger population of the north-central highlands, the century-long recession clearly had depressed tax revenues. The only reason for the jump in these revenues between 1780 and 1790 (see Table 6.5) was the administrative decision to have the suboffices temporarily remit their income to the Quito office, instead of sending the funds directly to the nearest treasury office (*caja real*).[64]

Exports from the north-central highlands

Despite the declining *obraje* economy, textiles remained the principal export of the north-central highlands. According to some estimates, *obrajeros* and cottage producers still made 250,000–750,000 pesos worth of cloth, hats, and rugs. The bulk of these textiles went to markets in New Granada, but as much as one-third may have been consumed locally. *Obrajeros* often paid their laborers in cloth, not cash, forcing the largely Amerindian work force to consume any surplus product.[65]

---

62. *Ibid.*

63. See AGI, Quito 478–482B, Cuentas de la Aduana de Guayaquil, 1780–1808.

64. Fernández Martínez, *La alcabala en la Audiencia de Quito*, 111–12.

65. The figures on late colonial cloth production are only very crude estimates. Robson Tyrer indicates that minimal estimates for value of cloth production are 1 or 2 million pesos in the heyday of the *obraje* economy in the seventeenth century. He estimates that this production declined 50–75 percent by 1800. Tyrer, "Demographic and Economic History," 221–24, 252, and 323.

By the late colonial period, merchants sent most exportable goods northward through Popayán. In 1791, for example, customs inspectors in Popayán collected over 70 percent of the taxes levied on goods from Quito.[66] Only very small amounts of cloth or artisan products went to the coast, which received this sort of merchandise from Cuenca. Moreover, customs accounts from Popayán list cloth as the only significant export from the north-central sierra. The remaining commodities were either exempt from the sales tax, escaped the notice of inspectors, or paid only insignificant amounts.

The dwindling of cloth exports registered at the customs office in Popayán provides additional evidence of the textile industry's overall decline. Inspectors in Popayán recorded an average of 702 *cargas* (mule loads) of cloth between 1782 and 1802, worth approximately 91,000 pesos.[67] Customs revenues rose from 1,978 pesos in 1782 to a high of 4,204 pesos in 1797, and thereafter declined precipitously. In 1802, the customs officers in Popayán recorded only 100 *cargas* of cloth, worth a mere 395 pesos in taxes (see Table 6.6). Although legal cloth exports had recovered to 458 *cargas* in 1814, that figure had dropped again to 257 *cargas* in 1824.[68]

The sales tax receipts for the north-central sierra indicate that the regional economic decline produced a serious imbalance between imports and exports. By the late colonial period, the region probably imported between 200,000 pesos and 400,000 pesos in European and colonial merchandise annually.[69] This was much below the import levels in Guayaquil and probably represented a 50-percent drop for the highlands from the late seventeenth century.[70] At the same time, cloth exports through Popayán, which accounted for most of the region's earnings, never exceeded 150,000–200,000 pesos annually, leaving a substantial deficit.[71] Some of this shortfall might be explained by a general tendency among customs inspectors in New Granada to undervalue *Quiteño* exports or by the con-

---

66. Robson Tyrer lists a total of 850 *cargas* of cloth exported from Quito. As Table 6.6 indicates, nearly 590 *cargas* passed through Popayán and paid customs duties – a total of 71 percent. Tyrer, "Demographic and Economic History," 262.

67. AGI, Quito, 519, Alcabalas de Popayán, 1782–1803.

68. *Ibid.*

69. This estimate is based on figures presented by Carlos Presenti on imports in 1780 and projecting the total value of imports from customs receipts. Both are extremely speculative and give only the most general estimate of imports. AGI, Quito, 240, Copia de Informe, 31 agosto 1780; and Fernández Martínez, *La alcabala en la Audiencia de Quito*, 157–60.

70. For an estimate of imports in the seventeenth century, see Tyrer, "Demographic and Economic History," 241, 270.

71. These figures are estimates calculated from the export figures in AGI, Quito, 519, Alcabalas de Popayán, 1782–1802. These figures probably represented approximately 70 percent of total export earnings.

Table 6.6. *Cloth exported from the North-central sierra
through Popayán, 1782-1802*

Year	Cargas of Cloth	Taxes Collected (in pesos de ocho)
1782	522.5	1,978
1783	708.0	2,741
1784	749.5	2,815
1791	589.5	2,222
1792	693.5	2,751
1793	814.5	3,175
1794	828.5	3,226
1795	1,005.5	3,903
1796	896.25	3,469
1797	1,064.0	4,204
1798	620.5	2,424
1799	853.5	3,317
1800	586.0	2,229
1801	502.0	1,958
1802	100.5	395
Total	10,534.25	40,807

Source: AGI, Quito, 519, Alcabalas de Popayán,
1782-1802.

traband trade. Invisible earnings, however, also played a central role in easing this apparent deficit. Quito was the kingdom's capital, and the Bourbon Reforms promoted a substantial increase in the size of the bureaucracy and public sector outlays. Government salaries and other miscellaneous payments totaled at least 150,000 pesos annually, disbursed from the regional taxes and remittances from treasuries in Cuenca and Guayaquil.[72] The growing size of bureaucratic salaries and government transfer payments probably explain how elites afforded the rising level of European imports. In effect, the late colonial state promoted a reallocation of resources from the coastal export economy, the south highlands, and the Amerindian communities to support the consumption of highland elites. This shift of wealth may well explain why highland elites proved so complacent, despite the harmful effects of Bourbon trade policies on local manufacturing. Although bureaucratic jobs and government subsidies helped the *Quiteño* upper classes over the short run, they also made

---

72. For these figures, see: AGI, Quito, 420–29, Cuentas de la Caja de Quito, 1780–1803; Fernández Martínez, *La alcabala en la Audiencia de Quito*, 66–69; and AGI, Quito, 407, Razon de los empleos, Quito, 12 marzo 1783; AGI, Quito, 409, José García de Leon y Pizarro to José de Gálvez, Quito, 2 julio 1783.

Table 6.7. *Sales tax revenues in Cuenca, 1786-1803*

Year	Total	American Imports	European Imports	Local Trade
1786	9,061	3,718	3,121	2,220
1787	8,852	2,715	3,247	2,890
1788	5,490	2,434	1,050	2,006
1789	7,088	3,064	1,738	2,286
1790	7,972	2,150	2,538	3,284
1791	6,611	2,147	870	3,594
1792	9,015	2,890	2,667	3,458
1793	8,523	2,893	401	5,229^a
1794	11,543	2,765	451	8,327^a
1795	8,151	3,327	1,498	3,326
1796	7,479	2,979	1,444	3,056
1797	8,193	2,372	2,010	3,811
1798	10,400	2,642	1,627	6,131
1799	9,319	3,545	1,748	4,026
1800	10,235	3,364	2,871	4,000
1801	6,822	3,105	1,307	2,410
1802	10,653	2,922	1,631	6,100
1803	10,216	2,946	2,578	4,692
Total	155,623	51,978	32,797	70,848

^{a}Debts are included in these figures.
Source: AGI, Quito, 459, Alcabalas de Cuenca, 1786-1803.

the regional economy directly dependent on the colonial state and indirectly dependent on the prosperity of the coastal and south highland economies.

Cuenca and the south highland trade

Customs taxes from the province of Cuenca demonstrate the modest scale of the regional economy and its overall stability from 1786 to 1803. Total revenues normally fluctuated annually between 6,000 pesos and 10,000 pesos, approximately one-half the amount collected in the Quito office (see Table 6.7).[73] After all, the region supervised by the Cuenca customs network had less than 30 percent of the population of the north-central sierra. The bulk of these sales tax revenues (54 percent) came from

73. Although Loja operated its own state-controlled customs house from 1786, I located none of its accounts in Quito or Seville. As a result, Table 6.7 includes data only from the Cuenca region, which had subordinate offices in Cañar, Jabon y Oña, Gualaseo, Paute, and Azogues. Since the Cuenca province had approximately 80 percent of the population of the south sierra and dominated the regional economy, the accounts from its customs house undoubtedly represent overall trends for the entire southern zone.

levies on American and European imports. The only other important items were the varied taxes on local production and commerce: the tax on rural properties accounted for 20 percent of the total, and charges on legal contracts amounted to 12 percent.[74]

Cuenca's import trade

Unlike Guayaquil or Quito, the Cuenca region imported more American than European merchandise during the late colonial period. Colonial goods produced 51,978 pesos in tax receipts, while European imports yielded only 32,797 pesos from 1786 to 1803 (see Table 6.7). Apparently the elite market for European luxury goods – such as cloth, clothing products, artisan goods, and wines – remained small in the south highlands. Iron, wines, brandy, paper, ink, wax, hats, agave, pita, dyes, and raw cotton formed the bulk of the colonial produce sold in the region.[75] Merchants also imported dyes and cotton in abundance to support the local cottage textile industry, which probably explains why tax receipts on American goods continually exceeded returns on European luxuries.

Lima merchants dominated the regional import trade in Cuenca; 73 percent of the goods introduced into Cuenca came from the Viceroyalty of Peru (see Table 6.8). Only 14 percent of the imported merchandise came from the coast, but Lima-based commercial houses also controlled most of this commerce. Taken together these two trade circuits accounted for an average of 87 percent of the imported goods coming to the south highlands from 1786 through 1803 (see Table 6.8).

Merchants in Quito managed the northern trade networks, but they seldom introduced more than 15 percent of the imported taxed merchandise. The only exception was in 1802, when northern traders captured 64 percent of the legal import market in Cuenca, following the return of neutral trade (see Table 6.8). All of these goods from Quito were European wares; apparently the advent of neutral trade allowed merchants in New Granada to restock their storehouses more rapidly than Peruvian traders. Tax receipts from European goods introduced into Quito had reached high levels during that period, and the northerners must have sent their surplus southward for a few years (see Table 6.5).

Peruvian merchants controlled most of the trade routes supplying colonial imports to the Cuenca region. In 1802, for example, nearly 22 percent of this American merchandise came through Guayaquil, princi-

---

74. The remaining commercial levies on *pulperías* and foodstuffs accounted for the remainder. AGI, Quito, 459, Alcabalas de Cuenca, 1786–1803.
75. Silvia Palomeque, "Historia económica de Cuenca y sus relaciones regionales (desde fines del siglo XVIII a principios del XIX), *Segundo encuentro de historia y realidad económica y social del Ecuador*, 3 vols. (Cuenca, 1978), 1:97–98, 114.

Table 6.8. *Origin of European and American goods imported into Cuenca, 1786-1803*

Year	Highlands	Coast	Viceroyalty of Peru
1786	4.6%	17.7%	77.7%
1787	7.0%	4.0%	89.0%
1788	10.0%	15.0%	75.0%
1789	11.0%	21.0%	68.0%
1790	3.0%	14.0%	83.0%
1791	24.0%	24.0%	52.0%
1792	4.0%	4.0%	92.0%
1793	4.0%	50.0%	46.0%
1794	12.0%	31.0%	57.0%
1795	13.0%	4.0%	83.0%
1796	4.0%	7.0%	89.0%
1797	4.0%	26.0%	70.0%
1798	19.0%	24.0%	57.0%
1799	9.0%	11.0%	80.0%
1800	15.5%	1.5%	83.0%
1801	15.0%	9.0%	76.0%
1802	64.0%	28.0%	8.0%
1803	27.0%	18.5%	54.5%
Total	13.0%	14.0%	73.0%

Source: AGI, Quito, 459, Alcabalas de Cuenca, 1786-1803.

pally wines, dyes, iron, paper, wax, pita, and artisan goods. Some of these goods, like pita and hats from Jipijapa, came originally from the coast, but the rest originated in Peru. Raw cotton and soap from northern Peru and Loja represented nearly 52 percent of the value of colonial imports in 1802. In addition, merchants from these southern regions sent artisan goods, foodstuffs, leather, mules, and sugar, which accounted for 8 percent of the taxable merchandise. The remainder (mostly cloth, foodstuffs, artisan goods, cochineal, cinnamon, and *anís*) came from the north-central sierra.[76] The principal raw materials for the cloth trade emanated from Peru, while the remaining imports came from a diverse group of regional suppliers.

The customs taxes on rural properties, internal consumption, local trade, and legal transactions often equaled or exceeded the amounts levied on either American or European imports. These tax receipts still only represented one-fifth of the sums collected in the north-central sierra and

76. *Ibid.*

a mere fraction of the amounts raised along the coast.[77] The bulk of these revenues came from the levies on rural estates and legal transactions.[78] Thus, taxation in the south highlands remained light, which undoubtedly proved conducive to the overall growth of the regional textile industry.

Cuenca's export trade

Peruvian merchants controlled the export of locally produced cottons and woolens, shipping approximately 54 percent of them by the sea route from Guayaquil by the early nineteenth century. The rest went overland through Piura.[79] The major markets were in Peru, Chile, and the Guayaquil region. In 1802, for example, the trade permits issued by the Cuenca customs officials indicated that cloth valued at 85,728 pesos went to Lima, with 84,179 pesos in textiles going to Guayaquil, 42,748 pesos to Chile, and 20,333 pesos to northern Peru.[80] Merchants shipped cloth valued at only 2,497 pesos to the central sierra and an additional 2,035 pesos worth of textiles to Panama.[81]

The tax revenues collected on cloth leaving Guayaquil rose steadily throughout the late colonial period. Sales taxes collected on *tocuyos* and *bayetas* from the south highlands (shown in Table 6.9) rose from 1,397 pesos in 1780 to 3,228 pesos in 1808. Some of these textiles undoubtedly went to clothe wage workers in the cities and slaves on coastal plantations, with the rest going to Peru. By the late colonial period, producers in Cuenca had captured virtually all of the textile market in Guayaquil, effectively shutting out producers from the north-central highlands.

The other major outlet for southern cloth was the overland route to Piura. Taxes collected on cloth from the south sierra rose to a peak of 3,378 pesos in 1800 and declined thereafter (see Table 6.9). This overland route was not any more expensive than shipping goods by sea, and it required less in cash outlays by merchants.[82] The major impediment was the 6-percent sales tax collected in Piura, twice the amount levied in Guayaquil.[83] The relatively small amount of cloth taxed in Piura, however, amounted to under 25 percent of the total cloth trade, not the 40–

77. AGI, Quito, 478–482B, Cuentas de la Aduana de Guayaquil, 1779–1808; Fernández Martínez, *La alcabala en la Audiencia de Quito*, 71–118, 157–67.
78. These two *ramos* account for approximately 75 percent of the non-import taxes at the customs house in Cuenca for most years. AGI, Quito, 459, Alcabalas de Cuenca, 1786–1803.
79. Silvia Palomeque, "Loja y en el mercado interno colonial," *HISLA*, 2 (1983): 36, Cuadro I.
80. Palomeque, "Historia económica de Cuenca," 114, Cuadro 3.
81. *Ibid.*
82. Palomeque, "Loja en el mercado interno colonial," 37–39.
83. AGI, Quito, 531, Alcabalas de Piura, 1789–1809.

Table 6.9. *Taxes on exports from Cuenca, 1780-1809*
(in pesos de ocho reales)

Year	To Piura[a]	To Guayaquil
1780	No records	1,397
1781	No records	1,788
1782	No records	1,786
1783	No records	1,486
1784	No records	1,130
1785	No records	947
1786	No records	1,524
1787	No records	1,303
1788	No records	1,484
1789	1,340	1,122
1790	1,319	1,038
1791	1,171	1,260
1792	1,352	1,366
1793	1,218	1,582
1794	1,167	1,740
1795	1,047	1,820
1796	3,733	12
1797	1,500	1,312
1798	1,973	2,578
1799	1,854	2,338
1800	3,378	2,991
1801	1,080	2,600
1802	1,328	No records
1803	1,429	No records
1804	952	No records
1805	706	2,363
1806	907	2,241
1807	1,505	3,349
1808	662	3,228
1809	633	No records
Total	30,254	47,127

[a]Goods passing from Cuenca to Piura paid a 6 percent *alcabala*, while those passing to Guayaquil paid only 3 percent. As a result, the true value of the goods going to Piura was approximately one-half the value of the goods paying taxes at the coastal port.

Source: AGI, Quito, 478-482B, Cuentas de la Aduana de Guayaquil, 1780-1808; AGI, Quito, 531, Alcabalas de Piura, 1789-1809.

50 percent estimated from examining the trade permits for the early nineteenth century.[84] Apparently the high sales tax encouraged merchants to avoid registering their cargoes with customs officials in Piura or, at least, to bribe them and avoid paying the full 6-percent tax levy. In any case, the taxes collected in Piura probably represented only approximately one-half the real trade in cloth taking that overland trade route.

The south highlands apparently experienced no long-term trade deficits, at least until the export trade declined during the independence wars. Local textile exports reached a minimum of 110,000 pesos annually, and, together with annual outlays of approximately 25,000 pesos in government salaries, they probably equaled the value of imports.[85] The prosperity of the entire south highland economy, however, rested with the Peruvian merchant-entrepreneurs, who organized the putting–out system of manufacturing and sold the merchandise in Peru. Once these merchants abandoned their business in the south highlands during the dislocations of the independence era, a prolonged commercial decline ensued, leading to economic autarky.[86]

The Bourbon Reforms promoted the development of economic regionalism rather than an integrated network of markets in the Kingdom of Quito. By the late colonial period, commercial connections for the kingdom's three major markets in Quito, Guayaquil, and Cuenca extended throughout the Spanish Pacific. The Guayaquil region had expanded its commercial links with traders from Mexico City to Lima, supplying cacao and other coastal products in exchange for a wide range of European and American goods. These external connections far overshadowed the port's traditional role as the major commercial outlet for the sierra. Likewise, after cloth producers in the north-central sierra lost Peruvian markets to foreign competition, they sent most of their textiles to New Granada. Northern merchants also gradually gained an advantage over Guayaquil suppliers by the early nineteenth century, providing the majority of the European imports entering the Quito market. The south sierra developed its primary commercial ties with the Viceroyalty of Peru and the coast,

84. Palomeque, "Loja en el mercado interno colonial," 36.
85. Palomeque, "Historia económica de Cuenca," 114. This figure probably accounted for over 90 percent of the region's export earning, other than *cascarilla*. The figures for the export of cloth through Piura were adjusted upwards to attain this figure, so that they represented 44 percent of the total export earnings. This amounted to approximately 50,000 pesos annually, a minimal figure. The figure for the amounts exported through Guayaquil were calculated from the sales tax figures listed in Table 6.9 (multiplying the tax figure by 33.33). This was done to correspond to the amounts given by Silvia Palomeque from the libros de guía, see her "Loja en el mercado interno colonial," 36.
86. The *cascarilla* trade also declined during this period; see AGI, Quito, 276, Matias Lopez Escudero, "Expediente sobre el libre comercio de Cascarilla," Cuenca, 15 octubre 1790.

exchanging local cloth through Guayaquil and the overland route via
Piura. These commercial links to external markets within the empire
ultimately proved far more important than the mutual economic ties
binding these economic centers of the kingdom together. In the end, this
produced three relatively weak market systems rather than a single, uni-
fied national market.

The commercial system imposed by the Bourbon monarchs also promoted economic dependency. Although trade liberalization allowed
coastal planters to expand their commercial links with imperial markets
and the international economy, Lima and Mexico City merchants controlled the commercial life of this booming coastal zone. In addition,
Lima commercial houses dominated the cottage textile industry of the
south highlands. Even in the depressed north-central sierra, local elites
depended on merchants in Guayaquil and New Granada. Highland elites
also became increasingly reliant on the economic benefits derived from
the expanding colonial government in Quito, which channeled funds
from the more prosperous coastal and southern economies to the capital's
bureaucratic and service sectors.

When the independence struggles led to the breakdown of this powerful state, commercial life in the kingdom suffered. Conflicts in Europe
curtailed the supply of luxury imports, and the colonial state's slow-
motion collapse between 1809 and 1830 disrupted commercial trade networks throughout the Pacific. Quito's ties with New Granada declined,
and the disintegration of the colonial state apparatus removed the transfer
payments from Cuenca and Guayaquil, which supported the bureaucratic
and service sectors so central to the capital's economy. Once merchants
from Lima also began to abandon the cottage textile industry in the south
sierra, a major commercial recession enveloped that region. Only Guayaquil managed to maintain some measure of prosperity. The cacao trade
to New Spain and Europe remained vigorous, even after the disruptions
in the Atlantic trade.[87] Many other coastal exports, however, marketed
throughout the Pacific, declined along with the imperial trading system.
In short, as the late colonial commercial system disintegrated, the economies of the Kingdom of Quito experienced difficult, unpredictable
times. The future held decline, not prosperity.

87. Cacao imports to New Spain averaged 356,063 pesos in value between 1825 and 1828. See
    John Kicza, "Mexican Merchants and Their Links to Spain, 1750–1850," in Kenneth J. Andrien
    and Lyman L. Johnson, eds., *The Political Economy of Spanish America in the Age of Revolution, 1750–
    1850* (Albuquerque, NM, 1994), Table 4, 127.

PART II

Reform and political conflict

7

Political turmoil and economic decline, 1690–1778

By the late seventeenth century, the political regime in the Kingdom of Quito had become deeply divided by partisan conflicts. Like most important provinces, Quito was governed by an *audiencia*, but the justices were all venal officeholders with strong political, business, and social ties to regional elites. As a result of these relationships, the judges continually became enmeshed in local factional squabbles, making it impossible for them to dominate the political arena and respond consistently to metropolitan dictates. The same problems plagued the small coterie of fiscal officials and provincial magistrates, whose powers had been diminished over time by concessions to local magnates. The *corregidores de indios* in the region, for example, had lost their control over the collection of Amerindian tribute in 1734 to private tax farmers. For the most part, metropolitan governments in Madrid paid scant attention to strengthening the weak judicial state apparatus in Quito, unless local political conflicts in the kingdom became too disruptive. As a result, state policies most often evolved from the complex interplay of self-interested peninsular and creole elite factions, occasionally moderated by political pressures from local middle, laboring, or peasant classes. It was a time of endemic political conflict.

Persistent economic malaise in the Kingdom of Quito made matters of public policy particularly disruptive in this highly charged political environment. On three separate occasions – in 1711, 1738, and 1765 – crown policies and local socioeconomic problems intermingled to provoke bitter discord, which paralyzed the political process in the kingdom. During their tenures as president of the *audiencia*, two political outsiders, Juan de Sosaya (1707–16) and José de Araujo y Rio (1736–47), caused serious imbroglios when they began blatantly advancing their political and business interests during periods of acute economic distress. The last major crisis emerged when Viceroy Pedro Messía de la Cerda attempted to wrest control of the lucrative sales and cane liquor taxes from local elites in 1765. This action threatened to undermine the local economy in Quito, and it incited a major insurrection in the city, which overthrew the *audiencia* and established a popular government that ruled until the arrival of royal troops over one year later. In each of these cases, consensus within the political system broke down as crown officials, local creole elites, and even the popular sectors divided over how to deal with the pressing economic problems in the kingdom. In short, economic decline formed the backdrop for disruptive political conflicts in Bourbon Quito.

By 1766, the corrupt institutions of the judicial state had proven incapable of sustaining royal authority in the *audiencia* district. Crown officials and local elites had failed to restore economic prosperity or even maintain order as political life degenerated into a barely disguised scramble among interest groups to loot what remained of the region's economic assets. As a result, in the aftermath of the 1765 Quito uprising the Madrid government dismissed any plans for moderate reforms and turned to more drastic solutions. In 1778, the crown initiated a complete overhaul of the political system, establishing a new administrative order grafted onto the older judicial state founded by the Habsburgs in the sixteenth century.

The French trade and the case of Juan de Sosaya

The first major political altercation in eighteenth-century Quito erupted after the demographic and economic crises of the 1690s. The succession wars in Spain had undermined the decrepit system of *flotas* and *galeones*, giving French traders an opportunity to enter the Pacific and sell large quantities of European cloth, which captured lucrative markets formerly supplied by Quito's *obrajeros*. Some enterprising Peruvian and Mexican merchants added to these woes by taking advantage of the glut in oriental goods in Acapulco and shipping them illegally throughout South America.[1] This led to a steady decline in the price of *Quiteño* woolens, particularly in the Lima market. Merchants and cloth producers in Quito remained divided over how to deal with these dire economic circumstances, which subverted Quito's traditional role in the colonial economic order.

During these hard times, Juan de Sosaya, a prominent Lima merchant, purchased the *audiencia* presidency in Quito for 20,000 pesos, assuming his duties in March 1707.[2] Sosaya found his new post filled with unex-

---

1. This glut occurred because oriental goods could no longer be sent easily to Europe during the War of the Spanish Succession; in fact, by 1706 the merchant guild (*consulado*) of Lima claimed that the Mexican trade comprised 90 percent of all Peruvian commerce. See George Robertson Dilg, "The Collapse of the Portobelo Fairs: A Study in Spanish Commercial Reform, 1720–1740" (Ph.D. diss., Indiana University, 1975), 35.
2. Archivo General de Indias (hereafter cited as AGI), Quito, 106, Real decreto, Madrid, 25 mayo 1706. Sosaya wanted the post for himself or his cousin Pedro de Sosaya, a leading member of

pected challenges. Apart from the daunting economic problems facing the government and local elites, the ruling *audiencia* was rent by incessant factional disputes.

The judges of Quito's high court were an extremely eccentric and fractious group, which undoubtedly contributed to the political divisions in the province. One justice, Cristóbal de Ceballos, was infamous for his unorthodox religious beliefs. At his birthday party, for example, Ceballos claimed to see the virgin arise from a meat pie (*empanada*). He then sought to hold a special mass, celebrating "our Lady of the *Empanada*," but the bishop immediately took stern steps to quell the cult.[3] Another judge, Juan de Ricauarte, was notorious for his domestic discord. Ricauarte allegedly beat his wife and even tried to poison her when she took refuge in a convent. This colorful but quarrelsome group fought among themselves in a shifting series of temporary alliances.[4]

The predecessor of Juan de Sosaya as president, Francisco López Dicastillo, had been an ambitious but arrogant leader whose actions only worsened the existing climate of political discord in the court.[5] On 25 June 1705, for example, López Dicastillo prompted a dispute on the bench by ordering a local rancher, Juan de Villacis, to send a herd of cattle to the capital for the city's butcher shops. Villacis hoped to delay compliance until his cattle fattened, so that he could fetch a higher price for them. When López Dicastillo threatened to bring the cattle to Quito by force, Villacis appealed the decision to the *audiencia* on a day when the president had left the chamber early.[6] The principal political foe of López Dicastillo, *oidor* Juan de Ricauarte, agreed to consider the case, but the president's staunch ally, Judge Tomás Fernández Pérez, objected and

the Lima merchant guild; the men were allegedly business partners. Federico González Suárez, *Historia general de la República del Ecuador* (Quito, 1970 edn.), 835.

3. Mark A. Burkholder and D. S. Chandler, *Biographical Dictionary of Audiencia Ministers in the Americas, 1687–1821* (Westport, CT, 1982), 85.

4. AGI, Quito, 128, Francisco López Dicastillo to crown, Quito, 6 junio 1704 and 30 diciembre 1704; Quito 103, Consulta, Madrid, 17 abril 1716.

5. The arrival of a new president usually altered the configuration of factional alignments in Quito, as politicians tried to curry favor with their new leader and gain a temporary advantage. Evidence of this sort of jockeying for political position is evident in the complaint of Justice Fernando de Sierra Osorio that his colleagues Lorenzo Lastero de Salazar and Tomás Fernández Pérez tried to block his appointment to succeed Attorney Antonio de Ron as judge for the revision of land titles (*venta y composición de tierras*). In the squabbles over the Sosaya case, Sierra Osorio and Lastero de Salazar often sided together in defense of the president. AGI, Quito, 128, Fernando de Sierra Osorio to crown, Latacunga, 24 September 1708; AGI, Quito, Escribanía de Cámara, 913A, Autos de Juan de Sosaya, Quito, 14 septiembre 1707.

6. The city council of Quito had written on 10 August 1705 complaining about numerous irregularities in the government of López Dicastillo, harmful to the indigenous population working in the textile mills and their traditional villages. AGI, Quito, 102, Consulta, Madrid, 1 diciembre 1708.

rose to leave the court chamber, thus preventing a quorum and delaying a hearing.[7] The two justices exchanged insults, apparently drew weapons, and created such a ruckus that the remaining *oidor*, Fernando de Sierra Osorio, had to intercede to prevent violence.[8]

Before Sierra Osorio could calm the quarreling justices, President López Dicastillo returned with a friend, Cristóbal de Xijón. Xijón immediately intervened in the dispute on behalf of Fernández Pérez and began to manhandle Justice Ricauarte. Order was not restored until a constable arrived, took Xijón to jail, and separated the feuding judges. López Dicastillo only exacerbated the dispute later that evening when he went to the city jail himself and secured the release of Xijón.[9] Although this move ended the disgraceful episode, bitter feelings endured. Each side in the dispute wrote a series of angry letters to Spain for over a decade, prompting the Council of the Indies to order Fernández Pérez transferred to Santo Domingo and Ricauarte to Panama.[10] Both justices remained on duty in Quito when Sosaya arrived in 1707, however, and their mutual animosity continued to poison the political atmosphere in the capital.[11]

Despite such lingering factional strife, the presidency of Quito must have seemed a valuable prize to an enterprising merchant clan such as the Sosayas. Controlling access to the overland roads passing through Quito and the sea lanes to the Pacific port of Guayaquil could prove a tremendous boon for any Lima merchant house engaging in legal or contraband commerce, particularly during the lean years following the collapse of the fleet system and the French incursions. Nevertheless, such aspirations were also bound to arouse jealousy among the kingdom's faction-ridden elites. While some prominent families could benefit from

7. López Dicastillo had a low opinion of most of the judges, especially Juan de Ricauarte. He wrote the crown in 1704 about Ricauarte's domestic problems and suspended the judge over the matter. The viceroy, however, forced Dicastillo to reinstate the justice. Fernández Pérez apparently insulted Ricauarte in the court chambers about the scandalous rumors concerning his strained relationship with his wife. AGI, Quito, 128, Francisco López Dicastillo to crown, Quito, 6 junio 1704 and 30 diciembre 1704; AGI, Quito, 103, Consulta, Madrid, 17 abril 1716.

8. The witnesses disagreed over whether or not the judges drew weapons. According to Sierra Osorio, who separated the feuding men, neither did so. AGI, Quito, 102, Consulta, Madrid, 1 diciembre 1708; AGI, Quito, 103, Consulta, Madrid, 17 abril 1716.

9. López Dicastillo inflamed the situation even further by threatening to put Ricauarte in chains; the stubborn judge replied that he would seek redress before the viceroy once again to thwart the president. The president also ordered the court to remove the order confiscating Xijón's possessions, which also outraged his enemies, such as Ricauarte. AGI, Quito, 102, Consulta, Madrid, 1 diciembre 1708.

10. AGI, Quito, 128, López Dicastillo to crown, Quito, 30 diciembre 1704; AGI, Quito, 128, Fernando de Sierra Osorio to crown, Quito, 24 septiembre 1708; AGI, Quito, 102, Consulta, Madrid, 1 diciembre 1708; and AGI, Quito, 103, Consulta, Madrid, 17 abril 1716.

11. The Council of the Indies did not make its final ruling on this case until 1720. See AGI, Quito, 103, Consulta, 17 abril 1716; 4 abril 1720.

allying with the new president, many others had long chafed under the restrictive control of Lima merchants such as the Sosayas and yearned for greater economic freedom. Regardless of their inclination, however, most local merchants and cloth producers faced serious economic problems after the influx of French cloth. They were extremely sensitive to any possibility that a merchant like the new president might enact policies to weaken their economic interests further.

Rumors quickly circulated that Juan de Sosaya used his powers to trade in contraband cacao, cloth, and oriental goods through Guayaquil, where the president's close friend, Juan de Meléndez, served as *corregidor*.[12] Indeed, many of the president's foes even speculated that such abuses were merely a continuation of Sosaya's previous contraband activities, begun while serving as admiral of the fleet and later magistrate in Guayaquil. Some rumormongers even alleged that one load of contraband worth 57,000 pesos went to Chancay, south of Lima, to the home of the president's cousin and business partner, Pedro de Sosaya, a prominent member of the Lima *consulado*.[13] Such tales did not endear Juan de Sosaya to many in the beleaguered merchant and cloth-manufacturing communities of Quito.

When the *corregidor* of Quito, Juan Gutiérrez Pelayo, intercepted a cargo of trade goods in 1708, apparently containing illicit Chinese cloth, many blamed the president. This rumor gained added currency when two *audiencia* justices, Lorenzo Lastero de Salazar and Cristóbal de Ceballos, refused to unpack the merchandise before sending it to the royal treasury *caja*. When Gutiérrez Pelayo insisted on opening the crates, both justices suspended the magistrate and exiled him in retaliation. After the treasury officers released the goods unopened to the president's partner (who later sold them openly in Quito), Gutiérrez Pelayo and other angry citizens wrote Madrid demanding an investigation.[14] Moreover, Sosaya's enemies gained a powerful ally when Diego Ladrón de Guevara, the bishop of Quito, became interim viceroy of Peru in 1710. The bishop had feuded so openly with the president that Sosaya was preparing to expel him from the city; only the prelate's appointment as viceroy interrupted his plans.[15]

12. AGI, Quito, 103, Minutas del Consejo de Indias, Madrid, 14 febrero 1711.

13. *Ibid.*; AGI, Quito, 267, Instrucciones de la pesquisa contra Juan de Sosaya, Madrid, 11 julio 1711.

14. Among those opposing Juan de Sosaya were the following: Antonio Gómez, *regidor* of the Guayaquil *cabildo*; Antonio Zerero, that city's *depositario general*; and in Quito, Magistrate Gutiérrez Pelayo, Francisco Medina Davila, Félix de Luna, Juan Bauptista del Castilla Caveza de Vaca, and Juan de Medrano. AGI, Quito, 103, Minutas del Consejo de Indias, Madrid, 14 febrero 1711. According to Sosaya, Gutiérrez Pelayo became his enemy when the president closed down the magistrate's gambling house in Quito. AGI, Escribanía de Cámara, 913A, Auto de Juan de Sosaya, Quito, 14 septiembre 1707.

15. González Suárez, *Historia general*, 849.

With Ladrón de Guevara as the viceroy of Peru, Sosaya faced an imposing array of enemies dedicated to his political destruction.

As numerous letters from prominent citizens denouncing Juan de Sosaya arrived in Madrid, a case against the president mounted. His accusers first charged that Sosaya had earned the enormous sum of 884,787 pesos in the contraband trade. In addition, the president allegedly supplied meat to Quito at inflated prices, which had nearly provoked a riot among the poor in the urban parishes. According to the president's critics, only the intercession of the priors of Santo Domingo and La Merced and the parish priests in the *barrios* averted an uprising.[16] His enemies also claimed that Sosaya had conspired with mill owners to force local Amerindians to buy cloth at artificially high prices. Moreover, he supposedly engaged in nepotism, naming a notorious debtor and malcontent, Vicente Caguenas, to head a local hospital and even allowed parties and dances in the house of an "immoral woman" during the solemn holiday of Saint Rose.[17] It was a serious set of allegations, which the Council of the Indies could not ignore.

During the War of the Spanish Succession, French and English contrabandists threatened to usurp much of the Indies trade, which made the Madrid government loathe to tolerate any shenanigans from colonial officials serving in strategic posts, such as Juan de Sosaya. In a rare display of administrative vigor, the Council of the Indies named Juan Bautista de Orueta y Irusta – a justice on the Lima court serving as interim governor of Panama – to head a special investigation (*pesquisa*) of the allegations against Sosaya in 1711. The council's instructions to Orueta also named him interim president of the *Audiencia* of Quito and authorized him to suspend Sosaya, exile him (along with Justices Ceballos and Lastero de Salazar), and remove Justices Ricauarte and Sierra Osorio from the case. The council further empowered Orueta to confiscate the assets of Sosaya, fine him 4,000 pesos (and the implicated justices 2,000 pesos each), and send the president to prison in Spain. The councilors clearly believed the worst about Juan de Sosaya, a merchant-politician apparently abusing his powers.[18]

16. AGI, Quito, 267, Francisco Xavier de Luna to crown, Quito, 3 agosto 1718.
17. AGI, Quito, Instrucciones de la pesquisa contra Juan de Sosaya, Madrid, 11 julio 1711; AGI, Quito, 102, Consulta, Madrid, 14 febrero 1711 and 11 junio 1711. The Caguenas case was a complicated one. He allegedly purchased the post of *alcalde provincial* for 6,000 pesos but was prohibited from serving because of outstanding debts. The *audiencia* ordered his arrest, but he escaped and found refuge in the church of La Merced. His friend, Juan de Ricauarte, prevailed on his ally, President Sosaya, to free Caguenas and appoint him to head the hospital. The action outraged the enemies of Caguenas, who charged that he had embezzled funds. AGI, Quito, 267, Instrucciones de la pesquisa contra Juan de Sosaya, Madrid, 11 julio 1711.
18. Burkholder and Chandler, *Biographical Dictionary*, 245; AGI, Quito, 267, Instrucciones de la

Given the complex political undercurrents in Quito, after arriving in 1712 Orueta found it difficult to remain impartial. His superior, Interim Viceroy Ladrón de Guevara, along with many prominent citizens of Quito and Guayaquil, clearly wanted Sosaya convicted. On the other hand, the president had a formidable array of his own allies, including Justices Juan de Ricauarte, Cristóbal de Ceballos, Fernando de Sierra Osorio, and José de Laysequilla, who had replaced Fernández Pérez and allegedly planned to marry the sister-in-law of Sosaya.[19] In addition, the president lingered in Quito to defend himself until Orueta demanded his departure, threatening to fine him 10,000 pesos.

With Sosaya gone, the special investigator moved against the president's allies in the *audiencia* and began gathering evidence. Orueta first suspended Justices Cristóbal de Ceballos and Lorenzo Lastero de Salazar for allegedly suppressing evidence of Sosaya's contraband activities. Later Orueta removed Justices Juan de Ricauarte and Fernando de Sierra Osorio for their spirited defense of the controversial Vicente Caguenas.[20] These high-handed actions outraged the supporters of Sosaya, who allegedly harassed prosecution witnesses and even threatened the investigator himself. Amidst this tumult, Orueta removed Justice José de Laysequilla and suspended Sierra Osorio a second time – shortly after having reinstated him – for partisanship.[21] As Orueta explained to the Council of the Indies, the suspensions were justified because of the "excesses committed by the president and the other ministers of this *Audiencia* of Quito over the execution of this investigation."[22]

In the end, Juan Baptista de Orueta presented a case before the Council of the Indies based on the testimony of forty-four witnesses in Quito and thirty-one in Guayaquil, roundly condemning Juan de Sosaya. Nevertheless, the councilors found this evidence so weak that they exonerated the accused in 1713, despite earlier suspicions. They also reinstated Sosaya as president of the *audiencia* and gave him 12,000 pesos in restitution. They even reversed the suspensions of José de Laysequilla, Cristóbal de Ceballos, Fernando de Sierra Osorio, and Lorenzo Lastero de Salazar.[23]

pesquisa contra Juan de Sosaya, Madrid, 11 julio 1711; AGI, Quito, 102, Consulta, Madrid, 14 febrero 1711.

19. AGI, Quito, 103, Consulta, Madrid, 16 febrero 1719; AGI, Quito 128, Juan Baptista de Orueta to crown, Quito, 3 abril 1713.

20. *Ibid.*; González Suárez, *Historia general*, 850; AGI, Quito, 267, Instrucciones de la pesquisa contra Juan de Sosaya, Madrid, 11 julio 1711.

21. According to Orueta, José de Laysequilla had planned to marry the sister-in-law of Sosaya until the investigation began. The justice then abandoned his plans but still remained an ally of the beleaguered president. AGI, Quito, 103, Consulta, Madrid, 16 febrero 1719.

22. AGI, Escribanía de Cámara, 913A, Juan Bautista de Orueta to Council of the Indies, Quito, 10 febrero 1717.

23. Juan de Ricauarte remained in Quito until after the investigation, when he moved to Bogotá

The accusers of Sosaya paid heavy fines and suffered exiles ranging from two to six years.[24]

Despite the unequivocal resolution of the case, tensions persisted in Quito as President Sosaya sought vengeance on his foes. Juan de Sosaya wrote the Council of the Indies, for example, condemning Joseph de Llorente – his principal enemy on the court – for poor work habits, gambling, and failing to vote on any controversial court cases.[25] Sosaya received his greatest satisfaction, however, by witnessing the downfall of his most dogged foe, Bishop Diego Ladrón de Guevara. As viceroy, Ladrón de Guevara had angered both the Lima merchant guild and the Council of the Indies by his unabashed support of the French trade and his rumored contraband activities.[26] In 1712, for example, the viceroy had allowed French traders to unload their cargoes in Callao, ostensibly so that the government could collect tax revenues from the sale of this merchandise. The *consulado* opposed the decision vigorously but to no avail. One of the signers of the guild's protest was the president's cousin Pedro de Sosaya, an indication that the powerful Sosaya family played a role in publicizing the interim viceroy's questionable actions.[27] By 1716, the Council of the Indies relieved Ladrón de Guevara dishonorably, and as a result of his judicial review (*residencia*) the former bishop was fined 40,000 pesos for his transgressions.[28]

In the end, vengeance also came for the enemies of Juan de Sosaya. On his way to take office in 1729, the president-designate of Quito, Dionisio de Alcedo y Herrera, met Sosaya in Cartagena, by then an aged and broken man. One of the elderly president's enemies in Quito, a young justice named Simón de Ribera y Aguado, apparently had dishonored Sosaya by living openly with the old man's youthful wife, Michaela de Otañon. When Sosaya attempted to seek redress in Spain for this disgrace, Ribera blocked the trip, claiming that the former president intended to abscond with his wife's dowry. According to Alcedo, Sosaya even feared

and served as a substitute *oidor* during the suppression of the Quito tribunal (1718–22). He then returned to serve again in the reestablished court in Quito in 1722. Fernández Pérez went to Santo Domingo in 1716; he retired from that court in 1723 and took up the post of dean of the Cathedral at Cuzco in 1724. AGI, Quito, 103, Consulta, Madrid, 18 agosto 1724.

24. AGI, Escribanía de Cámara, 913A, Residencia de Juan de Sosaya, Madrid, no date; AGI, Quito, 103, Consulta, Madrid, 10 febrero 1717.

25. AGI, Quito, 267, Sosaya to crown, Quito, 5 abril 1713; AGI, Quito, 130, Joseph de Llorente to crown, Quito, 20 junio 1725.

26. See Geoffrey Walker, *Spanish Politics and Imperial Trade 1700–1789* (Bloomington, IN, 1979), 61–62, 80, 83; AGI, Lima, 779, Minutas y instrucciones y cartas de las ordenes dadas a Luis de Alarcón para tomar la residencia al virrey obispo de Quito, Madrid, 1 octubre 1714.

27. Manuel Moreyra y Paz Soldán, *El tribunal del consulado de Lima: Cuaderno de Juntas, (1706–1720)*, 3 vols. (Lima, 1956), 2:282–88.

28. Walker, *Spanish Politics*, 61–62.

that Ribera and his wife had hired assassins to murder him in Cartagena.[29] It was a sordid end to a case replete with political intrigue, corruption, and scandal. It also undermined the power and credibility of the royal government in the Kingdom of Quito.

The collapse of the Portobelo fairs and the case against José de Araujo y Rio

During the presidency of Dionisio de Alcedo y Herrera (1729–37), the commercial order responsible for Quito's economic prosperity in the previous century continued its decline. Although French interlopers were gone from the Pacific by the 1720s, the crown and trade monopolists in both Spain and the Indies failed to reestablish a fleet system capable of serving South America. The Portobelo Fair of 1731, for example, had proven disastrous for the merchants in Lima and Quito, as Spanish traders descended from the isthmus and sold their goods directly in the viceregal capital. The resulting flood of European wares and contraband goods during the decade damaged the Lima merchant guild's power and further undermined the already declining markets for Quito's cloth.[30]

Merchants and mill owners in the *Audiencia* of Quito were divided over how best to respond to these diverse challenges. Some wanted the crown to limit European cloth imports and guarantee markets in Lima for Quito's *paños*, while others focused on gaining greater access to northern markets in New Granada. Regardless of their solutions to the problem of economic decline, however, merchants and mill owners in the kingdom shared the anxiety of the Lima merchant guild about the prospect of a projected trade fair in 1739. Should the influx of legal and contraband goods rival that following the fair of 1731, the economic life of the *audiencia* district would suffer another serious blow.

Despite these nagging economic woes, the new president of Quito, José de Araujo y Rio, eagerly paid 26,000 pesos for the post in 1732, even carrying his petition to the court in Madrid.[31] Like Juan de Sosaya,

---

29. AGI, Quito, 204, Dionisio de Alcedo to crown, Quito, 12 enero 1729.
30. These economic problems were exacerbated in 1718 when the crown created the Viceroyalty of New Granada and also suppressed the *Audiencia* of Quito, transferring its justices to other provinces. Although the crown abandoned this experiment in 1722, reopened the *audiencia* once again, and placed it under the jurisdiction of the Viceroyalty of Peru, the changes further disrupted political life in the kingdom. These problems arose anew in 1739 when the crown restored the Viceroyalty of New Granada, placing the high court of Quito under its jurisdiction. González Suárez, *Historia general*, 929. For a more detailed discussion of the political disruptions caused by the suppression of the court, see Mark A. Burkholder and D. S. Chandler, *From Impotence to Authority: The Spanish Crown and the American Audiencias, 1687–1808* (Columbia, MO, 1977), 38.
31. These were pesos of 10, not 8, reales. Luis Ramos Gómez, *Las noticias secretas de América de Jorge*

Araujo came from a notable Lima merchant family, undoubtedly anxious to control the strategic trade routes passing through the *audiencia* district during the coming trade fair.[32] The father of the new president had made his fortune in commerce and served as a prominent member of the Lima *consulado*, and his younger brother, Francisco, remained active in the guild. Their brother-in-law and business associate Victorino Montero del Aguila was also a rising merchant and held the magistracy in Piura-Paita.[33] With José de Araujo installed as president of Quito and Montero in control of Paita, a key center for the Pacific contraband trade, the Araujo clan was well positioned to benefit from any legal or illicit commercial opportunities arising from the trade fair of 1739.

When José de Araujo arrived in Riobamba, south of the capital, he met a distinguished delegation of the enemies of his predecessor, President Dionisio de Alcedo. They included the bishop, Andrés Paredes de Arendariz, Justices Juan de Luxán de Vedía and Estéban de Olais, and the district treasurer, Fernando García Aguado. Alcedo was a strong-willed ruler with close ties to the Lima *consulado*, having served as its representative in Spain before assuming the presidency.[34] In Quito he had alienated much of the creole establishment by surrounding himself with a coterie of outsiders closely allied to the Lima guild. On the other hand, José de Araujo was a creole merchant with strong socioeconomic ties in the *audiencia* district. In addition his brother-in-law, Victorino Montero, was an outspoken critic of the Lima merchant guild who had long argued for loosening the monopoly of the *consulado* and for promoting greater competition in colonial commerce.[35] The arrival of José de Araujo undoubtedly presented a clear threat to Alcedo and his partisans. At the same time, the new president offered local creoles the hope of greater economic freedom from the *consulado* and access to political power.

Only two days after the arrival of José de Araujo y Rio on 28 December 1736, Dionisio de Alcedo wrote a long letter to Madrid denouncing the new president.[36] Alcedo contended that his successor had purchased his

---

Juan y Antonio de Ulloa (1735–1745), 2 vols. (Madrid, 1985), 1:55; and AGI, Quito, 266, Cédula, Madrid, 16 mayo 1732.

32. Contemporaries charged that Quito was a center of the contraband trade, and many merchants dubbed Guayaquil the principal entrepôt for illicit oriental goods from the Pacific. Jorge Juan and Antonio de Ulloa, *Discourse and Political Reflections on the Kingdoms of Peru*, ed. and trans. John J. TePaske and Besse Clement (Norman, OK, 1978), 49.

33. Moreyra y Paz Soldán, *El tribunal del consulado*, 2:230, 253, 258, 261, 262; Guillermo Lohmann Villena, "Victorino Montero del Aguila y su Estado político del reyno del Perú," *Anuario de Estudios Americanos*, 31 (1974): 767–69; and Ramos, *Las noticias secretas*, 1:55.

34. Ramos, *Las noticias secretas*, 1:61; Walker, *Spanish Politics*, 164; AGI, Quito, 122, Relación de méritos de Dionisio de Alcedo y Herrera, Madrid, 1727.

35. Lohmann Villena, "Victorino Montero," 776–77.

36. The most detailed description of the political conflicts resulting from the denunciations of José

position, not gained it on merit, and intended to use his powers to engage in illegal trade. To bolster his allegations, Alcedo claimed that Araujo had stopped in Acapulco on his way from Spain and bought contraband oriental goods, which he sent in a shipment of over 130 mule loads that arrived in Quito on December 26. Alcedo concluded that the new president and his brother-in-law, Montero, intended to use these goods to start a large-scale mercantile business in the city.[37] Lorenzo Nates, deputy of the Lima merchant guild in Quito, corroborated these allegations in a letter to the crown in 1738. Nates complained that the *Quiteño* merchants were too dispirited to descend to Cartagena, despite news of the fleet's arrival, because the president's contraband goods had flooded Quito's marketplaces, lowered prices, and ruined many traders.[38] In December of 1738, a group of merchants in Quito wrote that José de Araujo continued introducing contraband goods, leading to the "annihilation, ruin, and destruction of the province."[39] In addition, Spanish observers Jorge Juan and Antonio de Ulloa blamed Araujo for tolerating the blatant sale of contraband merchandise in Quito.[40] The message to the crown was clear: the trade fairs in Cartagena and Portobelo were doomed if merchants like Araujo glutted viceregal markets with cheaper contraband merchandise before the galleons even unloaded.[41]

Always a combative and acerbic man, José de Araujo defended himself and lashed out at his foes. He denied carrying any contraband items and claimed that his enemies exaggerated the amounts of merchandise entering Quito: the trade goods were only to pay for his trip to the capital. Moreover, Araujo charged that his principal accusers in Quito, the *fiscal* of the *audiencia*, Juan de Valparda (the son-in-law of Alcedo), and two Spanish-born merchants, Lorenzo Nates and Simón Alvarez Monteserín, wanted only to discredit him and pursue their own political and economic agenda.[42] Their strategy involved identifying Araujo as a partisan of the

---

de Araujo; see Luis Ramos Gómez, "La estructura social Quiteña entre 1737 y 1745 según el proceso contra José de Araujo," *Revista de Indias*, 51:191 (1991): 25–56.

37. Ramos, *Las noticias secretas*, 1:60–63.
38. *Ibid.*, 1:61.
39. *Ibid.*, 1:64.
40. TePaske and Clement, *Discourse and Political Reflections*, 19, 42–68.
41. Araujo claimed that most of the goods belonged to his brother-in-law Victorino Montero and to Antonio Balanzategui. Montero, however, was a close business associate of the new president, who had quarreled with members of the Lima guild. Balanzategui (a cousin of Araujo's wife) was a peninsular merchant involved in the Cartagena trade, which was also largely outside the control of the *consulado*. Such connections were bound to raise objections among members of the Lima merchant guild and its former agent, Dionisio de Alcedo. AGI, Quito, 134, José de Araujo y Rio to crown, Quito, 6 agosto 1739; 4 febrero 1740.
42. Simón Alvarez de Monteserín was the uncle of Lorenzo Nates and the brother-in-law of another

city's creole population, in order to enflame the passions of the local peninsular-born Spaniards and conceal their own greed and nepotism.[43]

President Araujo and his enemies clashed bitterly and often during the next year. When Araujo intervened in the election of city council magistrates (*alcaldes ordinarios*) on behalf of his allies (Joaquín Laso de la Vega and Tomás Guerrero), the treasury comptroller, José Suárez de Figueroa, nullified the election by declaring the president's candidates debtors to the crown and thus unfit to serve.[44] Suárez also complained that Araujo had interfered illegally in the sale of aldermanships on the city council and exercised tyrannical control over the church. The president's enemies even claimed that Araujo had interfered with the mails, illegally raised and funded a presidential guard, supported gambling establishments, granted illicit commercial licenses, suppressed local *aguardiente* stills, and perpetrated a host of other abuses aimed at promoting his friends and punishing anyone who dared oppose him.[45]

The treasury comptroller, José Suárez de Figueroa, had already run afoul of President Araujo during a long and convoluted examination of Quito's *caja real*. Reports had circulated for decades about gross irregularities in the treasury office. From 1723, members of the *audiencia* had complained of their inability to control the administration of royal finances. The judges even requested – unsuccessfully – the privilege of having the court audit treasury records, instead of the distant Tribunal of Accounts in Lima. When officials in Cartagena complained of declining yearly subsidies (*situados*) from Quito (during the tense years in the relationship between Spain and Britain), the Madrid government ordered an investigation in 1737.[46] Since Quito had failed to send its yearly

opponent of Araujo, Antonio Pastrana, whom the president had rejected as a candidate for the city council in 1737. Ramos, "La estructura social Quiteña entre 1737 y 1745," 33.

43. AGI, Quito, 133, José de Araujo to crown, 22 febrero 1737.

44. Suárez even charged that the treasurer, Fernando García Aguado, had gained the favor of Araujo by giving him a bribe of 5,000 pesos to manipulate the election of the *alcaldes*. See Ramos, "La estructura social Quiteña entre 1737 y 1745," 29–30.

45. One of the president's most controversial edicts involved suppressing the local stills producing *aguardiente*. Although the president claimed he wanted only to restrain alcohol abuse, his enemies charged that he and Montero really conspired to sell their own imported Peruvian liquor and wanted to use the edict to destroy all local opposition. AGI, Quito, 135, Pedro Gómez Andrade and Juan de Luján y Vedía to crown, Quito, 20 octubre 1745; see also Ramos, *Las noticias secretas*, 1:65–66, and Ramos, "La estructura social Quiteña entre 1737 y 1745," 41.

46. AGI, Quito, 129, Diego de Zárate to crown, Quito, 26 septiembre 1723, 25 noviembre 1733, and 11 febrero 1724; AGI, Quito, 129, Consulta, Madrid, 3 julio 1724; AGI, Quito, 129, Dionisio de Alcedo to crown, Quito, 15 mayo 1731; AGI, Quito, 133, José de Araujo to crown, Quito, 7 octubre 1738; AGI, Quito, 175, Quinquenio de 1730, Quito, 20 diciembre 1730; AGI, Quito, 175, Quinquenio de 1732, Quito, 1732; AGI, Quito, 133, Dionisio de Alcedo to crown, Quito, 15 mayo 1731; AGI, Quito, 133, Consulta, Madrid, 31 marzo 1740; AGI, Quito, 175, Manuel Gerónimo de la Cerda to crown, Quito, 30 mayo 1732; AGI, Quito, 141, Fernando

accounting to Lima for decades, the crown demanded that the treasury officers remit a detailed report for the previous five years. After the *Quiteños* finally complied, officials in Madrid found that debts under the tenure of Comptroller José Suárez de Figueroa and Treasurer Fernando García Aguado had reached 333,546 pesos.[47]

Fighting for their political survival, both treasury officers wrote a number of letters to Madrid, blaming the other for any shortfalls. Tales of nepotism, botched tax farming contracts, bribery, and graft abounded, implicating both men and most of the city's political elite. Few public officials could remain neutral in the resulting conflict, including President Araujo, an ally of García Aguado.[48] Amidst this struggle, it is no small wonder that José Suárez wrote to Madrid condemning his enemy, Araujo. In all likelihood, this mutual hostility lay behind the president's decision to jail the irascible comptroller. In any case, the Council of the Indies gave the job of investigating the Quito treasury to *oidor* Manuel Rubio de Arévalo, who had just received a promotion from Quito to the viceregal court in Bogotá. Rubio did not actually begin his inquiries, however, until 17 May 1740.[49]

The trade fair of 1739 further complicated the turbulent political affairs of Quito and added to the president's list of opponents. Longstanding tensions between the merchants of Quito and Lima had worsened by the time the Spanish fleet docked in Cartagena in late 1738. The Lima merchants claimed that the Quito traders had abused their privilege of participating in the Cartagena fair in 1731 by selling legal and contraband goods throughout the viceroyalty before the Peruvians had returned from the later Portobelo exchange.[50] The situation for the *Limeños* became even more difficult with the outbreak of war with England in 1739. The threat of an English attack on Portobelo forced the Lima merchants to seek refuge with their silver inland at Quito, then ruled by the guild's powerful enemy, José de Araujo y Rio.[51]

de García Aguado to crown, Quito, 2 octubre 1738; José de Suárez to crown, 13 enero 1732, 10 noviembre 1736; 5 marzo 1737; AGI, Quito, 141, Consulta, Madrid, 14 agosto 1737; and AGI, Quito, 133, Informe del fiscal, Madrid, 31 marzo 1740.

47. Ramos, "La estructura social Quiteña entre 1737 y 1745," 37.

48. According to one of his severest critics, the treasurer, Fernando García Aguado, had also used public funds earmarked for the subsidy at Cartagena to buy cloth at that city. He then allegedly sold the goods, used the proceeds to repay the subsidy, and pocketed the profits. This sort of freelance mercantile activity was bound to run afoul of the more established members of the Lima merchant guild and may be one additional reason why García Aguado favored Araujo over his foes in the *consulado*. See AGI, Quito, 175, Manuel Gerónimo de la Cerda to crown, Quito, 30 mayo 1732.

49. Ramos, "La estructura social Quiteña entre 1737 y 1745," 46.

50. Ramos, *Las noticias secretas*, 1:120–30.

51. Dilg, "Collapse of the Portobelo Fairs," 238–51.

Soon after the Peruvian merchants arrived in Quito, squabbles arose with the president, who still harbored a grudge against many in the Lima *consulado* for the denunciations of its deputy, Lorenzo Nates, and its former agent, Dionisio de Alcedo y Herrera. When the guild members in Quito agreed to band together and trade with the Spaniards in Cartagena only as a group, for example, Araujo undermined them by granting licenses for selected merchants to trade individually at the Caribbean port. These independent merchants allegedly paid handsomely for these licenses, but they also made considerable sums selling their European merchandise to viceregal retailers. Meanwhile, the loyal guild members and their silver languished in Quito.[52] In a long and angry letter to the crown, the guild's commissioner in Quito, Manuel Labeano, explained this problem and also charged that the president had demanded bribes, had allowed locals to charge them exorbitant prices for services like moving their specie upland to Quito, and had extorted over 100,000 pesos from the guild to provision Cartagena after the English attack in 1741.[53] Araujo defended himself vigorously against these charges, making it clear that he had no sympathy for his old enemies in the Lima *consulado*. Indeed, he seemed to relish having them under his control during this critical trade fair.[54]

Given the many controversies surrounding the troubled tenure of José de Araujo y Rio in Quito, the Council of the Indies authorized a special investigation of the president on 14 August 1739. After compiling a list of twenty separate charges, ranging from trading in contraband goods to gambling, the council named a trusted justice of the *audiencia*, Pedro Martínez de Arizala, to head the inquiry. Martínez de Arizala had the power to suspend Araujo and assume the presidency ad interim, exile him, confiscate his property, and levy heavy fines against all wrongdoers.[55] As in the investigation of Juan de Sosaya, the council appeared willing to believe the guilt of Araujo, another merchant apparently abusing his powers for profit at a critical period for the empire.

Delays and administrative complications hindered the investigation from the outset. By the time legislation authorizing an inquiry reached Quito in October 1739, Martínez de Arizala had resigned from the bench and entered the Franciscan order, rendering him ineligible to head the

52. Profits from this trade could be high, since merchants usually brought goods worth 30,000–50,000 pesos to Lima and sold them at high prices, while goods from the galleons remained bottled up in Cartagena. Ramos, *Las noticias secretas*, 1:179; TePaske and Clement, *Discourse and Political Reflections*, 47.

53. Dilg, "Collapse of the Portobelo Fairs," 238; Ramos, *Las noticias secretas*, 1:180.

54. AGI, Quito, 134, Araujo to crown, Quito, 17 septiembre 1741.

55. Ramos, *Las noticias secretas*, 1:100–01; Ramos, "La estructura social Quiteña entre 1737 y 1745," 33–36. AGI, Quito, 105, Consulta, Madrid, 12 junio 1747.

probe. The council had named no alternate, and the inclusion of the *Audiencia* of Quito in the Viceroyalty of New Granada that same year only delayed further action. In fact, the Madrid government failed to resolve the problem until early in 1742, when it named an old enemy of Araujo, Manuel Rubio de Arévalo, to lead the investigation.[56]

Although Rubio de Arévalo had been transferred to the Bogotá court, he still resided in Quito, serving as the special investigator of the Quito treasury. With these combined commissions, Rubio de Arévalo wielded tremendous political power in the capital, which he quickly used to gain support among the president's many enemies – especially *fiscal* Juan de Valparda, *oidor* José de Quintana y Azevedo, and those who had denounced Araujo in 1736 and 1738. Within weeks of receiving his commission, Rubio de Arévalo had removed Araujo from office, confiscated his property, fined him 2,000 pesos, and exiled the former president to Tumbes.[57]

The investigation of José de Araujo proved a bitter, partisan affair.[58] The former president's friends, Justices Luxán and Gómez Andrade, wrote the crown in 1745 denouncing Rubio de Arévalo for abusing his powers, collecting an excessive amount in salary and expenses, obstructing testimony favorable to Araujo, and favoring his allies. These critics related a particularly ugly incident involving Rubio and his son Benito. Apparently the two men and their slave went, armed, to the house of a debtor, Francisco Xavier Piedrahita, and threatened to use force in the arrest.[59] When Justices Gómez Andrade and Luján confronted Rubio de Arévalo over this abuse of his powers, the special prosecutor retaliated by suspending both men. One year later the inspector removed two other Araujo supporters, Treasurer Fernando García Aguado and the new comptroller, Juan de Ibarguren. As one influential Araujo supporter, Fernando Félix Sánchez Orellana, warned, Rubio's high-handed actions threatened "a civil war in the city, whose fatal consequences I cannot predict."[60]

Despite these setbacks, events began to turn in favor of Araujo by 1745, when the beleaguered president's original term had expired and the crown decided not to renew the interim appointment of Rubio de

---

56. González Suárez, *Historia general*, 1055; Ramos, "La estructura social Quiteña entre 1737 y 1745," 36–38.
57. Ramos, Las noticias secretas, 1:100–02; González Suárez, *Historia general*, 1055.
58. According to Luis Ramos Gómez, the allies of Araujo were frequently linked by kinship ties. For further details on these family networks, see Ramos, "La estructura social Quiteña entre 1737 y 1745," 32–33, 39–40.
59. AGI, Quito, 135, Juan de Luján and Estéban de Olais to crown, Quito, 10 diciembre 1746; AGI, Quito, 135, Juan de Luján and Pedro Gómez Andrade to crown, Quito, 20 octubre 1745.
60. AGI, Quito, 135, Fernando Félix Sánchez Orellana to crown, Quito, 30 octubre 1745.

Arévalo. Instead, the Madrid government named Fernando Félix Sánchez Orellana the new *audiencia* president. Sánchez Orellana came from a powerful creole family tied to Araujo, and along with his allies on the *audiencia* – Estéban de Olais, Pedro Gómez Andrade, and Juan de Luján – the new president proved capable of neutralizing the power of Rubio de Arévalo.[61] After answering charges in Quito in 1744, José de Araujo then fled to Lima and from there eventually made his way to Madrid by 14 November 1746. With a sympathetic ally as president of Quito, José de Araujo used his presence at court to refute the largely unsubstantiated charges of Rubio de Arévalo. In the end Araujo was acquitted on all twenty counts by the Council of the Indies on 8 August 1747.[62]

After reaching this decision, the council meted out stern punishments for the accusers of José de Araujo. Dionisio de Alcedo y Herrera was removed from his post as president of Panama and fined 10,000 pesos – 4,000 for the crown and 6,000 as compensation for Araujo. The council then suspended Manuel Rubio de Arévalo for eight years and José Suárez de Figueroa for four years, levying substantial fines on both men. Moreover, each of the citizens who had raised charges against Araujo received a heavy fine along with exile or prohibition from holding public office. As for the former president, José de Araujo y Rio received over 12,000 pesos in damages and the presidency of Guatemala for two years – the time he had unjustly lost as president of Quito during his suspension.[63] By removing the irascible Araujo from Quito, however, the Council of the Indies avoided the kind of costly reprisals that had characterized the aftermath of the Sosaya case over thirty years before. Despite the clear resolution of the case, the prestige and power of the *audiencia* had again suffered enormous damage.

The Quito Insurrection of 1765

The collapse of the Portobelo fairs and the beginning of legalized sailings by individual register ships only added to the economic problems in Quito by encouraging the importation of larger amounts of European cloth. These difficulties increased with the rise in foreign cloth imports after 1763, when Spanish overseas trade began to recover from the disruptions of the Seven Years' War.[64] Profits for mill owners continued their decline, bankruptcies abounded, and the economic prospects of

61. Ramos, *Las noticias secretas*, 1:334.
62. *Ibid.*, 1:334–36; González Suárez, *Historia general*, 1056–65.
63. Ramos, *Las noticias secretas*, 1:334–36; González Suárez, *Historia general*, 1056–65.
64. Antonio García–Baquero González, *Cádiz y el Atlántico (1717–1778)*, 2 vols. (Seville, 1976), 1:370; 2:173.

elites and the lower classes diminished, especially in the north-central sierra.

In March of 1764 the viceroy of New Granada, Pedro Messía de la Cerda, provoked a groundswell of hostility in Quito by transferring control over the cane liquor monopoly (*estanco de aguardiente*) and the *alcabala* from local tax farmers to the royal treasury *caja*. Although the sales and *aguardiente* levies yielded approximately 16 percent of the total income flowing into the central treasury in Quito, these sums still came to less than one-third the amount collected in Bogotá, a city of roughly similar size.[65] As a result, the viceroy hoped to end the inefficient tax farming system, increase tax receipts, and boost the Quito treasury's yearly subsidy to the coastal defenses at Cartagena.[66] Many *Quiteños* bitterly opposed these actions, however, maintaining that increasing these two key imposts and draining larger amounts of specie for the subsidy to Cartagena would devastate the declining urban economy. In such a time of economic distress, the local citizenry sought concessions from the crown, not enhanced fiscal pressure.

The *audiencia* in Quito played only a minor part in the emerging controversy over tax reform. The court's long history of weak leadership and factionalism left it little credibility with the viceroy. The justices had all purchased their positions, served long tenures in the city, and allegedly developed strong connections to local elites.[67] Two members of the bench, Félix de Llano and José de Cistué, were reputedly partisans of Antonio Solano de Salas, the current tax farmer for the *aguardiente* monopoly.[68] As a result, Messía de la Cerda failed to consult the *audiencia* and sent his own representative, Juan Díaz de Herrera, to enact the reforms.[69] The viceroy's high-handed actions ensured that any protest movement would bypass the traditional center of regional political power, the *audiencia*.

---

65. See Anthony McFarlane, "The 'Rebellion of the Barrios': Urban Insurrection in Bourbon Quito," *Hispanic American Historical Review*, 69 (May 1989): 286.

66. The *Audiencia* of Quito had been part of the Viceroyalty of New Granada since only 1739, and Messía de la Cerda apparently hoped to use the tax policies to extend his powers in the region, as well as increase taxes. AGI, Quito, 398, Pedro Messía de la Cerda to *Audiencia* of Quito, Bogotá, 9 marzo 1764.

67. McFarlane, "Rebellion of the Barrios," 290; for evidence of the *audiencia* president's local economic connections, see AGI, Quito, 135, Pedro Gómez de Andrade to crown, Quito, 20 octubre 1745.

68. Both men had been partisans of the deceased former president of the *audiencia*, the Marqués de Selva Alegre, along with Solano de Salas. Burkholder and Chandler, *Biographical Dictionary of Audiencia Ministers*, 88–89, 192; see also Juan Romualdo Navarro, "Noticia secreta de la revolución de Quito de 1765," in Pablo Herrera, ed., *Antología de prosistas Ecuatorianos*, 2 vols. (Quito, 1895), 1:239.

69. AGI, Quito, 398, Pedro Messía de la Cerda to *Audiencia* of Quito, Bogotá, 9 marzo 1764.

In this tense political atmosphere, the *audiencia* judges struggled to distance themselves from the tax reform policies. When the viceroy named *oidor* Félix de Llano special justice (*juez conservador*) to implement the *aguardiente* monopoly, he warned of the policy's dangers. The new regulations required all estate owners to supply only *miel* (syrup refined from sugar cane) to the crown monopoly, which would then manufacture it into bottled *aguardiente* and sell it.[70] The justice claimed that the sugar estates would operate at a loss if they did not bottle and sell their own cane liquor and warned that creole producers, the clerical corporations, and city bootleggers would even promote violence to impede the fiscal innovations.[71] The new sales tax reforms offended elites by calling for more effective collection procedures and a higher assessment on rural estates. According to Justice Luis de Santa Cruz, the *juez conservador* of this new administration, opponents feared that higher taxes would bankrupt estates and even hurt those clerical organizations holding the mortgages on rural properties.[72]

A controversy in 1764 foreshadowed these objections to the reforms, when a prominent creole, Melchór Rivadeneyra, proposed changing the tax farming contract for the *aguardiente* monopoly along the basic lines demanded by Messía de la Cerda.[73] Since its establishment in 1746, local sugar producers sold predetermined amounts of bottled cane liquor to the royal monopoly at fixed prices. Rivadeneyra offered a higher price for the tax farming contract if he could set the prices for *aguardiente*, buy only as much syrup and distilled liquor as he could sell, and establish a factory to bottle cane liquor himself. Prominent sugar growers and the city's clerical corporations wrote vehement denunciations to the *cabildo*. If Rivadeneyra won the contract, opponents claimed that farmers would abandon sugar cultivation and plant wheat, resulting in an 80-percent drop in land values and the abandonment of many estates.[74] Under this intense local pressure, Rivadeneyra withdrew his bid for the tax farming contract.[75] The strength of the opposition to this alteration of the monopoly agreement only one year earlier should have warned Díaz de Herrera to proceed cautiously in Quito. He did not.[76]

---

70. AGI, Quito, Decreto, Bogotá, 9 marzo 1764.

71. AGI, Quito, 398, Félix de Llano to Pedro Messía de la Cerda, Quito, 20 noviembre 1764.

72. AGI, Quito, 398, Luis de Santa Cruz to Pedro Messía de la Cerda, Quito, 1 febrero 1765.

73. Archivo Nacional de Historia, Quito (hereafter cited as ANH-Q), Presidencia de Quito, 1764, 58, ff. 30–32, Melchór de Rivadeneyra to treasury officials, Quito, no date.

74. ANH-Q, Presidencia de Quito, 1764, 58, ff. 22–25, Prelados de religiones y hacendados, trapicheros, y vecinos to *Audiencia* of Quito, Quito, no date.

75. ANH-Q, Presidencia de Quito, 1764, 58, ff. 35–43, José de Cistué to treasury officials, Quito, 17 febrero 1764.

76. Díaz de Herrera justified his actions by accusing Félix de Llano of importing contraband goods from Lima, claiming that this explained his opposition to the new taxes; Díaz de Herrera was

With the *audiencia* powerless to deter Díaz de Herrera, clerical and lay opponents of the reforms, led by the prominent landowner Francisco de Borja, petitioned to convene a rare open meeting of the creole-controlled city council (*cabildo abierto*) on 7 December 1764.[77] The recommendations of the open meeting and the petitions circulated by Borja demanded an end to the dangerous royal reforms. These documents explained that the new administrations drew needed specie from the economy, overtaxed provincial agriculture, and led to an increase in drunkenness and vice. Moreover, all of these problems exacerbated the poverty of the province, caused by foreign cloth imports and the resulting depression of the traditional textile trade.[78]

Although hardly a coherent political manifesto, the petitions and pronouncements of the *cabildo abierto* asserted indirectly the city elite's right to have a voice in fiscal matters.[79] The creole oligarchy's purpose in calling for political representation, however, was to articulate their long-standing economic demands – for tax concessions, the restoration of their oligopoly "rights" in textile manufacturing, and protection against European cloth imports. All aimed to restore regional economic prosperity. During this growing protest, the viceroy and his commissioner ordered the immediate enforcement of the new tax policies.[80]

The viceroy of New Granada risked much by ignoring the creole protest arising from the *cabildo abierto*. A list of large landowners in the sugar zones of Quito and Ibarra in 1768 included many powerful creole families. In addition, the sales tax records indicate that over 70 percent of the city's bottled cane liquor came from the estates of only six wealthy and distinguished citizens: the Marqués de Sánchez Orellana, Diego Donoso, Juan de Chiriboga (the father-in-law of Francisco de Borja), General Manuel de la Peña, Joseph de Grijalva, and the *audiencia* president, Ma-

equally suspicious of the motives of Luis de Santa Cruz and José de Cistué and accused all three of inciting creole opposition to the tax reforms. AGI, Quito, 398, Juan Díaz de Herrera to Pedro Messía de la Cerda, Quito, 18 enero 1765.

77. McFarlane, "Rebellion of the Barrios," 287–96.
78. *Ibid.*
79. Relying on an argument articulated by John L. Phelan in his study of the 1781 Comunero Revolt in New Granada, McFarlane finds evidence in these documents of a relatively sophisticated constitutional argument – opposing the viceroy's right to impose taxes without honoring the traditional forms of "bureaucratic representation." This argument, linking taxation with some form of local representation, is patterned on the constitutional explanations provided for the Comunero Revolt in Spain in 1521 and the revolt of the British North American colonies from 1765. Regardless of whether or not the documents display the sophisticated legal reasoning that McFarlane attributes to them, they do outline very directly the economic and political agenda articulated by *Quiteño* elites since the economic crisis began late in the previous century. See *ibid.*; and John L. Phelan, *The People and the King: The Comunero Revolution in Colombia* (Madison, WI, 1978), 172–86.
80. AGI, Quito, 398, Pedro Messía de la Cerda to cabildo of Quito, Bogotá, 6 mayo 1765.

nuel Rubio de Arévalo.[81] The clergy held numerous mortgages on these lucrative sugar-producing estates and also engaged directly in sugar cultivation and the *aguardiente* trade. The Jesuits, in particular, owned some of the very best sugar estates along the Mira and Chota Rivers in Ibarra. The administrator of the cane liquor monopoly even complained in 1755 that the Jesuits alone supplied over 56 percent of the city's *aguardiente*.[82] In short, the new tax reforms posed a threat to the economic welfare of Quito's upper class and united the normally faction-ridden elites in a coalition against crown policy.

The plebeians of the *barrios* had long despised new taxes, and the government's attempt to control the production and sale of *aguardiente* provoked their immediate anger. Cane liquor and corn wine (*chicha*) were popular drinks among the poor, and any effort to interfere with their marketing and consumption was bound to provoke dissent. Moreover, many plebeians made their living by operating bootleg stills, manufacturing *aguardiente* from the syrup provided by local landowners. A few even owned illegal bars or stores that sold *aguardiente* and corn wine to their plebeian customers.[83] A reform of the cane liquor monopoly would have undercut this black market of stills and bars, probably raised the price of alcoholic beverages, and disrupted the ties between plebeians and elite suppliers. When rumors spread in the *barrios* that the *aguardiente* produced by the new monopoly was adulterated and that the factory in the Plaza de Santa Bárbara had redirected the city's scarce water supply, causing shortages, many in the parishes called openly for an uprising.

The reform of the sales tax also threatened to disrupt the urban marketplace and cause additional hardships for the middle- and lower-class citizenry of the *barrios*.[84] The *alcabala* reforms of 1765 demanded higher fixed tax assessments on all small freeholders in the parishes. Such fixed rents were particularly threatening, since they did not change in times of abundance or dearth and could ruin small farmers after a bad harvest. The freeholders also had little access to mortgage loans or other forms of

81. ANH-Q, Presidencia de Quito, 1714–1774, 362, ff. 206–19, Cuenta de Cargo y Descargo tomadas a dn Manl. de Guevara durante el tiempo que desempeño el cargo de admr. de Alcabalas corrido desde 31 Mayo de 1765 hasta 30 de Septre. de 1768; AGI, Quito, 430, Cuenta general del encabezamiento de alcabalas de Quito, 1768–1775, Quito; Javier Ortiz de la Tabla y Ducasse, "Panorama económico y social del corregimiento de Quito (1768–1775)," *Revista de Indias*, 145–46 (1975): 84–97. Rubio de Arévalo was restored to his position in Quito in 1757 and ascended to the interim presidency through seniority when the Marqués de Selva Alegre died in 1761. See Burkholder and Chandler, *Biographical Dictionary of Audiencia Ministers*, 302.

82. ANH-Q, Estancos, Caja 3, Informe de Fernando de Merisalde y Chacón, Quito, 8 agosto 1755.

83. AGI, Quito, 398, Félix de Llano to Pedro Messía de la Cerda, Quito, 20 noviembre 1764.

84. The most recent and detailed study of the Quito Insurrection and its links to the plebeian citizenry of the *barrios* is by Martin Minchom, *The People of Quito, 1690–1810: Change and Unrest in the Underclass* (Westport, CT, 1994) 229–31.

credit. To compete with foodstuffs grown on the larger estates, small-scale producers had to reduce costs by avoiding taxes. The *alcabala* reforms also attempted to tighten regulations on untaxed goods brought into the city by peddlers. Taken together, these measures could have weakened the ties between the city and its hinterland and destroyed the comparative advantage of small producers and food suppliers, two key pillars of the underground economy. Indeed, when crown authorities began preliminary surveys in the *barrios* of San Roque and San Sebastián, rumors abounded about taxing the rocks in the streams and babes in the womb.[85] By 1765 the urban *plebe* were prepared to join disgruntled elites in an unprecedented popular alliance against the crown.[86]

For many of Quito's elite and plebeian citizens, the reforms of the *alcabala* and *aguardiente* administrations posed serious dangers to their material welfare. Moreover, the crown had imposed such risky policies without even consulting the city's prominent clerical and lay leadership, whom the *barrio* residents traditionally had entrusted with protecting their political fortunes. As a result, these fiscal innovations had the potential to unite the citizenry of the capital, at a time when the traditional institutions of government proved unable to provide redress.[87] It was an ominous and potentially explosive situation.

On 22 May 1765 the angry citizens of Quito erupted in a massive popular riot directed against the building housing the *aguardiente* factory and *aduana* in the Plaza de Santa Bárbara. Although *pasquinades* (placards) had warned of an impending uprising, the relative calm of the previous weeks had lulled authorities into inactivity. Preparations for the upcoming festival of Corpus Christi apparently gave the plebeians and perhaps some clerical and creole conspirators an opportunity to plan united action. In any case, when the church bells, drums, and fireworks sounded at eight in the evening, crowds assembled from the southern parishes of San Roque and San Sebastián before the hated customs and factory building. The city's butchers, peddlers, small farmers, and shop owners apparently led the rioters, who proceeded to destroy the building in a relatively disciplined and methodical manner.[88] Several members of the *audiencia*

85. AGI, Quito, 398, Juan Díaz de Herrera to crown, Quito, 18 enero 1765; Luis de Santa Cruz to Pedro Messía de la Cerda, Quito, 1 febrero 1765.

86. According to Martin Minchom, the plebeians played a central and leading role in the insurrection to come. Minchom, *The People of Quito*, 231.

87. The plebeians, particularly in the southern parishes, were liable to rise up in support of a number of causes. Ties with a local faction of Franciscans, for example, led the residents of nearby San Roque to riot against the abuses of an outside inspector, sent by the order to investigate the local chapter in Quito in 1747–48. See González Suárez, *Historia general*, 1094; Martin Minchom, "Urban Popular Society in Colonial Quito, c.1700–1800" (Ph.D. diss., University of Liverpool, 1984), 332–46.

88. Juan de Velásco, *Historia del reino de Quito*, 2 vols. (Quito, 1971 edn.), 1:144; McFarlane, "Re-

and the clergy (who claimed to have tried unsuccessfully to prevent the destruction) commented on the presence of masked rioters, allegedly members of the creole elite trying to conceal their identities.[89] Some local authorities saw further evidence of creole collusion with the mob when few members of the elite rallied to the high court's call to arms or its request later that all loyal subjects illuminate their houses in a show of solidarity with the crown.[90] The crowd apparently grew to over 4,000 and refused to disband until the *audiencia* agreed to pardon all the demonstrators and abolish the hated tax reforms.[91] Even after the mob dispersed, an uneasy calm prevailed, and in the next few weeks several riots nearly broke out in the city's *barrios*.[92]

These tensions erupted in a second riot on 24 June 1765, during the feast of Saint John. The city *corregidor* and a small group of peninsular Spaniards, on a patrol to reassert royal authority, precipitated the outburst by killing two young men in the parish of San Sebastián. The riot that followed was apparently spontaneous, violent, and directed against the native-born Spaniards in the city. A popular force numbering several thousand, initially led by plebeians from San Sebastián and San Roque, besieged the peninsulars and government officials in the central square (Plaza Mayor), where they fought from eleven at night until four the next morning. Then the beleaguered Spaniards hastily retreated to their homes or the sanctuary of the religious houses. Members of the creole elite remained suspiciously neutral throughout the uprising, although some observers claimed that a few priests and prominent landowners joined the rioters.[93]

Order was not restored until Justice Luis de Santa Cruz and several clergymen spread rumors that Amerindians had entered the parish of San

bellion of the Barrios," 305. Martin Minchom makes the very interesting and plausible case that the *barrio* of San Roque, which had a recent history of economic decline and unrest, played the leading role in the initial phase of the insurrection, and he tends to downplay the importance of the butchers. See Minchom, *The People of Quito*, 210–15; 228–33.

89. According to Minchom, the tradition of wearing masks had a long symbolic importance in Andean festivals, but he concludes that "this evidence of elite and clerical involvement is . . . highly indirect." Minchom, *The People of Quito*, 227–28.

90. AGI, Quito, 398, bishop of Quito to crown, Quito, 24 mayo 1765; Gregorio Hurtado de Mendoza to crown, Quito, 24 mayo 1765; *Audiencia* of Quito to crown, Quito, 24 mayo 1765; McFarlane, "Rebellion of the Barrios," 310–19.

91. Díaz de Herrera escaped to the parish church of Santa Bárbara. See AGI, Quito, 398, Manuel Sánchez Osorio to Pedro Messía de la Cerda, Quito, 26 mayo 1765.

92. Reports of minor unrest also reached Quito from Ibarra, Otavalo, Tabacundo, Latacunga, and Riobamba. See AGI, Quito, 398, Pedro Messía de la Cerda to *Audiencia* of Santa Fe, Bogotá, 21 junio 1765.

93. The *audiencia* ministers provided no names to substantiate these charges. See AGI, Quito, 398, *Audiencia* of Quito to crown, Quito, 2 julio 1765.

Blas to join the riot.[94] The prospect of hundreds or even thousands of Amerindians demanding an end to their tax obligations undoubtedly tempered the enthusiasm of some Spaniards and *mestizos* involved in the uprising. It also hastened the submission of the royalists. With the local creole elite and the Jesuits serving as mediators, the *audiencia* capitulated to the rioters. The judges agreed to surrender all royal weapons to the crowd, expel the peninsular Spaniards from the city within seven days, and grant a general pardon for all demonstrators.[95] The rioters consented to naming new *barrio* captains drawn from the principal creole families of the city, an indication of their continued willingness to defer to local elites. To affirm this agreement, the plebeians assembled in the Plaza Mayor on 4 July 1765, returned captured royal arms, and proclaimed their allegiance to the king. Despite this show of loyalty, the riot of Saint John's Day effectively suspended royal government in Quito, as power rested with an uneasy coalition of creoles and plebeians.[96]

After the June uprising, the popular movement entered a new and more radical phase. The success of the riots in May and June apparently emboldened some plebeian leaders to seek a wider political and social role in Quito. According to Attorney José de Cistué (a bitter opponent of the rioters), leaders in the *barrios* began to administer the sales tax and stamped paper monopoly, to threaten the lives of key citizens, to place former criminals in positions of power, and to encourage Amerindians to stop paying taxes.[97] Attacks on property continued, and some bold plebeian leaders demanded jurisdiction over local justice in their neighborhoods. These "radicals" also sought to control the movement of Europeans in the city, granting passes for limited periods only to those conducting approved business.[98] Moreover, the creole noblemen, chosen as *barrio* captains after the June riot, complained about the need to bribe the obstreperous plebeian leaders to curtail lawlessness and other criminal excesses in the parishes. Rumors even spread that leaders in the *barrios* had com-

94. McFarlane, "Rebellion of the Barrios," 312.

95. Two of the justices who had originally expressed reservations about the new tax policies, José de Cistué and Félix de Llano, had to flee the ire of the protesters and seek refuge outside of the city. AGI, Quito, 399, José de Cistué to Pedro Messía de la Cerda, Quito, 10 marzo 1766.

96. The new deputies – the Conde de Selvaflorida, Nicolás Calixto de Alarcón, Mariano Pérez de Ubillus, Joseph Laso de la Vega, and Francisco de Borja – represented the principal creole families of the city. AGI, Quito, 398, *Audiencia* of Quito to Pedro Messía de la Cerda, Quito, 13 julio 1765; McFarlane, "Rebellion of the Barrios," 310–17; Minchom, *The People of Quito*, 227, 230–31.

97. According to information given by Cistué, the names of the *barrio* leaders indicate that they were mostly from creole and middle-class *mestizo* families – two were silversmiths, usually the most prestigious of the artisan guilds, and one held the post of lieutenant of the city jail. AGI, Quito, 398, José de Cistué to Pedro Messía de la Cerda, Guanacas, 9 septiembre 1765.

98. McFarlane, "Rebellion of the Barrios," 315–19.

municated with dissident groups in other parts of the kingdom, threatening to expand the scope of the unrest. This growing lower-class militancy reached a peak when some popular leaders apparently demanded independence from Spain, even offering the crown of the "kingdom" to the Conde de Selvaflorida.[99] The movement begun in May had evolved into a full-scale insurrection, threatening the colonial order.

Tensions within the coalition government ultimately undermined its power and hastened the return of royal control. The violence of the June riot and its extreme xenophobia alienated any peninsulars and their creole kinsmen who might otherwise have sympathized with the economic grievances of the protesters. The growing radicalism of some plebeian leaders also alarmed elites, leading still more to abandon the popular alliance. Even the city council and its former spokesman Francisco de Borja became ardent defenders of the crown and civic order by late summer in 1765.[100] Latent distrust between *mestizos* and Amerindians also emerged, further weakening the popular government. In short, the class and ethnic divisions present in *Quiteño* society gradually undermined the fragile popular coalition after the *audiencia* met the principal demands of the demonstrators. On 1 September 1766, when a royal army entered Quito under the command of the conciliatory governor of Guayaquil, Juan Antonio de Zelaya, the divided citizenry welcomed the soldiers warmly.[101]

Zelaya managed to restore order in Quito by the time he handed over the *audiencia* presidency to his successor, José de Diguja, in 1767. The divisions among the local elites and the popular classes remained acute, and President Diguja (who ruled until 1778) had no real trouble maintaining peace in the city. Even the expulsion of the Jesuits in 1767, which caused such unrest in Mexico, led to only sporadic trouble in the kingdom. Nevertheless, the judicial state remained weak, as public revenues lagged behind expectations and subsidies to Cartagena suffered. In short, preserving the peace did little to raise crown revenues needed to support the imperial designs of Madrid.

The socioeconomic changes in the Kingdom of Quito formed the backdrop for some of the most divisive political confrontations in the eighteenth century. As the highland textile business faltered, so too did the position of all social classes dependent on the colonial market economy.

99. McFarlane asserts that this incident was part of an "exaggerated" account, but it was widely known by contemporaries and has appeared in the standard history of the period, without such qualifications. González Suárez, *Historia general*, 1137.

100. An epidemic in 1765 apparently also played a role in calming the rebellious spirit. See Minchom, *The People of Quito*, 227.

101. González Suárez, *Historia general*, 1139; see also McFarlane, "Rebellion of the Barrios," 324.

This overall pattern of economic decline and social instability heightened factionalism, as various groups competed to control the institutions of government and manipulate them for partisan interests. Under such pressures the power of the judicial state began to ebb, as government officials became enmeshed in a constantly shifting array of factional alignments. In short, economic decline and imperial policies combined to produce a corrupt and divided political system, incapable of maintaining a workable consensus.

The political imbroglios surrounding the tenures of Juan de Sosaya and José de Araujo y Rio produced remarkably similar problems in Quito. Both men were prominent Lima merchants, interested in using public office to advance their own political and business concerns. The arrival of a new president often produced changes in partisan alignments; the resulting tensions could erupt into serious conflicts when leaders such as Sosaya and Araujo also threatened the economic balance of power in the district. In these two cases serious political crises emerged, paralyzing the state until the Council of the Indies interceded to resolve the impasse.

By 1765, the institutions of government were so fragile that efforts to reform the tax structure prompted a complete breakdown of the traditional political order. Although creole elites and the plebeians managed to rule the capital city for over one year, socioeconomic tensions endemic to colonial society led to the dissolution of the popular government. This collapse demonstrated that the colonials could neither unite to govern themselves nor force meaningful concessions from the crown.[102] As a result, the decline of the textile industry, sugar production, and even the urban underground economy continued apace. A legacy of mistrust and fear also remained after 1765, dividing the city's social groups and inhibiting any further resistance to crown policies.

The Quito Insurrection also convinced crown policy makers that the decrepit judicial institutions in Quito needed sweeping changes, not just moderate fiscal innovations. As a result, in 1778 the Madrid government dispatched a special investigator, José García de Leon y Pizarro, to overhaul the political system in Quito and to reinvigorate its administrative structure. It was a clear break with the past, one that promised serious challenges for the elites and the plebeians during an era of economic decline.

102. Whereas John L. Phelan found a common ideology emerging during the Comunero Revolt in New Granada in 1781, no such evidence exists for Quito. This explains why the revolt failed to spread outside of the capital and its hinterland, and also why the popular alliance fractured so quickly after assuming power in 1765. See Phelan, *The People and the King*, passim. For a dissenting view, see McFarlane, "Rebellion of the Barrios," passim.

8

The price of reform, 1778–1830

When José García de Leon y Pizarro arrived in the Kingdom of Quito in 1778, he began implementing a series of policies aimed at making the administrative structure of the state more centralized and efficient. These innovations formed part of an empire-wide program of reform to realize the ambitious fiscal, commercial, and defense goals of King Charles III (1759–88) and his ministers. García Pizarro was a well-connected politician, given extraordinary political, judicial, fiscal, and military powers by the Madrid government. Despite formidable local opposition, he used this authority and influence to become the towering political figure to rule in Quito during the eighteenth century. Employing a mixture of ruthlessness, administrative skill, and political cunning, García Pizarro succeeded in creating a strong bureaucratic state structure that helped to shape the socioeconomic evolution of the kingdom well into the early republican period.

García Pizarro and his successors proved remarkably successful in revitalizing the state and extracting large amounts of revenue from the modest regional economies of the *audiencia* district. As government fiscal accounts – drawn from the principal treasuries in Quito, Guayaquil, and Cuenca – attest, new tax levies, more efficient collection procedures, and the imposition of royal monopolies all contributed to a substantial influx of income.[1] Such increases in tax receipts also indicate a dramatic expan-

---

1. These treasury records provide vital evidence about the long-term impact of public policy on the socioeconomic development of the kingdom in the critical period from the onset of the inspection in 1778 to the consummation of independence in 1830. Despite their importance, some critics – such as D. A. Brading – have argued that the uncritical use of these data can present a confusing mixture of "facts and figments," particularly about the economic evolution of Spanish America. See D. A. Brading, "Facts and Figments in Bourbon Mexico," *Bulletin of Latin American Research*, 4 (1985): 61–64. Some vehement criticisms also appear in Henry Kamen and Jonathan Israel in "Debate: The Seventeenth-Century Crisis in New Spain: Myth or Reality?" *Past and Present*, 97 (November 1982): 144–56. Other critics have simply urged using greater care with the accounts. See for example, Samuel Amaral, "Public Expenditure Financing in the Colonial Treasury: Analysis of the Real Caja de Buenos Aires Accounts," and Javier Cuenca Esteban, "Of Nimble Arrows

sion of state power, which hinged fundamentally on access to secure, predictable financial resources. Over time, however, these predatory fiscal policies disrupted business, trade, and capital accumulation in the Kingdom of Quito.

The high-handed polices of José García de Leon y Pizarro left a legacy of high taxes, intrusive government economic regulations, and official corruption that endured into the early republican era. Although his opponents in Quito criticized García Pizarro for presiding over a government riddled with fraud, nepotism, and intimidation, authorities in Spain failed to prosecute the great "reformer and state builder." As a result, successive colonial regimes continued to exploit regional economies and local discontent continued. In fact, this intrusive and often corrupt state contributed to unrest leading to the outbreak of an autonomy movement in Quito by 1809 that would contribute to the ultimate breakdown of the Spanish American empire. The disruptions of this independence era led to the virtual collapse of the colonial state apparatus, but its heritage continued. Although diminished in power, the early national state carried on the colonial tradition of exploiting, not developing, the economic potential of the newly independent nation.

Reform and public finance

The Bourbon monarchs made few changes in the decentralized, patrimonial fiscal bureaucracy in the Kingdom of Quito until the late eighteenth century. Apart from placing the administration of the government monopoly on cane liquor (*aguardiente*) and the sales tax (*alcabala*) under direct state control in 1765, the crown did little to increase the colonial government's administrative and fiscal powers. Three separate treasury offices administered the royal revenues in Quito, Guayaquil, and Cuenca.[2] Although the treasury *caja* in Quito was supposed to serve as a clearinghouse for surplus income from the other two offices, in practice Guayaquil and Cuenca seldom sent sizable sums to the capital.[3] There was no ef-

and Faulty Bows: A Call for Rigor," both in *Hispanic American Historical Review*, 64 (May 1984): 287–95.

2. The jurisdictional lines of these three *cajas reales* varied over time and depended on the taxes collected, but generally the Quito office controlled the provinces of Ibarra, Otavalo, Quito, Latacunga, Ambato, and Riobamba. Cuenca controlled Chimbo, Guaranda, Cuenca, Loja-Zaruma, and Alausí. Guayaquil exercised jurisdiction over Guayaquil, Puertoviejo, Punta de Santa Elena, Machala, Baba, Yaguache, Babahoyo, Daule, and Puná.

3. In Guayaquil, treasury remittances to Quito ranged from nothing to a high of 75,691 pesos reached in 1766, one year after the Quito Insurrection. Archivo General de Indias (hereafter cited as AGI), Contaduría, 1377, 1576, 1577, and Quito, 407, 469–475, and 477, Cuentas de la Caja de Guayaquil, 1714–1804. Remittances from Cuenca ranged from nothing to 46,445 pesos

fective supervision of the collection and disbursement of royal funds, except for periodic audits by the Tribunal of Accounts in distant Lima and later Bogotá.[4] After the Quito Insurrection of 1765, it became apparent that this fiscal apparatus had to be transformed into a more centralized bureaucracy if the crown hoped to raise revenues and revitalize royal authority in the Kingdom of Quito.

This process of reform only began in earnest with the arrival of José García de Leon y Pizarro. García Pizarro was a protégé of several key Spanish officials, including José de Gálvez, the powerful minister of the Indies.[5] Gálvez engineered the appointment of García Pizarro as *visitador*, president-regent (the newly created post of presiding officer), treasury subdelegate, and captain general (with supreme military power) in the *Audiencia* of Quito. This union of political, fiscal, judicial, and military power under the control of one man was unprecedented in the kingdom. Coincidentally, in 1778 the crown had to fill four vacancies on the *audiencia*, leaving only two experienced justices with any real political influence in Quito when García Pizarro arrived. The president augmented his political clout by arranging the marriage of his daughter to Juan Josef de Villalengua y Marfil, the most influential of these two *audiencia* judges. After his brother Ramón was named governor of Guayaquil, the García Pizarro "political family" effectively controlled the most important positions of power in the district. These circumstances allowed the ruthless and supremely able José García de Leon y Pizarro to dominate politics in the *Audiencia* of Quito.

Less than a year after arriving in Quito, García Pizarro wrote a letter to José de Gálvez outlining the economic woes of the kingdom and proposing a number of remedies. The new president claimed that European cloth imports had driven *Quiteño* woolens from colonial markets, which

reached in 1774. AGI, Contaduría, 1534, and Quito, 453–458, Cuentas de la Caja de Cuenca, 1722–1803.

4. From the creation of the Tribunal of Accounts in Lima in 1605 until the establishment of the tribunal in Bogotá (the capital of the newly created Viceroyalty of New Granada) in 1739, the *cajas* in the *Audiencia* of Quito remained under Lima's jurisdiction. The Bogotá tribunal's authority continued until 1776, when the crown created a separate audit court in Quito, independent of the viceregal capital. See María Luisa Laviana Cuetos, "Organización y funcionamiento de las cajas reales de Guayaquil en la segunda mitad del siglo XVIII," *Anuario de Estudios Americanos*, 37 (1980): 314.

5. According to his son's memoirs, García Pizarro held the magistracies of Lorca, Ubeda, Jerez, and Baeza, where he came to the attention of the minister of Grace and Justice, Manuel de Roda, who had him work on several government problems. In the discharge of his duties García Pizarro formed friendships with Gaspar Melchór de Jovellanos, Pedro Rodríguez Campomanes, Rafael de Músquiz, and finally José de Gálvez, who became his patron thereafter. See José García de Leon y Pizarro, *Memorias de la vida del excmo. señor d. José García de Leon y Pizarro*, 3 vols. (Madrid, 1894), 1:11–14; 3:125–26.

hindered trade and created a shortage of specie in the district. Even Guayaquil, with its emergent cacao economy, lacked an adequate labor force to develop its agricultural and commercial sectors effectively. Local silver mines had the potential to provide some relief, but high mercury prices curtailed production. As a result, García Pizarro proposed three remedies: limiting sales of European textiles by one-half to one-third, providing cheap mercury to stimulate mining, and subsidizing the importation of 300–400 black slaves each year to ease any labor shortages.[6]

Although the president's letter represented many of his subjects' pressing needs, it failed to impress the Madrid government. Gálvez and the Council of the Indies handed the suggestions over to the inspector general of Peru, Jorge Escobedo, who ridiculed them as utterly naive and impractical. Escobedo informed the council that *Quiteño* cloth was inferior to European imports; mercury was already in short supply for the proven mines of Peru, Bolivia, and Mexico; and slave labor was too expensive for work in the Guayaquil region. The council concurred.[7]

Stung by this rebuke, President García Pizarro completely abandoned efforts to wring concessions from Madrid for his subjects. Never one to jeopardize his own career ambitions, the president instead decided to follow the successful reform model outlined by his mentor José de Gálvez in New Spain. This involved implementing a far-reaching program of administrative, fiscal, and military reforms aimed at increasing state power and exploiting what remained of the kingdom's economic resources.

The foundation of García Pizarro's reform policies rested on the creation of a new, centralized state fiscal bureaucracy headed by the *Dirección general de rentas* in 1783.[8] The reforms removed jurisdiction over the collection of lucrative taxes, such as Amerindian tribute, the *alcabala*, and several royal monopolies (*aguardiente, tabaco, naipes,* and *pólvora*), from the treasury *cajas* and placed it under the control of the *Dirección general* and its subtreasuries scattered throughout the realm. Fiscal officers deposited only surplus income from these subtreasuries in the local treasury *cajas*. Officials of the *Dirección general de rentas* answered only to the local office of the Tribunal of Accounts, residing in Quito since 1776.[9]

6. AGI, Quito, 410, José García de Leon y Pizarro to José de Gálvez, Quito, 18 junio 1782; also summarized in Federico González Suárez, *Historia general de la república del Ecuador* (Quito, 1970 edn.), 1199–1202.

7. AGI, Quito, Informe del fiscal, Madrid, 20 junio 1782 and 28 junio 1782.

8. This new fiscal bureaucracy was established by royal decree on 10 March 1777. See Douglas Alan Washburn, "The Bourbon Reforms: A Social and Economic History of the Audiencia of Quito, 1760–1810" (Ph.D. diss., University of Texas at Austin, 1984), 129.

9. AGI, Quito, 407, Razón de los empleos de Rl hacda que hay establecidos en Quito y sus provincias y los sujetos destinados en ellos, segun proviene la Real Orden de 12 marzo de este año

The new president created three separate tribunals in Quito, one to collect the *alcabala*, a second for the manufacture and sale of *aguardiente*, and a third to supervise three other monopolies (*tabaco, naipes,* and *pólvora*). A comptroller, administrator, and several clerks staffed the agencies. These three offices each supervised subtreasuries (*recepturías*) in Alausí, Latacunga, Ambato, Riobamba, and Guaranda. The province of Guayaquil had its own network of offices controlling tax collection, while in Cuenca the levies remained under the jurisdiction of the treasury *caja*.[10] All these various tribunals, however, gave an annual accounting to the main office of the *Dirección general de rentas* in Quito.

The administration of tribute revenues fell to a separate fiscal agency under the control of the *Dirección general*, established after the census (*numeración*) of the Amerindian population conducted by *fiscal* Juan Josef de Villalengua y Marfil. The jurisdiction of the main office in Quito extended over subtreasuries in Ibarra, Otavalo, Ambato, Cuenca, Riobamba, and Latacunga. Only Guayaquil was outside the jurisdiction of Quito, and its treasury did not begin operations until 1785.[11] Surplus income from the tribute offices also went to the nearest treasury *caja*.

The number of fiscal offices increased dramatically during the tenure of García Pizarro, who ensured his control over the government by filling the new posts with kin, friends, and political allies. Of course, his brother Ramón already held the strategic governorship of Guayaquil, and his son-in-law Villalengua was the *fiscal* of the *audiencia*.[12] The key position of *director de rentas* went to the personal secretary of the *visitador*, Agustín Martín de Blas, while another political ally, Pedro Josef de Franco, received the comptrollership.[13] Positions in important subordinate offices usually went to trusted peninsulars or well-connected creoles, such as Josef de Renxijo, a partisan of Villalengua who became *contador de tributos* in Quito.[14] García Pizarro further solidified his control by giving his allies

---

de 1783, Quito. This information is summarized in Washburn, "The Bourbon Reforms," 129–32; and Laviana Cuetos, "Organización y funcionamiento," 314; AGI, Quito, 411, Juan Antonio de Asilona to José de Gálvez, Quito, 18 octubre 1778; AGI, Quito, 409, Instrucción y ordenanza para el régimen y govierno de la Dirección General de Rentas de Tabacos, Alcavalas, Aguardiente, Pólvora, y Naipes de Quito y provincias comprehendidas en el distrito de sus reales cajas, Quito, 3 julio 1783.

10. *Ibid.*

11. Laviana Cuetos, "Organización y funcionamiento," 314.

12. Villalengua was also a cousin of the new bishop of Cuenca, José de Carrión y Marfil. González Suárez, *Historia general,* 1206, 1219, 1247.

13. AGI, Quito, 267, Pesquisa contra José García de Leon y Pizarro. This *legajo* contains numerous documents providing details about the way García Pizarro abused his patronage appointments. See also AGI, Quito, 264, José García de Leon y Pizarro to José de Gálvez, Guayaquil, 19 marzo 1778.

14. AGI, Quito, 232, Hoja de servicio de Josef de Renxijo, Quito 1795.

officerships in the newly created disciplined militia regiments.[15] In this way, the García Pizarro clan exercised unparalleled political dominance in the *audiencia* district.

The fiscal reforms begun by José García de Leon y Pizarro represented a concerted effort to create a more centralized colonial state, capable of extracting more wealth from these Andean regional economies. This was a difficult task. The highland textile industry already suffered from a prolonged recession, and the cacao economy of the coast was just experiencing the beginnings of its export boom with the advent of *comercio libre* in 1778. The key problem before García Pizarro and his allies was how to use this reinvigorated state apparatus to increase tax receipts during a period of such fundamental economic change.

Public finance and the colonial state

Despite these problems, the rapid rise in revenues flowing into the three major treasury districts of Quito, Guayaquil, and Cuenca demonstrate the success of José García de Leon y Pizarro's reforms.[16] In Quito, for example, income rose from only 127,196 pesos in 1778 to 497,807 pesos in 1803, an average annual growth rate of 5.4 percent.[17] Income in Gua-

---

15. Allan J. Kuethe, *Military Reform and Society in New Granada, 1773–1808* (Gainesville, FL, 1978), 118–25.

16. I have chosen to use the accounts of the treasury districts rather than the *Dirección general de rentas* to evaluate the effectiveness of the reform policies. These records provide a more extensive time series and facilitate comparisons both with the pre-reform period and with other revenues not under the jurisdiction of the *Dirección general de rentas*. Although the amounts remitted from the treasuries of the *Dirección general de rentas* represent surplus income, rather than the gross amounts collected, they still show the profits of these agencies – a good measure of the outcome of the reforms. In a recent critique, D. A. Brading has pointed out some of the problems in working with these materials, particularly when attempting to measure economic performance. He argues instead that historians ought to rely on the accounts of the individual offices of the *Dirección general*. In previous sections of this study, I have used such data in ways that Brading suggests. I believe the treasury records are a more accurate index of the outcome of state policies, however. For a summary of Brading's position, see D. A. Brading, "Comments on 'The Economic Cycle in Bourbon Central Mexico: A Critique of the *Recaudación del diezmo líquido en pesos*,' I," *Hispanic American Historical Review*, 69 (August 1989): 537–38.

17. Although some scholars have criticized recent studies of the treasury accounts for failing to adjust for fluctuations in basic commodity prices, the figures presented in this study are not deflated. Complete price data have simply not been compiled for the entire period from 1690 to 1830. The preliminary price figures that I have collected for the period 1750–90 from the records of rural estates, commercial sales, and tax materials, however, show no inflationary trend, in marked contrast to Mexico. In fact, these data (using 1755 as the base year) show a slight deflationary trend: the price index – compiled from figures for cane liquor, beans, corn, *paño azul*, and potatoes – actually declines 11 percent by 1790. While hardly conclusive, these figures suggest that prices remained relatively static or even declined slightly during the late colonial period. As a result, changes in the nominal figures for treasury receipts were apparently not

yaquil manifested a similar pattern of growth, from 78,909 pesos in 1777 to 213,107 pesos in 1804 – a yearly growth rate of 3.8 percent annually. This trend also held for Cuenca, where the growth in treasury receipts started a few years earlier. Revenues began to rise in 1775 from only 41,463 pesos to 155,196 pesos by 1802, for an average annual growth rate of 4.7 percent.[18] This growth in public revenues throughout the *Audiencia* of Quito was even more rapid than in much wealthier provinces such as Mexico, a clear indication of the state's control over economic output in the province.[19]

The success of the colonial state in raising income in the Quito treasury district depended on new tax levies and more efficient collection procedures. Levels of taxation in the declining economy of the north-central *sierra* remained low until the reform period (see Table 8.1). Then income

influenced significantly by price fluctuations, as in Mexico. The price data used to compile this index come from the following sources: Archivo Nacional de Historia, Quito (hereafter cited as ANH-Q), Haciendas, Caja 3, Estado de las haciendas de Chaquibamba y Lloa, Caja 5, Libro de recivos de la hacienda de San Antonio de Quaxara desde 1 agosto hasta fin de septiembre 1767; Caja 8, Libro de recivo de estas haciendas de San Yldefonso del Colegio Mayor de Sn. Luis, que empieza a correr desde 1 dic. 1759; Caja 14, Cuentas de las haciendas de San Xavier, El Palmar, y San Pedro, 1774–1780; Cuentas ajustadas a dn Francisco Auzeco Echea de las haciendas de Santiago, Carpuela, Chaluayaco, Caldera, Concepción, Chamanal, y Tumbaviro, desde 12 junio 1776 hasta 28 marzo 1778; Cuentas ajustadas a dn Simon Fuentes y Vivero, Comisionado de las Temporalidades de Tacunga desde 31 diciembre 1776 hasta 5 mayo 1778; Caja 20, Cuentas del Obraje y Haciendas de San Ildefonso desde 30 marzo 1780 hasta 31 enero 1787; ANH-Q, Temporalidades, Caja 8, Cuentas dadas por dn Joaquín de Merizalde y comisionado de las Temporalidades de Cuenca, año 1772; and Robson Brines Tyrer, "Demographic and Economic History of the Audiencia of Quito: Indian Population and the Textile Industry, 1600–1800" (Ph.D. diss., University of California at Berkeley, 1976), 188. These price trends are not unique. Indeed, few of South America's regional economies experienced the inflationary trends seen in eighteenth-century Mexico. According to a recent study by Enrique Tandeter, an overall increase in the indigenous population, expanded agricultural production, rising internal trade, and the expansion of European commerce in South America all increased the demand for American silver, which also helps to explain the overall decline of agricultural prices. See Enrique Tandeter, *Coercion and Market: Silver Mining in Colonial Potosí, 1692–1826* (Albuquerque, NM, 1993), 115– 16. For a comparison of prices in Quito to other regions of the empire, see two important studies of colonial prices: Enrique Tandeter and Nathan Wachtel, eds., *Precios y producción agraria: Potosí y Charcas en el siglo XVIII* (Buenos Aires, 1983); and Lyman Johnson and Enrique Tandeter, eds., *Essays on the Price History of Eighteenth-Century Latin America* (Albuquerque, NM, 1990).

18. In these calculations of total income, I have subtracted the amounts listed as carryover funds, such as *debido cobrar, depósitos, existencia, fianzas*, and *reintegros*. These amounts sometimes reached over 50 percent of the total income in certain years, thus distorting dramatically the amounts of money actually flowing into the treasuries each year. AGI, Quito, 419, 429, Cuentas de la Caja de Quito, 1778, 1803; AGI, Quito 469, 471, Cuentas de la Caja de Guayaquil, 1777, 1804; AGI, Quito, 453, 458, Cuentas de la Caja de Cuenca, 1775, 1802.

19. According to figures provided by John J. TePaske and Richard Garner, the rate of growth in public revenues in the treasury office in Mexico City ranged from 2.9 percent to 3.3 percent annually from 1775 to 1809. See Richard L. Garner, "Further Consideration of Facts and Figments in Bourbon Mexico," *Bulletin of Latin American Research*, 6 (1986): 59.

Table 8.1. *Income, Quito caja, 1702–1803*

Year	Commerce & Production	Indian	Bureaucratic	Clerical	Monopolies	Remittances	Loans	Mining	Misc.	Total
1702-04	109,009	66,779	56,577	24,365	13,554		1,880		3,179	275,343
1705-09	41,129	25,286	3,607	18,670	9,808			8,852	1,547	108,899
1710-14	78,843	112,621	68,055	3,285	41,618				2,247	306,669
1715-19	57,551	123,401	36,937	10,472	16,769				8,930	254,060
1720-24	57,070	130,612	50,997	15,418	11,613			62	1,868	267,640
1725-29	70,495	132,053	26,441	22,685	17,645				10,222	279,541
1730-34	94,488	169,822	38,824	18,139	28,778			69	1,593	351,713
1735-39	95,697	262,524	61,482	6,032	27,649			276	572	454,232
1740-44	89,502	159,602	55,295	4,029	21,525	231,543			1,040	562,536
1745-49	164,768	330,961	98,607	14,197	42,876	65,936	25		30,340	747,710
1750-54	111,873	248,101	58,098	13,567	21,709	39,304			15,406	508,058
1755-59	151,562	261,923	38,356	55,669	37,970	17,179		5	40,823	603,487
1760-64	180,098	306,001	72,891	70,095	45,951	219,028			69,147	963,211
1765-69	226,547	209,532	66,517	135,744	33,386	70,236		2	3,863	745,827
1770-74	164,071	281,004	52,711	144,514	48,195	38,637			25,987	755,119
1775-79	173,588	331,291	87,231	122,315	44,845	89,327		9	14,023	862,629
1780-84	339,556	529,813	163,948	496,422	153,543	704,075	56,055	26	45,255	2,488,693
1785-89	295,006	526,959	97,978	710,235	381,523	453,031	15,464	70	28,104	2,508,370
1790-94	362,975	664,928	124,914	307,342	89,085	585,541	47,154	28	36,826	2,218,793
1795-99	308,211	751,039	120,255	255,856	155,326	356,059	50,923		146,781	2,144,450
1800-03	290,069	644,643	88,463	347,029	105,592	343,598	115,471	52	105,627	2,040,544
All	3,462,108	6,268,895	1,468,189	2,796,080	1,348,960	3,213,494	286,972	9451	593,380	19,447,529

Note: The following years are missing from the AGI, Seville, and the ANH, Quito: 1706-10, 1716-17, 1733, 1740, and 1786. In several years, particularly early in the eighteenth century, some tax categories generated no income; when this occurs, blank spaces appear in the table.

Sources: ANH, Quito, Real Hacienda 10, 11, Cuentas de la Caja de Quito, 1702-1705, 1739; AGI, Contaduría, 1539-1540, Quito, 140-144, 173, 175, 416-429, Cuentas de la Caja de Quito, 1711-1803.

levels increased rapidly. Remittances from the Guayaquil and Cuenca treasuries played an important role in this process, rising from only 38,637 pesos in the period from 1770 through 1774 to over 700,000 pesos ten years later (see Table 8.1). Significant increases in revenues collected in the Quito district itself also revealed enhanced state control over local resources. Clerical taxes, for example, increased 500 percent after the onset of the *visita*, largely because of the confiscation of Jesuit wealth after 1767. Likewise, royal monopolies accounted for 5–15 percent of the total income in Quito.[20] Income levels from traditional taxes, such as Amerindian tribute and levies on trade and production, also rose rapidly after 1778 (see Table 8.1). These increases are even more striking, given the overall stagnation or decline in the population under the jurisdiction of the Quito treasury office.

Remittances from the *Dirección general de rentas* also played a key role in the rising tax receipts at the Quito treasury office. In 1778, the new fiscal bureaucracy remitted only 86,519 pesos to Quito; by 1803, officials from the various offices of the *Dirección general* sent 211,775 pesos. Increased yields from Amerindian tribute and the cane liquor monopoly accounted for much of this rise in revenues. Tribute returns climbed from 51,050 pesos in 1778 to over 195,000 pesos in 1801, while *aguardiente* taxes jumped from 14,952 pesos in 1778 to 44,246 pesos in 1803.[21]

The *visita* of José García de Leon y Pizarro also strengthened state fiscal control in the Guayaquil region, as collections of tax revenues increased and became more predictable. Before the reform period, public revenues remained dependent on port taxes, but yields were erratic (see Table 8.2). García Pizarro's establishment of a new customs house (*aduana*) and the monopolies on cane liquor and tobacco in 1778 ended these problems. Income from taxes on commerce and production increased from 130,174 pesos in the five years before the *visita* to over 600,000 pesos between 1800 and 1804 (see Table 8.2). Contributions from the *Dirección general* also played an increasingly important role in total income levels, rising from only 28,774 pesos in 1778 (30 percent of total income) to 169,014 pesos by 1804 (79 percent of total income).[22] Increased yields from clerical taxes, as in Quito, stemmed from the crown's control over the former Jesuit properties, while rising tribute receipts resulted from more efficient

---

20. I have included the returns from the *aguardiente* monopoly with levies on commerce and production rather than with royal monopolies. The funds were profits from the manufacture and sale of cane liquor, made from locally grown sugar cane. As a result, they represented local production and trade more directly than any other monopoly in the Quito district.

21. These figures are compiled from the following *legajos*: AGI, Quito, 418–29, Cuentas de la Caja de Quito, 1778–1803.

22. These data are compiled from AGI, Quito, 469, 472–77, Cuentas de la Caja de Guayaquil, 1778–1804.

Table 8.2. *Income, Guayaquil caja, 1714-1804*

Year	Commerce & Production	Indian	Bureaucratic	Clerical	Monopolies	Remittances	Loans	Mining	Misc.	Total
1714	4,810	3,060	67		63			26		8,026
1715-19	24,477	5,789	1,140		5,806			130	13,682	51,024
1720-24	33,618	2,497	1,455		1,688				53,880	91,138
1725-29	50,882	5,133	2,013		431				17,713	76,172
1730-34	47,506		3,771		1,796					53,073
1735-39	12,505		362		1,180					14,047
1740-44	63,389				3,945				57,760	125,094
1745-49	80,801	12,425			2,107				20,936	116,269
1750-54	18,848		364		498	75,000		630		95,340
1755-59	73,742	1,017	3,345	5,053	2,530	28,000		410	50,949	165,046
1760-64	74,598	15,375	21,004	7,797	3,327	1,645		120	11,525	135,391
1765-69	119,452	17,903	4,053	23,218	2,404	53,752		17,180	11,278	249,240
1770-74	130,174	16,344	6,272	15,782	5,554	68,966		800	5,003	248,895
1775-79	186,426	30,022	21,814	22,874	44,098	64,384		2,500	7,788	379,906
1780-84	449,571	38,080	46,452	52,602	181,581	97,032		1,924	25,824	893,066
1785-89	357,861	63,453	25,706	8,700	122,836	124,029	866	6	39,260	742,717
1790-94	423,069	61,651	17,681	1,822	130,288	9,932	9,786	20	25,157	679,406
1795-99	478,918	58,711	25,082	1,247	113,774	1,090	9,427	34	19,600	707,883
1800-04	619,603	65,753	21,745	55,183	79,252	102,723	6,227	17	172,421	1,122,924
All	3,250,250	397,213	202,326	194,278	703,158	626,553	26,306	23,797	532,776	5,956,657

Note: The following years are missing from the AGI, Seville, and the ANH, Quito: 1730, 1734, 1736-1739, 1750-1752. In several years, particularly early in the eighteenth century, some tax categories generated no income; when this occurs, blank spaces appear in the table.

Sources: AGI, Contaduría, 1377, 1576-77; Quito, 407, 469-75, 477.

tax collection procedures and the influx of Andean migrants seeking work on coastal plantations.[23] In short, the reforms of García Pizarro established firm governmental control over the coastal economy, just as the export boom commenced after 1778.

The development of state fiscal control was least successful in Cuenca, where the *Dirección general de rentas* collected only Amerindian tribute. Government power had always been notoriously weak in the south highlands. The public revenues (shown in Table 8.3) fluctuated between 37,598 pesos (1755–59) and 89,492 pesos (1760–64), with the bulk of these meager amounts coming from Amerindian tribute.[24] After the onset of the reform period, however, remittances from the local office of the tribute administration rose from nearly 146,000 pesos (1775–79) to over 270,000 pesos (1795–99).[25] The only other lucrative levies were on regional commerce, which went from 30,739 pesos (1770–74) to nearly 90,000 pesos (1795–99).[26] Revenue increases in Cuenca were modest, and the tax base remained virtually unchanged from early in the century (see Table 8.3). After the reforms, the state collected revenues more consistently but did not extend its fiscal control over any new economic sectors.

The dramatic rise in per capita tax rates in the late colonial period provides graphic evidence of the growing fiscal control of the Bourbon state. In the Quito district, for example, each citizen paid an average of 13 reales by the late eighteenth century.[27] At the same time, per capita taxes on Amerindians doubled during the period, from 4 reales to 8 reales.[28] Creoles, peninsulars, and castes paid approximately 22 reales.

23. Michael T. Hamerly, *Historia social y económica de la antigua provincia de Guayaquil, 1763–1842* (Guayaquil, 1973), 65–79; and María Luisa Laviana Cuetos, *Guayaquil en el siglo XVIII: recursos naturales y desarrollo económico* (Seville, 1987), 104–13.

24. Amerindian tribute accounted for 51–86 percent of the total income in the Cuenca district before the reform period. Cuenca's small European population paid virtually nothing in taxes until 1770, apart from minor exactions on regional trade and production. AGI, Contaduría, 1534, Quito, 453, Cuentas de la Caja de Cuenca, 1722–1775.

25. These remittances normally accounted for between 50 percent and 60 percent of total income. See AGI, Quito, 453–458, Cuentas de la Caja de Cuenca, 1775–1803.

26. Bureaucratic and clerical taxes experienced only modest increases, while royal monopolies were an insignificant source of funds until 1780–84, when they began to yield over 13,000 *pesos*. See Table 8.3.

27. I calculated the amount of taxes per capita by using the population figures taken from the following sources: AGI, Quito, 381, 412, Numeración de Juan Josef de Villalengua, 1780; Martin Minchom, "Demographic Change in Eighteenth-Century Ecuador," in M. Delaunay and M. Portais, eds., *Equateur 1986*, 3 vols. (Paris, 1989), 1:179–96; Laviana Cuetos, *Guayaquil en el siglo XVIII*, 77–159. I then divided these figures by the income from taxes in each treasury district, after subtracting the carryover funds.

28. I used the ethnic breakdowns in the census materials and divided each racial-ethnic group by the amount collected from the taxes levied against them. In the case of the Amerindians, I

Table 8.3. *Income, Cuenca caja, 1722-1803*

Year	Commerce & Production	Indian	Bureaucratic	Clerical	Monopolies	Remittances	Loans	Mining	Misc.	Total
1722-24	5,970	29,024	12,411	114	265				3,128	50,912
1725-29	11,120	38,390	11,800		956			22	2,940	65,228
1730-34	10,348	26,099	10,448		1,662			30	308	48,895
1735-39	1,910	3,195	375					14	120	5,614
1740-44										
1745-49	1,517	10,334	137		14				30	12,032
1750-54	21,966	33,340	9,513					59	1	64,879
1755-59	10,143	22,846	4,003		466				140	37,598
1760-64	24,699	56,405	7,535		605			48	200	89,492
1765-69	18,928	36,975	7,054						1,672	64,629
1770-74	30,739	125,459	6,270	1,225	6,015	526		1,675	3,197	175,106
1775-79	66,054	145,999	15,000		8,412		28	1,889	18,157	255,539
1780-84	58,366	192,828	17,035		13,777		450	3,905	22,989	309,350
1785-89	68,005	208,386	13,747	882	14,566		4,791	3,236	18,373	331,986
1790-94	80,285	259,268	26,062	46,043	16,246		26,247	2,974	11,446	468,571
1795-99	89,030	271,872	24,774	52,010	36,106	30,000	19,347	2,808	14,914	540,861
1800-03	67,785	207,479	45,776	18,490	65,012		39,508	1,049	81,348	526,447
All	566,865	1,667,899	211,940	118,764	164,764	30,526	90,371	17,709	178,963	3,047,139

Note: The following years are missing from the AGI, Seville, and the AHN, Quito: 1734, 1736-1747, 1749, and 1772. In several years, particularly early in the eighteenth century, some tax categories generated no income; when this occurs blank spaces appear in the table.

Sources: AGI, Contaduría, 1534, Quito, 453-58, Cuentas de la Caja de Cuerca, 1722-1803.

Tax levels in Cuenca remained significantly lower. Nevertheless, per capita taxes rose from 2.5 reales to 3.3 reales. Taxes on Amerindians doubled, while significant increases also fell on the European and caste populations, whose per capita tax burden rose from under 1 real to over 6 reales annually.[29] The most dramatic rise, however, took place in the Guayaquil district, where per capita taxes soared from 11 reales in 1765 to over 48 reales by 1780. Coastal Amerindians saw their per capita tax burden increase from 4 reales to 6 reales, while the white and caste populations endured a tremendous expansion of their taxes from 13 to 75 reales by the turn of the century.

State control over local resources in the *audiencia* district reached extremely high levels, particularly when compared to other European colonial systems. Although a great economic and military power, England was never able to levy taxes so effectively in its relatively prosperous North American colonies. Despite the decline of textile manufacturing in the north-central highlands, taxpayers in the Quito district paid twice as much in per capita taxes as the English colonists in North America.[30] The amounts paid in Guayaquil dwarfed anything collected in the thirteen English colonies. In fact, the per capita tax burden in Guayaquil reached nearly twice the amounts paid in England itself, which reputedly had among the highest tax levels in western Europe.[31] By the late colonial period, the reforms of García Pizarro created a state fiscal apparatus as powerful and exploitative as any in the world.

The large number of regressive taxes also had serious repercussions for the socioeconomic evolution of the kingdom. Apart from a tremendous increase in the tax burden, the amounts collected in direct taxes (levied on income and wealth) tended to fall as a percentage of total income from 1780 to 1805.[32] In the Quito district, these generally more pro-

---

assumed that they paid only tribute; thus, their per capita tax burden is a bare-minimum figure. I also subtracted the figures for the slave populations from the totals for the Europeans and castes, assuming that the bondsmen paid no taxes.

29. This rise clearly reflects the minimal levels of taxes paid by non-Amerindians in the south highlands before the reform period.

30. Taxpayers in Cuenca paid approximately the same amounts in per capita taxes as the English colonists, but the economic output of the south highlands was hardly comparable. For sources indicating the tax burdens in English North America, see Edwin Perkins, *The Economy of Colonial America* (New York, 1980), 124–43. Information on the necessary currency conversions needed to make these comparisons may be found in John J. McCusker, *Money and Exchange in Europe and North America, 1600–1775: A Handbook* (Chapel Hill, NC, 1978), 3–12.

31. Perkins, *The Economy of Colonial America*, 129; Peter Mathias, *The First Industrial Nation: An Economic History of Britain, 1700–1914* (London, 1969), 32–50.

32. Calculating the amounts in direct taxes is difficult. Some levies collected for the sales tax on local estates, for example, might be considered levies on wealth and income. So might some royal monopolies, such as the one on tobacco. At the same time, income from the administration of former Jesuit properties might or might not be considered direct taxes. For the purposes of

gressive taxes fell from 51 percent of total income to 43 percent during this period, while in Cuenca they dropped from 76 percent to 59 percent. Direct levies accounted for only 14 percent of total income in Guayaquil.[33] As a result, more regressive indirect taxes (mostly levied on sales, commerce, and consumption) accounted for most of the tax increases. Even direct taxes, however, could be burdensome and regressive. In Quito and Cuenca, for example, Amerindian tribute accounted for the majority of direct taxes, but assessments for this head tax seldom varied according to the income potential of taxpayers.[34] Consequently, any tax increase fell disproportionately on the exploited Amerindian communities of the highlands. The extremely high level of indirect taxes along the coast (86 percent) also penalized the most rapidly growing economic zone. Such policies effectively transferred wealth from the coast and the poorest highland groups to those elites working in nonproductive bureaucratic jobs in Quito and to metropolitan Spain.

The remarkable financial success of García Pizarro's reforms rested upon the state's ability to draw taxes from regional economies, regardless of whether they experienced cycles of growth or recession. Although the crown imposed few additional levies after 1778, new state administrations extracted much higher levels of public revenues from local economies, particularly in Guayaquil and Quito. Guayaquil had paid relatively low taxes early in the century, but once the export economy began to grow, the crown increased the tax burden tremendously. Quito, however, experienced no such prosperity during the century; instead the state drew

---

this exercise, however, I used the following entries as direct taxes: *novenos, pulperías,* Amerindian tribute – *tributos, encomiendas,* and *tributos de forasteros* – *media anata,* the *monte píos, mesadas, media anata eclesiastica, temporalidades,* and *cascarilla.* For an article that examines these issues for Great Britain and France, see Peter Mathias and Patrick O'Brien, "Taxation in Britain and France, 1715–1810. A Comparison of the Social and Economic Incidence of Taxes Collected for the Central Governments," *Journal of European Economic History,* 5:3 (1976): 601–50.

33. While the income from direct taxes rose in Quito from 4,128,654 pesos in the years 1700–79 to 4,866,704 pesos in the brief period 1780–1805, the percentage of total income did fall. Likewise, in Cuenca direct taxes rose from 657,628 pesos (1720–79) to 1,287,756 pesos (1780–1803), and in Guayaquil direct taxes went from 273,157 pesos (1710–79) to 570,453 pesos (1780–1804). See ANH-Q, Real Hacienda, 10, 11, Cuentas de la Caja de Quito, 1702–05, 1739; AGI, Contaduría, 1539–40, Quito, 140–44, 173, 175, 416–24, Cuentas de la Caja de Quito, 1711–1803; AGI, Contaduría, 1377, 1576–77; Quito, 407, 469–75, 477, Cuentas de la Caja de Guayaquil, 1710–1804; and AGI, Contaduría 1534, Quito, 453–58, Cuentas de la Caja de Cuenca, 1722–1803.

34. *Ibid.* The assessments were fixed and did not vary (except in exceptional cases, like natural disasters) in response to crop yields. In the largely agrarian Amerindian villages, this meant the tax burden became particularly onerous after bad harvests. In addition, the tribute rates in the north-central highlands had been set at artificially high levels, apparently to encourage Amerindians to seek work on the *obrajes* or Spanish rural estates. The decline of the highland economy precluded this option in most areas by the late colonial era.

markedly increased tax receipts from a declining regional economy. The overriding aim of García Pizarro, his cronies, and their superiors in Spain was to extract resources from the *audiencia*, regardless of the cost. The Bourbon Reforms had surely come to the Kingdom of Quito but at a very high price.

State expenditures and public policy

From the *visita general* of José García de Leon y Pizarro, the colonial state directed royal funds to meet imperial rather than local needs. Each year the colonial treasuries spent whatever was necessary to meet local government expenses and sent the remainder to Cartagena, and thence to Spain. During periods of expanding revenues, such as the late eighteenth century, state officials shipped increasingly large sums of money to Cartagena, rather than spending it within the *audiencia* district. Remittances to Spain increased from only 109,299 pesos in the period 1700–04 to over 1,098,427 pesos between 1800 and 1803 (see Table 8.4). Moreover, the percentage of total expenditures sent to Spain rose from 37 percent to over 56 percent during those same years. García Pizarro and his successors had changed the fiscal priorities in government spending markedly.

The only other major expenses of the Quito treasury were administrative and defense outlays. Administrative costs rose steadily during the century, reaching a high of 755,034 pesos between 1795 and 1799. Nevertheless, their share of total expenditures dropped from a high of 58 percent between 1710 and 1714 to an average of only 25 percent after the *visita general*. The money spent on local defense, however, grew from insignificant amounts early in the century to over 385,688 pesos, when García Pizarro established the new disciplined militia system in the region (see Table 8.4). Despite increasing remittances to Spain, fiscal reform clearly exacted a heavy price in rising administrative and defense expenditures.

In both Guayaquil and Cuenca, remittances to Quito rose sharply during the century. The sums shipped from Guayaquil to Quito were particularly impressive. According to the data in Table 8.5, the coastal treasury sent only 52,626 pesos to Quito between 1770 and 1774; after the García Pizarro reforms, however, remittances reached 531,784 pesos (1785–89). The Cuenca *caja* also sent between 212,708 pesos (1780–84) and 359,293 pesos (1795–99), which averaged approximately 70 percent of the treasury's total expenses (see Table 8.6). These funds from Guayaquil and Cuenca formed a large portion of the annual subsidy sent from Quito to Cartagena.

The Guayaquil and Cuenca treasuries also allocated increasing sums

Table 8.4. *Expenditures, Quito caja, 1702-1803*

Year	Remittances	Clerical	Administ.	Defense	Loans	Misc.	Total
1702-04	109,299	11,459	124,635	18,389	6,300	22,085	292,167
1705-09	89,073	2,780	44,420	1,000	2,100	18,306	157,679
1710-14	91,039	23,832	188,225		7,700	12,407	323,203
1715-19	131,286	10,098	125,308		5,600	11,162	283,454
1720-24	100,475	26,476	134,237		8,400	9,641	279,229
1725-29	136,298	24,384	134,507		4,200	4,567	303,956
1730-34	171,914	42,039	207,360		10,500	9,077	440,890
1735-39	254,250	55,854	185,725		10,500	34,924	541,253
1740-44	339,020	3,950	47,810	151,834	8,400	2,408	553,422
1745-49	416,458	96,890	406,119		10,500	6,292	936,259
1750-54	265,481	64,788	187,659		11,200	11,951	541,079
1755-59	297,079	49,213	213,148	13,294	10,500	14,199	597,433
1760-64	584,480	60,131	198,279	24,729	10,500	30,851	908,970
1765-69	255,665	37,580	225,883	171,509	12,500	23,080	726,217
1770-74	297,831	46,248	253,551	115,065	11,400	53,606	777,701
1775-79	502,170	49,381	321,531	194,339	7,300	39,417	1,114,138
1780-84	1,381,856	71,246	402,590	329,747	26,350	113,010	2,324,799
1785-89	967,435	35,255	508,976	281,572	8,400	91,359	1,892,997
1790-94	1,230,930	101,149	508,927	385,688	9,654	66,422	2,302,770
1795-99	1,118,378	34,405	755,034	226,332	11,346	32,445	2,177,940
1800-03	1,098,427	44,269	510,430	255,527	8,400	41,279	1,958,332
All	9,838,844	891,427	5,684,354	2,169,025	201,750	648,488	19,433,888

Note: The following years are missing from the AGI, Seville, and the ANH, Quito: 1706-1710, 1716-1717, 1724-1726, 1733, 1740, 1786. In several years. particularly early in the eighteenth century, some tax categories generated no income; when this occurs, blank spaces appear in the table.
Source: ANH, Quito, Real Hacienda, 10, 11, Cuentas de la Caja de Quito, 1702-1705, 1739; AGI, Contaduría, 1539-1540, Quito, 140-144, 173, 175, 416-429, Cuentas de la Caja de Quito, 1711-1803.

for local administration and defense. Administrative costs in Guayaquil rose from only 46,023 pesos between 1770 and 1774 to over 433,823 pesos in the period 1800–04 (see Table 8.5). Likewise, the cost of government operations in Cuenca nearly doubled between 1770 and 1795 (see Table 8.6). Defense spending, however, escalated most dramatically in Guayaquil. García Pizarro made the strategic port city the centerpiece of his military reforms, causing defense expenditures to rise to nearly 250,000 pesos between 1800 and 1804 (see Table 8.5). On the other hand, military outlays were never extensive in Cuenca, which played an insignificant role in the defense of the realm.

Despite increased expenses, the treasury system in the Kingdom of

Table 8.5. *Expenditures, Guayaquil caja, 1714-1804*

Year	Remittances	Clerical	Administ.	Defense	Shipyards	Loans	Misc.	Total
1714		615	2,089	1,651				4,355
1715-19		615	2,446	1,294				4,355
1720-24	11,545	2,460	16,782	2,417	29,932		853	63,989
1725-29	8,393	3,033	13,347	1,989	21,984		1,685	50,431
1730-34		1,845	4,767	57	27,678		125	34,472
1735-39	25,000	615	1,491	1,026	7,841		4,385	40,358
1740-44	15,000	2,209	10,544	48,285	44,676		24,762	145,476
1745-49	39,134	4,342	26,779	7,240	4,746		219	82,460
1750-54		11,020	6,429	1,011	86,696		1,446	106,602
1755-59	333	6,256	21,787	2,522	49,596		43,406	123,900
1760-64	67,194	1,920	17,918	12,953	308			100,293
1765-69	170,191	6,117	33,330	37,192	5,074		7,691	259,595
1770-74	52,626		46,023	55,190	89,987		4,000	247,826
1775-79	149,561		74,739	110,520			2,545	337,365
1780-84	509,267	809	111,748	219,862	16,967		9,821	868,474
1785-89	531,784	2,737	193,297	90,448	1,706	4,750	5,932	830,654
1790-94	339,803	4,136	98,850	85,642	864		16,758	546,053
1795-99	330,329		213,334	214,628			200	758,491
1800-04	426,829		433,823	249,368			324	1,110,344
All	2,676,989	48,729	1,329,523	1,143,295	388,055	4,750	124,152	5,715,493

Note: The following years are missing from the AGI, Seville, and the ANH, Quito: 1730, 1734, 1736-1739, and 1750-1752. In several years. particularly early in the eighteenth century, some tax categories generated no income; when this occurs, blank spaces appear in the table.
Source: AGI, Contaduría, 1377, 1576-1577, Quito, 407, 469-475, 477.

Quito became increasingly centralized and responsive to metropolitan needs by the late colonial period. The treasuries extracted escalating amounts of revenue, both from growing coastal export zones and declining regional economies in the north-central highlands. Moreover, increased remittances from Guayaquil and Cuenca to Quito allowed the state to transfer ever larger sums to Cartagena and Spain. Funds were no longer retained to support local economies as in earlier years, except for defense and administration, which primarily increased the coercive power of the state and subsidized loyal colonial elites in government posts or the military.

The reforms of García Pizarro in the Kingdom of Quito demonstrate clearly that crown policy aimed to increase revenues, not to promote any lasting economic development in the kingdom. Such policies primarily involved tightening administrative and fiscal controls. Crown policies clearly discriminated against manufacturing, trade, or agricultural cen-

Table 8.6. *Expenditures, Cuenca caja, 1722-1803*

Year	Remittances	Clerical	Administ.	Defense	Misc.	Total
1722-24	30,468	10,525	13,845		794	55,632
1725-29	43,497	9,619	12,063	255	629	66,063
1730-34	32,064	2,101	8,031	1,000	4,187	47,383
1735-39	3,064		1,290	400		4,754
1740-44						
1745-49		2,636	2,333			4,969
1750-54	21,325	5,618	17,147		4,000	48,090
1755-59	35,100	4,184	12,797			52,081
1760-64	27,630	3,234	15,380			46,244
1765-69	45,150	2,064	7,115		4,625	58,954
1770-74	111,990		50,921	1,874	76,362	241,147
1775-79	127,207		75,819	4,620	18,594	226,240
1780-84	212,708		69,232		44,621	326,561
1785-89	248,485	6,156	62,017	6,501	14,569	337,728
1790-94	322,712	35,795	90,726	5,865	3,964	459,062
1795-99	359,293	56,815	83,542	540	11,041	511,231
1800-03	260,107	50,611	81,974	6,848	3,106	402,646
All	1,880,800	189,358	604,231	27,903	186,492	2,888,784

Note: The following years are missing from the AGI, Seville, and the ANH, Quito: 1734, 1736-1747, 1749, and 1772. In several years. particularly early in the eighteenth century, some tax categories generated no income; when this occurs, blank spaces appear in the table.

Sources: AGI, Contaduría, 1534, Quito, 453-58, Cuentas de la Caja de Cuenca, 1722-1803.

ters, such as the north-central *sierra*. As Archbishop Antonio Caballero y Góngora, the viceroy of New Granada (1782–89) observed, the decline of Quito's textile industry was entirely fitting, because agriculture and mining were "the appropriate function of the colonies," while manufactured goods like cloth "ought to be imported from the metropolis."[35] As the fiscal accounts from the Kingdom of Quito indicate, however, even favored regions, such as the coastal export economy around Guayaquil, paid exceedingly high taxes by the late colonial period.

Reform and corruption

How could García Pizarro have imposed policies so blatantly exploitative and detrimental to long-term economic development in the kingdom?

---

35. Quoted in John Lynch, "The Origins of Spanish American Independence," in Leslie Bethell, ed., *The Independence of Latin America* (Cambridge, 1987), 16.

Answers to this question began to emerge after the president left Quito in 1783 to assume a post on the Council of the Indies. Rumors had reached Madrid that José García de Leon y Pizarro and his "political family" had ruled despotically in Quito, intimidating the creole aristocracy and the church, extorting bribes to enrich his clan, selling public offices, and using the militia to enforce his corrupt designs.[36] These allegations also implicated Ramón García Pizarro in Guayaquil.[37] García Pizarro and his allies allegedly used whatever means were possible to raise revenues for the benefit of the crown and themselves.

José García de Leon y Pizarro remained a powerful force on the Council of the Indies, but the death of his patron José de Gálvez in 1787 left him more politically vulnerable to the charges. On 9 October 1788, the crown ordered a full investigation of the alleged wrongdoing in Quito.[38] When the viceroy of New Granada, Francisco de Gil y Lemos, received the order to begin an inquiry, he entrusted the task to Fernando de Quadrado y Valdenebro, one of the few eighteenth-century justices renowned for his personal and professional honesty. According to the bishop of Quito, Quadrado was a very "rare bird," because "integrity with money and integrity with women is miraculous in these provinces."[39]

Although Fernando de Quadrado quickly ran afoul of García Pizarro's successor and son-in-law Juan Josef de Villalengua, he doggedly set about compiling a strong case against the former president and his "political family."[40] Despite threatening reports that José García de Leon y Pizarro had paid large sums from the Quito treasury to bribe high officials in

---

36. AGI, Quito, 272, Francisco de Gil y Lemos to Fernando de Quadrado, Santa Fe, 26 enero 1789.
37. Several prominent citizens in the port city wrote to Madrid denouncing the governor's corruption and involvement in the contraband trade, his attempts to intimidate the city council, and his creation of a virtual monopoly over the export of tobacco and cacao for himself and a few cronies. AGI, Quito, 271, Anonymous to crown, Guayaquil, 4 diciembre 1787; AGI, Quito, 271, Joaquín Pareja to crown, Guayaquil, 4 mayo 1789; AGI, Quito, 271, Antonio Marcos to crown, Guayaquil, 19 diciembre 1787.
38. AGI, Quito, 272, Francisco de Gil y Lemos to Fernando de Quadrado, Santa Fe, 26 enero 1789.
39. Mark A. Burkholder, "Honest Judges Leave Destitute Heirs: The Price of Integrity in Eighteenth-Century Spain," in Richard K. Matthews, *Virtue, Corruption, and Self-Interest: Political Values in the Eighteenth Century* (Bethlehem, PA, 1994), 257.
40. News of the investigation outraged García Pizarro's successor, Villalengua, who denounced Quadrado and his allies as notorious foes of the former president. The viceroy discounted these complaints, citing Villalengua's close family and political connections to the García Pizarro clan. Moreover, Gil y Lemos was a conservative military man, suspicious of the innovations sponsored by García Pizarro, particularly the expensive fiscal bureaucracy that he had created in Quito. AGI, Quito, 267, Francisco de Gil y Lemos to Antonio Porlier, Santa Fe, 14 mayo 1789. AGI, Quito, 272, Francisco de Gil y Lemos to Fernando de Quadrado, Santa Fe, 26 enero 1789; AGI, Quito, 267, Juan Josef de Villalengua to Antonio Porlier, Quito, 3 abril 1789, 18 mayo 1789; 18 junio 1789; Juan Josef de Villalengua to Francisco de Gil y Lemos, Quito, 26 marzo 1789, 28 marzo 1789, 1 abril 1789, 14 mayo 1789, 30 mayo 1789, 19 junio 1789.

Spain, Quadrado persisted in uncovering a host of abuses.[41] The former president had allegedly extorted over 230,000 pesos in bribes from every public official in Quito, even taking 20,000 pesos from the bishop.[42] Quadrado also questioned García Pizarro's famous fiscal innovations, claiming that much of the money from the administration of Jesuit assets came from the sale of land, not the skillful management of the properties. The special investigator found corruption so rampant in the *Dirección general de rentas* that he recommended an investigation of its agencies.[43] In short, Justice Quadrado claimed to have sufficient evidence to prove that García Pizarro and his successor, Juan Josef de Villalengua, had promoted nepotism, corruption, intimidation, and deep political divisions in the kingdom.

Villalengua and his allies impeded the investigation at every turn, and by 1790 the whole affair had degenerated into a series of charges and counter charges.[44] It became apparent that only the Madrid government's intervention could resolve the political deadlock in Quito. After a careful review of the evidence, members of the Council of the Indies, surprisingly, decided not to mete out any punishments. To calm the political situation, the council made Juan Josef de Villalengua the president-regent of the *Audiencia* of Guatemala and sent Ramón García Pizarro to serve as governor in Salta. As for Fernando de Quadrado, the council supported his efforts to uncover the truth about corruption in Quito and Guayaquil but acknowledged that he had far exceeded their original instructions. His charge had been merely to investigate certain specific accusations, not to probe into every aspect of the García Pizarro clan's activities in Quito. In the end, the council ordered the new president, Juan Antonio de Mon y Velarde, to complete the investigation quickly and promote harmony in the Kingdom of Quito. The councilors made no further mention of any alleged abuses of their colleague José García de Leon y Pizarro, and the affair conveniently ended.[45]

---

41. AGI, Quito, 267, Carta reservada, Fernando de Quadrado to Francisco de Gil y Lemos, Quito, 21 marzo 1789.
42. AGI, Quito, 267, Resúmen del dinero, plata labrada, y alajas de oro, piedras y perlas que resultan del información averse regalado a la señora Pizarro, Quito, no date; González Suárez, *Historia general*, 1207–22.
43. AGI, Quito, 267, Fernando de Quadrado to Francisco de Gil y Lemos, Quito, 18 mayo 1789.
44. An interesting insight into Villalengua's character may be found in his response to a royal order demanding the establishment of institutions to care for smallpox victims in 1785. In 1787 Villalengua responded by recommending, as a cost-saving measure, housing the smallpox victims with the city's indigents in the old *Casa de Ejercicios* of the Jesuits. The crown wisely disapproved of the plan to expose the ill-nourished urban poor to a highly contagious disease such as small-pox. See Jacques A. Barbier and Lynda deForest Craig, "Lepers and Hospitals in the Spanish Empire: An Aspect of Bourbon Reform in Health Care," *Ibero-Amerikanisches Archiv*, 11:4 (1985): 401.
45. *Ibid.* Although the power of the García Pizarro clan in Quito was broken, the careers of José

Although José García de Leon y Pizarro had created a strong administrative state, he also manipulated it cynically for his own ends. The "great reformer" was only a supremely successful and ruthless practitioner of the traditional politics of corruption, nepotism, and intimidation in Quito. The very powers vested in him by the reformist Spanish crown and the newly reinvigorated colonial state contributed mightily to his "success" in imposing this apparently tyrannical regime. García Pizarro made no attempt to use this powerful political apparatus to promote socioeconomic development in Bourbon Quito; he just drained its wealth for the metropolis, himself, and his political cronies.

As the colonial treasury accounts indicate, after García Pizarro's departure the strong, activist colonial state continued to exploit regional economies in the kingdom until the onset of the independence period. Despite the overall decline of the economy in the north-central highlands, the accounts for the Quito treasury show substantial revenue increases until 1803.[46] These revenue figures provide eloquent testimony to the success of this more exploitative and efficient state apparatus. The spiraling level of taxation also did little to promote even the coastal export economy. In the end, the Bourbon Reforms left a legacy of government intervention and predatory fiscal policies that severely limited the long-term economic prospects of the Kingdom of Quito.

The legacy of state activism in the independence and early republican eras

Sporadic discontent among all sectors of society with the exploitative policies of the colonial state undoubtedly contributed to the outbreak of a full-fledged movement for political autonomy in the kingdom in 1809 (after news of the French invasion of Iberia arrived). Nevertheless, the inability of two creole-led provisional *juntas* in 1809 and 1810 to gain widespread popular support throughout the kingdom led to their rapid downfall; even a revolt in Guayaquil in 1820 failed to expand beyond

and Ramón García de Leon y Pizarro and Juan Josef de Villalengua y Marfil continued to prosper. Ramón García Pizarro eventually became president of the *Audiencia* of Charcas, where he remained until the independence movements in South America, while Juan Josef de Villalengua was named to the Order of Charles III and promoted to the Council of the Indies in late 1794. Kuethe, *Military Reform*, 125; and Burkholder and Chandler, *Biographical Dictionary*, 358.

46. The last systematic colonial fiscal accounts that I found in the Spanish and Ecuadorian archives were for 1803, for Quito and Cuenca, and 1804 for Guayaquil. Extant accounts exist for the "cajas nacionales de Quito" for 1812 and 1813. See AGI, Quito, 458, Cuentas de la Caja de Cuenca, 1803; AGI, Quito, 477, Cuentas de la Caja de Guayaquil, 1804; AGI, Quito, 429, Cuentas de la Caja de Quito, 1803; and AGI, Quito, 415, Cuentas de las Cajas nacionales de Quito, 1812–1813.

the coast.[47] Formal independence did not come until the insurgent armies of Simón Bolivar's trusted lieutenant José Antonio de Sucre won the Battle of Pichincha in 1822. The downfall of the colonial system, however, only unleashed the pressures of regionalism and disunity.

In the chaotic years of the independence struggle (1809–22) the strong, centralized colonial state disintegrated in the Kingdom of Quito. Before the incorporation of the old *audiencia* district (now called Ecuador) into the Republic of Gran Colombia in 1822, the fiscal bureaucracies of Quito, Guayaquil, and Cuenca operated virtually independently. Even after joining the Colombian union, this fiscal decentralization continued apace. By the creation of the Republic of Ecuador in 1830, the strong activist state established by the Bourbons had essentially disappeared. As the new republic's finance minister complained in 1831, the nation was really three separate fiscal entities operating from Quito, Guayaquil, and Cuenca.[48]

The early history of the new republic was a long and generally inconclusive struggle between centralists and regionalists (who advocated creating local, autonomous, ad hoc *juntas* to collect and disburse government funds).[49] Amidst this conflict, the state proved effective only in promoting minimal levels of public order and foreign security. As a result, the fiscal records were sporadically kept and usually incomplete. The national government in Quito was never able to gain accurate data on the economy, formulate a rational tax code, create a professional bureaucracy, or overcome the elite's intransigent opposition to paying even the minimal levels of taxation needed to run the government.[50]

The best, most comprehensive study of the political economy in the early republic – by Linda Alexander Rodríguez – indicates that taxes remained regressive and perpetually inadequate. Total government income from 1830 to 1861 rose slowly from 554,000 pesos to 1,276,000 pesos.[51] It was not until the 1850s that republican income levels matched those of the late Bourbon period. Despite these problems, important continuities with the colonial fiscal regime persisted. Indirect taxes remained a crucial source of government funds. The customs duties collected at

47. For a good summary of these independence movements, see Demetrio Ramos Pérez, *Entre el Plata y Bogotá: cuatro claves de la emancipación Ecuatoriana* (Madrid, 1978).
48. At this time Cauca was also included in the republic and was cited as the fourth fiscal district. See Linda Alexander Rodríguez, *The Search for Public Policy: Regional Politics and Government Finances in Ecuador, 1830–1940* (Berkeley, CA, 1985), 56.
49. *Ibid.*, 55.
50. *Ibid.*, 54.
51. The fiscal data for Ecuador are sporadic for the early nineteenth century. To facilitate comparisons with the colonial period I used figures taken from Linda Rodríguez going up to 1861, rather than 1830, in order to get an adequate sample of the accounts capable of illustrating the basic fiscal trends.

Guayaquil, for example, accounted for 34–64 percent of all public revenues.[52] The cacao economy of Guayaquil had recovered from the dislocations of the independence period, and exports from the port rose rapidly by the 1830s.[53] Direct taxes such as Amerindian tribute and the tithe also remained important sources of national income.[54] Tithe revenues rose from under 40,000 pesos in 1832 to 117,723 pesos in 1861, but the tax never formed much more than 8 percent of the national income.[55] Amerindian tribute was a more lucrative levy, fluctuating between 147,289 pesos and 205,652 pesos. It also accounted for approximately 13–36 percent of all government receipts until its abolition in 1857.[56] The tobacco and cane liquor monopolies also produced very little during these turbulent early years of the republic.[57] The one significant departure from the colonial fiscal system was the reliance on foreign loans.[58] Nevertheless, the policies of republican governments continued the colonial precedent of placing enormous relative tax burdens on Amerindians and the export economy of the coast.[59]

The expenditures of the Ecuadorian state reflect the low income levels and chaotic political situation in the early nineteenth century. Until the 1840s, the military received 57–74 percent of all public revenues; most of the rest went to defray administrative expenses.[60] The amounts spent on defense declined by the 1840s, but the cost of servicing foreign debts and paying the bureaucracy more than compensated for any military savings. The republican government's fiscal priorities, however, differed markedly from those of the Bourbon state, which never allocated more than 16 percent of its total expenditures for defense; loan repayments during the colonial period were also insignificant outlays. This need to support the military establishment reveals the republican state's institutional weakness and the endemic political disorders of the early nineteenth century. At the same time, the amounts spent on the bureaucracy matched outlays during the colonial period. The monies expended on servicing the foreign and domestic debts also corresponded to the funds remitted to Spain during the late colonial era. Even after independence,

52. *Ibid.*, 187.
53. Hamerly, *Historia social y económica*, 121.
54. Rodríguez, *Search for Public Policy*, 62.
55. *Ibid.*, 66.
56. *Ibid.*, 63.
57. *Ibid.*, 215.
58. *Ibid.*, 75–78.
59. For a discussion of the failures of coastal elites to protect their regional economic interests during the independence era, see David J. Cubitt, "Economic Nationalism in Post-Independence Ecuador: The Commercial Code of 1821–1825," *Ibero-Amerikanisches Archiv*, 11:1 (1985): 65–82.
60. Rodríguez, *Search for Public Policy*, 223.

the beleaguered Ecuadorian state still sent relatively large allocations of public money to outsiders, proving that the drain of local capital continued throughout the early nineteenth century.[61]

The treasury records of the national state in Ecuador indicate clearly the onset of fiscal decentralization. The tax base and income levels of the government continued to shrink until the 1850s, and public finances depended largely on taxes levied against the coastal export economy and the Amerindian population. Government spending also went almost exclusively to service the military, the bureaucracy, and the burgeoning national and provincial debts. As a result, state intervention in the economy declined, but public policy also perpetuated regional and social inequities and foreign dependency, which did little to help the new nation surmount its many socioeconomic difficulties.

From the late 1770s, the colonial and early national states pursued policies that interfered in specific and major ways with autonomous economic development in the Kingdom of Quito. The state directed public funds away from productive enterprises and sent out large amounts of money, first to Spain and later to foreign creditors. In addition to these transfers of capital, the state imposed a number of fiscal and legal policies that blocked or impeded development. In short, the colonial and early national states failed to promote an institutional environment capable of sustaining enterprise and development.[62]

Colonial fiscal policies led to several important constraints on the socioeconomic development of the kingdom. The decline of the highland textile manufactures during the eighteenth century undermined the fragile economic integration of the north-central highlands (from Ibarra to Riobamba) and reinforced these daunting geographical barriers to devel-

61. State finances in Cuenca from 1779 to 1861 demonstrate the congruence of provincial- and national-level trends. Income at the Cuenca treasury ranged between 50,000 pesos and 110,000 pesos – far less than the 150,000 pesos collected in the best years of the late colonial period. The tax base of Cuenca also shrank. The only significant sources of revenue were Amerindian tribute, which produced over 40 percent of all income, followed by the sales tax at 7 percent, and loans at just over 5 percent. In addition, the treasury remitted only 2 percent of the regional income in Cuenca annually. Likewise, Cuenca exercised little fiscal control over the districts of Loja, Alausí, Gualaceo, Jaén, and Azogues, which sent declining yearly remittances of taxes. Military and administrative expenses together accounted for over 70 percent of the provincial budget, with most of the rest going to pay the public debt. See Leonardo Espinosa, "Política fiscal de la provincia de Cuenca: reseña histórico – presupuestaria – 1779–1861," *Segundo encuentro de historia y realidad económica y social del Ecuador*, 3 vols. (Cuenca, 1978), 1:1–75.

62. For an intriguing examination of this process in Mexico, see John Coatsworth, "The Limits of Colonial Absolutism: The State in Eighteenth-Century Mexico," in Karen Spalding, ed., *Essays in the Political, Economic, and Social History of Colonial Latin America* (Newark, DE, 1982) 25–51; and idem, "Obstacles to Economic Growth in Nineteenth-Century Mexico," *American Historical Review*, 83:1 (February 1978): 80–100.

opment. The state's rigid enforcement of sales tax regulations on a declining cloth trade clearly raised transaction costs in overland commerce,
retarded the evolution of highland markets, and contributed to the
greater isolation of regional trading centers. Indeed, high levels of per
capita taxation undoubtedly played a role in undermining colonial manufacturing throughout the highlands by the early nineteenth century.

The regressive character of Bourbon fiscal levies also hindered agricultural production in the highlands. The sales tax levied on rural estates
and on foodstuffs sold in the cities and towns unquestionably raised food
prices and interfered with the regional trade in rural produce. Even direct
taxes (levied on wealth and income) such as Amerindian tribute also
inhibited rural production, because the fixed tax rates seldom changed in
response to periods of either hardship or prosperity.[63] Other direct levies
on the church drained capital from this organization, which traditionally
played an important role in the agrarian economy. The state-run *Administración de temporalidades*, for example, directed profits from the former
Jesuit estates to Spain instead of reinvesting them in the sorts of regional
socioeconomic enterprises formerly supported by the Society.

The onerous taxes levied in the Guayaquil region also cut into commercial and agricultural profits. The state imposed an *alcabala* on the
sale of cacao, for example, and an additional customs duty when it left
the port city. Cacao estates also paid the tithe and the sales tax, both
levied against estimated rural production. Moreover, all imported goods
paid the *alcabala* and a port duty ranging from 4 percent to 7 percent,
depending on the origin of the product. Such goods paid an additional
sales tax at each subsequent sale. Royal monopolies on locally produced
goods such as tobacco further raised prices and lessened the profit margins
of coastal producers. In addition, the sales tax paid on foodstuffs and
textiles from the *sierra* boosted prices in Guayaquil. Freer trade also
brought imports of European cloth, which damaged both highland cloth
manufacturing and the export trade in *Quiteño* woolens. By the late eighteenth century, these fiscal and commercial policies had raised per capita
taxes for coastal residents to among the highest in the world. None of
these policies proved devastating to the relatively buoyant coastal export
economy, but taken together they created an institutional environment
concerned primarily with exploiting, not promoting, economic development.

The success of the colonial state – established by José García de Leon
y Pizarro – in extracting resources from the kingdom and shipping them

---

63. For a discussion of the problems caused by head taxes in peasant communities, see James C.
Scott, *The Moral Economy of the Peasant: Rebellion and Subsistence in Southeast Asia* (New Haven, CT,
1976): 99–110.

to Spain impeded development and even lessened the prospects for future growth and prosperity. Public investment in the economy was negligible, in contrast to the previous century, when viceregal treasury officials routinely spent much larger sums in the colony than they shipped to Spain.[64] The drain of money to the metropolis undoubtedly hindered capital accumulation and investment in the *audiencia* district. This was the legacy of García Pizarro.

In the first three decades of independence, republican governments had the opportunity to end this corrupt political order, remove many of the fiscal impediments to growth, and stop the hemorrhage of wealth abroad, all of which had impeded economic progress from the late colonial period. Although the new governments did eliminate some constraints on the private sector, republican fiscal policies continued many onerous colonial levies and failed to create a markedly improved environment for development. Amerindian tribute, high customs duties, and levies on agriculture continued as the main sources of public revenues. Such regressive taxes drained resources from productive sectors, inhibited market expansion, and exacerbated the traditional communications and geographical barriers within the nation. Moreover, shifting resources to largely unproductive sectors such as the military and the bureaucracy and the need to service the burgeoning public debt nullified any limited gains realized from ending revenue transfers to Spain. The frequent collapse of the central government in the political disorders of the period – particularly the vacillation between centralism and federalism – created an ever more chaotic environment for investment, enterprise, and development. In short, the republican states proved weaker and less overtly exploitative than their colonial predecessor but equally unenlightened.

---

64. By the period 1681 to 1690, for example, Lima treasury officials remitted only 5 percent of their outgo to Spain and spent the remainder in the viceroyalty. See Kenneth J. Andrien, *Crisis and Decline: The Viceroyalty of Peru in the Seventeenth Century* (Albuquerque, NM, 1985), 67.

9

Conclusion: the state and regional development

The major market economies in the Kingdom of Quito – centered on Quito, Guayaquil, and Cuenca – proved incapable of generating ongoing, autonomous growth during the period from 1690 to 1830. The evolution of manufacturing, agrarian, and commercial sectors in these regions was frequently circumscribed by state policies designed to benefit Spain, regardless of their long-term consequences in the kingdom. Colonial governments directed public funds away from local enterprises and sent large amounts of money to support imperial defenses and the needs of metropolitan Spain. Crown taxes, monopolies, and market regulations also hindered growth by siphoning investment capital and savings from productive sectors and by failing to promote an institutional environment capable of maintaining enterprise and economic vitality.

Although deep political divisions emerged after the onset of the independence era in Quito by 1809, the tradition of an activist state survived the breakup of the empire. The newly independent governments of Gran Colombia and later Ecuador merely lacked the power and authority of their colonial predecessor, not the desire to continue public sector interventions. The weakened national regimes transferred wealth abroad, now to repay ill-conceived foreign loans, and continued many of the basic taxes, monopolies, and market regulations that had hindered economic development in the colonial period. Republican states enacted policies that helped to promote weak, divided market economies during much of the nineteenth century.

The state and the market economy

The rugged geography of the north Andes imposed numerous barriers to the growth and integration of regional markets in the Kingdom of Quito. The Andean cordillera and an extensive system of rivers promoted scattered settlement patterns across the narrow mountain valleys, making transportation and communication particularly difficult. The private and public sectors never invested sufficient capital resources to improve roads, technology, and other infrastructure, resulting in high transportation costs and inadequate sources of information about the internal economy. As a result, the growth of large domestic markets for basic consumption items (with their relatively low profit margins) languished. Given these constraints, the principal economic problem in the kingdom was finding a lucrative export product capable of generating sufficient specie needed to pay for luxury imports.

The decline of the obrajes

For over a century peninsular and creole elites in the north-central sierra found such an exportable commodity: manufactured woolen cloth (*paños, bayetas,* and *jergas*) sent to Lima and New Granada. The highland textile manufactories served as the foundation of the regional economy until epidemics, natural disasters, and the introduction of large amounts of European cloth combined to erode the prosperity of the *obraje* sector by the early eighteenth century. Such problems only worsened as the Spanish crown extended trade liberalization, leading to even greater foreign cloth imports. Mill owners still sold their cheapest textiles to New Granada, but they had lost ground in the more lucrative Lima market to foreign rivals. As a result, foreign competition restricted the market share available for Quito's mills, whose net output fell 50–75 percent by the 1780s.

The textile economy of the north-central highlands had evolved during the sixteenth century in a business environment closely regulated by the state. The crown effectively promoted an oligopoly in textile production by licensing only elite-run enterprises and by providing the legal means to recruit Amerindian laborers. The most successful mill owners prospered in this protected environment by establishing family-owned businesses, uniting *obrajes* with food-producing estates and sheep ranches in a single integrated enterprise. Such rural estate complexes brought together many key factors of production, which minimized cash outlays and reduced the problem of procuring raw materials. These textile mills, however, employed no sophisticated machinery or production techniques capable of lowering the unit cost of production, as in modern factories. Instead, the *obraje* internalized many market functions, supplying important material inputs needed for manufacturing. This organizational structure worked well in the protected markets of the seventeenth century, but it proved incapable of increasing product quality or lowering prices to compete with European imports. By allowing foreign textiles to enter colonial markets, the crown effectively doomed the *obraje* sector to decadence.

The falling demand for locally produced woolens from the early eighteenth century prompted a slow agrarian decline in much of the north-central highlands. Most Spanish rural enterprises had organized the abundant land and labor resources in the countryside to export textiles, not food or livestock. Geographical barriers and high transport costs limited the ability of most *hacendados* to move from exporting cloth to selling bulk crops in distant colonial markets. Attempts at finding a suitable cash crop, such as sugar cane, proved impractical for most regional producers, particularly after the crown placed the *aguardiente* and sales tax administrations under direct state control in 1765. Then, only the religious orders or the wealthiest elites could muster the political clout and the economic resources needed to profit from textile production. By the late eighteenth century, even these large-scale enterprises had become less lucrative.

The decline in textile production had negative repercussions on regional commerce and state revenues. The sale of woolens financed the importation of European luxury goods and provided the specie for domestic enterprise, regional trade, and the fiscal needs of the colonial state. As cloth exports declined, so too did imports and commerce. By the 1780s, government customs houses in the formerly dominant north-central highlands produced only one-third of the fiscal receipts collected annually in the Guayaquil *aduana*, which supervised a region with only a fraction of its population.

During this period the city of Quito evolved from a manufacturing to more of an administrative and service oriented economy. The reforms of García Pizarro led to a proliferation of bureaucratic jobs, which went to members of the peninsular and creole elites. Most of the city's middle and lower classes eked out a living from a marginal underground economy, working in small shops or as servants, peddlers, and hucksters. Relatively small putting-out industries also evolved, producing cloth, artisan goods, and art work, but such enterprises could not compensate for the decline of the *obrajes*. As the crown enforced higher taxes and administrative controls in the city, however, even many of these economic activities suffered. Such enterprises actually failed to generate much specie, and they often depended on lax enforcement of market regulations and tax laws. Even the elite's bureaucratic jobs depended entirely on continued state patronage. With the disorders caused by epidemics, natural disasters, and the wars of independence, the urban market in Quito declined steadily.

The decline of the *obraje* economy and the rising importance of the south highlands and the coast had a profound effect on the Amerindian population. Many Andeans had already left their traditional ethnic communities to participate in regional market economies, working on Spanish estates and in the chief cities. By the eighteenth century, larger numbers of Amerindians migrated from depressed provinces in the north-central highlands to regions of greater opportunity, which encouraged the development of the south sierra and later the coastal export boom. Those who remained behind faced diminished economic prospects, high taxes, and political repression, leading to the outbreak of highland Amerindian uprisings later in the colonial period.

The political economy of the south sierra

As the *obraje* economy deteriorated, a prosperous cotton and woolen textile industry emerged in the south highlands. The institutions of the colonial state were notoriously lax in the region, particularly about collecting taxes, which attracted Amerindian migrants and served as an indirect economic stimulus. Cloth manufacturing was concentrated in the local Amerindian villages, where merchants operating from Lima, northern Peru, and Guayaquil organized a cottage or putting-out system of production. These entrepreneurs usually supplied raw cotton and wool, while the Andeans used traditional techniques of spinning and weaving to produce cheap, durable cloth. The Amerindians benefitted by gaining additional income from this growing cottage industry to supplement any earnings from agriculture. The merchants also made substantial profits by marketing their wares throughout the more advanced network of regional markets in the Pacific by the late eighteenth century. Even the crown gained modest tax revenues from these transactions, which supplied the more profitable export economies of Peru with the sort of cheap cottons and woolens that European producers could not furnish in sufficient quantities.

The Spanish agricultural economy of the south highlands also experienced steady growth during the eighteenth century. The success of most peninsular- and creole-owned estates depended on the demand for agricultural products in local highland markets, Guayaquil, and northern Peru. Other landowners prospered by supplying a local tree bark, *cascarilla*, rich in quinine, to European and colonial markets. South highland landlords seldom participated in the cottage textile industry, but the trade in rough cloth undoubtedly stimulated the local agrarian economy and promoted the introduction of European luxury items.

Once the imperial system started its slow collapse by 1810, the state-regulated market economy in the Andes became more volatile and unpredictable. The disruptions to regional market exchanges led merchant houses to abandon their manufacturing concerns in the south highlands, and textile exports fell to near insignificance by 1830. This cottage textile industry simply lacked the capital, scale, and marketing connections to survive without its merchant backers. The Amerindian villagers involved in cloth manufacturing lost a lucrative source of income, forcing many over time to emigrate to the coast. The Spanish *hacendados*, however, continued to prosper. Their estates were not directly connected to the local textile trade, and they extended their domination of the southern countryside.

The coastal export boom

The crown's decision to extend imperial free trade between 1778 and 1789 played a major role in the coastal cacao boom. *Comercio libre* opened markets in the Pacific, Mexico, and Europe to coastal cacao, leading to the growth of coastal exports. The Spanish crown's efforts to maximize fiscal receipts concentrated public sector institutions and government expenditures in regions, such as the coast, connected to wider imperial and international trading circuits. Peninsular and creole elites took advantage of the new commercial opportunities to establish large numbers of cacao plantations along the extensive river network of the coastal plain, and during the 1790s production of this crop increased dramatically. The fertile coastal soils also produced copious yields of tobacco, sugar, and hardwoods, but the cultivation and export of cacao formed the economic core of the coastal economy, until the demand for the crop declined in the 1840s.

After the advent of *comercio libre*, large- and medium-sized cacao plantations developed rapidly in the parishes of Baba, Babahoyo, Palenque, and Machala. Abundant rainfall, a hot climate, and cheap riverine transportation in these zones all contributed to the expansion of the export economy. In addition, the cacao regions produced the only major trade commodity in the Kingdom of Quito capable of generating large amounts of hard cash to ease the specie shortages accompanying the decline of the textile trade.

Although cacao plantations linked the productivity of the coast to the international economy, outside merchant houses apparently reaped the largest profits from the export economy. Coastal planters lacked the access to credit and the commercial connections needed to market their crops, and they relied instead on large mercantile companies based in Lima, Mexico City, and Spain. These commercial houses also gained by introducing European wares. The state too reaped a share from the cacao bonanza, as per capita tax rates along the coast increased markedly.

The state and regional development

State policies established much of the context for regional socioeconomic development in the Kingdom of Quito during the eighteenth century.

Although the early Bourbon Reforms represented a patchwork of fiscal, bureaucratic, commercial, religious, and military policies, they still extended many important regulatory controls over basic economic relationships. Spain's decision to allow European cloth imports, for example, severely undermined colonial manufacturing centers in the north-central highlands. Over time, however, the whole corpus of laws, institutions, and fiscal impositions had a profound cumulative economic impact by organizing important commercial ties among local, regional, and international markets for the benefit of the metropolis.

Amidst the wrenching socioeconomic changes of the eighteenth century, interest groups in the kingdom tried desperately to control the political arena. The implementation of crown policies most often arose from the complex interplay among self-interested metropolitan and colonial elite factions, sporadically influenced by political pressures from the middle and lower classes. The apex of local power over state policy came with the Quito Insurrection of 1765, when a broad popular coalition swept aside the *audiencia* and effectively ruled the capital city and its hinterland. After the popular government collapsed in 1766, however, the crown reasserted its control. Scarcely twelve years after the insurrection, metropolitan authorities sent José García de Leon y Pizarro with a mandate to overhaul the kingdom's political and administrative structure.

The level of state intervention in the kingdom's regional economies rose dramatically after the "reforms" of García Pizarro and his cronies. The failed Quito Insurrection left elite and plebeian groups deeply divided and pessimistic about influencing state policies. The president and his cronies used this "propitious" opportunity to reinvigorate the administrative state, co-opt much of the local elite with bureaucratic jobs, and maximize tax receipts and remittances to the metropolis. By enlarging the government bureaucracy, García Pizarro was able to expand the number of royal monopolies, tighten commercial regulations, and increase receipts from levies on the Amerindian population, the church, trade, and production. In the depressed north-central highlands, for example, state income rose from 860,000 pesos in the period 1775–79 to nearly 2,500,000 pesos in the subsequent quinquennium.

By the late colonial period, state intervention in the economy had become steadily more direct, consistent, and damaging to economic development. Commercial regulations, royal monopolies, and regressive taxes impeded manufacturing, agriculture, and commerce. The fiscal burden needed to support the newly expanded bureaucracy and to meet the needs of Spain imposed real economic costs; per capita tax rates skyrocketed. By escalating the fiscal burdens on exploited Amerindian communities in the kingdom, the colonial state also did much to exacerbate the gap between rich and poor, diminishing opportunities for any wider economic prosperity. Moreover, heavy taxes on cacao exports curtailed the prospects for savings and investment in the export sector.

Colonial fiscal and commercial policies also contributed to regionalism, not the development of an integrated national market. By the late eighteenth century, the major markets of Quito, Guayaquil, and Cuenca maintained commercial links to regional trading partners outside of the kingdom. In each case, these outside commercial connections proved stronger than the economic bonds among the three market centers themselves. Decaying manufacturing zones in the north-central highlands, for example, sold cheap woolens primarily to New Granada. At the same time, expanding commercial links between coastal exporters and market centers like Mexico City and Lima overshadowed the importance of trade with the highlands. The south sierra prospered by sending local cloth and *cascarilla* to the Viceroyalty of Peru. In the end, this produced three relatively weak market systems, dependent on government-supported trading networks and merchant houses centered in Cartagena, Lima, or Mexico City.

Independence seriously restricted state fiscal and regulatory control, but the new national regimes continued many burdensome policies of the past. Amerindian tribute, high customs duties, restrictive commercial regulations, and levies on consumption and agricultural production all survived. Even transfers of wealth abroad persisted, this time to repay foreign creditors. The combination of regressive taxes, excessive regulations, and socioeconomic policies that discriminated against the poor all inhibited production and domestic consumption. Under these conditions, the diminished market economies became more fragmented, contributing to the endemic regionalism and political disunity of the early republican period.

In pre-industrial societies, such as the Kingdom of Quito, growth in aggregate demand was vital for sustained development. This required an expansion of consumer demand and foreign trade, sufficient capital accumulation to promote investment, and the direction of public funds to support economic infrastructure. The fiscal policies of the Bourbon and early republican states did none of these things. Instead, government policies hindered Amerindians from reaping any substantial benefits from the market economy and from using any surplus resources to expand internal consumption. Public sector interventions also inhibited domestic savings and investment, which limited many potentially salutary benefits from regional export economies. The state promoted policies that created a discriminatory, arbitrary, and irrational economic environment for promoting sustained, autonomous development. In the end, Spanish colonialism exacted far too high a price, promoting patterns of dependent development that endured well beyond the independence of Ecuador in 1830.

Appendix 1

Major Jesuit landholdings, 1767

Estate	Location
COLEGIO MÁXIMO	
1. Pedregal y Vallevicioso	Quito
2. Pintac (g)	Quito
3. Chillo	Quito
4. Pinllocoto	Quito
5. Ychubamba	Quito
6. Tanalagua	Quito
7. Guatus	Quito
8. Niebli y Pinguilla con Irubí	Quito
9. Cayambe	Quito
10. Quadras de Semillán	Quito
11. El Colegio	Quito
12. Yúrac y Yúrag	Quito
13. Santiago	Ibarra
14. Carpuela y Chaluayaca	Ibarra
15. Caldera	Ibarra
16. Pimanpiro	Ibarra
17. Santa Lucía	Ibarra
18. Tigua	Latacunga
COLEGIO DE PROVINCIA	
1. Concepción, Lomagorda y San Judas	Ibarra
2. Chamanal, Santa Lucía, Pisquer, Cabuyal, y Guagrabamba	Ibarra
3. Tumbaviro	Ibarra
4. Cotacache y Calera	Ibarra
5. San Pablo, Agualongo y La Laguna	Ibarra
6. Naxiche, Pigua, Shuyo, Zilipo, Guambayna, Provincia, y Quisapincha	Quito

Estate   *Location*

MISIONES DE MAINAS
1. Yaroquí   Quito
2. Cangagua o Guachalá   Quito
3. Caraburo   Quito
4. Urapanta (pamba)   Quito

COLEGIO Y SEMINARIO DE SAN LUÍS
1. San Ildefonso (Trapiche, Tontapi, Quinchibamba, Patalo,
   Llagua, Cunugyaco, Pacobamba, Chiquito)   Ambato
2. Alangasí   Quito
3. Pazuchuoa   Quito
4. Santa Clara   Quito
5. Cotocollao   Quito

CASA DE NOVICIADO
1. Conrogal   Quito
2. Lloa   Quito

CASA DE EXERCISIOS
1. Chaquibamba   Quito

COLEGIO DE IBARRA
1. Quajara   Ibarra
2. Pisquer, Mira, Guaquer   Ibarra
3. Chorlavi y Caranqui   Ibarra
4. Calera   Ibarra
5. Lulunqui   Ibarra

COLEGIO DE LATACUNGA
1. Obraxe   Latacunga
2. Calera   Latacunga
3. Collas   Latacunga
4. Saquisilí   Latacunga
5. Ysinlivi y Guasumbinio   Latacunga
6. Cotopilaló   Latacunga
7. Ylito   Latacunga
8. Guanailín (Guanaila)   Latacunga
9. Tiobamba   Latacunga
10. Tontapi   Latacunga
11. Tacaló   Latacunga
12. San Blas Pamba   Latacunga

Estate	*Location*
COLEGIO DE AMBATO	
1. Miraflores y Quadras	Ambato
2. Obraje y Batan	Ambato
3. Guaslan	Ambato
4. Sebañon	Ambato
5. Gualcanga	Ambato
6. Chiquicha	Ambato
7. Calera y Pitula	Ambato
8. Guambaló	Ambato
COLEGIO DE RIOBAMBA	
1. Cicalpa, Cunug, Pogio	Riobamba
2. San Xavier de Patate y Leyto	Riobamba
3. Cagualí y Macaxi	Ambato-Riobamba
4. Cuzubamba	Ambato
5. Pangur	Ambato
COLEGIO DE CUENCA	
1. San Xavier	Cuenca
2. San Pedro y Tasque	Cuenca
3. Machangara y Zaucay	Cuenca
4. Racor	Cuenca
5. Tontapali	Cuenca
6. Portete	Cuenca
7. Gualdaleg	Cuenca
8. Guarangos	Cuenca
9. Guayansapá	Cuenca
COLEGIO DE LOJA	
1. Toma y Catamayo	Loja
2. Punsara	Loja
3. Hatelo	Loja
4. Alamala	Loja
COLEGIO DE GUAYAQUIL	
1. Soledad	Guayaquil
2. San Xavier	Guayaquil
3. Tumbes	Guayaquil
4. Santa Catalina	Guayaquil
5. Guaig	Guayaquil

Estate   *Location*

  6. San Pedro, Las Palmas   Guayaquil
  7. Palmar   Guayaquil
  8. Guare   Guayaquil
  9. Chilintomo   Guayaquil
 10. Salinas y Zurumilla   Guayaquil

Source: AGI, Quito 242, Estado que manifiesta los productos de la haciendas, Fincas, y
   Rentas que gozaron los Regulares expatriados de la Provincia de Quito . . . y los gastos
   ordinarios y extraordinaries de cada Colegio, 15 noviembre 1784; Nicholas P. Cushner,
   Farm and Factory: The Jesuits and the Development of Agrarian Capitalism in Colonial Quito,
   1600–1767 (Albany, NY, 1982), 189–91; Federico González Suárez, *Historia general*
   de la República del Ecuador (Quito, 1970), 1160–63.

Appendix 2

Major Jesuit lands sold by the Administración de temporalidades

Hacienda complex	Location	Price	Buyer
Quajara, Chamanal	Ibarra	80,000	Carlos Araujo. (Sold in 1793 to Mariano y Agustín Valdivieso.)
Lulunque	Ibarra	9,000	Joaquín Reyes
Caldera, Chaluayaca, Cotacache, Laguna, Agualongo	Ibarra	140,000	Pedro Calixto
Santiago	Ibarra	51,000	Mariano Donoso (Later sold to J. Saldumbide.)
Tumbaviro	Ibarra	75,000	Jq. Rivadeneyra
Concepción	Ibarra	180,000	J. A. Chiriboga
Chorlavi	Ibarra	14,500	C. Vélez Alava
Pisquer, Guaquer	Ibarra	45,800	J. Paz Guerrero
Naxiche	Quito	?	Mariano Estrada
Pintag	Quito	61,600	Josef Aguirre
Conrogal	Quito	43,000	Mig. Ponce
Ychubamba	Quito	12,500	Ant. Azpiazu
Tigua, Pazuchoa, Chillo,	Latacunga Quito		
Pinllocoto	Quito	98,400	Mq. SelvaAlegre
Pedregal, Vallevicioso	Quito	100,000	Pedro Ante
Cayambe	Quito	45,000	Man. Larrea Zurbano, María Gijon Chiriboga
Chaquibamba	Quito	20,000	F. Nieto Araujo

Hacienda complex	Location	Price	Buyer
Santa Clara, Pazuchua	Quito	8,500	Jos. Guarderas
Ychubamba	Quito	12,500	Ant. Aspiazu
Lloa	Quito	7,913	Vicente Melo. (Later sold to Nicolás Carrion.)
Conrogal	Quito	43,000	Miguel Ponce
Cotocollao	Quito	16,000	J. Hidalgo Reira. (Later sold, 1802, to Antonio Acosta.)
Cangagua, Yaroquí, Caraburu, Urapamba	Quito	60,000	G. Sánchez. (Later sold for 35,000 to Javier Villacis.)
Tanlagua, Guatus, Niebli	Quito	26,000	Mq. Miraflores
Yúrac, Yúrag	Quito	61,600	Jos. Aguirre
Cotopilaló	Latacunta	33,500	I. Solano Sala
Ysinlivi	Latacunga	3,621	M. Benavides
Tontapi	Latacunga	7,600	Pablo Razines
Saquisilí	Latacunga	3,700	Mq. Miraflores
San Blas Pamba	Latacunga	115	Mq. Miraflores
Ylito	Latacunga	553	Mq. Miraflores
Tacaló	Latacunga	1,000	Mq. Miraflores
Collas	Latacunga	8,008	Josef Espinoza
Guanaylín	Latacunga	5,251	Baltasara Teran
Tiobamba	Latacunga	6,500	Josef Espinoza
San Ildefonso	Ambato	128,000	A. Valdivieso
Gualcanga, Ypolongo	Ambato	1,302	Pedro Zevallos
Chiquicha	Ambato	5,500	Pedro Zevallos
Miraflores	Ambato	4,204	A. Villacreses
Pitula	Ambato	52,000	Juan de Erdoyza
Sebañon	Ambto	9,000	Andrés Salazar
Guaslan	Ambato	5,615	Juana Costales
San Xavier, Leyto	Riobamba	28,300	Balt. Carriedo
Cuzubamba	Riobamba	17,000	Pablo Martínez
Cagualí	Riobamba	5,000	Mariano Donoso
Cicalpa	Riobamba	22,720	Balt. Carriedo

Hacienda complex	Location	Price	Buyer
Portrete, Guarangos Guayansapá, Tontapali Racor, San Pedro, San Xavier, Gualdeleg	Cuenca	89,318	Juan Chica
Machangara	Cuenca	10,050	M. Valdivieso
Bisil	Cuenca	230	Josef de Tapia
Toma, Alamala, Hatillo, Punsara	Loja	40,575	Balt. Carrion
Salinas, Zurumilla	Guayaquil	2,667	Miguel Olmedo
Soledad, Guare, Chilintomo, San Pedro, Santa Catarina	Guayaquil	20,000	Miguel Olmedo
Palmar, San Xavier, San Pedro	Guayaquil	61,500	Silv. Gorostiza
Salinas, Zurumilla	Guayaquil	2,666	Mig. Olmedo
Total		1,786,808	

Source: ANH-Q, Temporalidades, Caja 3, Remates de Haciendas, 1789–1791; Caja 14, Remates de Haciendas, 1779–1783; Caja 16, Remates de Haciendas, 1784; Caja 19, Remates de Haciendas, 1783; Caja 21, Remates de Haciendas, 1785–1787; Caja 22, Remates de Haciendas, 1787–1805.

Glossary

Administración de temporalidades: State agency that administered the former properties of the Jesuits, after their expulsion in 1767

aduana: State customs house

aguardiente: Alcoholic beverage refined from sugar cane in the Ecuadorian highlands

alcabala: Several taxes levied directly or indirectly on the sale of goods. An *alcabala* of 3 percent was charged on commercial sales of European and colonial goods; the *alcabala del cabezón* was an indirect tax levied against the predicted value of the goods produced on rural estates; the *alcabala del viento* was a levy of 3 percent on local goods entering the city gates of most urban areas; *escrituras y contratos públicos* were levies on all legally sanctioned sales of property

alcalde del crimen: Criminal justice in an *audiencia*

alcaldes ordinarios: Members of a city council, usually elected by a restricted electorate of urban elites

almojarifazgo de entrada: Port taxes collected on imports to Guayaquil; assessed at 3 percent on Spanish goods, 5 percent on American goods, and 7 percent on European (non-Spanish) products

almojarifazgo de salida: Port tax of 2.5 percent on all local goods exported from Guayaquil, except cacao, which paid a 3-percent sales tax

añil: Indigo

Armada del mar del sur: Spanish Pacific fleet

astillero: Shipyard

avería: Fleet or convoy tax assessed by value or by cubic volume

barrios: Popular district or semi-rural parish of a city

bayeta: Coarse, inexpensive woolen fabric

cabildo: City council

cabildo abierto: A meeting of the city council, usually open to a selected citizenry of urban elites

cabuya: A fibrous plant (comparable to hemp) found in the coastal region, used for ship cordage

caja real: Royal treasury office or the strongbox found in that office

califate: Caulker, particularly in the Guayaquil shipyard

capellanía: Chantry; an endowment, usually funded in cash or by a lien against property, paying 3–5 percent interest on the principal, to fund a chaplaincy or the periodic celebration of masses for the deceased

cascarilla: A tree bark rich in quinine found in the south highlands

cédula: A royal edict

censo: A long-term loan or lien most often advanced by clerical organizations guaranteed by collateral, usually property, bearing 3–5 percent interest

comercio libre: A decree in 1778 that began establishing free trade within the Spanish Empire; the final decree installing this more liberal trade system came in 1789

concierto: A full-time resident worker on a Spanish rural estate

cofradía: A religious brotherhood or confraternity

consulado: A merchant guild, usually with the privilege of serving as the court of first instance in commercial cases within its jurisdiction

copey: Tar-like substance found in the coastal region, used for pitch in the Guayaquil shipyard

corona: An Amerindian emigrant to a region, whose ties with his/her home community could no longer be verified by authorities (see *forastero*)

corregidor de indios: Spanish rural magistrate in charge of an Amerindian province (*corregimiento*), usually larger than a parish and certainly smaller than an *audiencia* district

chagro: An urban shop selling foodstuffs

chicha: Corn beer, commonly drunk by the Andean population, particularly for social and ritual occasions

chorillo: A small urban textile mill producing coarse woolen cloth

diezmo: Clerical tithe (10 percent) collected on rural agricultural produce of European origin; usually farmed out to an elite tax collector called a *diezmero*

encomendero: Holder of an *encomienda* grant

encomienda: A grant of Amerindian towns to a creole or peninsular, who had the right to receive a portion of the tribute collected in these communities in return for protecting the welfare of the inhabitants

estanco: A royal monopoly on the production and sale of a given product, such as *aguardiente*, playing cards, tobacco, or gunpowder

estopa: Caulking material made from the skin of a coastal coconut

fianza: A security bond, often posted by public officials to ensure their honesty in office

fiscal: Attorney of the *audiencia*

forastero: An Amerindian living as a resident alien in a settlement other than his/her place of birth; usually the emigrant's place of origin could be determined by crown authorities

forastero corona: See *corona*

galpones: Small rural landholdings, which frequently had a small textile mill

gañanes: Agricultural workers, frequently contracted or assigned to corveé labor on Spanish estates

gatera: Urban peddlers, most often Amerindian women

gobernación: Governorship; an administrative district that was usually larger than or had some particular importance (often strategic) that separated it from a *corregimiento*

gremio: Guild

guachapelí: A coastal hardwood tree similar to oak, used in shipbuilding

guía: Trade permit issued to merchants listing origin and destination of all trade goods; after selling their goods merchants had to secure a receipt (*tornaguía*) attesting that they had paid the required sales taxes at the approved destination

hacendado: Owner of a *hacienda*

hacienda: A Spanish landed estate, often involved in mixed farming and sometimes in textile production

hato: A ranch that frequently formed part of an integrated *obraje*-estate complex

jergas: A cheap, rough woolen cloth, usually lower in quality than *bayeta*

kuraka (variant *curaca* and plural *kurakakuna*): A Quichua term for a native ethnic lord or leader of an Amerindian community

lienzo: A rough cotton cloth, usually produced by the cottage system

llactayo (variant *llactayuc* and plural *llactakuna*): A Quichua term for a tributary; it came from the root *llacta* or *llajta*, which referred to an Andean territorial entity (town, village, or province) with its own local dieties and with its own inhabitants, resources, and socioeconomic infrastructure

matrícula: A list of taxpayers, usually for Amerindian communities

mayorazgo: An entail

mayordomo: A steward or manager of an estate or enterprise

merced: A grant, usually of land or pensions

miel: Syrup made from sugar cane and often refined into *aguardiente*

minifundia: Very small landholdings

mita (Quichua *mit'a*): A Spanish reworking of the Incaic cyclical corveé, used to man Spanish textile mills, mines, or estates

mitayo (Quichua *mitayu* or *mit'ayuq*): An Amerindian fulfilling *mita* obligations

naipes: Playing cards

numeración: A census

obraje: A mill or workshop producing woolen textiles

obrajero: Owner of an *obraje*

obrajes de comunidad: An *obraje* founded on an *encomienda* grant, theoretically owned by the Amerindians to help them meet communal tribute obligations

obrajuelo: A small, and usually illegal, textile workshop that most often produced cheap, low-quality woolen cloth

oidor: Civil justice in an *audiencia*

padrón: An official census

palos maría: A coastal wood similar to pine, often used for masts in the shipyard at Guayaquil

paño: The highest-quality woolen cloth produced in the Kingdom of Quito

paño azul: Blue-colored *paño*, usually died with indigo

páramo: High-altitude, humid grasslands used for pasturage in the northern Andes

pardo: Someone of mixed racial ancestry, usually with some African blood

pasquinade: Placard or handbill, usually publicizing a major event such as a riot or demonstration

pesquisa: A crown investigation of a specific set of allegations

plebe: The plebeian sector

polvillo: A wheat fungus that periodically attacked the northern Andes

préstamos: Direct loans

protector de indios: An attorney of the *audiencia* entrusted with pleading cases before that body involving Amerindians

pulpería: Licensed retail store selling foodstuffs, various beverages, and drygoods

quintal: Hundredweight

quinto: One-fifth; most often a tax on silver of one-fifth of production

recepturía: A suboffice of one of the tax-collecting agencies under the jurisdiction of the *Dirección general de rentas*

rédito: Interest payments on a loan or *censo*

regatona: Urban marketwoman

repartimiento de mercancías: Forced distribution of European merchandise to Amerindian communities, usually by the *corregidor de indios*

residencia: Judicial review of a crown officer upon the completion of his term of office

sarampión: Measles

situado: A subsidy from a royal treasury to maintain frontier provinces or key defense establishments

socorro: An advance of money, clothing, food, or tools to a worker

sombrería: A hat-manufacturing establishment

tabardillo: Various types of fevers

tocuyo: A cheap, inexpensive cotton cloth, usually produced by the cottage system

tornaguía: See *guía*

viruelas: Smallpox

visita: A crown inspection tour or general investigation of a region

visitador: Official conducting a *visita*

Bibliography

Archival sources

Archivo General de Indias, Seville
  Contaduría, legajos 1416, 1417, 1419A, 1420B, 1421–27, 1428A, 1500–02, 1540
  Escribanía de Cámara, legajos 913A, 914A, 914B, 914C, 915A, 915C, 916A, 916B
  Estado, legajos 54, 72
  Indiferente General, legajo 555A
  Audiencia de Guatemala, legajo 13
  Audiencia de Lima, legajos 346, 347, 364, 409–10, 779
  Audiencia de Quito, legajos 69, 72–75, 102–06, 122–41, 149, 150, 161, 170–76, 181, 204, 210, 219, 228, 229, 230, 232–234, 235, 237–62, 263–67, 271, 272, 275, 276, 291, 296, 377, 398, 399, 403, 407–12, 416–28, 430, 435, 436, 445, 447, 448, 453–60, 470–79, 481, 482A, 482B, 492, 494, 497, 500, 504, 506, 507, 519, 527, 531, 537, 592
  Audiencia de Santa Fe, legajos, 772, 803, 955, 957, 971
  Mapas y Planos, Panama, 134, 247

Archivo Nacional de Historia, Quito
  Alcabalas, cajas 1–33
  Carnicerías y Pulperías, cajas 1–5
  Cedularios, cajas 5–20
  Censos y Capellanías, cajas 5–45
  Diezmos, cajas 1–11
  Empadronamientos, cajas 1, 5, 8, 15, 17, 26, 27
  Encomiendas, cajas 3, 4
  Estancos, cajas 2–5
  Haciendas, cajas 1–35
  Indígenas, cajas 95–103
  Obrajes, cajas 9–22
  Notarías, tomos 308, 326
  Presidencia de Quito, tomos 58, 359–61, 395,
  Real Hacienda, cajas 9–15
  Rebelliones, cajas 1–6
  Ropas, cajas 1–10
  Temporalidades, cajas 1–29
  Tierras, cajas 60–80

Tributos, cajas 10, 12, 15,
Vínculos y Mayorazgos, cajas 2–6

Printed primary sources

Alcedo, Antonio de. *Diccionario geográfico histórico de las Indias Occidentales o America*. Vols. 205–08 of *Biblioteca de autores Españoles*. Madrid: Editorial Atlas, 1967 edition.

Borrero Crespo, Maximiliano. *Orígenes Cuencanos*. 2 vols. Cuenca: Universidad de Cuenca, 1962.

"Orígenes Cuencanos." *Revista del Centro Nacional de Investigaciones Genealógicas y Antropológicas*, 2 (Julio 1981): 117–36.

"Origenes Cuencanos (Apéndice)." *Revista del Centro Nacional de Investigaciones Genealógicas y Antropológicas*, 3 (Noviembre 1981): 9–98.

Burkholder, Mark A., and Chandler, D. S. *Biographical Dictionary of Audiencia Ministers in the Americas, 1687–1821*. Westport, CT: Greenwood Press, 1982.

Costales, Jaime. "Los ordenanzas de obrajes." *Boletín de Informaciones Científicas Nacionales*, 119 (1986): 17–62.

García de Leon y Pizarro, José. *Memorias de la vida del excmo. señor d. José García de Leon y Pizarro*. 3 vols. Madrid: Sucesores de Rivadeneyra, 1894.

Guzmán, José Alejandro. *Títulos nobiliarios en el Ecuador*. Madrid: Asilo de Huérfanos del Sagrado Corazón de Jesús, 1957.

Hamerly, Michael T. "Un censo olvidado: el padrón de vecinos de 1738." *Revista del Archivo Histórico de Guayas*, 15 (Junio 1979): 71–90.

Jara, Alvaro, and TePaske, John J. *The Royal Treasuries of the Spanish Empire in America*. Vol. 4, *Eighteenth-Century Ecuador*. Durham: Duke University Press, 1990.

Juan, Jorge, and Ulloa, Antonio de. *Discourse and Political Reflections on the Kingdoms of Peru*. Edited and translated by John J. TePaske and Besse Clement. Norman: University of Oklahoma Press, 1978.

Relación histórica del viaje a la America meridional. 2 vols. Edited by Miguel M. Rodríguez Navarro and Miguel Rodríguez San Vicente. Madrid: Fundacíon Universitaria Española, 1978 edition.

Jurado Naboa, Fernando. *Los descendientes del Benalcázar en la formación social Ecuatoriana, siglos XVI–XX*. 5 vols. Quito: Servimpress, 1984–85.

Laviana Cuetos, María Luisa, ed. *Francisco de Requena y su descripción de Guayaquil*. Seville: Escuela de Estudios Hispano-Americanos, 1984.

Lohmann Villena, Guillermo. *Los americanos en las órdenes nobiliarias, 1529–1900*. Madrid: Consejo Superior de Investigaciones Cientificas, 1947.

Magdaleno, Ricardo. *Títulos de Indias: Catálogo XX del Archivo General de Simancas*. Valladolid: Casa Martín, 1954.

Mendiburu, Manuel. *Diccionario histórico biográfico del Perú*. 15 vols. Lima: Imprenta Enrique Palacios, 1931–38.

Miño Grijalva, Manuel, ed. *La economía colonial: relaciones socio-económicas de la Real Audiencia de Quito*. Quito: Editoral Nacional, 1984.

Moreno Egas, Jorge. "Resúmen alfabético del primer libro de matrimonios de españoles de la parroquia de El Sagrario de Quito, 1723–1764." *Revista del Archivo Histórico de Guayas*, 14 (Diciembre 1978): 81–182.

"Resúmen alfabético del segundo libro de matrimonios de españoles de la

Parroquia de El Sagrario de Quito 1764–1805." *Revista del Centro Nacional de Investigaciones Genelógicas y Antropológicas*, 3 (Noviembre 1981): 195–281.

Moreno Yánez, Segundo E. "Formulario de las ordenanzas de Indios: una regulación de las relaciones laborales en las haciendas y obrajes del Quito colonial y republicano." *Ibero-Amerikanisches Archiv*, 5:3 (1979): 227–41.

Moreyra y Paz Soldán, Manuel. *El tribunal del consulado de Lima: Cuaderno de Juntas (1706–1720)*. 3 vols. Lima: Instituto Histórico del Perú, 1956.

Ortiz de la Tabla Ducasse, Javier. "Las ordenanzas de obrajes de Matías de Peralta para la Audiencia de Quito: régimen laboral de los centros textiles coloniales ecuatorianos." *Anuario de Estudios Americanos*, 33 (1976): 471–541.

Ortiz de la Tabla Ducasse, Javier, Fernández Martínez, Montserrat, and Agueda Rivera, Garrido. *Cartas de Cabildos Hispanoamericanos: Audiencia de Quito*. Seville: Escuela de Estudios Hispano-Americanos, 1991.

"Padrón de Santa Barbara en 1768." *Museo Histórico (Quito)*, 56 (1978): 93–122.

Ramos Gómez, Luis. *Recopilación de leyes de los reynos de las Indias*. 4 vols. Madrid: Ediciones Cultura Hispánica, 1973 edition.

Las noticias secretas de América de Jorge Juan y Antonio de Ulloa (1735–1745). 2 vols. Vol. 2, *Edición crítica del texto original*. Madrid: Consejo Superior de Investigaciones Científicas, 1985.

Robles y Chambers, Pedro. *Contribución para el estudio de la sociedad colonial de Guayaquil*. 3 vols. Guayaquil: Litografia e imprenta de la Reforma, 1938.

Romualdo Navarro, Juan. "Noticia secreta de la revolución de Quito de 1765." In *Antología de Prosistas Ecuatorianos*. 2 vols. Edited by Pablo Herrera. Quito: Imprenta del Gobierno, 1895.

Rumazo, Jose, ed. *Documentos para la historia de la Audiencia de Quito*. 8 vols. Madrid: Afrodisio Aguado S.A., 1948–49.

Salomon, Frank, and Urioste, George L. *The Huarochirí Manuscript: A Testament of Ancient and Colonial Andean Religion*. Austin: University of Texas Press, 1991.

Solórzano y Pereyra, Juan de. *Política Indiana*. Vols. 252–56 of *Biblioteca de autores Españoles*. Madrid: Editorial Atlas, 1972 edition.

"Sublevación de Quito en protesta por la Aduana y los Estancos." *Museo Histórico (Quito)*, 2 (1950): 16–54.

Torres Ramírez, Bibiano, and Ortiz de la Tabla, Javier, eds. *Reglamento y aránceles reales para el comercio libre de España a Indias de 12 de octubre de 1778*. Seville: Escuela de Estudios Hispano-Americanos, 1979 edition.

Velásco, Juan de. *Historia del reino de Quito*. 2 vols. Quito: Casa de la Cultura, 1977–78 edition.

Villavicencio, Manuel. *Geografía de la República del Ecuador*. Quito: Corporación Editorial Nacional, 1984 edition.

Secondary works: books

Alchon, Suzanne Austin. *Native Society and Disease in Colonial Ecuador*. Cambridge: Cambridge University Press, 1991.

Andrien, Kenneth J. *Crisis and Decline: The Viceroyalty of Peru in the Seventeenth Century*. Albuquerque: University of New Mexico Press, 1985.

Assadourian, Carlos Sempat. *El sistema de la economía colonial: mercado interno, regiones y espacio económico*. Lima: Instituto de Estudios Peruanos, 1982.

Bakewell, P. J. *Silver Mining and Society in Colonial Mexico: Zacatecas, 1546–1700*. Cambridge: Cambridge University Press, 1971.

Barbier, Jacques A. *Reform and Politics in Bourbon Chile, 1755–1796*. Ottawa: University of Ottawa Press, 1980.

Basile, David Giovanni. *Tillers of the Andes: Farmers and Farming in the Quito Basin*. Chapel Hill: University of North Carolina Press, 1974.

Berg, Maxine, *The Age of Manufactures*. Oxford: Oxford University Press, 1986.

Braudel, Fernand. *Civilization and Capitalism, 15th–18th Century*. Vol. 1, *The Structures of Everyday Life: The Limits of the Possible*. Translated by Sian Reynolds. New York: Harper and Row, 1981 edition.

Civilization and Capitalism, 15th–18th Century. Vol. 2, *The Wheels of Commerce*. Translated by Sian Reynolds. New York: Harper and Row, 1982 edition.

Civilization and Capitalism, 15th–18th Century. Vol. 3, *The Perspective of the World*. Translated by Sian Reynolds. New York: Harper and Row, 1984 edition.

Afterthoughts on Material Civilization and Capitalism. Translated by Patricia Ranum. Baltimore: Johns Hopkins University Press, 1977.

Burkholder, Mark A., and Chandler, D. S. *From Impotence to Authority: The Spanish Crown and the American Audiencias, 1687–1808*. Columbia: University of Missouri Press, 1977.

Cardoso, Fernando Henrique, and Faletto, Enzo. *Dependency and Development in Latin America*. Berkeley: University of California Press, 1971 edition.

Castillo, Abel Romeo. *Los gobernadores de Guayaquil del siglo XVIII*. Guayaquil: Archivo Historíco de Guayas, 1978 edition.

Chiriboga, Manuel. *Jornaleros y gran propietarios en 135 años de exportación cacaotera (1790–1925)*. Guayaquil: Consejo Provincial de Pichincha, 1980.

Clayton, Lawrence A. *Caulkers and Carpenters in a New World: The Shipyards of Colonial Guayaquil*. Athens: Ohio University Press, 1980.

Cochran, Thomas C. *Frontiers of Change: Early Industrialism in America*. Oxford: Oxford University Press, 1981.

Contreras, Carlos C. *El sector exportador de una economía colonial: La costa del Ecuador entre 1760 y 1820*. Quito: Ediciones Abya-Yala, 1990.

Coronel Feijóo, Rosario. *El valle sangriento: de los indígenas de la coca y el algodón a la hacienda cañera Jesuita: 1580–1700*. Quito: Ediciones Abya-Yala, 1991.

Costales, P. Peñaherrera de, and Costales, Alfredo. *Historia social del Ecuador*. 4 vols. Quito: Casa de la Cultura, 1964–65.

Cushner, Nicholas. *Farm and Factory: The Jesuits and the Development of Agrarian Capitalism in Colonial Quito, 1600–1767*. Albany: S.U.N.Y Press, 1982.

Dahlgren, Erik W. *Les relations commerciales et maritimes entre la France et les cotes de l'Ocean Pacifique*. Vol. 1, *Le commerce de la Mar du Sud jusqu'a la Paix d'Utrech*. Paris: Librairie Ancienne Honoré Campion Editeur, 1909.

Deler, J. P., and Gómez, N. *El manejo del espacio en el Ecuador: Etapas claves*. Quito: Centro de Investigación Geográfica, 1983.

DeVries, Jan. *The Economy of Europe in an Age of Crisis, 1600–1750*. Cambridge: Cambridge University Press, 1976.

Escobedo Mansilla, Ronald. *El tributo indígena en el Perú (siglos XVI–XVII)*. Pamplona: Ediciones Universidad de Navarra, 1979.

Estrada Ycaza, Julio. *El puerto de Guayaquil.* 2 vols. Guayaquil: Archivo Histórico de Guayas, 1973.

Fernández Martínez, Montserrat. *La alcabala en la Audiencia de Quito, 1765–1810.* Cuenca: Casa de la Cultura Ecuatoriana, 1984.

Fisher, John. *Commercial Relations between Spain and Spanish America in the Era of Free Trade, 1778–1796.* Liverpool: Centre for Latin American Studies, University of Liverpool, 1985.

Fisher, J[ohn] R. *Silver Mines and Silver Miners in Colonial Peru, 1776–1824.* Liverpool: Centre for Latin American Studies, University of Liverpool, 1977.

Floud, Roderick. *An Introduction to Quantitative Methods for Historians.* Princeton: Princeton University Press, 1975.

Frank, Andre Gunder. *Latin America: Underdevelopment or Revolution.* London: Monthly Review Press, 1969.

Capitalism and Underdevelopment in Latin America. New York: Monthly Review Press, 1970.

García-Baquero González, Antonio. *Cádiz y el Atlántico (1717–1778).* 2 vols. Seville: Escuela de Estudios Hispano-Americanos, 1976.

González Suárez, Federico. *Historia general de la República del Ecuador.* Quito: Casa de la Cultura Ecuatoriana, 1970 edition.

Guevara, Darío. *Las mingas en el Ecuador.* Quito: Editorial Universitaria, 1957.

Gutmann, Myron P. *Toward the Modern Economy: Early Industry in Europe, 1500–1800.* New York: Knopf, 1988.

Hamerly, Michael T. *Historia social y económica de la antigua provincia de Guayaquil, 1763–1842.* Guayaquil: Archivo Histórico de Guayas, 1973.

El comercio de cacao de Guayaquil durante el período colonial: un estudio cuantitativo. Guayaquil: Historia Marítima del Ecuador, 1976.

Haring, Clarence. *The Spanish Empire in America.* New York: Harcourt, Brace, and World, 1963 edition.

Harris, Olivia, Larson, Brooke, and Tandeter, Enrique, eds. *La participación indígena en los mercados surandinos: estratégias y reproducción social. Siglos XVI a XX.* La Paz: CERES, 1987.

Hawke, G. R. *Economics for Historians.* Cambridge: Cambridge University Press, 1980.

Hopkins, Terence K., and Wallerstein, Immanuel, eds. *World-Systems Analysis: Theory and Methodology.* New York: Academic Press, 1982.

Hudson, Pat. *The Industrial Revolution.* London: Edward Arnold, 1992.

Jenkins, D. T., and Ponting, K. G. *The British Wool Textile Industry, 1770–1914.* Aldershot, U.K.: Scolar Press, 1987.

Johnson, Lyman, and Tandeter, Enrique, eds. *Essays on the Price History of Eighteenth-Century Latin America.* Albuquerque: University of New Mexico Press, 1990.

Knapp, Gregory. *Geografía Quichua de la sierra del Ecuador: núcleos, dominios y esfera.* Quito: Ediciones Abya-Yala, 1987.

Kuethe, Allan J. *Military Reform and Society in New Granada, 1773–1808.* Gainesville: University of Florida Press, 1978.

La Force, James C. *The Development of the Spanish Textile Industry.* Berkeley: University of California Press, 1965.

Landázuri Soto, Alberto. *El régimen laboral indígena en la Real Audiencia de Quito.* Madrid: Imprenta de Aldecoa, 1959.

Laviana Cuetos, María Luisa. *Guayaquil en el siglo XVIII: recursos naturales y desarrollo económico.* Seville: Escuela de Estudios Hispano-Americanos, 1987.

Lloyd, Christopher. *The Structures of History.* Oxford: Blackwell, 1993.

Lynch, John. *Spain under the Habsburgs, 1589–1700.* Vol. 2. Oxford: Oxford University Press, 1969 edition.

The Spanish American Revolutions, 1808–1826. New York: Norton, 1973 edition.

McAlister, Lyle N. *Spain and Portugal in the New World, 1492–1700.* Minneapolis: University of Minnesota Press, 1984.

McCloskey, Donald N. *Econometric History.* London: Macmillan Press, 1987.

McCusker, John J. *Money and Exchange in Europe and North America, 1600–1775: A Handbook.* Chapel Hill: University of North Carolina Press, 1978.

McCuster, John J., and Menard, Russell R. *The Economy of British America, 1607–1789.* Chapel Hill, NC: University of North Carolina Press, 1985.

McFarlane, Anthony. *Colombia before Independence.* Cambridge: Cambridge University Press, 1993.

Malamud Rikles, Carlos. *Cádiz y Saint Malo en el comercio colonial Peruano (1698–1725)* Cádiz: Diputación de Cádiz, 1986.

Mathias, Peter. *The First Industrial Nation: An Economic History of Britain, 1700–1914.* London: Methuen, 1969.

Minchom, Martin. *The People of Quito, 1690–1810: Change and Unrest in the Underclass.* Boulder, CO: Westview Press, 1994.

Moreno Cebrián, Alfredo. *El corregidor de indios y la economía peruana en el siglo XVIII (los repartos forzosos de mercancías).* Madrid: Consejo Superior de Investigaciones Científicas, 1977.

Moreno Yánez, Segundo E. *Sublevaciones indígenas en la Audiencia de Quito, desde el comiezos del siglo XVIII hasta finales de la colonia.* Quito: Ediciones de la Universidad Católica, 1985 edition.

North, Douglass C. *Institutions, Institutional Change and Economic Performance.* Cambridge: Cambridge University Press, 1990.

Ortiz de la Tabla Ducasse, Javier. *Los encomenderos de Quito, 1534–1660: Origen y evolución de una élite colonial.* Seville: Escuela de Estudios Hispano-Americanos, 1993.

Palomeque, Silvia. *Cuenca en el siglo XIX: La articulación de una región.* Quito: Ediciones Abya-Yala, 1990.

Perkins, Edwin. *The Economy of Colonial America.* New York: Columbia University Press, 1980.

Pérez, Alquiles. *Las mitas en la Real Audiencia de Quito.* Quito: Imprenta del Ministerio del Tesoro, 1948.

Phelan, John Leddy. *The Kingdom of Quito in the Seventeenth Century: Bureaucratic Politics in the Spanish Empire.* Madison: University of Wisconsin Press, 1967.

The People and the King: The Comunero Revolution in Colombia, 1781. Madison: University of Wisconsin Press, 1978.

Quiroz, Alfonso W. *Duedas olvidadas: instrumentos de crédito en la economía colonial peruana, 1750–1820.* Lima: Pontificia Universidad Católica del Perú, 1993.

Ramón Valarezo, Galo. *La resistencia Andina: Cayambe, 1500–1800.* Quito: Ediciones Abya-Yala, 1987.

Ramos Gómez, Luis. *Las noticias secretas de América de Jorge Juan y Antonio de Ulloa (1735–1745)*. 2 vols. Vol. 1, *Estudio Histórico*. Madrid: Consejo Superior de Investigaciones Científicas, 1985.

Ramos Pérez, Demetrio. *Entre El Plata y Bogotá: cuatro claves de la emancipación Ecuatoriana*. Madrid: Ediciones Cultura Hispánica, 1978.

Rebolledo, Loreto G. *Comunidad y resistencia: el caso de Lumbisí en la colonia*. Quito: Ediciones Abya-Yala, 1992.

Rodríguez, Linda Alexander. *The Search for Public Policy: Regional Politics and Government Finances in Ecuador, 1830–1940*. Berkeley: University of California Press, 1985.

Roxborough, Ian. *Theories of Underdevelopment*. New York: Macmillan Press, 1979.

Rueda Novoa, Rocío. *El obraje de San Joseph de Peguchi*. Quito: Ediciones Abya-Yala, 1988.

Salomon, Frank. *Native Lords of Quito in the Age of the Incas: The Political Economy of North Andean Chiefdoms*. Cambridge: Cambridge University Press, 1986.

Salvucci, Richard J. *Textiles and Capitalism in Mexico: An Economic History of the Obrajes, 1539–1840*. Princeton: Princeton University Press, 1987.

Scott, James C. *The Moral Economy of the Peasant: Rebellion and Subsistence in Southeast Asia*. New Haven: Yale University Press, 1976.

Shepherd, James F. *A Balance of Trade for the Thirteen Colonies, 1768–1772*. New York: Garland Press, 1985 edition.

Socolow, Susan Migden. *The Bureaucrats of Buenos Aires, 1769–1810: Amor al Real Servicio*. Durham, NC: Duke University Press, 1987.

Spalding, Karen, ed. *Essays in the Political, Economic, and Social History of Colonial Latin America*. Newark: University of Delaware Press, 1982.

Spindler, Frank. *Nineteenth Century Ecuador: An Historical Introduction*. Fairfax, VA: George Mason University Press, 1987.

Stein, Stanley J., and Stein, Barbara H. *The Colonial Heritage of Latin America: Essays on Economic Dependence in Perspective*. New York: Oxford University Press, 1970.

Tandeter, Enrique, and Wachtel, Nathan, eds. *Precios y produción agraria: Potosí y Charcas en el siglo XVIII*. Buenos Aires: C.E.D.E.S., 1983.

Terán Najas, Rosmarie. *Los proyectos del Imperio Borbónico en la Real Audiencia de Quito*. Quito: Ediciones Abya–Yala, 1988.

Tilly, Charles. *Big Structures, Large Processes, and Huge Comparisons*. New York: Russell Sage Foundation, 1984.

Tracy, James D., ed. *The Political Economy of Merchant Empires: State Power and World Trade*. Cambridge: Cambridge University Press, 1991.

Twinam, Ann. *Miners, Merchants, and Farmers in Colonial Colombia*. Austin: University of Texas Press, 1982.

Vargas, José María. *La economía política del Ecuador durante la colonia*. Quito: Editorial Universitaria, 1957.

Wallerstein, Immanuel. *The Modern World-System*. Vol. 1, *Capitalist Agriculture and the Origins of the World-Economy in the Sixteenth Century*. New York: Academic Press, 1974

The Modern World-System. Vol. 2, *Mercantilism and the Consolidation of the European World-Economy, 1600–1750*. New York: Academic Press, 1980.

The Modern World-System. Vol. 3, *The Second Era of Great Expansion of the Capitalist World-Economy, 1730–1840s*. New York: Academic Press, 1989.

Walker, Geoffrey J. *Spanish Politics and Imperial Trade, 1700–1789.* Blooming-ton: Indiana University Press, 1979.
Weber, Max. *The Theory of Social and Economic Organization.* Translated by Talcott Parsons. New York: Free Press, 1968.
Wilson, Kax. *A History of Textiles.* Boulder, CO: Westview Press, 1979.

Secondary works: articles

Amaral, Samuel. "Public Expenditure Financing in the Colonial Treasury: Anal-ysis of the Real Caja de Buenos Aires Accounts." *Hispanic American Historical Review,* 64 (May 1984): 287–95.
Andrien, Kenneth J. "Economic Crisis, Taxes and the Quito Insurrection of 1765." *Past and Present,* 129 (November 1990): 104–31.
"The State and Dependency in Late Colonial and Early Republican Ecuador." In *The Political Economy of Spanish America in the Age of Revolution, 1750–1850,* edited by Kenneth J. Andrien and Lyman L. Johnson, 169–95. Albuquerque: University of New Mexico Press, 1994.
"Corruption, Self-Interest, and the Political Culture of Eighteenth-Century Quito." In *Virtue, Corruption, and Self-Interest: Political Values in the Eighteenth Century,* edited by Richard K. Matthews, 270–96. Bethlehem, PA: Lehigh University Press, 1994.
Assadourian, Carlos Sempat. "Modos de producción, capitalismo, y subdesar-rollo en América Latina." In *Modos de producción en América Latina,* ed-ited by Carlos Sempat Assadourian et al., 47–81. Buenos Aires: Ediciones Nueva Vista, 1973.
"La producción de mercancía dinero en la formación del mercado interno colonial: el caso del espacio peruano, siglo XVI." In *Ensayos sobre el de-sarrollo económico de México y América Latina (1500–1975),* edited by Enrique Florescano, 223–92. Mexico City: Fondo de Cultura Economica, 1979.
Barbier, Jacques A. "The Culmination of the Bourbon Reforms, 1787–1792." *Hispanic American Historical Review,* 57 (February 1977): 51–68.
"Peninsular Finance and Colonial Trade: The Dilemma of Charles IV's Spain." *Journal of Latin American Studies,* 12 (May 1980): 21–37.
"Venezuelan Libranzas, 1788–1807: From Economic Nostrum to Fiscal Im-perative." *The Americas,* 37 (April 1981): 457–78.
"Comercio neutral in Bolivarean America: La Guaira, Cartagena, Callao, and Buenos Aires." In *América Latina en la época de Simón Bolívar: la formación de las economías nacionales y los intereses económicos europeos, 1800–1850,* edited by Reinhard Liehr, 363–77. Berlin: Colloquium Verlag, 1989.
Barbier, Jacques A., and Craig, Lynda deForest. "Lepers and Hospitals in the Spanish Empire: An Aspect of Bourbon Reform in Health Care." *Ibero-Amerikanisches Archiv,* 11:4 (1985): 383–406.
Bauer, Arnold J. "The Church in the Economy of Spanish America: *Censos* and *Depósitos* in the Eighteenth and Nineteenth Centuries." *Hispanic American Historical Review,* 63 (November 1983): 707–33.
Bonifaz, Emilio. "Orígen y evolución de una hacienda histórica: Guachalá." *Boletín del Archivo Nacional de Historia,* 53 (1970): 338–50.
Borchart de Moreno, Christiana. "La transferencia de la propiedad agraria in-dígena en el corregimiento de Quito, hasta finales del siglo XVII." *Caravelle,* 34 (1980): 1–19.

"Composiciones de tierras en la Audiencia de Quito: el valle de Tumbaco a finales del siglo XVII." *Jahrbuch für Geschichte von Staat, Wirtschaft und Gesellschaft Lateinamerikas*, 17 (1980): 121–55.

"Composiciones de tierras en el Valle de los Chillos a finales del siglo XVII: una contribución a la historia agraria de la Audiencia de Quito." *Cultura*, 5 (1980): 139–78.

"La tenencia de la tierra en el Valle de Machachi a finales del siglo XVII." *Antropología Ecuatoriana*, 2–3 (1983–84): 143–71.

"La crisis del obraje de San Ildefonso a finales del siglo XVIII." *Cultura*, 24 (1986): 655–71.

"Las tierras de Licto, Punín, y Macaxí: factores para su diminución e intentos de restauración." *Revista Andina*, 6:2 (diciembre 1988): 503–24.

"Capital comercial y producción agrícola: Nueva España y Quito en el siglo XVIII." *Anuario de Estudios Americanos*, 46 (1989): 131–72.

"Mas alla del obraje: la producción artesanal en Quito, 1780–1830." *The Americas* (forthcoming).

Borchart de Moreno, Christiana, and Moreno Yánez, Segundo E. "La historia socioeconómica ecuatoriana (siglo XVIII): análisis y tendencias." *Revista de Indias*, 186 (1989): 379–409.

Brading, D. A. "Facts and Figments in Bourbon Mexico." *Bulletin of Latin American Research*, 4 (1985): 61–64.

Brading, David, Coatsworth, John H., and Lindo-Fuentes, Héctor. "Comments on 'The Economic Cycle in Bourbon Central Mexico: A Critique of the *Recaudación del diezmo líquido en pesos.*'" *Hispanic American Historical Review*, 69 (August 1989): 531–57.

Brenner, David. "The Origins of Capitalist Development: A Critique of Neo-Smithian Marxism." *New Left Review*, 104 (1977): 25–92.

Bromley, Rosemary D.F. "Disasters and Population Change in Central Highland Ecuador, 1778–1825." In *Social Fabric and Spatial Structure in Colonial Latin America*, edited by David J. Robinson, 85–115. Ann Arbor, MI: University Microfilms, 1979.

Mark A. Burkholder. "Honest Judges Leave Destitute Heirs: The Price of Integrity in Eighteenth-Century Spain." In *Corruption, Virtue, and Self-Interest: Political Values in the Eighteenth Century*, edited by Richard K. Matthews, 247–69. Bethlehem, PA: Lehigh University Press, 1994.

Caillavet, Chantal. "Les rouages economiques d'une societe miniere: echanges et credit. Loja: 1550–1630." *Bulletin l'Institut Français d'Études Andines*, 13 (1984): 31–63.

Chirot, Daniel, and Hall, Thomas D. "World-System Theory." *Annual Review of Sociology*, 8 (1982): 81–106.

Coatsworth, John. "Obstacles to Economic Growth in Nineteenth-Century Mexico." *American Historical Review*, 83 (February 1978): 80–100.

"The Limits of Colonial Absolutism: The State in Eighteenth-Century Mexico." In *Essays in the Political, Economic, and Social History of Colonial Latin America*, edited by Karen Spalding, 25–51. Newark, DE: University of Delaware Press, 1982.

Conniff, Michael. "Guayaquil through Independence: Urban Development in a Colonial System." *The Americas*, 33 (1977): 385–410.

Contreras, Carlos. "Balance de la historia económica del Ecuador." *HISLA*, 5 (1985): 127–34.

Cubitt, David J. "La composición social de una élite hispanoamericana a la

la producción textil en la economía de la Sierra en el siglo XIX." *Cultura*, 24 (1986): 531–43.

O'Brien, Patrick. "European Economic Development: The Contribution of the Periphery." *Economic History Review*, 2nd ser. 35 (February 1982): 1–18.

O'Phelan Godoy, Scarlett. "Vivir y morir en el mineral de Hualgayoc a fines de la colonia." *Jahrbuch für Geschichte von Staat, Wirtschaft, und Gesellschaft Lateinamerikas*, 30 (1993): 75–127.

Ortiz de la Tabla Ducasse, Javier. "Panorama económico y social del corregimiento de Quito (1768–1775)." *Revista de Indias*, 145–47 (1976): 83–98.

"El obraje colonial Ecuatoriano: aproximación a su estudio." *Revista de Indias*, 149–50 (1977): 469–541.

"La población ecuatoriana en la época colonial: cuestiones y cálculos." *Anuario de Estudios Americanos*, 37 (1980): 235–77.

"Obrajes y obrajeros del Quito colonial." *Anuario de Estudios Americanos*, 39 (1982): 341–65.

"La población tributaria del Ecuador colonial." *Cultura*, 24 (1986): 447–58.

Ouweneel, Arij, and Bijleveld, Catrien C. J. H. "The Economic Cycle in Bourbon Central Mexico: A Critique of the *Recaudación del diezmo líquido en pesos.*" *Hispanic American Historical Review*, 69 (August 1989): 479–530.

Packenham, Robert. "Holistic Dependency." *New World: A Journal of Latin American Studies*, 2 (1987): 12–48.

Palomeque, Silvia. "Historia económica de Cuenca y sus relaciones regionales (desde fines del siglo XVIII a principios del XIX)." In *Segundo encuentro de historia y realidad económica y social del Ecuador*. 77–128. 3 vols. Cuenca: I.D.I.S., 1978.

"Loja en el mercado interno colonial." *HISLA*, 2 (1983): 33–45.

Petitjean, Martine, and Saint-Geours, Ives. "La economía de cascarilla en el corregimiento de Loja." *Cultura*, 15 (1983): 171–207.

Platt, D. C. M. "Dependency in Nineteenth-Century Latin America: A Historian Objects." *Latin American Research Review*, 16 (1981): 113–29; 147–49.

Price, Jacob. "Economic Function and the Growth of American Port Towns in the Eighteenth Century." *Perspectives in American History*, 8 (1974): 123–75.

Quiroz, Alfonso W. "Reassessing the Role of Credit in Late Colonial Peru: *Censos, Escrituras* and *Imposiciones.*" *Hispanic American Historical Review*, 74 (May 1994): 193–230.

Ragin, Charles, and Chirot, Daniel. The World System of Immanuel Wallerstein: Sociology and Politics as History." In *Vision and Method in Historical Sociology*, edited by Theda Skocpol, 276–312. Cambridge: Cambridge University Press, 1979.

Ramos Gómez, Luis. "La estructura social Quiteña entre 1737 y 1745 según el proceso contra José de Araujo." *Revista de Indias*, 51:191 (1991) 25–56.

Romero, Carlos Marchán. "El sistema hacendario serrano, movilidad y cambio agrario." *Cultura*, 19 (1984): 63–106.

Sable, Charles, and Zeitlin, Jonathan. "Historical Alternatives to Mass Production: Politics, Markets and Technology in Nineteenth-Century Industrialization." *Past and Present*, 108 (August 1985): 133–76.

Salomon, Frank. "Indian Women of Early Colonial Quito as Seen through Their Testaments." *The Americas*, 44 (January 1988): 325–41.

Salvucci, Richard J. "Entrepreneurial Culture and the Textile Manufactories in

Eighteenth-Century Mexico." *Anuario de Estudios Americanos,* 39 (1982): 397–419.

Stern, Steve J. "New Directions in Andean Economic History: A Critical Dialogue with Carlos Sempat Assadourian." *Latin American Perspectives,* 12 (Winter 1985): 133–47.

"Feudalism, Capitalism, and the World-System in the Perspective of Latin America and the Caribbean." *American Historical Review,* 93 (October 1988): 829–72.

"Reply: Ever More Solitary." *American Historical Review,* 93 (October 1988): 886–97.

Taylor, William B. "Between Global Process and Local Knowledge: An Inquiry into Early Latin American Social History, 1500–1900." In *Reliving the Past,* edited by Olivier Zunz, 115–90. Chapel Hill: University of North Carolina Press, 1985.

Vergopoulis, Kostas. "Capitalism and Peasant Productivity." *Journal of Peasant Studies,* 5 (1978): 446–65.

Villalba, Jorge. "Los obrajes de Quito en el siglo XVII y la legislación obrera." *Revista del Instituto de Historia Eclesiástica Ecuatoriana,* 8 (1986): 43–212.

"Las haciendas de los Jesuitas en Pimampiro en el siglo XVIII." *Revista del Instituto de Historia Eclesiástica Ecuatoriana,* 7 (1983): 15–60.

Wallerstein, Immanuel. "Comments on Stern's Critical Tests." *American Historical Review,* 93 (October 1988): 873–85.

Unpublished material

Borchart de Moreno, Christiana. "La economía quiteña en un periodo de transición: circulación y producción manufacturera y artesanal entre colonia y república." Paper presented at the Latin American Studies Association meetings, Los Angeles, CA, 1992.

Bromley, Rosemary D. F. "Urban Growth and Decline in the Central Sierra of Ecuador." Ph.D. diss., University of Wales, 1977.

Dilg, George Robertson. "The Collapse of the Portobelo Fairs: A Study in Spanish Commercial Reform, 1720–1740." Ph.D. diss., Indiana University, 1975.

Minchom, Martin. "Urban Popular Society in Colonial Quito, c.1700–1800." Ph.D. diss., University of Liverpool, 1984.

Powers, Karen M. "Indian Migration and Socio-Political Change in the Audiencia of Quito." Ph.D. diss., New York University, 1990.

Tyrer, Robson Brines. "The Demographic and Economic History of the Audiencia of Quito: Indian Population and the Textile Industry, 1600–1800." Ph.D. diss., University of California at Berkeley, 1976.

Washburn, Douglas Alan. "The Bourbon Reforms: A Social and Economic History of the Audiencia of Quito, 1760–1810." Ph. D. diss., University of Texas at Austin, 1984.

Index